MENARDS Vacation & Small HOME PLANS

Vacation & Small Home Plans
is a collection of our best-selling vacation and small homes in a variety of architectural styles and sizes. A broad assortment is presented to match a wide variety of lifestyles and budgets. Each plan page features floor plans, a front view of the house, interior square footage of the home, number of bedrooms, baths, garage size and foundation types. All floor plans show room and exterior dimensions.

Technical Specifications
At the time the construction drawings were prepared, every effort was made to ensure that these plans and specifications meet nationally recognized building codes (BOCA, Southern Building Code Congress and others). Because national building codes change or vary from area to area some drawing modifications and/or the assistance of a professional designer or architect may be necessary to comply with your local codes or to accommodate specific building site conditions. We advise you to consult with your local building official for information regarding codes governing your area prior to purchasing your plans.

Blueprint Ordering - Fast & Easy
Your ordering is made simple by following the instructions on page 7. See page 6 for more information on which types of blueprint packages are available and how many plan sets to order.

Your Home, Your Way
The blueprints you receive are a master plan for building your new home. They start you on your way to what may well be the most rewarding experience of your life.

Current printing 5 4 3 2 1

COVER HOME is Plan #M09-007D-0060 and is featured on page 18.
Photo courtesy of Design America, Inc.

COVER HOME is Plan #M09-027D-0005 and is featured on page 19.
Photo courtesy of America's Home Plans.

MENARDS VACATION & SMALL HOME PLANS is published by Design America , Inc., 734 Westport Plaza, Suite 208, St. Louis, MO 63146. All rights reserved. Reproduction in whole or in part withoutwritten permission of the publisher is prohibited. © 2014.

Artist drawings and photos shown in this publication may vary slightly from the actual working drawings. Some photos are shown in mirror reverse. Please refer to the floor plan for accurate layout.

COPYRIGHT All plans appearing in this publication are protected under copyright law. Reproduction of the illustrations or working drawings by any means is strictly prohibited. The right of building only one structure from the plans purchased is licensed exclusively to the buyer and the plans may not be resold unless by express written authorization.

contents

2	Let Menards Make Your Dream Home A Reality
3	What's The Right Plan For You?
4	Our Blueprint Packages Offer...
5	Other Great Products More Helpful Building Aids...
6	What Kind Of Plan Package Do You Need?
7	How To Order Home Plans
8	Making Changes To Your Plan
9-223	Vacation & Small Home Plans
224	Home Plan Index

Let MENARDS Make Your Dream Home A Reality

"Thanks to MENARDS, finding and building our Dream Home has never been easier."

Thinking about building your dream home? Or, perhaps you are interested in a vacation home or downsizing to a smaller home? Choosing a home plan can be a daunting task.

This book of Vacation & Small Home Plans has been designed to make the search simple and easy. Browse the pages of this book and look for the style that best suits your family and your needs. These plans have been chosen from top designers from across the country and can provide to you the perfect home that will truly be a place of refuge for your whole family for years to come.

This book is the perfect place to begin your search for the home of your dreams. You will find the expected beauty you want and the functional efficiency you need, all designed with unmatched quality.

Also, keep in mind, this book contains helpful articles for understanding what kind of plan package you may need as well as other helpful building aids to make the process even easier. When you have made this decision visit your local MENARDS store to place your order and partner with one of their friendly team members to walk you through the process or order your home plans at www.Menards.com.

MENARDS is dedicated to assist you through the entire home decision process

What's The Right Plan For You?

Choosing a home plan is an exciting but difficult task. Many factors play a role in what home plan is best for you and your family. To help you get started, we have pinpointed some of the major factors to consider when searching for your dream home. Take the time to evaluate your family's needs and you will have an easier time sorting through all of the home plans offered in our magazine.

Budget:
The first thing to consider is your budget. Many items take part in this budget, from ordering the blueprints to the last doorknob purchased. When you find your dream home plan, visit the MENARDS® Building Materials Desk to get a cost-to-build estimate to ensure that the finished product will be within your cost range.

Family Lifestyle:
After your budget is deciphered, you need to assess you and your family's lifestyle needs. Think about the stage of life you are at now, and what stages you will be going through in the future. Ask yourself questions to figure out how much room you need now and if you will need room for expansion. Are you married? Do you have children? How many children do you plan on having? Are you an empty-nester?

Incorporate in your planning any frequent guests you may have, including elderly parents, grandchildren or adult children who may live with you.

Does your family entertain a lot? If so, think about the rooms you will need to do so. Will you need both formal and informal spaces? Do you need a gourmet kitchen? Do you need a game room and/or a wet bar?

Floor Plan Layouts:
When looking through our home plans, imagine yourself walking through the house. Consider the flow from the entry to the living, sleeping and gathering areas. Does the layout ensure privacy for the master bedroom? Does the garage enter near the kitchen for easy unloading? Does the placement of the windows provide enough privacy from any neighboring properties? Do you plan on using furniture you already have? Will this furniture fit in the appropriate rooms? When you find a plan you want to purchase, be sure to picture yourself actually living in it.

Experts in the field suggest that the best way to determine your needs is to begin by listing everything you like or dislike about your current home.

Exterior Spaces:
There are many different home styles ranging from Traditional to Contemporary. Flip through and find which style most appeals to you and the neighborhood in which you plan to build. Also think of your site and how the entire house will fit on this site. Picture any landscaping you plan on incorporating into the design. Using your imagination is key when choosing a home plan.

Choosing a home plan can be an intimidating experience. Asking yourself these questions before you get started on the search will help you through the process. With our large selection of multiple styles we are certain you will find your dream home in the following pages.

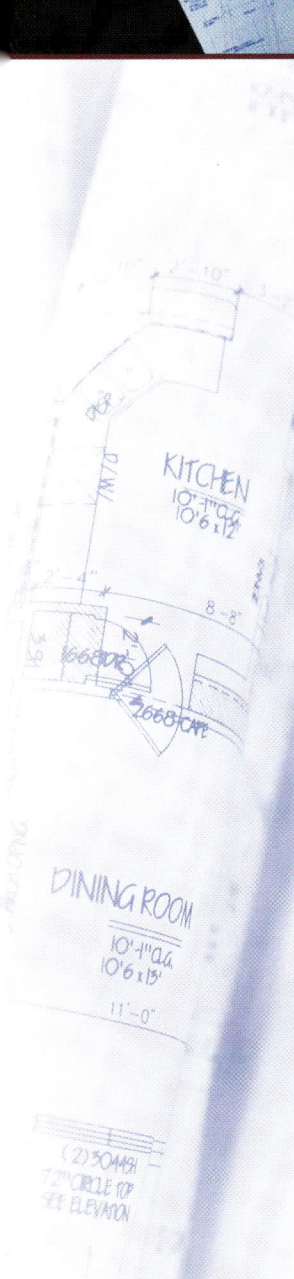

Our Blueprint Packages Offer...

*Quality plans for building your future,
with extras that provide unsurpassed value,
ensure good construction and long-term enjoyment.*

A quality home - one that looks good, functions well, and provides years of enjoyment - is a product of many things - design, materials, and craftsmanship.

But it's also the result of outstanding blueprints - the actual plans and specifications that tell the builder exactly how to build your home.

And with our BLUEPRINT PACKAGES you get the absolute best.
A complete set of blueprints is available for every design in this book. These "working drawings" are highly detailed, resulting in two key benefits:

- Better understanding by the contractor of how to build your home and...
- More accurate construction estimates.

Below is a sample of the plan information included for most of the designs in this magazine. Specific details may vary with each designer's plan. While this information is typical of most plans, we cannot assure the inclusion of all the following referenced items. Please contact customer service for plan specific information, including which of the following items are included.

1. Cover Sheet is the artist's rendering of the exterior of the home and is included with many of the plans. It will give you an idea of how your home will look when completed and landscaped.

2. Foundation plan shows the layout of the basement, crawl space, slab or pier foundation. All necessary notations and dimensions are included. See the plan page for the foundation types included. If the home plan you choose does not have your desired foundation type, see page 8 on how to customize your foundation to suit your specific needs or site conditions.

3. Floor Plans show the placement of walls, doors, closets, plumbing fixtures, electrical outlets, columns, and beams for each level of the home.

4. Interior Elevations provide views of special interior elements such as fireplaces, kitchen cabinets, built-in units and other features of the home.

5. Exterior Elevations illustrate the front, rear and both sides of the house, with all details of exterior materials and the required dimensions.

6. Sections show detail views of the home or portions of the home as if it were sliced from the roof to the foundation. This sheet shows important areas such as load-bearing walls, stairs, joists, trusses and other structural elements, which are critical for proper construction.

7. Details show how to construct certain components of your home, such as the roof system, stairs, deck, etc.

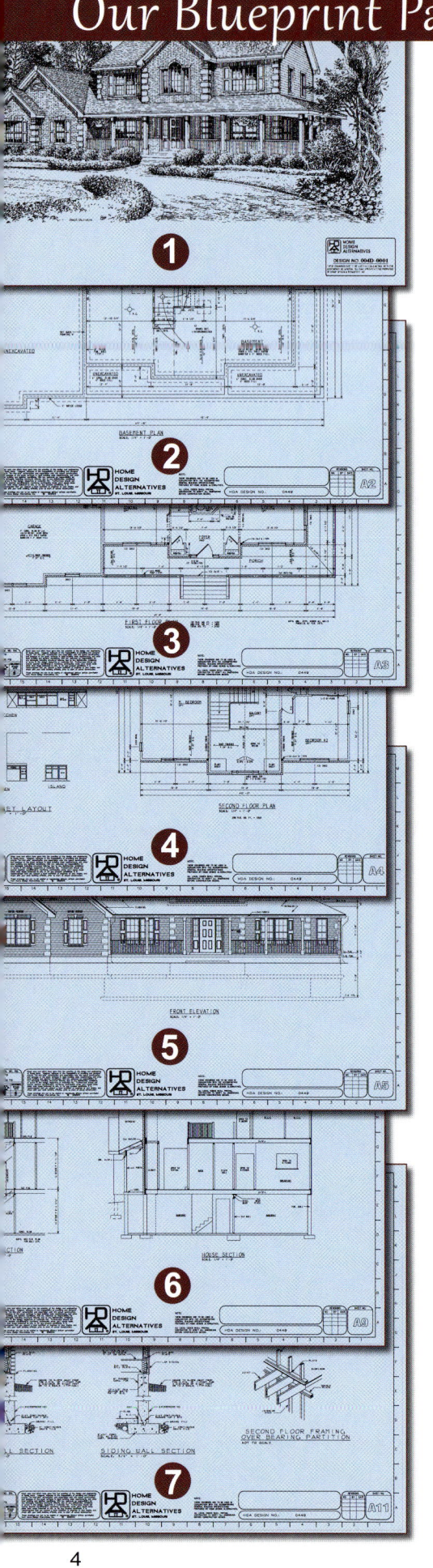

Other Great Products

The Legal Kit™

Home building can be a complicated process with many legal regulations being confusing. This Legal Kit was designed to help you avoid many legal pitfalls and build your home with confidence using the forms and contracts featured in this kit. Included are request for proposal documents, various fixed price and cost plus contracts, instructions on how and when to use each form, warranty statements and more. Save time and money before you break ground on your new home or start a remodeling project. Instructions are included on how to use the kit and since the documents are universal, they are designed to be used with all building trades. Since review by an attorney is always advised before signing any contract, this is an ideal way to get organized and started on the process. Plus, all forms are reproducible making it a terrific tool for the contractor and home builder.

Discount Price: $35.00 - Menards SKU 100-3422

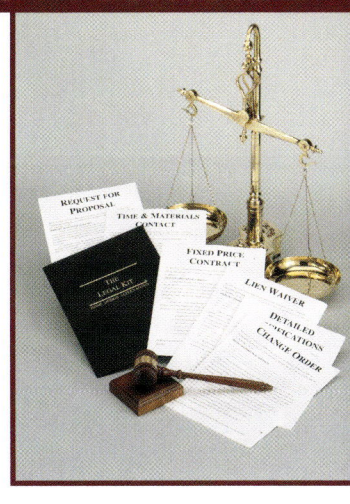

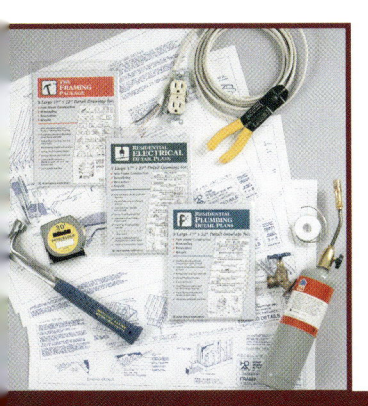

Detail Plan Packages
Framing, Plumbing and Electrical Plan Packages

Three separate packages offer home builders details for constructing various foundations; numerous floor, wall and roof framing techniques; simple to complex residential wiring; sump and water softener hookups; plumbing connection methods; installation of septic systems, and more. Packages include 3-dimensional illustrations and a glossary of terms. These drawings do not pertain to a specific home plan making them perfect for your building situation. Purchase one or all three.

Discount Price: $20.00 each or all three for $40.00 - Menards SKU 100-3422

More Helpful Building Aids...

Your Blueprint Package will contain the necessary construction information to build your home. We also offer the following products and services to save you time and money in the building process.

Material List

Material lists are available for all of the plans in this book. Each list gives you the quantity, dimensions and description of the building materials necessary to construct your home. The material list is intended to be used only in conjunction with the corresponding blueprints and specifications, and is not intended to be used solely for ordering purposes. Extreme care has gone into assuring that your material list is accurate. However, due to variations in local building practices and widely differing code requirements, the exact material quanities cannot be guaranteed. To receive a free home plan estimate call or visit any **MENARDS®** Building Materials Desk.

Discount Price: $125.00 - Menards SKU 100-3422

NOTE: Material lists are designed with the standard foundations only and will not include alternate or optional foundations. It is essential that you review the material list and the construction drawings with your builder and material supplier in order to verify product line, color, measurements, and descriptions of the materials listed.

Express Delivery

Most orders are processed within 24 hours of receipt. Please allow 7-10 business days for delivery. If you need to place a rush order, please call or visit any **MENARDS®** store to order by 11:00 a.m. Monday-Friday CST and specify you would like express service (allow 1-2 business days).

Discount Price: $60.00 - Menards SKU 194-4356

Customer Service

If you have questions about a plan, call our customer service department at 1-800-373-2646 Monday through Friday, 7:30am-4:30pm CST. Whether it involves design modifications, or specific plan questions, our customer service representatives will be happy to help you. We want your home to be everything you expect it to be.

What Kind Of Plan Package Do You Need?

Now that you've found the home you've been looking for, here are some suggestions on how to make your Dream Home a reality. To get started, order the type of plans that fit your particular situation.

Your Choices

☐ **The 1-Set Study Package** – We offer a One-set plan package so you can study your home in detail. This one set is considered a study set and is marked "not for construction." It is a copyright violation to reproduce blueprints.

☐ **The Minimum 5-Set Package** – If you're ready to start the construction process, this 5-set package is the minimum number of blueprint sets you will need. It will require keeping close track of each set so they can be used by multiple subcontractors and tradespeople.

☐ **The Standard 8-Set Package** – For best results in terms of cost, schedule and quality of construction, we recommend you order eight (or more) sets of blueprints. Besides one set for yourself, additional sets of blueprints will be required by your mortgage lender, local building department, general contractor and all subcontractors working on foundation, electrical, plumbing, heating/air conditioning, carpentry work, etc.

☐ **Reproducible Masters** – If you wish to make some minor design changes, you'll want to order reproducible masters. These drawings contain the same information as the blueprints but are printed on reproducible paper and clearly indicates your right to alter, copy or reproduce. This will allow your builder or a local design professional to make the necessary drawing changes without the major expense of redrawing the plans. This package also allows you to print copies of the modified plans as needed. The right of building only one structure from these plans is licensed exclusively to the buyer. You may not use this design to build a second or multiple dwelling(s) without purchasing another blueprint. Each violation of the Copyright Law is punishable in a fine. *Note: Plans are not returnable once the box has been opened.*

☐ **PDF File Format** – A complete set of construction drawings in an electronic format that allows you to resize and reproduce the plans to fit your needs. Since these are electronic files, we can send them to you within 24 hours (Mon-Fri, 7:30am-4:30pm CST) via email and save you shipping costs. They also offer printing flexibility by allowing you to print the size and number of sets you need. *Note: These are not CAD files and cannot be altered electronically. PDF Files are not returnable or refundable.*

☐ **Mirror Reverse Sets** – Plans can be printed in mirror reverse. These plans are useful when the house would fit your site better if all the rooms were on the opposite side than shown. They are simply a mirror image of the original drawings causing the lettering and dimensions to read backwards. Therefore, when ordering mirror reverse drawings, you must purchase at least one set of right-reading plans.

☐ **Right Reading Reverse Sets** – Right reading reverse is where the plan is a mirrored image of the original drawings, but all the text and dimensions read correctly. This option may not be available for all home plans, so please check the Home Plan Index on page 224 for availability.

☐ **Additional Sets** – Additional sets of the plan ordered are available for an additional cost of $45.00 each. Five-set, eight-set, reproducible and PDF File packages offer considerable savings. *Note: Available only within 90 days after purchase of plan package, PDF File, or reproducible masters of the same plan.*

COPYRIGHT

These plans are protected under Copyright Law. Reproduction by any means is strictly prohibited. The right of building only one structure from these plans is licensed exclusively to the buyer and these plans may not be resold unless by express written authorization from home designer/architect. You may not use this design to build a second or multiple dwelling(s) without purchasing another blueprint or blueprints or paying additional design fees. Each violation of the Copyright Law is punishable in a fine.

How To Order Home Plans

You've found your Dream Home, now what?
Follow these simple steps:

1. Review the article on page 6 to decide what type of plan package you need.
2. To order, call or visit any MENARDS® store and go to the Building Materials Desk or visit www.Menards.com.

To locate the nearest MENARDS® store, go to www.Menards.com and click on the Store locator.

Artist drawings and photos shown in this publication may vary slightly from the actual working drawings. Some photos are shown in mirror reverse or have been modified. Please refer to the floor plan for accurate layout.

Blueprint SKU Pricing
(prices subject to change)

PRICE CODE		1-SET STUDY	5-SET PLAN	8-SET PLAN	REPRO. MASTERS	PDF FILE
AAA	Menards SKU	194-3920	194-3933	194-3946	194-3959	194-3960
	Discount Price	$310	$410	$510	$610	$610
AA	Menards SKU	194-3962	194-3975	194-3988	194-3991	194-3995
	Discount Price	$410	$510	$610	$710	$710
A	Menards SKU	194-4000	194-4084	194-4165	194-4246	194-4250
	Discount Price	$470	$570	$670	$770	$770
B	Menards SKU	194-4013	194-4097	194-4178	194-4259	194-4260
	Discount Price	$530	$630	$730	$830	$830
C	Menards SKU	194-4026	194-4107	194-4181	194-4262	194-4265
	Discount Price	$585	$685	$785	$885	$885
D	Menards SKU	194-4039	194-4110	194-4194	194-4275	194-4280
	Discount Price	$635	$735	$835	$935	$935
E	Menards SKU	194-4042	194-4123	194-4204	194-4288	194-4290
	Discount Price	$695	$795	$895	$995	$995
F	Menards SKU	194-4055	194-4136	194-4217	194-4291	194-4295
	Discount Price	$750	$850	$950	$1050	$1050

OTHER PRODUCTS & BUILDING AIDS

MIRROR REVERSE*
Menards SKU 194-4327
Discount Price $15

RIGHT READING REVERSE*
Menards SKU 194-4328
Discount Price $150

2" x 6" WALLS
Menards SKU 194-4360
Discount Price $150

ADDITIONAL FOUNDATION
Menards SKU 194-4329
Discount Price $250

ADDITIONAL SETS**
Menards SKU 194-4330
Discount Price $45

MATERIAL LIST**
Menards SKU 100-3422
Discount Price $125

EXPRESS DELIVERY
Menards SKU 194-4356
Discount Price $60

LEGAL KIT
Menards SKU 100-3422
Discount Price $35

DETAIL PLAN PACKAGES
ELECTRICAL, PLUMBING & FRAMING - ALL SAME SKU
Menards SKU 100-3422
Discount Price $20 EA.
3 FOR $40

Please note: All blueprints are printed in response to your order, so we cannot honor requests for refunds. However, if for some reason you find that the plan you have purchased does not meet your requirements, you may exchange that plan for another plan in our collection within 90 days of purchase. At the time of the exchange, you will be charged a processing fee of 25% of your original plan package price, plus the difference in price between the plan packages (if applicable) and the cost to ship the new plans to you. Keep in mind, reproducible drawings can only be exchanged if the package is unopened and material lists can only be purchased within 90 days of purchasing the plan package. PDF Files are not returnable or refundable.

License To Build: When you purchase a "full set of construction drawings" from Design America, Inc., you are purchasing an exclusive one-time "License to Build," not the rights to the design. Design America, Inc. is granting you permission on behalf of the home plan designer to use the construction drawings one time for the building of your dream home. The construction drawings (also referred to as blueprints/plans and any derivative of that plan whether extensive or minor) are still owned and protected under copyright laws by the original designer. The blueprints/plans cannot be resold, transferred, rented, loaned or used by anyone other than the original purchaser of the "License to Build" without written consent from Design America, Inc. or the home plan designer.

*See page 6
**Available only within 90 days after purchase of plan package of same plan

Making Changes To Your Plan

We understand that it is difficult to find blueprints that will meet all your needs. That is why Design America, Inc. is pleased to offer plan modification services.

THINKING ABOUT CUSTOMIZING YOUR PLAN?

If you're like many customers, you may want to make changes to your home plan to make it the dream home you've always wanted. That's where our expert design and modification team comes in. You won't find a more efficient and economic way to get your changes done than by using our design services.

Whether it's enlarging a kitchen, adding a porch or converting a crawl space to a basement, we can customize any plan and make it perfect for your family. Simply create your wish list and let us go to work. Soon you'll have the blueprints for your new home and at a fraction of the cost of hiring an architect!

THE DESIGN AMERICA, INC. MODIFICATION ADVANTAGE

- We can customize any plan
- FREE cost estimates for your home plan modifications within 48 hours.
- Average turn-around time to complete the modifications is 2-3 weeks.
- One-on-one design consultations.

CUSTOMIZING FACTS

- The average cost for us to customize a house plan is typically less than 1 percent of the building costs — compare that to the national average of 7 percent of building costs.
- The average modification cost for a home is typically $800 to $1,500 (this does not include the cost of the reproducible blueprint, which is required to make plan changes).
- The average cost to modify a project plan is typically between $200-$500.

OTHER HELPFUL INFORMATION

- Feel free to include a sketch, or a specific list of changes you'd like to make.
- One of our designers will contact you within 48 hours with your free estimate.
- Upon accepting the estimate, you will need to purchase the reproducible/PDF set of plans.
- A contract, which includes a specific list of changes and fees will be sent to you for approval.
- Upon approving the contract, our designers will keep you up to date by emailing or faxing sketches throughout the project.
- Plan can be converted to metric.
- Barrier Free Conversion (accommodating a plan for special needs, transferring your living space for everyone).
- Customizing is also available for project plans, such as sheds, garages, apartment garages and more.

Easy Steps For Fast Service

Visit any **MENARDS**® Building Materials Desk and request a Custom Change Form.

Simply follow the instructions to receive your quote within two business days.

Plan #M09-027D-0005 on page 19.

MENARDS
Vacation & Small
HOME PLANS

The following pages include a collection of best-selling home plans featuring vacation and small homes that are designed for efficient and easy living. This collection of homes from some of the nation's leading designers and architects include functional floor plans, abundant storage, and many designed perfectly for narrow lots. Whether you're interested in a cozy bungalow or compact two-story, these small homes will welcome you and create the perfect atmosphere for quality family living in an enjoyable setting. We are excited to present this collection designed for functional living. Whatever your tastes or needs, we invite you to discover the home of your dreams.

Plan #M09-022D-0014 on page 16.

Plan #M09-072L-0024 on page 27.

Prestbury

MENARDS

Plan #M09-055L-0289

Photo, above - The stylish kitchen maintains a compact floor plan, perfect for high function, while it is only steps away from the great room and dining room.

Photo, left - This home highlights the kitchen with many of the most popular interior spaces surrounding it.

Photo, above - Stylish and sophisticated, the private master bath has a unique separate shower with sleek style. An oversized garden tub is sure to relieve stress for the homeowners in the private and amenity-filled master bath.

Photo, right - This homeowner moved the fireplace to act as a natural partition between the great room and the formal dining room. Arched entryways flank the see-through fireplace, while providing a bold symmetrical design element.

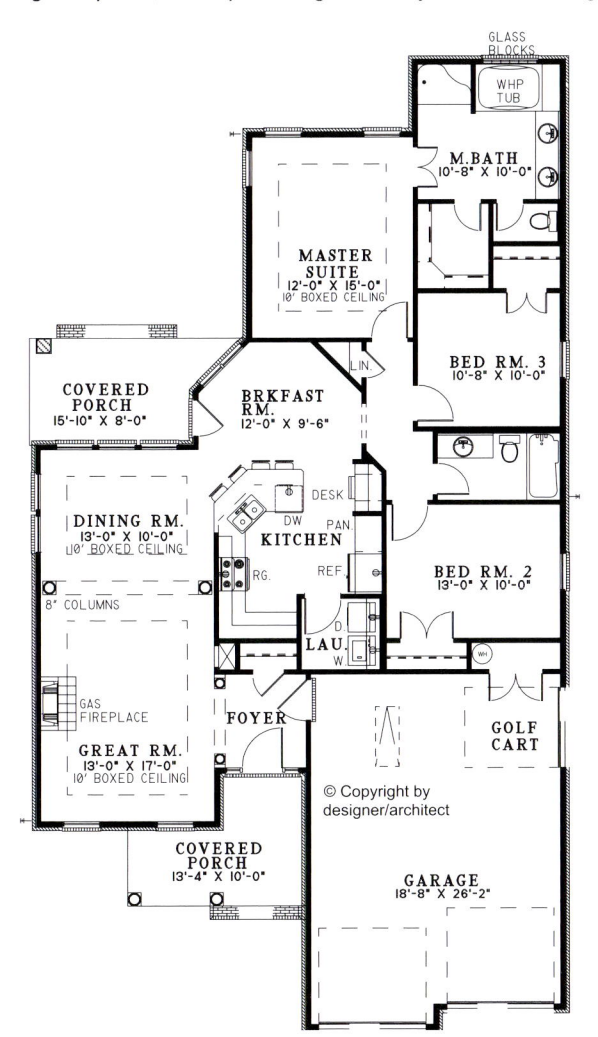

Plan #M09-055L-0289

Lavishing Southern Design

1,504 total square feet of living area

Width: 39'-6"   Depth: 72'-5"

3 bedrooms, 2 baths

2-car garage

Crawl space or slab foundation, please specify when ordering

Special features

The private master suite has its own luxury bath featuring an oversized tub and shower

A full bath is positioned between the two secondary bedrooms for convenience

Enjoy the outdoors on the covered porch directly off the breakfast room

Price Code C

To order this plan, visit the Menards Building Materials Desk or visit www.Menards.com.

Haddonfield

MENARDS

Plan #M09-077L-0097

Photo, above - Clean and effortless, the style of the great room is the perfect balance of formal and informal touches.

Photo, left - This angle of the kitchen shows off the stylish symmetry of the cabinetry and the center island work space.

Photo, above - Right off the foyer is a flex space that has been adapted here into a formal dining room with elegant chair rail details circumferencing the entire room.

Photo, right - Just one fine detail of the master bath, this corner tub is the perfect place to rinse away the day.

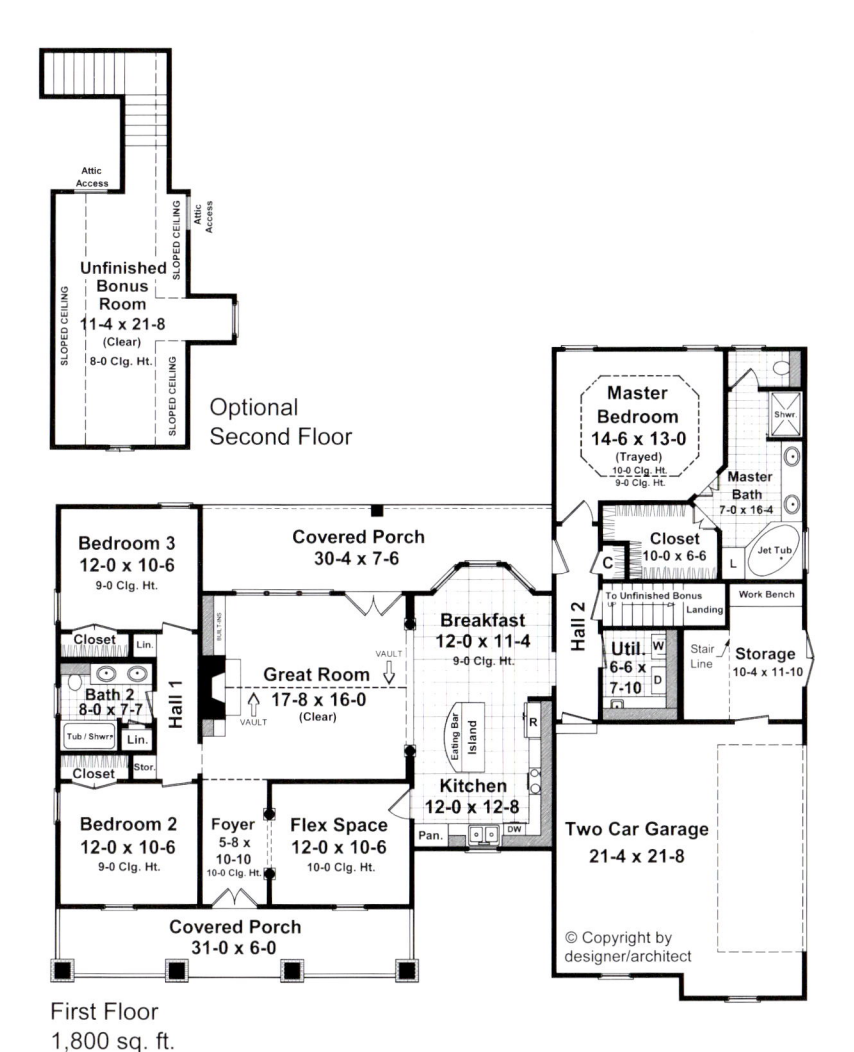

Plan #M09-077L-0097

Beautiful Brick And Siding Combination

1,800 total square feet of living area

Width: 65'-0" Depth: 56'-8"

3 bedrooms, 2 baths

2-car side entry garage

Slab, basement or crawl space foundation, please specify when ordering

Special features

Double doors open into the foyer crowned with a 10' ceiling

The vaulted great room opens into the kitchen and the bayed breakfast area with decorative columns

The unfinished bonus room has an additional 302 square feet of living area

Price Code E

First Floor
1,800 sq. ft.

To order this plan, visit the Menards Building Materials Desk or visit www.Menards.com.

Concord Grove

MENARDS

Plan #M09-041D-0006

Spacious Vaulted Great Room

1,189 total square feet of living area

Width: 36'-0"   Depth: 35'-8"

3 bedrooms, 2 1/2 baths

2-car garage

Basement foundation

Special features

All of the bedrooms are located on the second floor for added privacy

The dining room and kitchen have lovely patio views

The convenient half bath is located near the kitchen

Price Code AA

Rear View

Second Floor
574 sq. ft.

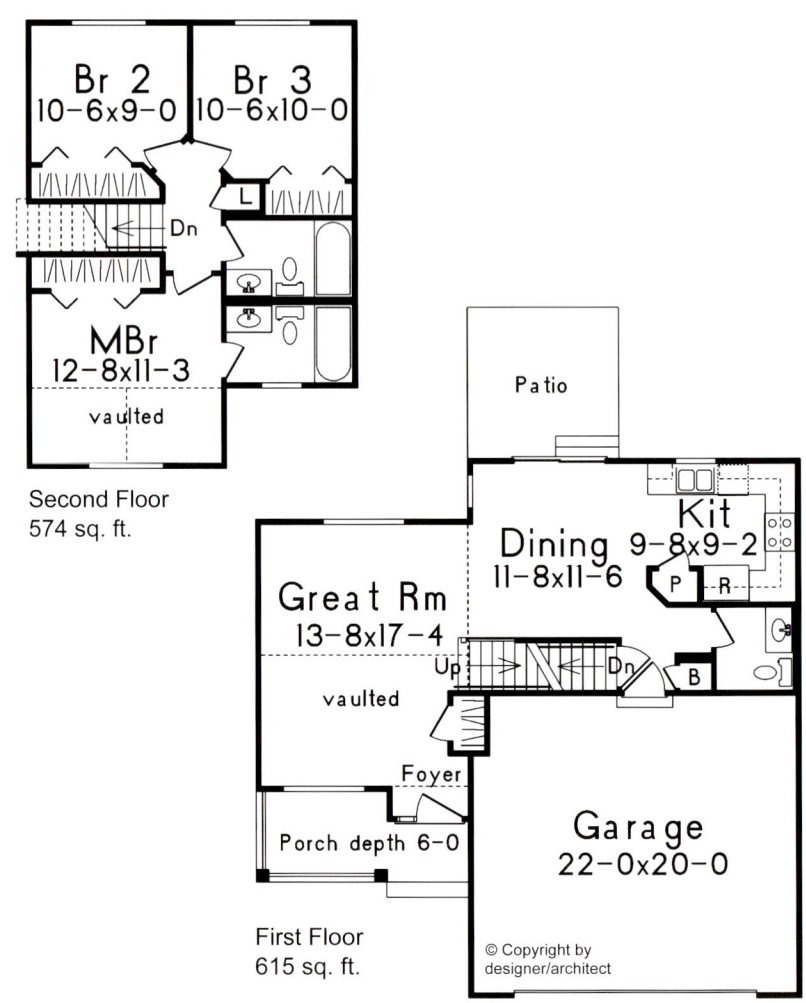

- Br 2: 10-6x9-0
- Br 3: 10-6x10-0
- MBr: 12-8x11-3 vaulted

First Floor
615 sq. ft.

- Great Rm: 13-8x17-4 vaulted
- Dining: 11-8x11-6
- Kit: 9-8x9-2
- Garage: 22-0x20-0
- Porch depth 6-0

© Copyright by designer/architect

14   To order this plan, visit the Menards Building Materials Desk or visit www.Menards.com.

MENARDS

Ashley Park

Plan #M09-007D-0054

Stylish Living For A Narrow Lot

1,575 total square feet of living area

Width: 38'-4"   Depth: 47'-0"

3 bedrooms, 2 1/2 baths

2-car garage

Basement foundation, drawings also include crawl space and slab foundations

Special features

The kitchen with corner windows features an island snack bar, an attractive breakfast room bay window, a convenient laundry area, and a built-in pantry

A luxury bath and walk-in closet adorn the master bedroom suite

Price Code B

Second Floor 773 sq. ft.

- MBr 12-0x14-8 vaulted
- Br 2 12-0x11-0
- Br 3 12-0x11-3 vaulted
- Hall

First Floor 802 sq. ft.

- Patio
- Brk'ft 10-0x10-2
- Kit 9-0x11-7
- Dining 12-0x11-0
- Laun.
- Hall
- Living 15-7x14-10
- Entry
- Porch
- Garage 19-4x20-4

© Copyright by designer/architect

Rear View

To order this plan, visit the Menards Building Materials Desk or visit www.Menards.com

15

Treebrooke

MENARDS

Plan #M09-022D-0014

Country Kitchen Is Center Of Living Activities

1,556 total square feet of living area

Width: 40'-0"   Depth: 44'-4"

3 bedrooms, 2 1/2 baths

2-car garage

Basement foundation

Special features

The country kitchen combines practicality with access to other areas for eating and entertaining

A three-way fireplace joins the dining and living areas

A plant shelf and vaulted ceiling highlight the master bedroom

Price Code B

Rear View

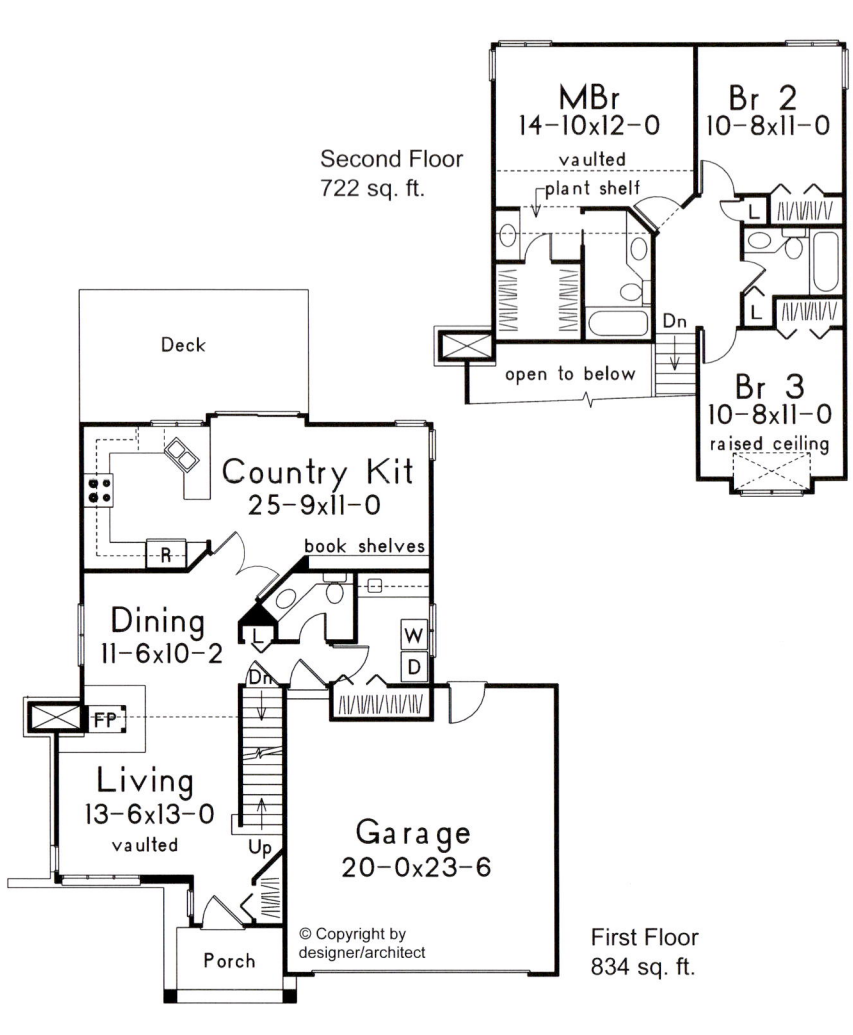

Second Floor 722 sq. ft.

MBr 14-10x12-0 vaulted

Br 2 10-8x11-0

plant shelf

open to below

Br 3 10-8x11-0 raised ceiling

Deck

Country Kit 25-9x11-0

book shelves

Dining 11-6x10-2

FP

Living 13-6x13-0 vaulted

Garage 20-0x23-6

Porch

© Copyright by designer/architect

First Floor 834 sq. ft.

16   To order this plan, visit the Menards Building Materials Desk or visit www.Menards.com

MENARDS

Wyndhurst

Plan #M09-065L-0006

Second Floor
558 sq. ft.

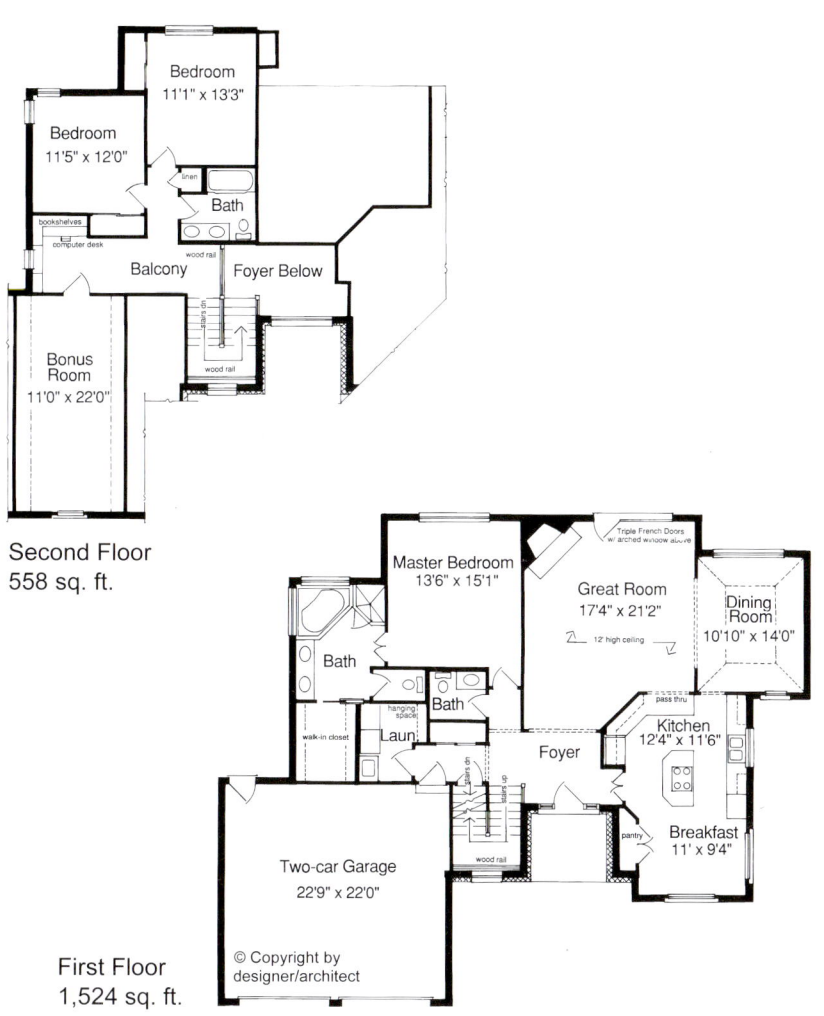

- Bedroom 11'5" x 12'0"
- Bedroom 11'1" x 13'3"
- Bath
- bookshelves
- computer desk
- Balcony
- Foyer Below
- Bonus Room 11'0" x 22'0"
- linen
- wood rail

First Floor
1,524 sq. ft.

- Master Bedroom 13'6" x 15'1"
- Great Room 17'4" x 21'2" — 12' high ceiling
- Dining Room 10'10" x 14'0" — Triple French Doors w/ arched window above
- Bath
- Bath
- Laun
- hanging space
- walk-in closet
- Foyer
- Kitchen 12'4" x 11'6" — pass thru
- Breakfast 11' x 9'4"
- pantry
- Two-car Garage 22'9" x 22'0"
- wood rail

© Copyright by designer/architect

Computer Area Is A Handy Feature

2,082 total square feet of living area

Width: 60'-0"   Depth: 50'-4"

3 bedrooms, 2 1/2 baths

2-car garage

Basement foundation

Special features

This home is designed with an insulated foundation system featuring pre-mounted insulation on concrete walls providing a drier, warmer and smarter structure

The master bedroom boasts a deluxe bath and a large walk-in closet

Natural light floods the breakfast room through numerous windows

The great room features a 12' ceiling, cozy fireplace and stylish French doors

The bonus room on the second floor has an additional 267 square feet of living area

Price Code C

To order this plan, visit the Menards Building Materials Desk or visit www.Menards.com.

Ashmont Woods

MENARDS

Plan #M09-007D-0060

Distinguished Styling For A Small Lot

1,268 total square feet of living area

Width: 38'-8"   Depth: 48'-4"

3 bedrooms, 2 baths

2-car garage

Basement foundation, drawings also include crawl space and slab foundations

Special features

Multiple gables, a large porch, and arched windows create a classy exterior

Innovative design provides openness in the great room, kitchen and the breakfast area

The secondary bedrooms have a private hall with bath

2" x 6" exterior wall framing available for an additional fee, please specify when ordering

Price Code B

Rear View

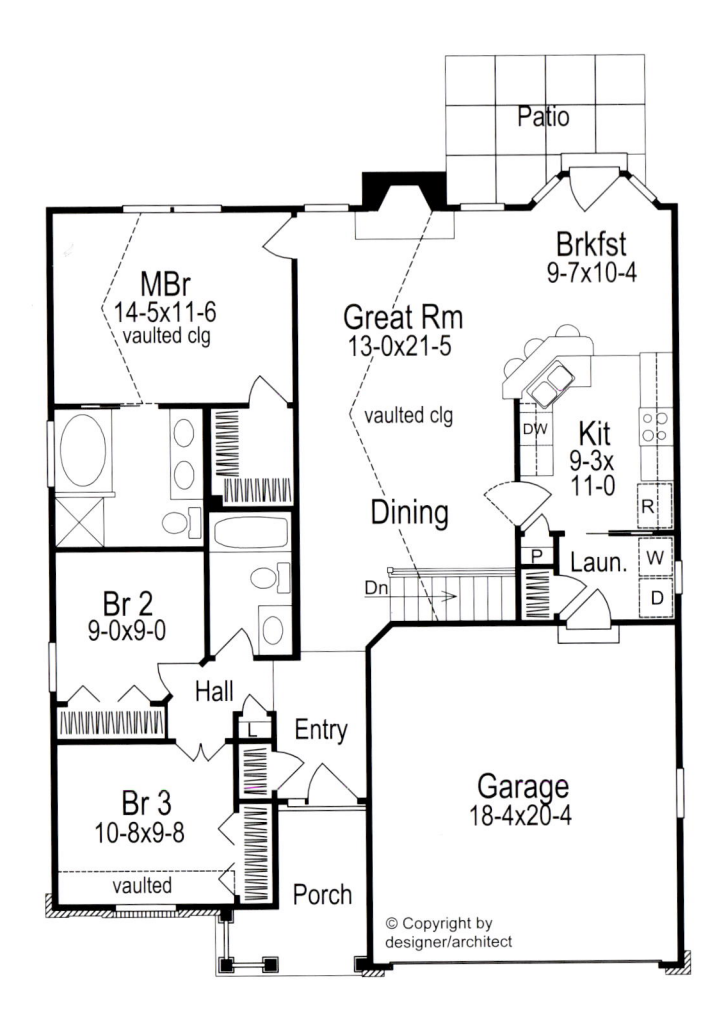

Patio

MBr 14-5x11-6 vaulted clg

Great Rm 13-0x21-5 vaulted clg

Brkfst 9-7x10-4

Kit 9-3x11-0

Dining

Br 2 9-0x9-0

Laun.

Hall

Entry

Br 3 10-8x9-8 vaulted

Garage 18-4x20-4

Porch

© Copyright by designer/architect

18   To order this plan, visit the Menards Building Materials Desk or visit www.Menards.com

MENARDS

Hermitage

Plan #M09-027D-0005

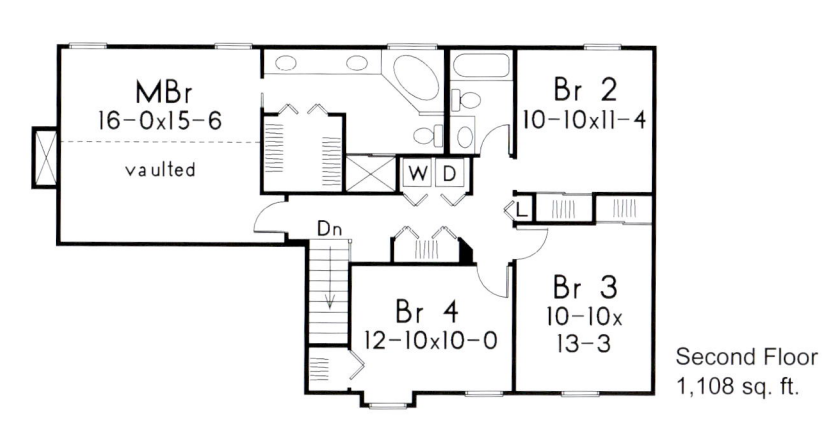

Second Floor
1,108 sq. ft.

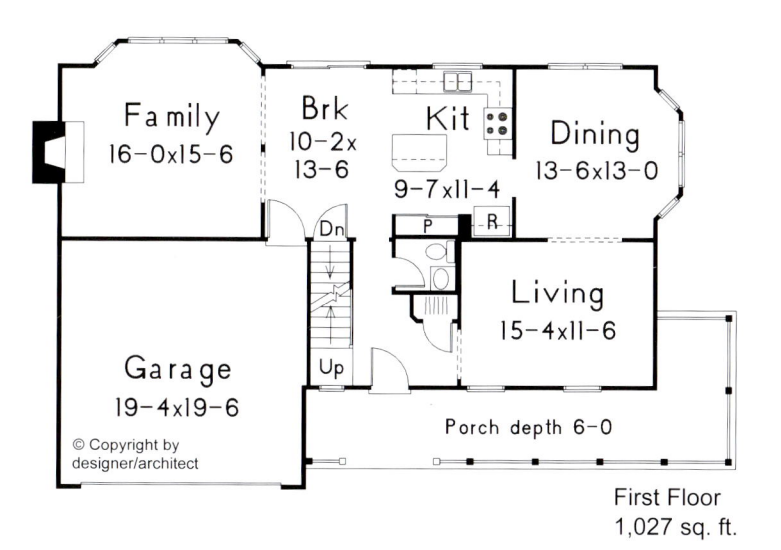

- MBr 16-0x15-6 vaulted
- Br 2 10-10x11-4
- Br 4 12-10x10-0
- Br 3 10-10x13-3

First Floor
1,027 sq. ft.

- Family 16-0x15-6
- Brk 10-2x13-6
- Kit 9-7x11-4
- Dining 13-6x13-0
- Living 15-4x11-6
- Garage 19-4x19-6
- Porch depth 6-0

© Copyright by designer/architect

Open Breakfast/Family Room Combination

2,135 total square feet of living area

Width: 48'-0"   Depth: 34'-0"

4 bedrooms, 2 1/2 baths

2-car garage

Basement foundation

Special features

The family room features extra space, an impressive fireplace, and a full wall of windows that joins the breakfast area creating a spacious entertainment area

The washer and dryer are conveniently located on the second floor

The kitchen features an island counter and a pantry

Price Code D

Rear View

To order this plan, visit the Menards Building Materials Desk or visit www.Menards.com.

Mannington

Plan #M09-013L-0022

Triple Dormers Create Terrific Curb Appeal

1,992 total square feet of living area

Width: 66'-2"   Depth: 62'-0"

4 bedrooms, 3 baths

2-car side entry garage

Basement, crawl space or slab foundation, please specify when ordering

Special features

Interesting angled walls add drama to many of the living areas including the family room, master bedroom, and breakfast area

The rear covered porch includes a spa and an outdoor kitchen with a sink, refrigerator, and a cooktop

Enter the majestic master bath to find a dramatic oversized corner tub

The bonus room above the garage has an additional 299 square feet of living area

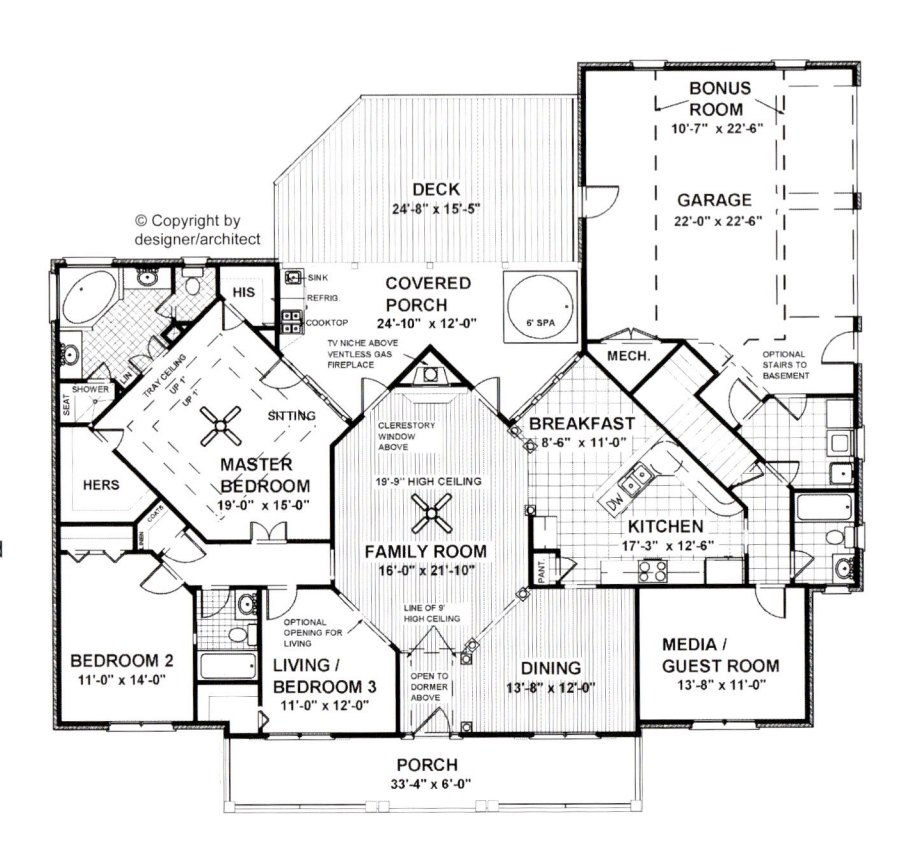

Price Code C

To order this plan, visit the Menards Building Materials Desk or visit www.Menards.com

MENARDS

Kalinda Cove

Plan #M09-072L-0013

Pleasant Country Cottage

1,283 total square feet of living area

Width: 51'-0"   Depth: 40'-0"

3 bedrooms, 2 baths

2-car garage

Basement foundation

Special features

The fabulous great room is located just off the front foyer and boasts a dramatic vaulted ceiling and a cozy fireplace

The efficient kitchen enjoys a pantry and a sunny breakfast room with deck access

Bedroom #2 boasts a cozy window seat

Price Code D

To order this plan, visit the Menards Building Materials Desk or visit www.Menards.com.

BARCLAY HILL

MENARDS

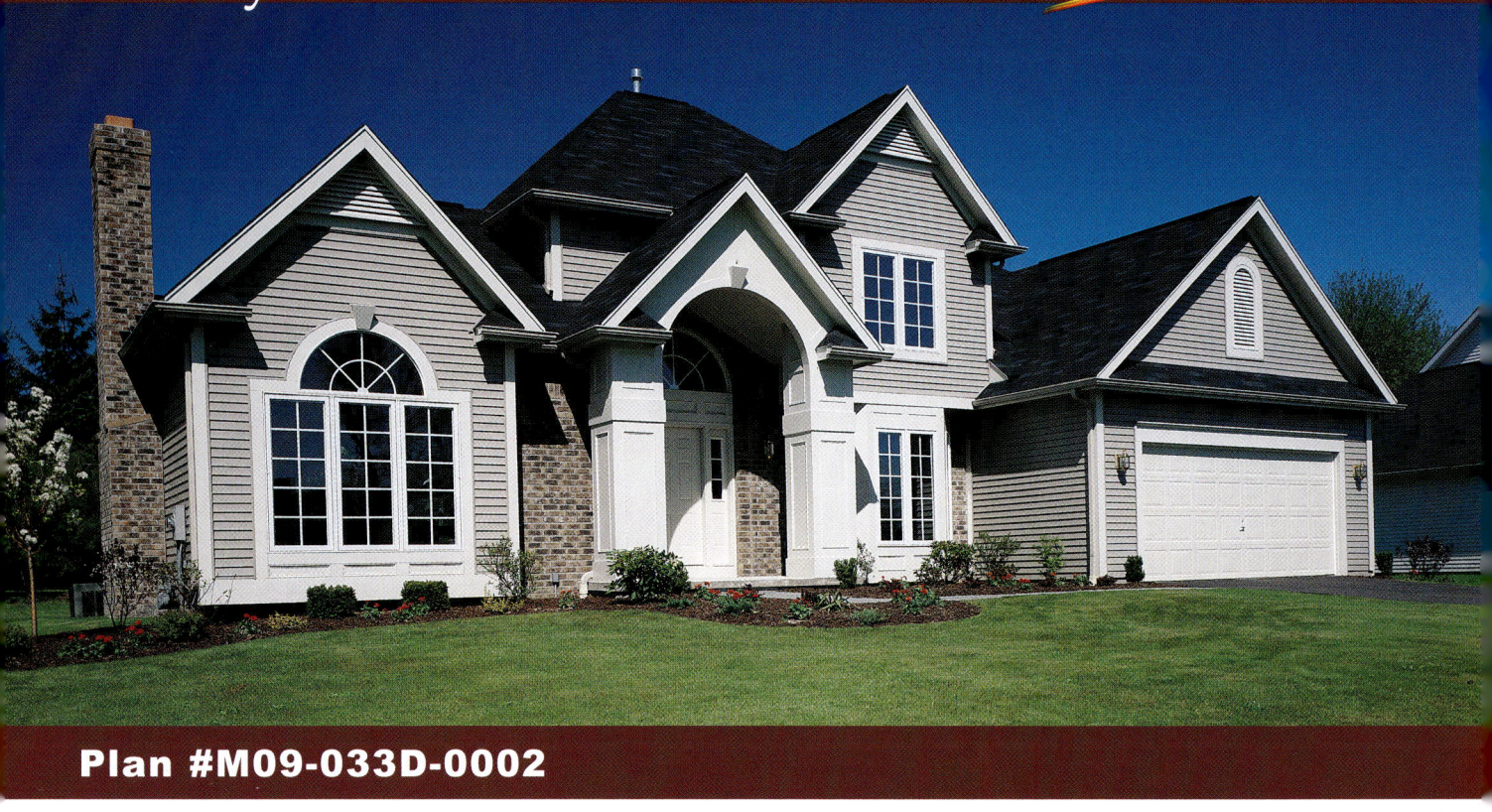

Plan #M09-033D-0002

Striking, Covered Arched Entry

1,859 total square feet of living area

Width: 61'-4"   Depth: 36'-0"

3 bedrooms, 2 1/2 baths

2-car garage

Basement foundation

Special features

A fireplace highlights the vaulted great room

The master bedroom includes a large walk-in closet and a private bath

The kitchen adjoins the breakfast room, which has easy access to the outdoors through glass sliding doors

Price Code D

Second Floor 789 sq. ft.

- Br 2: 10-8x11-3
- MBr: 11-10x17-2
- Br 3: 11-8x10-2

First Floor 1,070 sq. ft.

- Brk: 9-8x11-6
- Kit: 10-0x13-8
- Great Rm: 15-2x19-0 (vaulted)
- Dining: 11-8x11-2
- Garage: 21-8x21-8

© Copyright by designer/architect

Rear View

22 To order this plan, visit the Menards Building Materials Desk or visit www.Menards.com

MENARDS

Mooreland

Plan #M09-001D-0013

Traditional Exterior, Handsome Accents

1,882 total square feet of living area

Width: 60'-10"   Depth: 51'-2"

3 bedrooms, 2 baths

2-car garage

Basement foundation

Special features

A wide, handsome entrance opens to the vaulted great room with a fireplace

The great room and dining area are conveniently joined, but still allow privacy

A private covered porch extends the breakfast area

A practical passageway runs through the laundry room from the garage to the kitchen

Price Code D

Floor plan dimensions:
- MBr 15-0x14-4 vaulted
- Great Rm 24-0x17-0 vaulted
- Dining 11-8x12-0
- covered porch
- Kit 12-6x12-0
- Brk 11-6x9-0
- Br 3 11-0x11-3
- Br 2 12-0x11-5
- Foyer
- Porch
- Garage 20-0x20-7

© Copyright by designer/architect

Rear View

To order this plan, visit the Menards Building Materials Desk or visit www.Menards.com.

Oakglen Park

MENARDS

Plan #M09-065L-0002

Exciting Roof Lines

2,101 total square feet of living area

Width: 59'-4" Depth: 58'-10"

3 bedrooms, 2 1/2 baths

2-car garage

Basement foundation, crawl space foundation available for an additional fee

Special features

The sunken great room has a lovely balcony above

The octagon-shaped master bedroom is spacious and private

Luxurious amenities are located throughout this modest sized home

Price Code C

Second Floor
475 sq. ft.

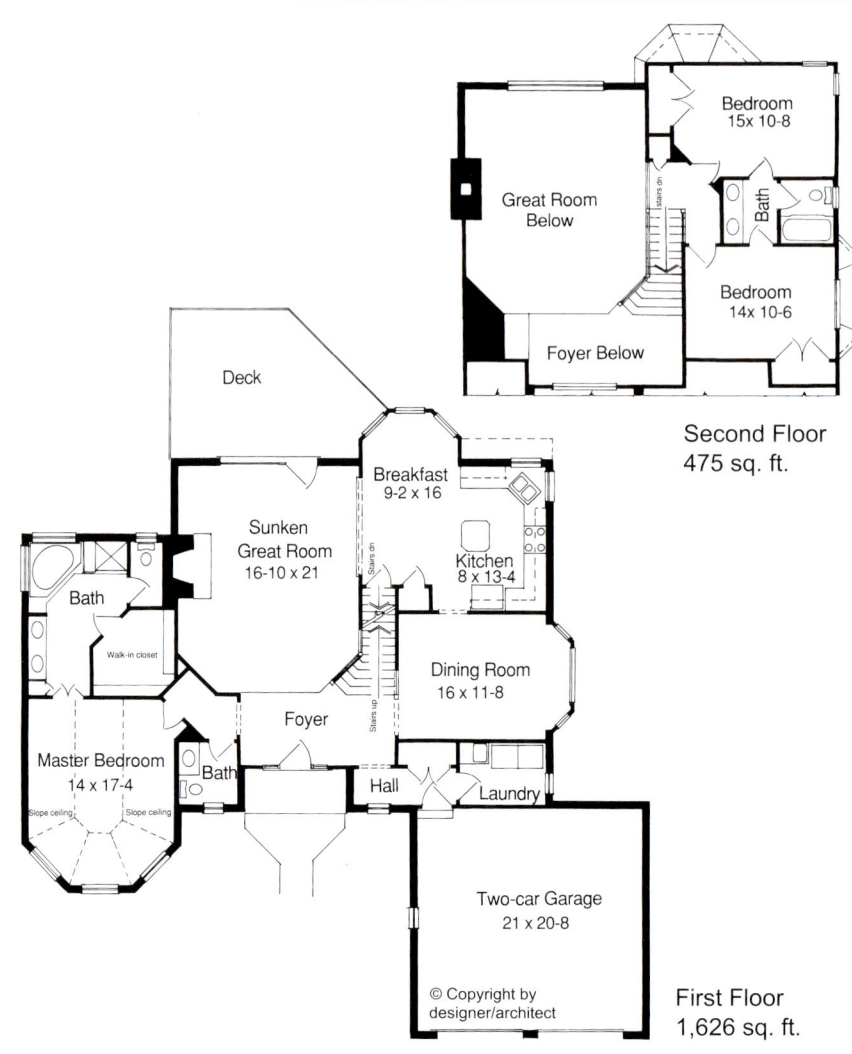

- Bedroom 15 x 10-8
- Great Room Below
- Bath
- Bedroom 14 x 10-6
- Foyer Below

First Floor
1,626 sq. ft.

- Deck
- Breakfast 9-2 x 16
- Sunken Great Room 16-10 x 21
- Kitchen 8 x 13-4
- Bath
- Walk-in closet
- Dining Room 16 x 11-8
- Foyer
- Master Bedroom 14 x 17-4
- Bath
- Hall
- Laundry
- Two-car Garage 21 x 20-8

© Copyright by designer/architect

24   To order this plan, visit the Menards Building Materials Desk or visit www.Menards.com

MENARDS

Dominique

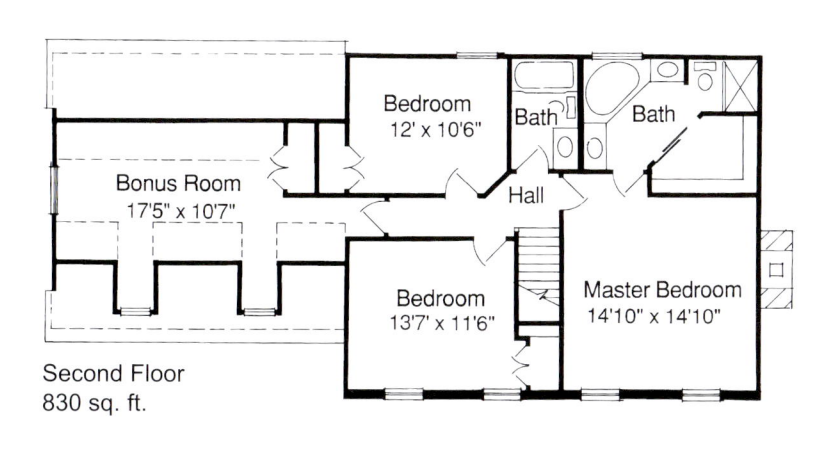

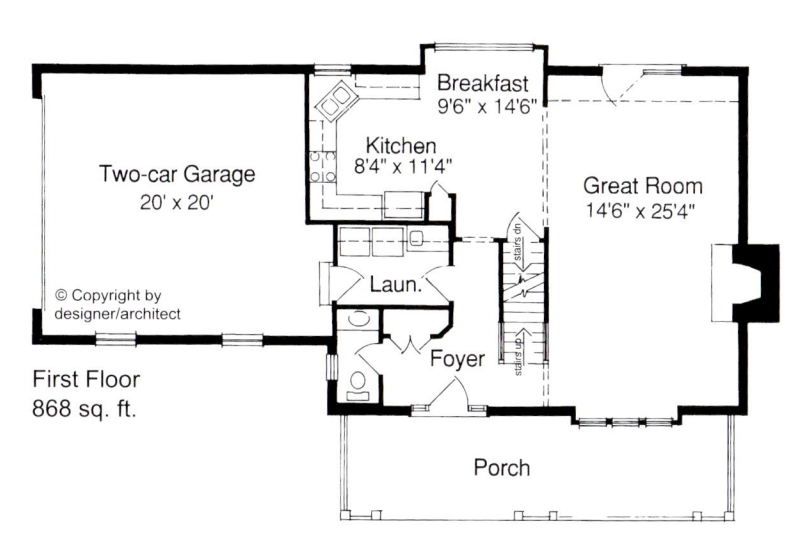

Plan #M09-065L-0166

Efficient Two-Story Home

1,698 total square feet of living area

Width: 57'-0"   Depth: 36'-4"

3 bedrooms, 2 1/2 baths

2-car side entry garage

Basement or crawl space foundation, please specify when ordering

Special features

The massive great room runs the entire depth of the home offering a view of the front porch and easy access to the backyard

The adjacent breakfast area offers a relaxed atmosphere and enjoys close proximity to the U-shaped kitchen

All of the bedrooms are located on the second floor, including the master bedroom that features a deluxe bath and a walk-in closet

The optional bonus room over the garage has an additional 269 square feet of living area

Price Code B

Second Floor 830 sq. ft.
- Bonus Room 17'5" x 10'7"
- Bedroom 12' x 10'6"
- Bath
- Bath
- Hall
- Bedroom 13'7" x 11'6"
- Master Bedroom 14'10" x 14'10"

First Floor 868 sq. ft.
- Two-car Garage 20' x 20'
- Breakfast 9'6" x 14'6"
- Kitchen 8'4" x 11'4"
- Laun.
- Foyer
- Great Room 14'6" x 25'4"
- Porch

© Copyright by designer/architect

To order this plan, visit the Menards Building Materials Desk or visit www.Menards.com.

Stellaville

MENARDS

Plan #M09-013L-0027

Spacious Country Kitchen

2,184 total square feet of living area

Width: 71'-2"   Depth: 58'-1"

3 bedrooms, 3 baths

2-car side entry garage

Basement, crawl space or slab foundation, please specify when ordering

Special features

The delightful family room has access to the screened porch for enjoyable outdoor living

The secluded master suite is complete with a sitting area, and a luxurious bath

The formal living room has a double-door entry easily converting it to a study or home office

Two secondary bedrooms have their own baths

The bonus room above the garage has an additional 379 square feet of living space

Price Code F

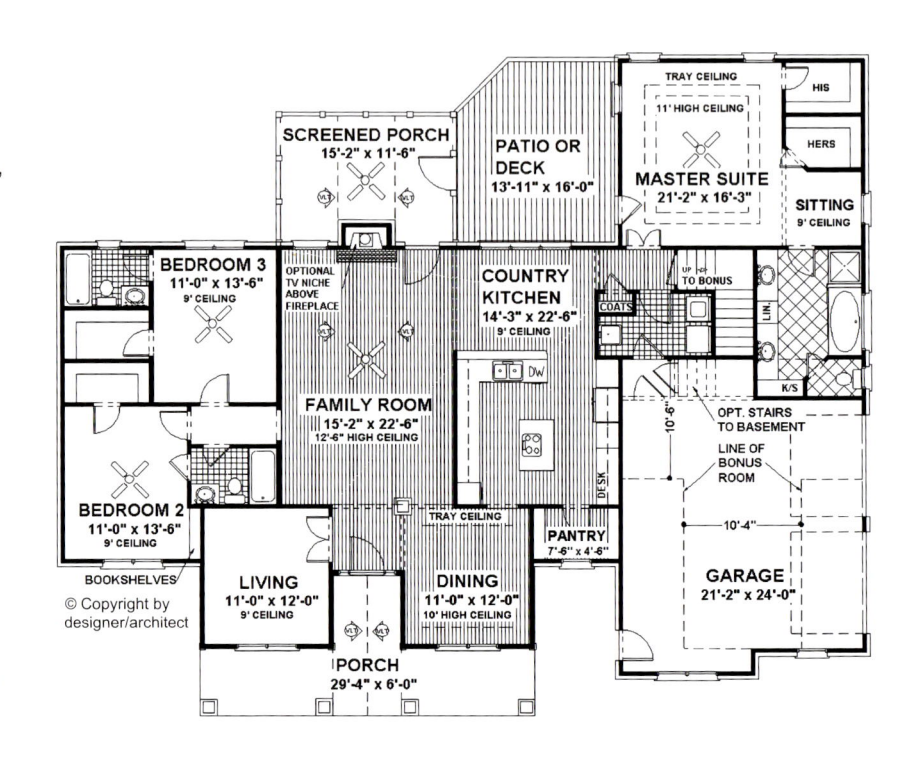

To order this plan, visit the Menards Building Materials Desk or visit www.Menards.com

MENARDS

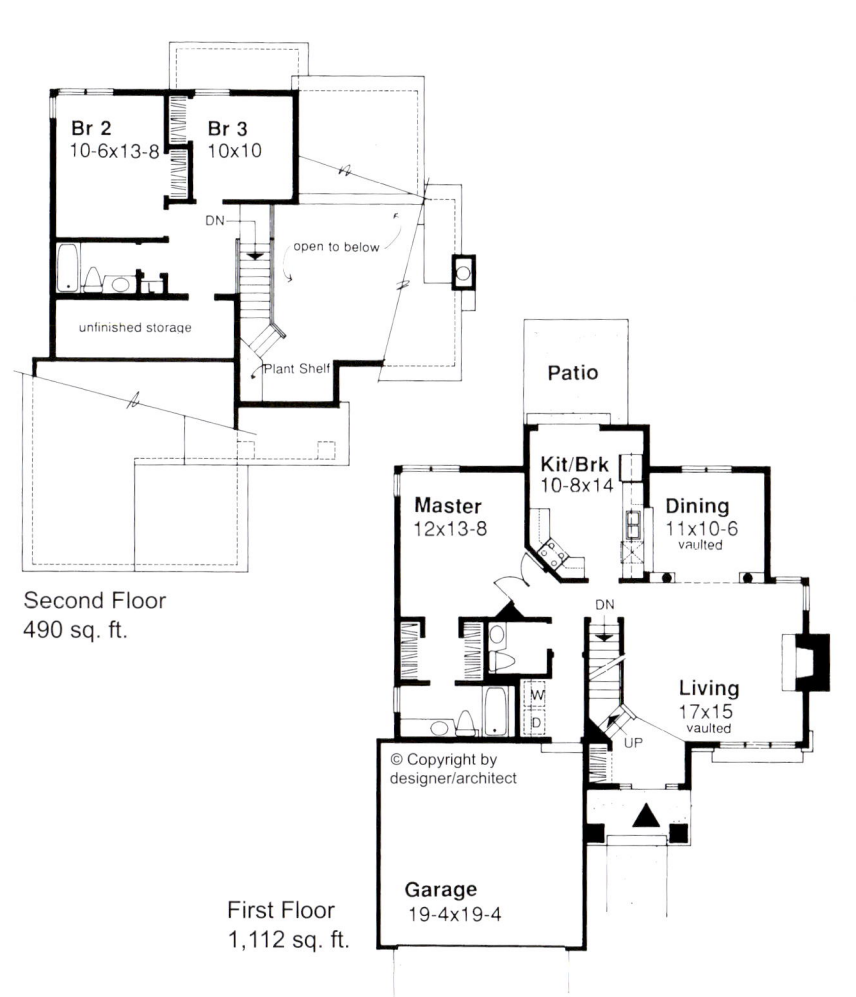

Boxberg

Plan #M09-072L-0024

Stunning Two-Story

1,602 total square feet of living area

Width: 43'-4"   Depth: 50'-0"

3 bedrooms, 2 1/2 baths

2-car garage

Basement foundation

Special features

The vaulted living room shines with a two-story window and a grand fireplace as a focal point

Columns define the entry into the formal dining room, while still maintaining an open feel

A double-door entry adds elegance to the master suite that also enjoys two closets and a private bath

Price Code D

Second Floor 490 sq. ft.
- Br 2: 10-6x13-8
- Br 3: 10x10
- unfinished storage
- Plant Shelf

First Floor 1,112 sq. ft.
- Patio
- Kit/Brk: 10-8x14
- Master: 12x13-8
- Dining: 11x10-6 vaulted
- Living: 17x15 vaulted
- Garage: 19-4x19-4

To order this plan, visit the Menards Building Materials Desk or visit www.Menards.com.

Hyde Place

MENARDS

Plan #M09-039L-0017

Covered Front Porch

1,966 total square feet of living area

Width: 48'-2"   Depth: 67'-5"

3 bedrooms, 2 1/2 baths

2-car side entry garage

Basement foundation

Special features

A private dining room remains the focal point when entering the home

The kitchen and breakfast area join forces to create a functional area

Lots of closet space can be found in all of the second floor bedrooms

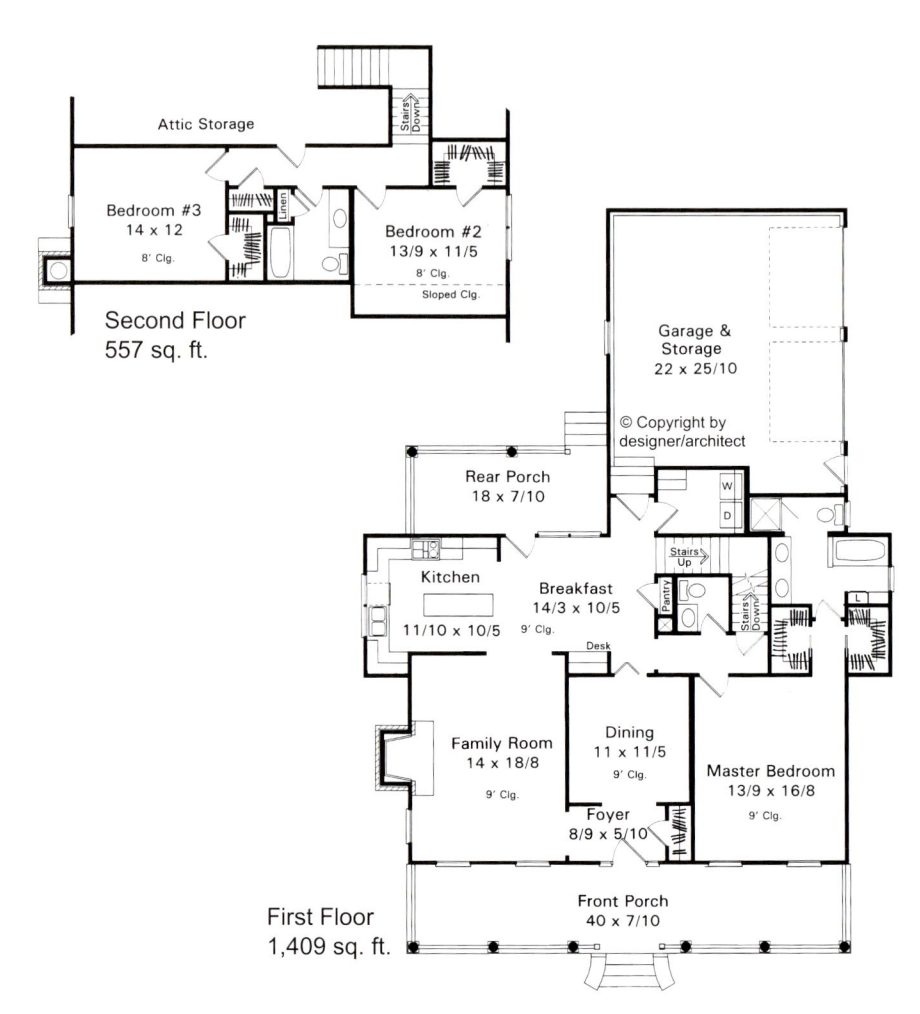

Price Code C

Second Floor 557 sq. ft.
- Attic Storage
- Bedroom #3 — 14 x 12 — 8' Clg.
- Bedroom #2 — 13/9 x 11/5 — 8' Clg. — Sloped Clg.

First Floor 1,409 sq. ft.
- Garage & Storage — 22 x 25/10
- Rear Porch — 18 x 7/10
- Kitchen — 11/10 x 10/5
- Breakfast — 14/3 x 10/5 — 9' Clg.
- Family Room — 14 x 18/8 — 9' Clg.
- Dining — 11 x 11/5 — 9' Clg.
- Master Bedroom — 13/9 x 16/8 — 9' Clg.
- Foyer — 8/9 x 5/10
- Front Porch — 40 x 7/10

© Copyright by designer/architect

To order this plan, visit the Menards Building Materials Desk or visit www.Menards.com.

MENARDS

Plan #M09-072L-0036

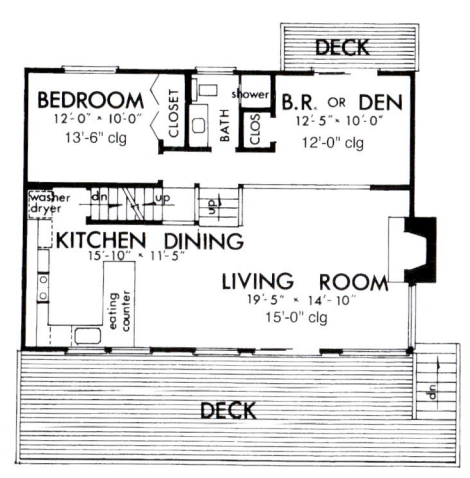

First Floor
936 sq. ft.

Second Floor
252 sq. ft.

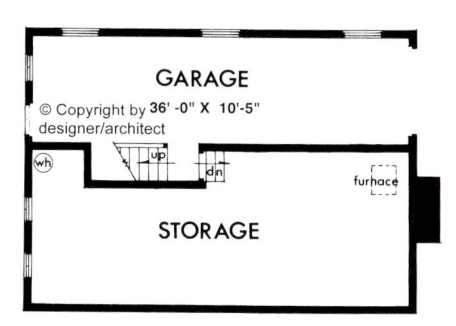

Lower Level

Wonderful Outdoor Living Spaces

1,188 total square feet of living area

Width: 38'-1"   Depth: 26'-0"

3 bedrooms, 2 baths

1-car drive under side entry garage

Walk-out basement foundation

Special features

The large living room with fireplace enjoys a ceiling height of 15' and has access to the large deck

The second floor bedroom is a nice escape with its own bath and private deck

A large eating counter in the kitchen creates casual dining space

Price Code D

To order this plan, visit the Menards Building Materials Desk or visit www.Menards.com.

Plan #M09-007D-0127

Luxury Home For Narrow Site Has Exciting Interior

2,158 total square feet of living area

Width: 32'-4"   Depth: 58'-0"

3 bedrooms, 2 1/2 baths

2-car garage

Basement foundation

Special features

The vaulted entry has a coat closet and built-in shelves with a plant shelf above

The two-story living room has tall dramatic windows flanking the fireplace

A laundry room and half bath are located near the kitchen

Price Code C

First Floor 1,125 sq. ft.

Second Floor 1,033 sq. ft.

Rear View

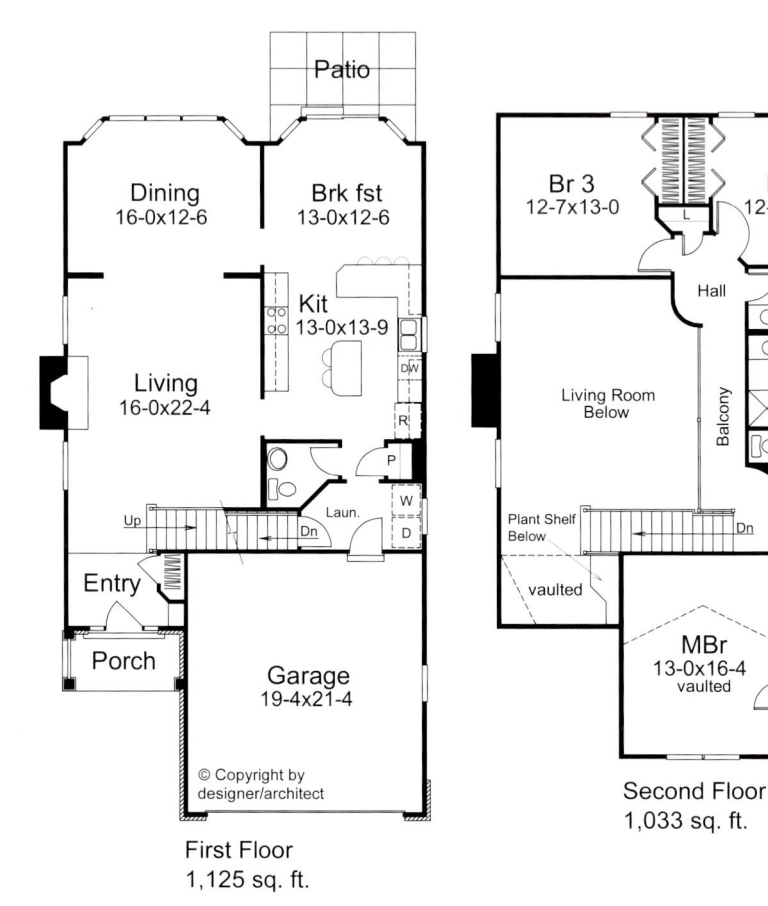

30 · der this plan, visit the Menards Building Materials Desk or visit www.Menards.com.

MENARDS

Anabel

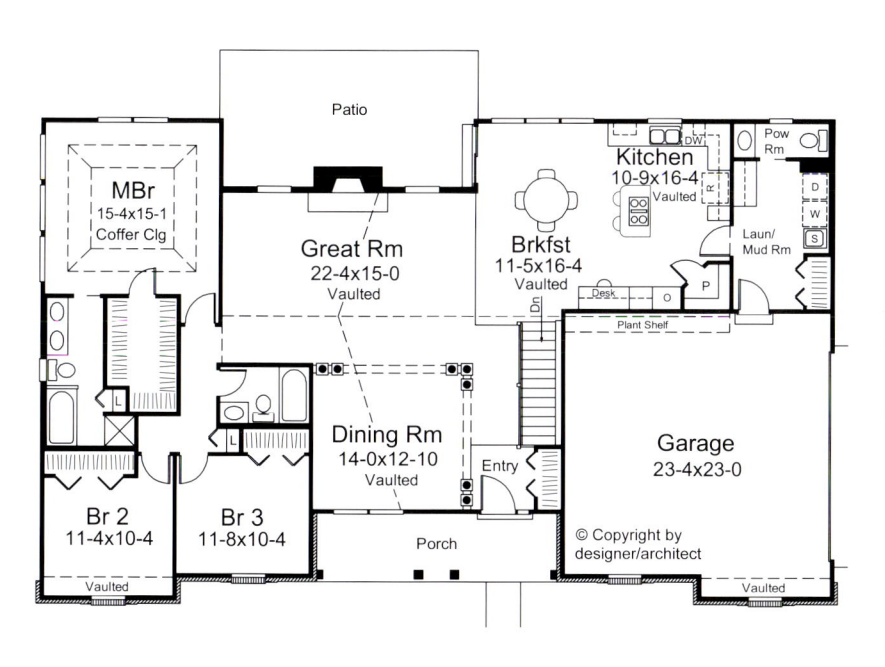

Plan #M09-121D-0002

Double Dormers And Gables Add Curb Appeal

2,025 total square feet of living area

Width: 70'-4"   Depth: 42'-8"

3 bedrooms, 2 1/2 baths

2-car side entry garage

Basement foundation

Special features

The cozy great room enjoys a 42" wood burning fireplace as the main focal point

The dining room has decorative columns and beams along with a vaulted ceiling

The vaulted kitchen has a versatile cooktop island with separate oven

An coffered ceiling tops the master bedroom

2" x 6" exterior wall framing available for an additional fee, please specify when ordering

Price Code B

Rear View

To order this plan, visit the Menards Building Materials Desk or visit www.Menards.com.

Floor Plan Rooms:
- MBr 15-4x15-1 Coffer Clg
- Patio
- Great Rm 22-4x15-0 Vaulted
- Kitchen 10-9x16-4 Vaulted
- Brkfst 11-5x16-4 Vaulted
- Laun/Mud Rm
- Pow Rm
- Dining Rm 14-0x12-10 Vaulted
- Garage 23-4x23-0
- Br 2 11-4x10-4 Vaulted
- Br 3 11-8x10-4
- Porch
- Entry

© Copyright by designer/architect

Riley

MENARDS

Plan #M09-121D-0021

Covered Country Front Porch

1,562 total square feet of living area

Width: 65'-0"   Depth: 46'-4"

3 bedrooms, 2 baths

2-car garage

Basement foundation

Special features

The vaulted breakfast room sits in a sunny bay window with sliding glass doors that access the rear patio

A convenient angled eating bar in the kitchen is perfect for casual meals and has enough dining space for five people

The spacious great room boasts a vaulted ceiling and a warming corner fireplace

Price Code A

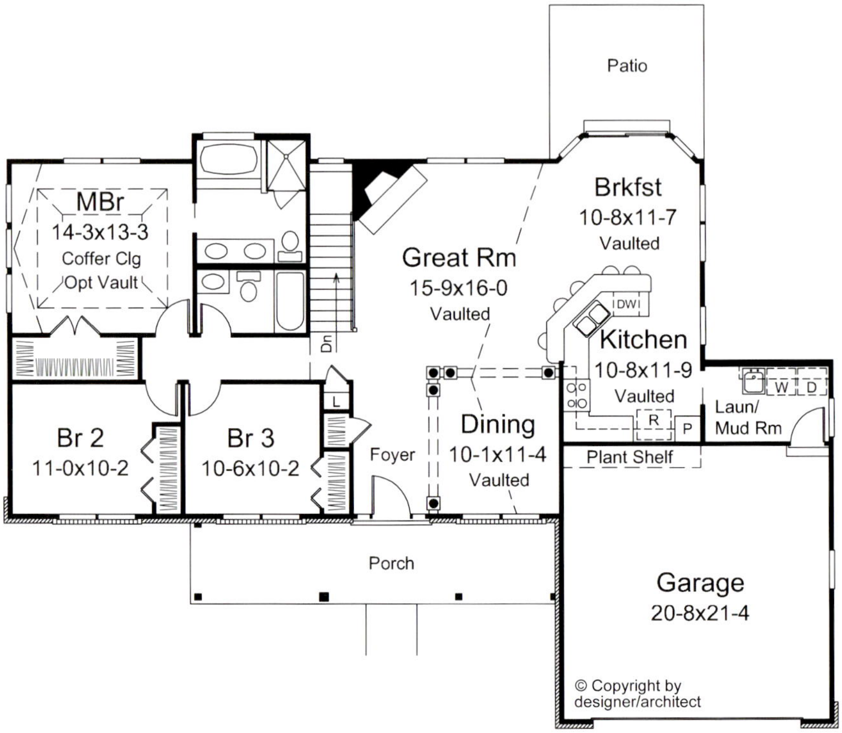

Rear View

To order this plan, visit the Menards Building Materials Desk or visit www.Menards.com

MENARDS

Fruitland

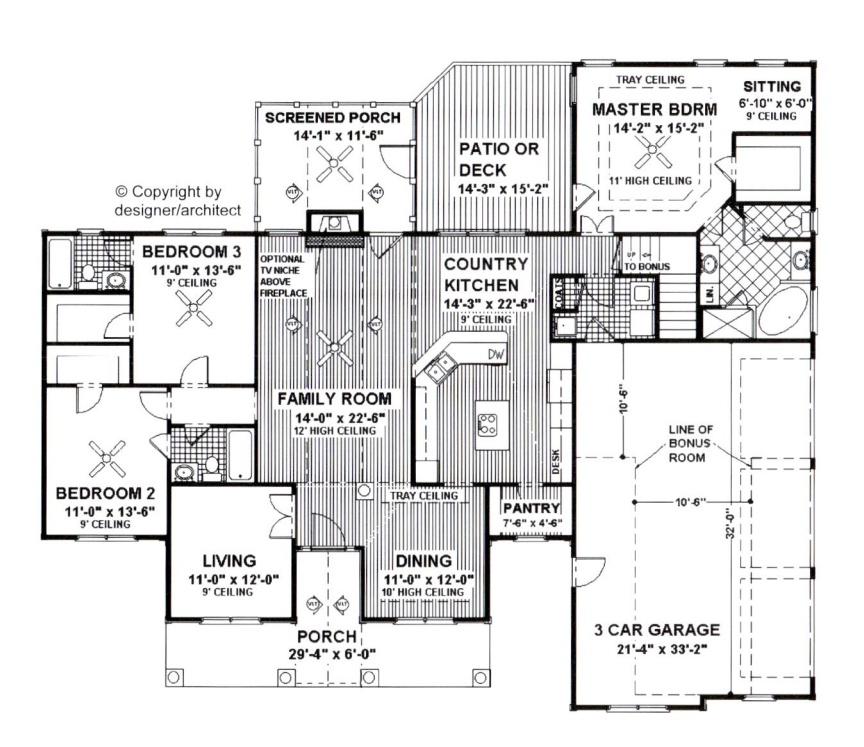

Plan #M09-013L-0025

Inviting Vaulted Entry

2,097 total square feet of living area

Width: 70'-2" Depth: 59'-0"

3 bedrooms, 3 baths

3-car side entry garage

Basement, crawl space or slab foundation, please specify when ordering

Special features

The country kitchen, family room, and dining area flow together for an open floor plan

The family room includes a TV niche making this a cozy place to relax

The sumptuous master bedroom includes a sitting area, a walk-in closet, and a full bath with double vanities

The bonus room above the garage has an additional 452 square feet of living space

Price Code D

To order this plan, visit the Menards Building Materials Desk or visit www.Menards.com.

Eatherton

Plan #M09-055L-0043

Built-In Pantry

1,654 total square feet of living area

Width: 49'-0"   Depth: 58'-6"

3 bedrooms, 2 baths

2-car garage

Walk-out basement, basement, crawl space or slab foundation, please specify when ordering

Special features

The U-shaped kitchen features tons of cabinetry, counter seating, and access to the dining room/hearth room

The great room has a sloped ceiling, a media center, and a fireplace

The master bath is accented with glass blocks above the whirlpool tub

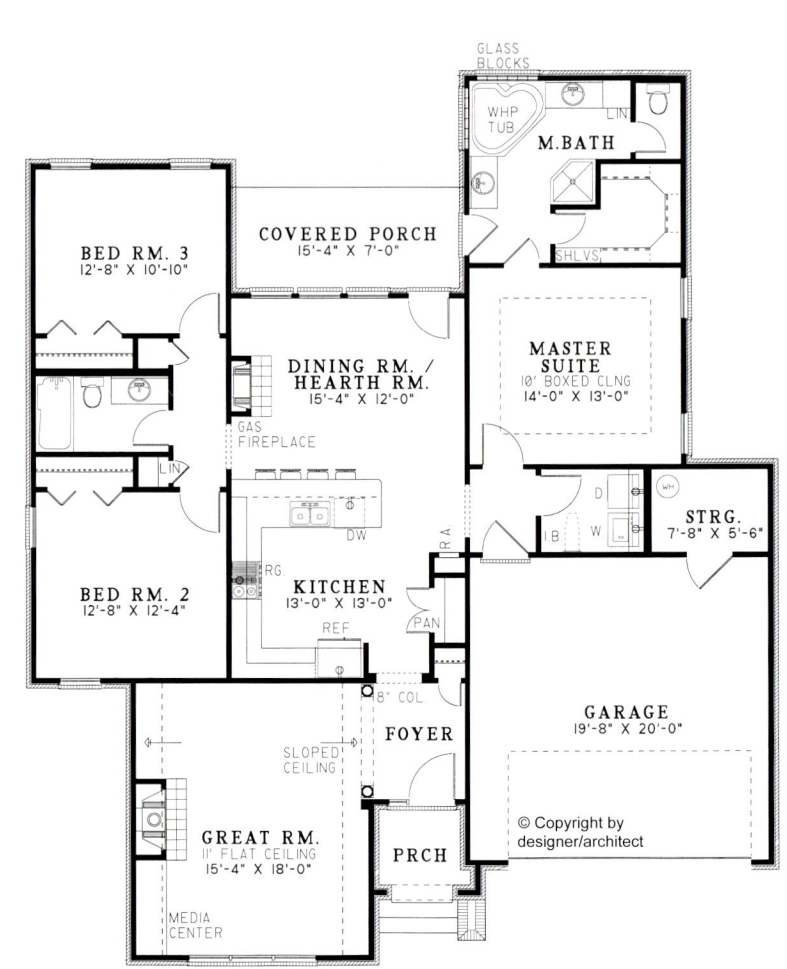

Price Code C

To order this plan, visit the Menards Building Materials Desk or visit www.Menards.com.

MENARDS

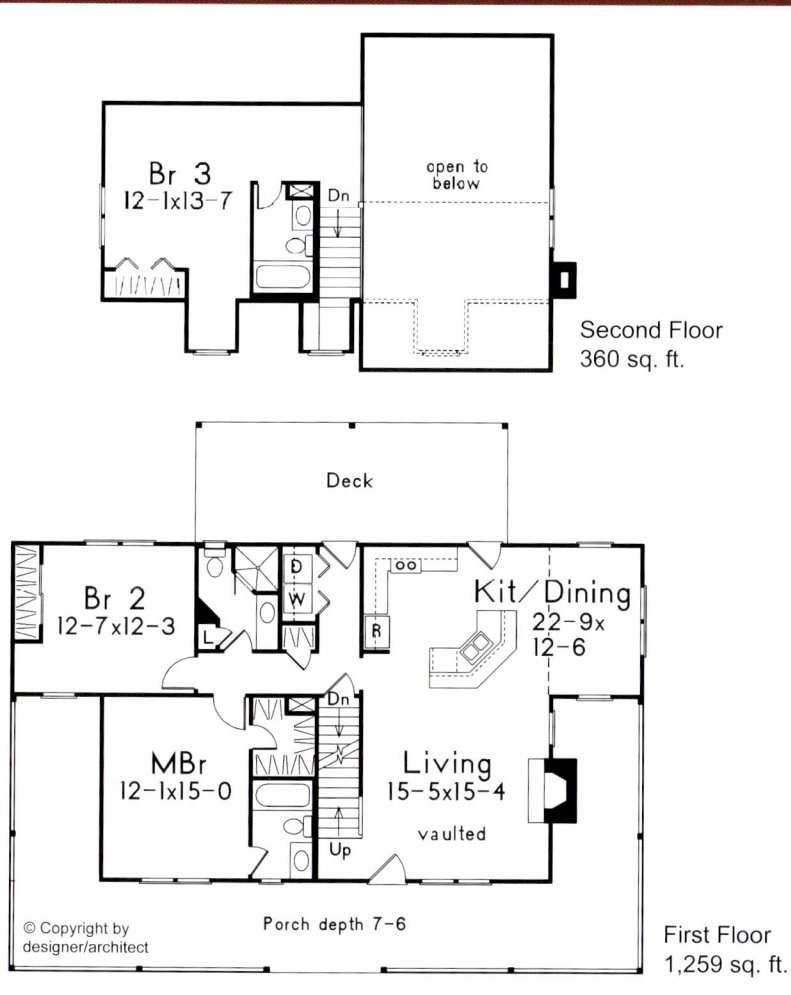

Hickory

Plan #M09-029D-0002

Country-Style Porch Adds Charm

1,619 total square feet of living area

Width: 52'-6"   Depth: 28'-2"

3 bedrooms, 3 baths

Basement foundation, drawings also include crawl space and slab foundations

Special features

The second floor private bedroom has a bath

The kitchen features an angled island snack bar and an adjacent dining area

The master bedroom has a private bath and a walk-in closet

The washer and dryer closet is centrally located for convenience

Price Code B

Br 3 12-1x13-7

Second Floor 360 sq. ft.

Deck

Br 2 12-7x12-3

Kit/Dining 22-9x 12-6

MBr 12-1x15-0

Living 15-5x15-4 vaulted

Porch depth 7-6

© Copyright by designer/architect

First Floor 1,259 sq. ft.

Rear View

To order this plan, visit the Menards Building Materials Desk or visit www.Menards.com.

35

Eureka

MENARDS

Plan #M09-122D-0001

Energy Efficient Two-Story Berm Home

1,105 total square feet of living area

Width: 33'-0"   Depth: 35'-0"

2 bedrooms, 1 1/2 baths

Slab foundation

Special features

Energy efficient home with 2" x 6" exterior walls

This fresh, modern design enjoys sleek window lines and a stucco exterior

The efficient U-shaped kitchen offers a tremendous amount of counterspace within reach for all sorts of kitchen tasks at hand

A tall sloped ceiling in the two-story living room gives this home an open and spacious feel all those who enter will appreciate

Price Code AAA

Rear View

Bedroom 2 11-9x11-4

Dining 9-4x7-8

Kitchen 9-0x9-0

Hall

Bath

Lndry

Living Rm 17-8x14-11
Sloped Clg.

Foyer

Patio

© Copyright by designer/architect

First Floor 880 sq. ft.

Bath

Bedroom 1 11-10x14-2

Open

Second Floor 225 sq. ft.

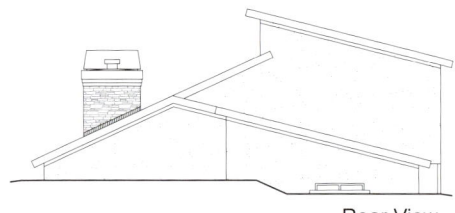

36   To order this plan, visit the Menards Building Materials Desk or visit www.Menards.com.

MENARDS

Yukon

Plan #M09-008D-0162

Terrific Design Loaded With Extras

865 total square feet of living area

Width: 26'-0"   Depth: 36'-0"

2 bedrooms, 1 bath

Pier foundation

Special features

The central living area provides an enormous amount of space for gathering around the fireplace

The outdoor ladder on the wrap-around deck connects the top deck with the main deck

The kitchen is bright and cheerful with lots of windows and access to the deck

Price Code AAA

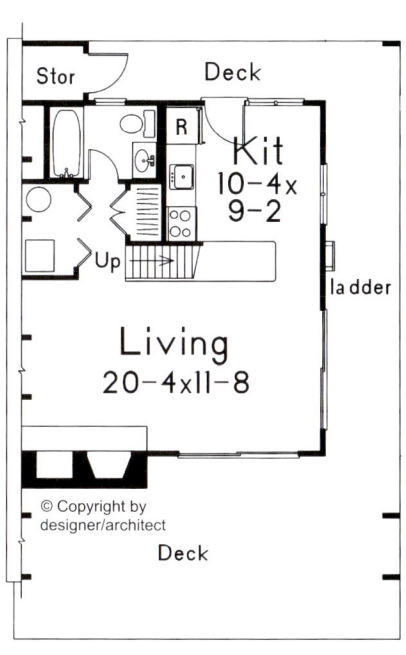

First Floor
495 sq. ft.

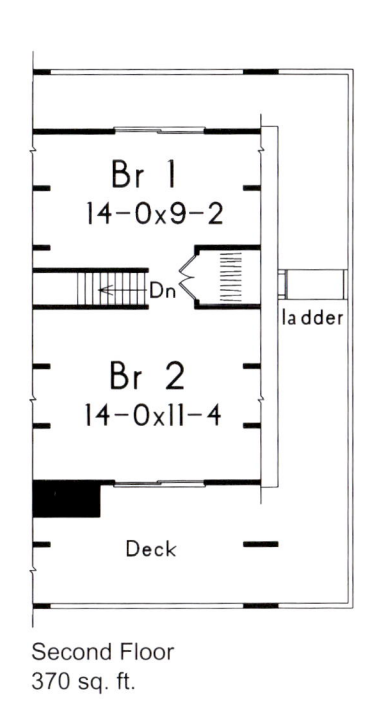

- Stor
- Deck
- Kit 10-4 x 9-2
- Up
- ladder
- Living 20-4 x 11-8
- Deck

Second Floor
370 sq. ft.

- Br 1 14-0 x 9-2
- Dn
- ladder
- Br 2 14-0 x 11-4
- Deck

To order this plan, visit the Menards Building Materials Desk or visit www.Menards.com

37

Lyn Lake

MENARDS

Plan #M09-007D-0198

Simple, Affordable Lake Home

1,142 total square feet of living area

Width: 30'-0"   Depth: 31'-0"

2 bedrooms, 1 1/2 baths

1-car side entry garage

Walk-out basement foundation

Special features

The living room has a bayed dining area with sliding glass doors to a large rear deck

The U-shaped kitchen has a separate laundry space and pass-through eating bar

The lower level consists of a hall bath, linen closet, and two bedrooms with walk-in closets and sliding glass doors to the patio

Price Code AA

Rear View

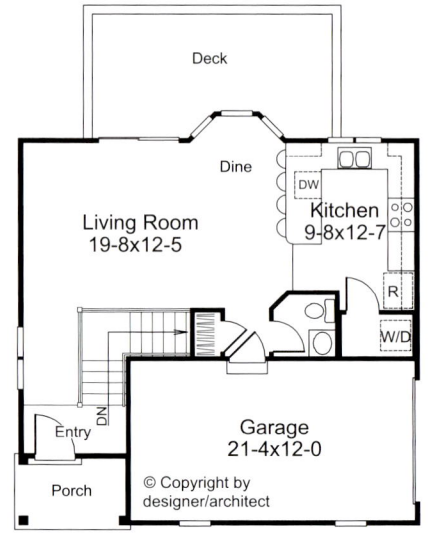

First Floor
572 sq. ft.

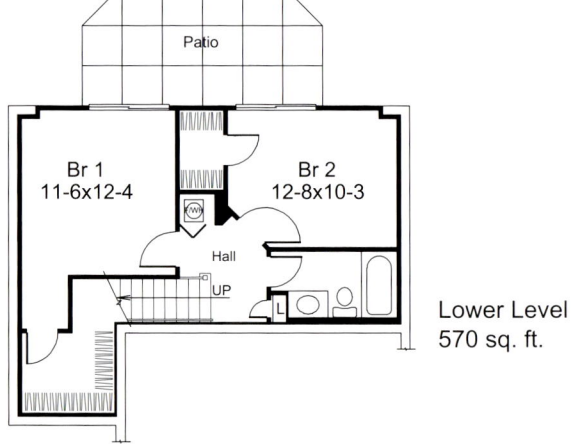

- Deck
- Dine
- Living Room 19-8x12-5
- Kitchen 9-8x12-7
- Entry
- Porch
- Garage 21-4x12-0

Lower Level
570 sq. ft.

- Patio
- Br 1 11-6x12-4
- Br 2 12-8x10-3
- Hall
- UP

To order this plan, visit the Menards Building Materials Desk or visit www.Menards.com

MENARDS

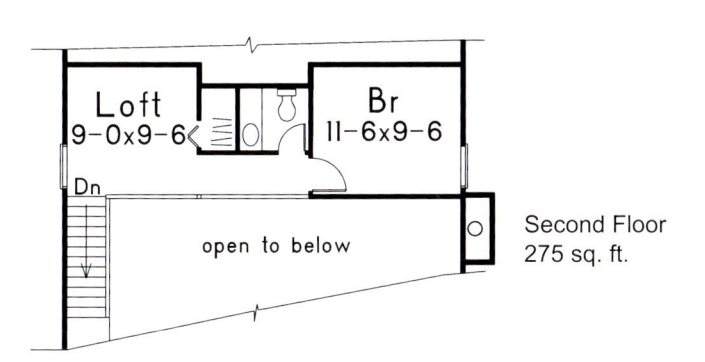

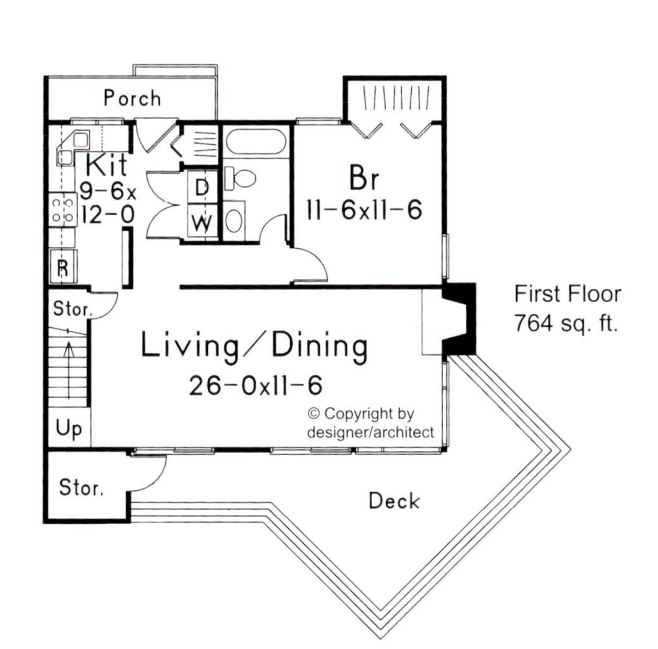

Chalet

Plan #M09-022D-0001

A Vacation Home For All Seasons

1,039 total square feet of living area

Width: 30'-0"   Depth: 33'-5"

2 bedrooms, 1 1/2 baths

Crawl space foundation

Special features

Cathedral construction provides the maximum in living area openness

Expansive glass viewing walls create an open feeling in the living/dining area

Simple, low-maintenance construction

This home has a charming second story loft arrangement

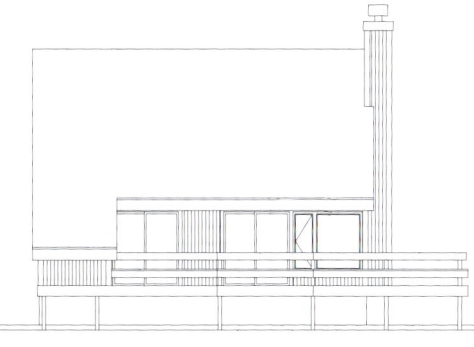

Price Code AA

Second Floor 275 sq. ft.
- Loft 9-0x9-6
- Br 11-6x9-6

First Floor 764 sq. ft.
- Porch
- Kit 9-6x12-0
- Br 11-6x11-6
- Living/Dining 26-0x11-6
- Stor.
- Deck

© Copyright by designer/architect

Rear View

To order this plan, visit the Menards Building Materials Desk or visit www.Menards.com.

Morfontaine

MENARDS

Plan #M09-077L-0026

Vaulted Great Room

1,501 total square feet of living area

Width: 61'-0"   Depth: 47'-4"

3 bedrooms, 2 baths

2-car garage

Slab, basement or crawl space foundation, please specify when ordering

Special features

The friendly covered front porch with arched openings invites guests inside the home and adds stunning curb appeal

The exquisite great room offers a vaulted ceiling and a grand fireplace flanked by built-in cabinets

The beautiful master bedroom features a trayed ceiling, two walk-in closets, and a plush bath with a garden tub

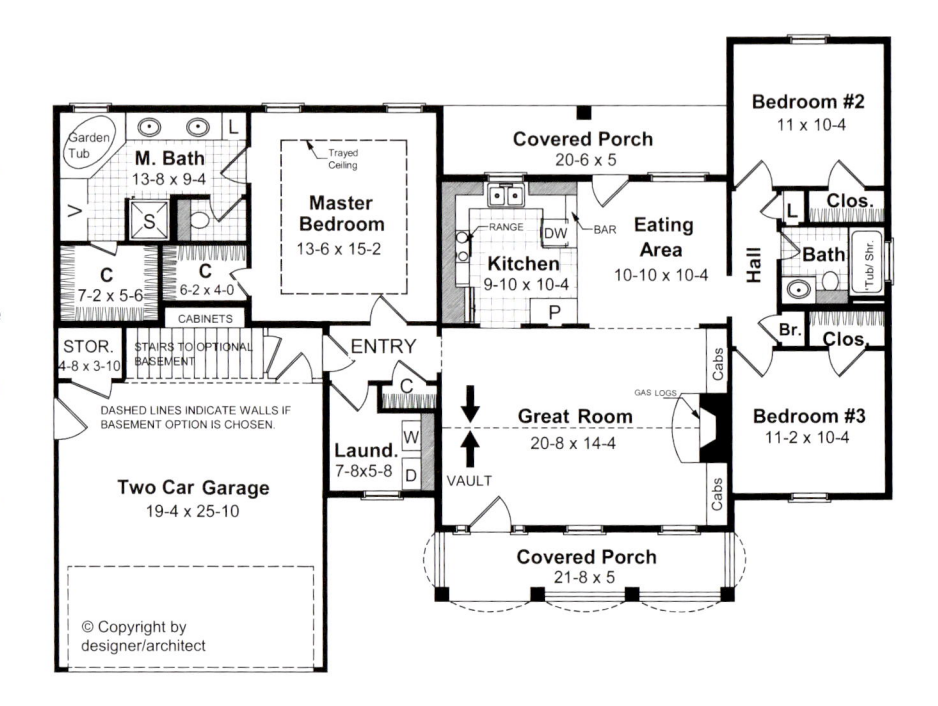

Price Code E

To order this plan, visit the Menards Building Materials Desk or visit www.Menards.com

MENARDS

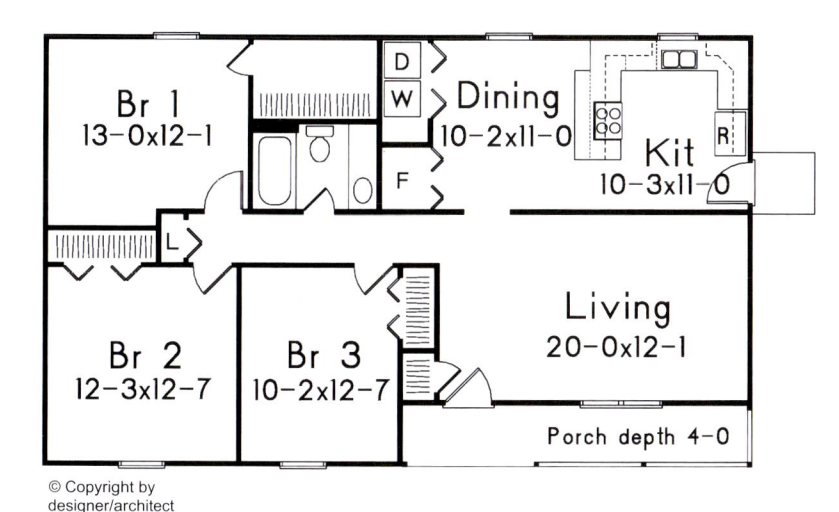

Manchester

Plan #M09-001D-0045

Country-Style With Spacious Rooms

1,197 total square feet of living area

Width: 46'-0"   Depth: 28'-0"

3 bedrooms, 1 bath

Crawl space foundation, drawings also include basement and slab foundations

Special features

The U-shaped kitchen includes ample workspace, a breakfast bar, a laundry area, and direct access to the outdoors

A large living room has a convenient coat closet

Bedroom #1 features a large walk-in closet

2" x 6" exterior wall framing available for an additional fee, please specify when ordering

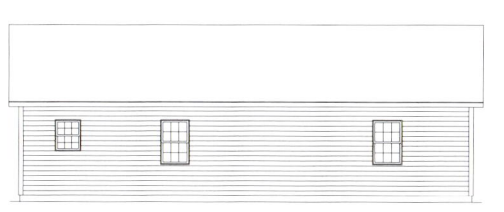

Price Code AA

Floor plan:
- Br 1: 13-0x12-1
- Dining: 10-2x11-0
- Kit: 10-3x11-0
- Br 2: 12-3x12-7
- Br 3: 10-2x12-7
- Living: 20-0x12-1
- Porch depth 4-0

© Copyright by designer/architect

Rear View

To order this plan, visit the Menards Building Materials Desk or visit www.Menards.com.

Mt. Pleasant

MENARDS

Plan #M09-024L-0002

Central Living Room Is Great For Gathering

1,405 total square feet of living area

Width: 42'-0" Depth: 51'-0"

3 bedrooms, 2 baths

Slab foundation

Special features

The compact design has all of the luxuries of a larger home

The master bedroom has its privacy away from the other bedrooms

The living room has a corner fireplace, access to the outdoors, and easily reaches the dining area and the kitchen

A large utility room near the kitchen has access to the outdoors

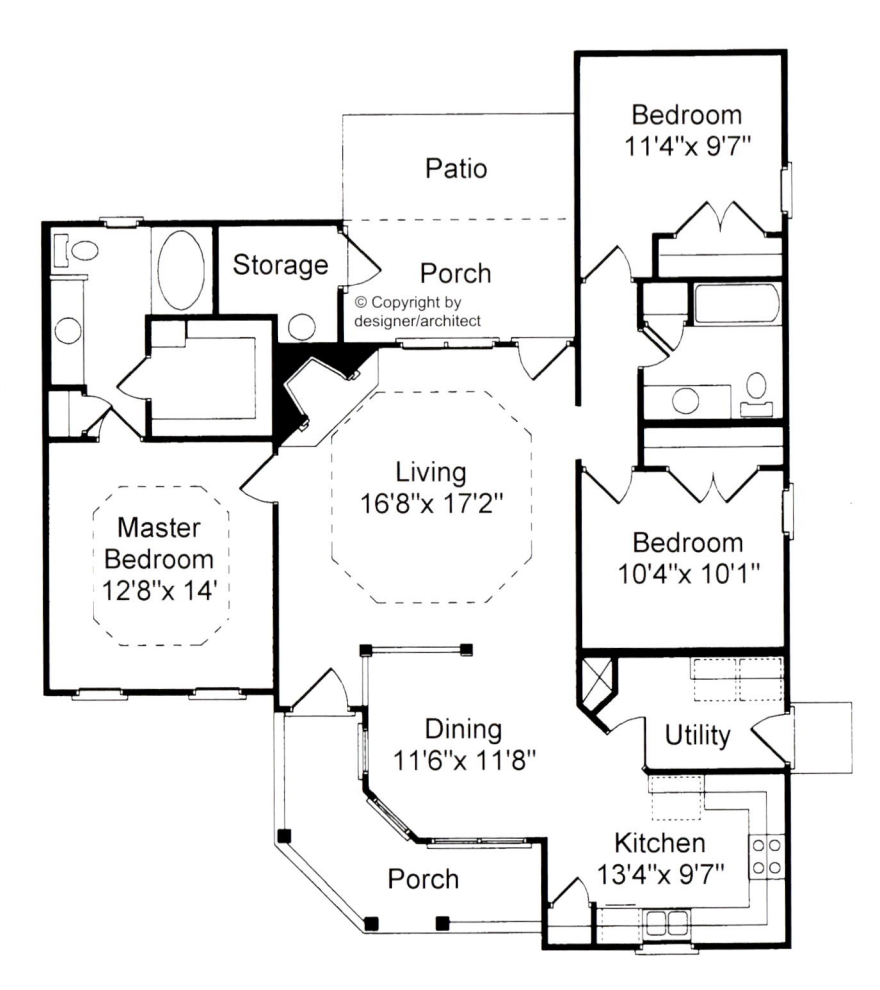

Price Code A

To order this plan, visit the Menards Building Materials Desk or visit www.menards.com.

MENARDS

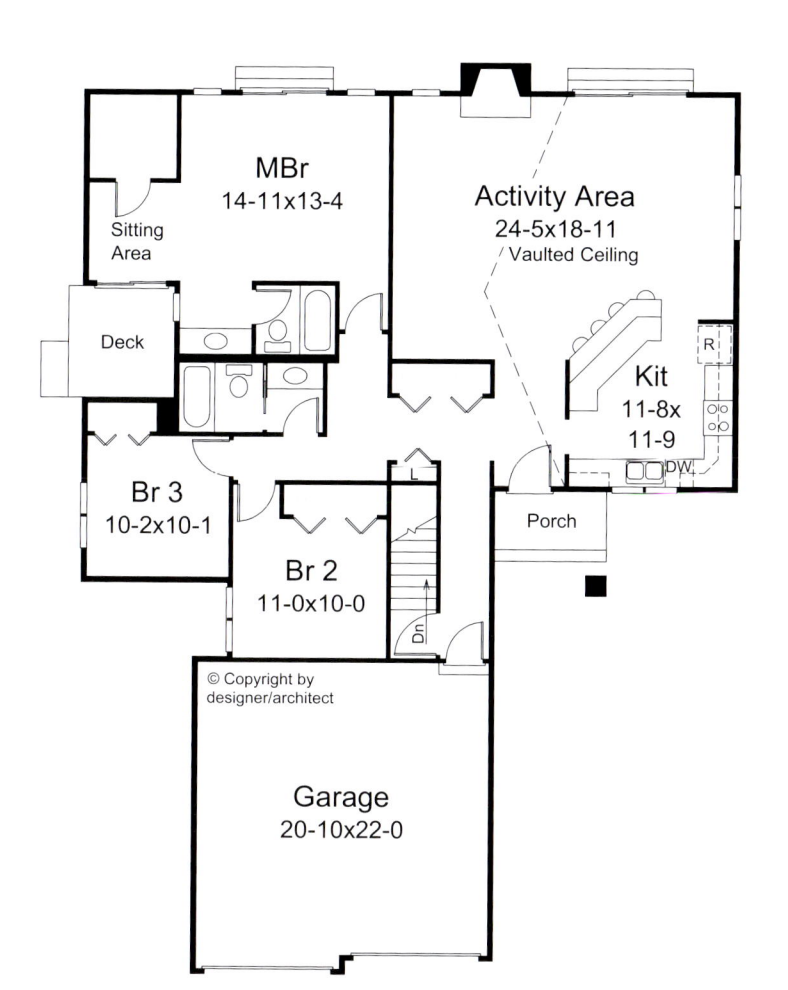

Cypress Hollow

Plan #M09-008D-0069

Multiple Gabled Roofs Add Drama

1,533 total square feet of living area

Width: 47'-0"   Depth: 65'-6"

3 bedrooms, 2 baths

2-car garage

Partial basement foundation, drawings also include crawl space foundation

Special features

The master bedroom accesses the outdoors through sliding glass doors onto a deck

A sloped ceiling adds volume to the large activity area

The activity area has access to the outdoors and is just steps away from the kitchen

A convenient utility room is located near the garage

Price Code B

Floor plan:
- MBr 14-11x13-4 (with Sitting Area and Deck)
- Activity Area 24-5x18-11, Vaulted Ceiling
- Kit 11-8x11-9
- Br 3 10-2x10-1
- Br 2 11-0x10-0
- Porch
- Garage 20-10x22-0

© Copyright by designer/architect

To order this plan, visit the Menards Building Materials Desk or visit www.Menards.com.

Zoey

MENARDS

Plan #M09-121D-0023

Handsome Ranch Home With Shingle Siding

1,762 total square feet of living area

Width: 41'-0"   Depth: 60'-4"

3 bedrooms, 2 baths

2-car garage

Basement foundation

Special features

The vaulted great room has a cozy fireplace and flows into the vaulted dining area

An island with eating bar in the kitchen is a perfect gathering spot for casual meals

A private bath, and a large walk-in closet are some of the amenities of the vaulted master bedroom

Price Code A

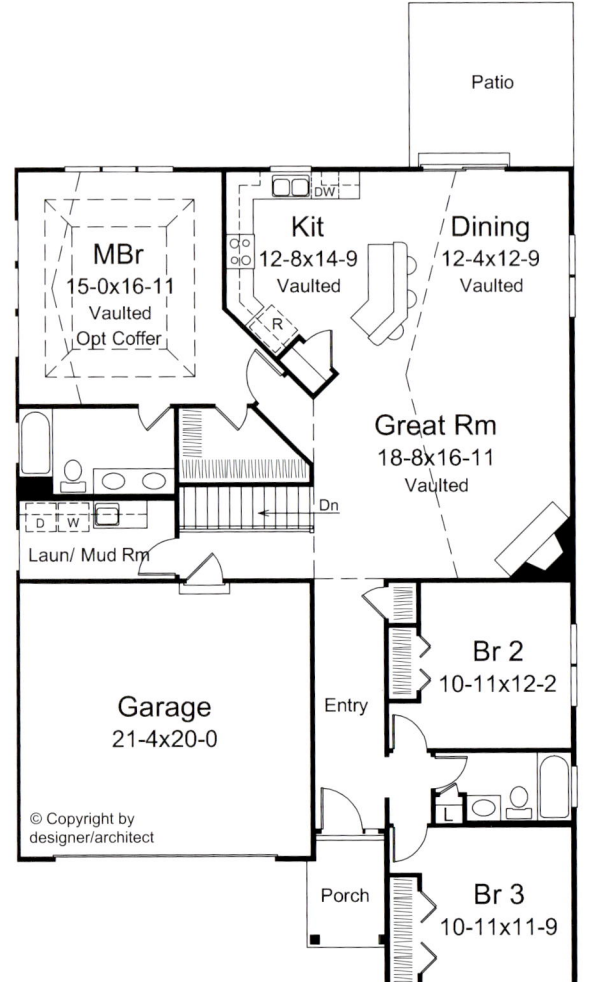

Rear View

Patio

MBr 15-0x16-11 Vaulted Opt Coffer

Kit 12-8x14-9 Vaulted

Dining 12-4x12-9 Vaulted

Great Rm 18-8x16-11 Vaulted

Laun/ Mud Rm

Garage 21-4x20-0

© Copyright by designer/architect

Entry

Br 2 10-11x12-2

Porch

Br 3 10-11x11-9

To order this plan, visit the Menards Building Materials Desk or visit www.Menards.com

MENARDS

Springwood

Plan #M09-037D-0009

Country Charm Wrapped In A Veranda

2,059 total square feet of living area

Width: 49'-8"   Depth: 38'-4"

3 bedrooms, 2 1/2 baths

2-car detached garage

Slab foundation, drawings also include basement and crawl space foundations

Special features

9' ceilings throughout the home

The sunny octagon-shaped breakfast room has a view of the veranda

The first floor master bedroom has a large walk-in closet and a deluxe bath

The secondary bedrooms and bath feature dormers and are near the cozy sitting area

Price Code C

Rear View

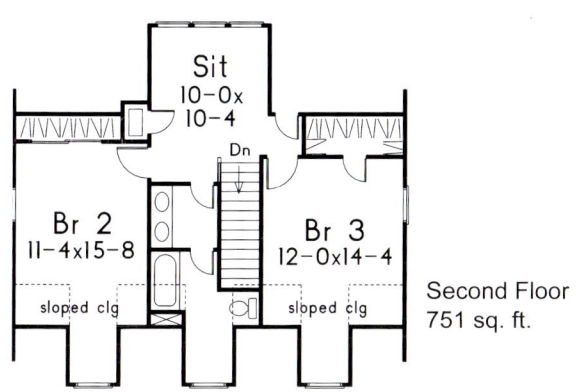

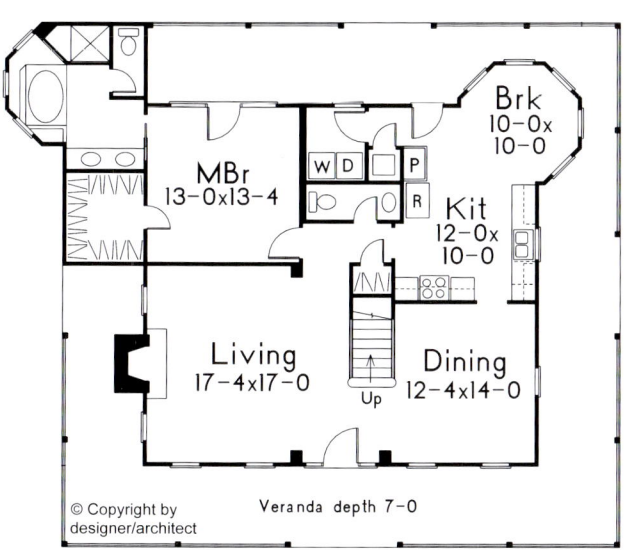

Second Floor 751 sq. ft.

- Sit 10-0 x 10-4
- Br 2 11-4 x 15-8 (sloped clg)
- Br 3 12-0 x 14-4 (sloped clg)

First Floor 1,308 sq. ft.

- MBr 13-0 x 13-4
- Brk 10-0 x 10-0
- Kit 12-0 x 10-0
- Living 17-4 x 17-0
- Dining 12-4 x 14-0
- Veranda depth 7-0

© Copyright by designer/architect

To order this plan, visit the Menards Building Materials Desk or visit www.Menards.com.

Eastwood Hill

MENARDS

Plan #M09-055L-0017

Built-In Computer Desk

1,525 total square feet of living area

Width: 51'-6"   Depth: 49'-10"

3 bedrooms, 2 baths

2-car garage

Slab, basement, walk-out basement or crawl space foundation, please specify when ordering

Special features

A corner fireplace is highlighted in the great room

A unique glass block window over the whirlpool tub in the master bath brightens the interior

An open bar overlooks both the kitchen and the great room

The breakfast room leads to an outdoor grilling and covered porch

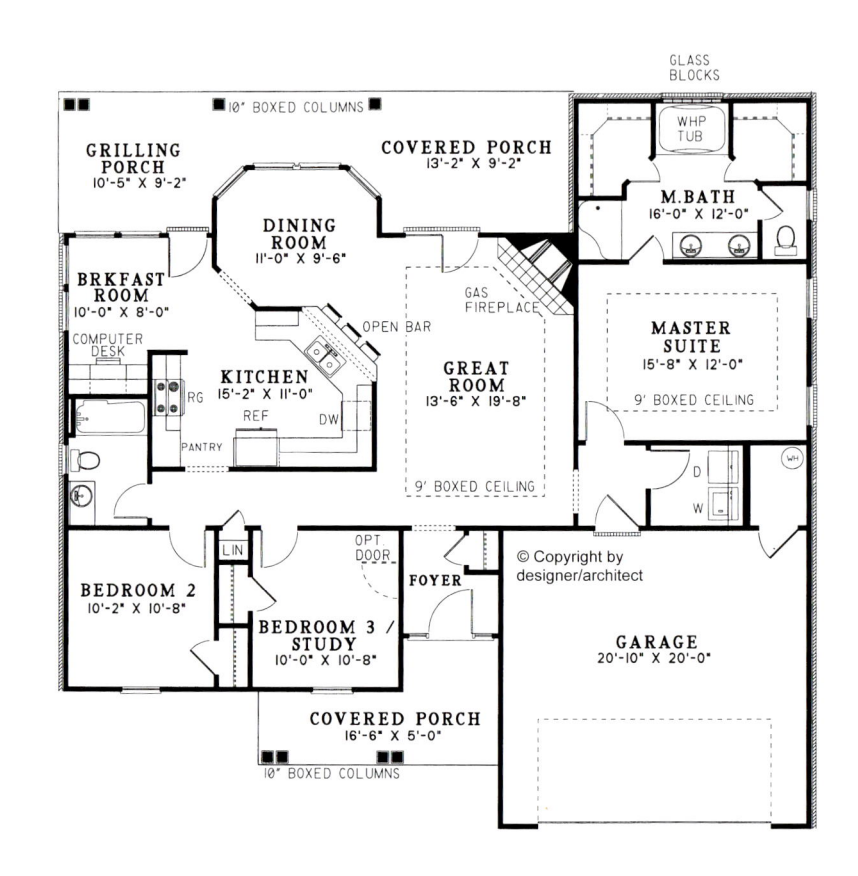

Price Code C

To order this plan, visit the Menards Building Materials Desk or visit www.menards.com.

MENARDS

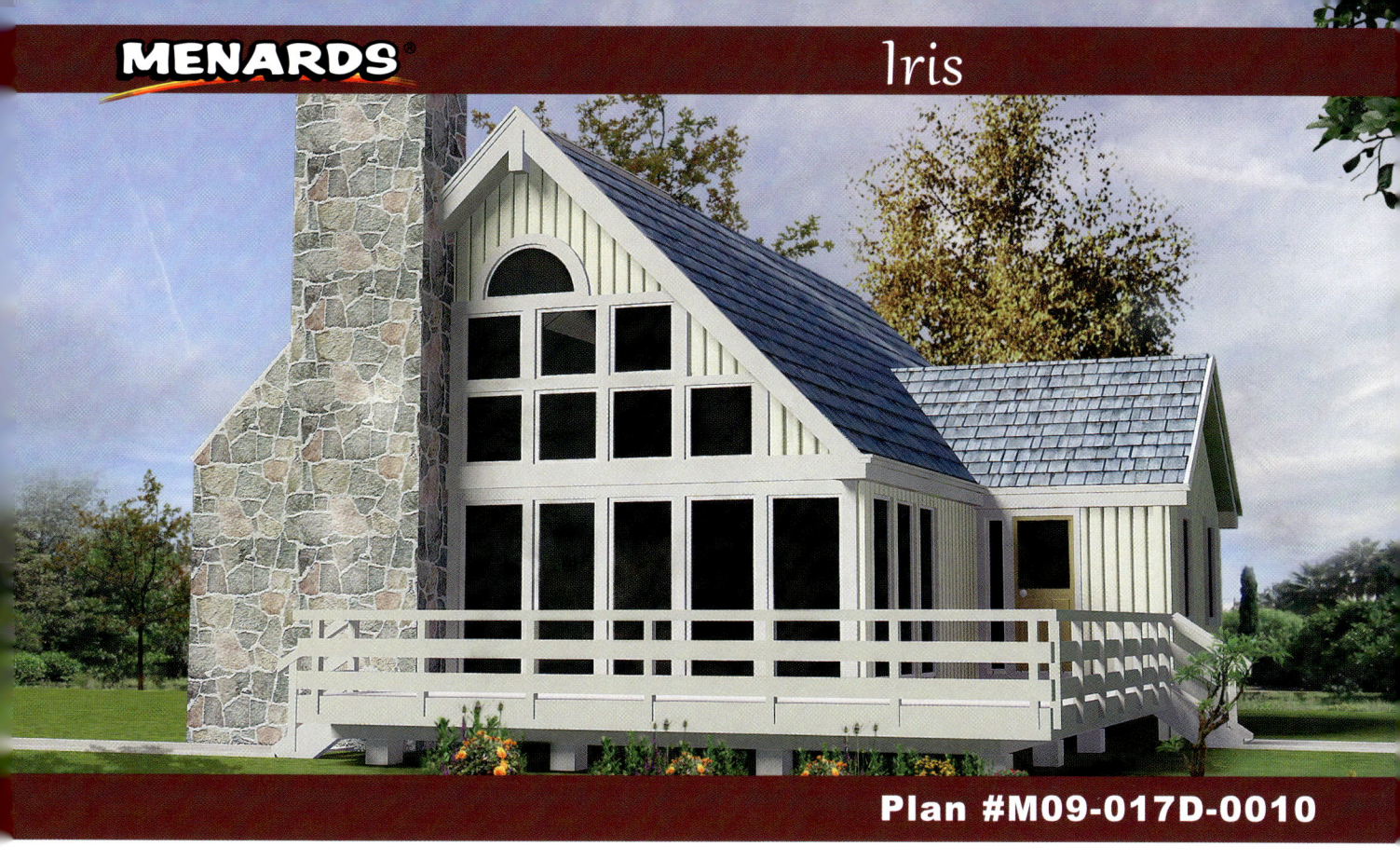

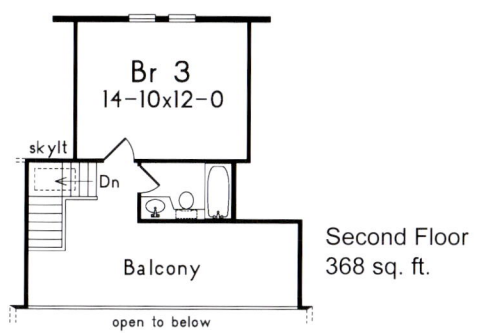

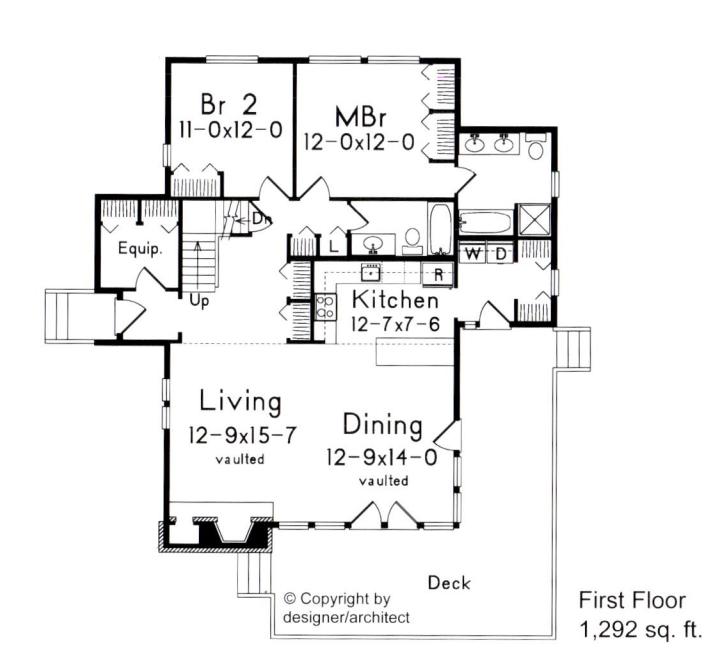

Iris

Plan #M09-017D-0010

Dramatic Expanse Of Windows

1,660 total square feet of living area

Width: 41'-5"   Depth: 44'-1"

3 bedrooms, 3 baths

Partial basement/crawl space foundation, drawings also include slab foundation

Special features

Energy efficient home with 2" x 6" exterior walls

The convenient equipment room has closet space for extra storage

The living and dining rooms look even larger with the openness of the foyer and kitchen

A large wrap-around deck is great for outdoor living

A broad balcony overlooks the living and dining rooms

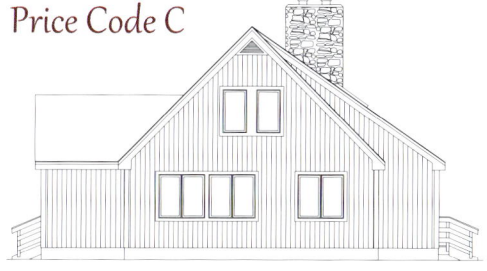

Price Code C

Br 3 14-10x12-0
skylt
Dn
Balcony
open to below
Second Floor 368 sq. ft.

Br 2 11-0x12-0
MBr 12-0x12-0
Equip.
Up
Kitchen 12-7x7-6
Living 12-9x15-7 vaulted
Dining 12-9x14-0 vaulted
Deck
© Copyright by designer/architect
First Floor 1,292 sq. ft.

Rear View

To order this plan, visit the Menards Building Materials Desk or visit www.Menards.com.

Jillian

Plan #M09-121D-0005

Cozy Corner Fireplace In The Great Room

1,562 total square feet of living area

Width: 65'-0"   Depth: 46'-4"

3 bedrooms, 2 baths

2-car garage

Basement foundation

Special features

The formal dining room is graced with an open feeling thanks to the beautiful vaulted ceiling and decorative corner columns

A wrap-around breakfast bar has enough seating for five people and overlooks the large and spacious great room

All of the bedrooms are located near each other for convenient family living

Price Code A

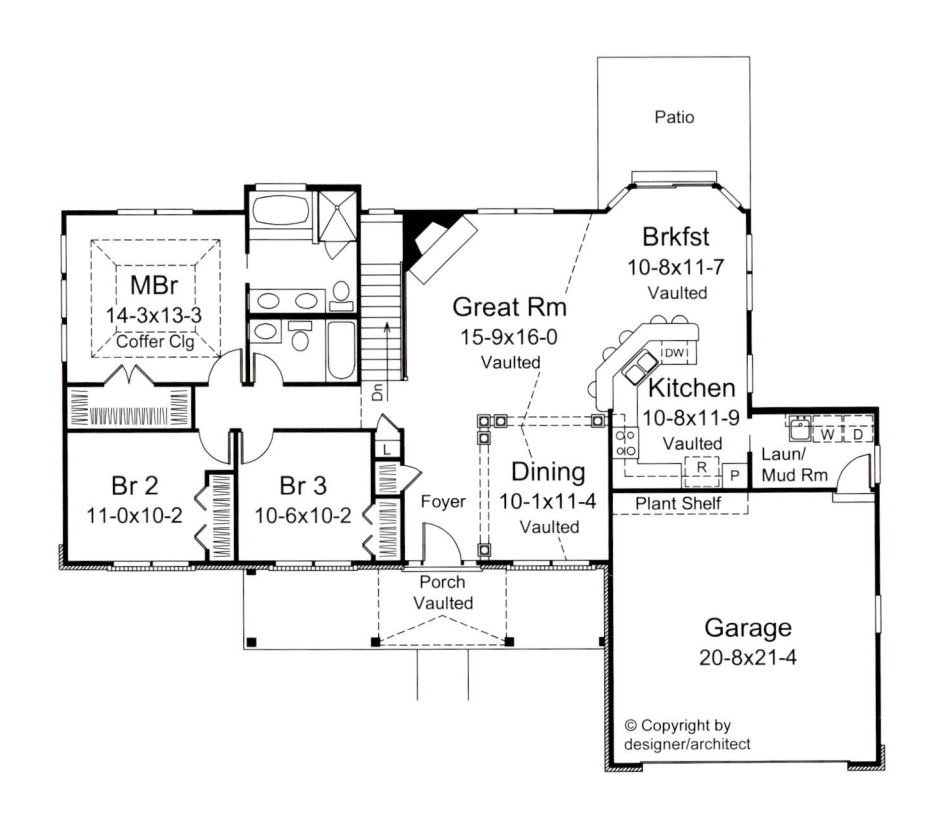

Rear View

48   To order this plan, visit the Menards Building Materials Desk or visit www.Menards.com.

MENARDS

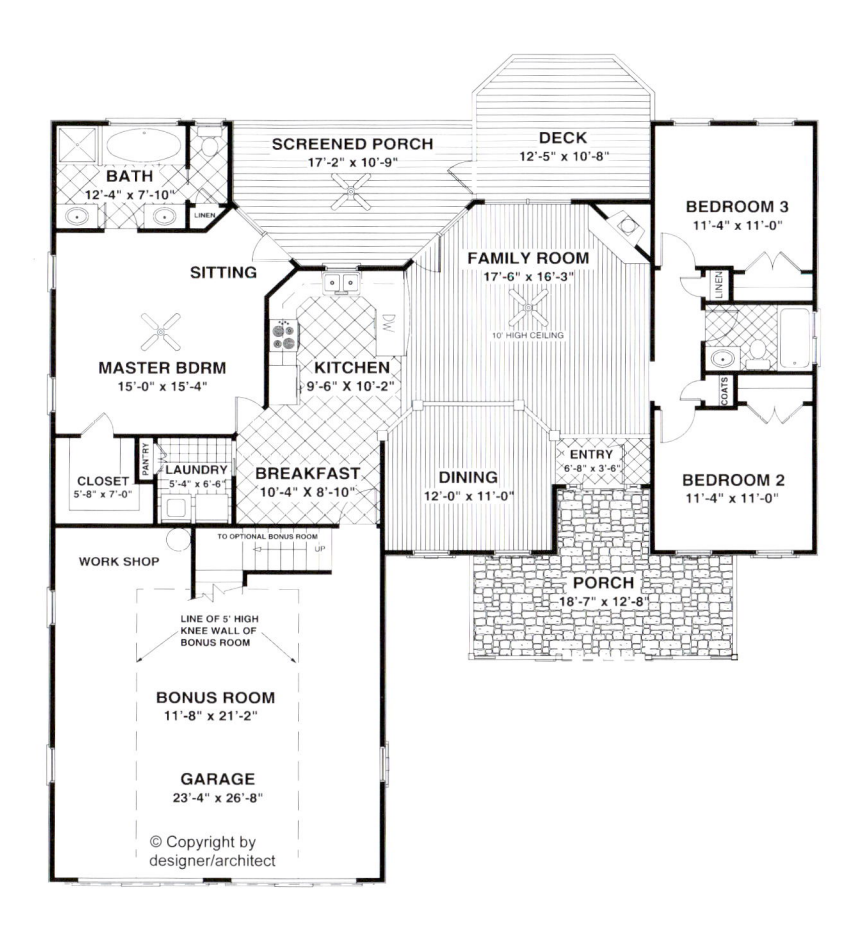

Martin House

Plan #M09-013L-0134

Inviting Stone Walkway

1,496 total square feet of living area

Width: 55'-0"   Depth: 58'-0"

3 bedrooms, 2 baths

2-car garage

Slab foundation

Special features

This country cottage features spacious open rooms and an easy flow from the welcoming front porch stone walkway to the breezy screened porch off of the family room and master bedroom

The family room features a cozy corner fireplace

Isolated from the secondary bedrooms, the master bedroom is an owner's retreat with a sitting area, a large walk-in closet, and a private bath with a separate tub and a shower

The bonus room above the garage has an additional 301 square feet of living area

Price Code E

To order this plan, visit the Menards Building Materials Desk or visit www.Menards.com.

WELLINGTON

MENARDS

Plan #M09-003D-0001

Practical Two-Story, Full Of Features

2,058 total square feet of living area

Width: 50'-0"   Depth: 38'-0"

3 bedrooms, 2 1/2 baths

2-car garage

Basement foundation, drawings also include slab and crawl space foundations

Special features

A handsome two-story foyer with balcony creates a spacious entrance area

The vaulted master bedroom has a private dressing area and a large walk-in closet

Skylights furnish the full baths with sunlight

The laundry closet is conveniently located

Price Code C

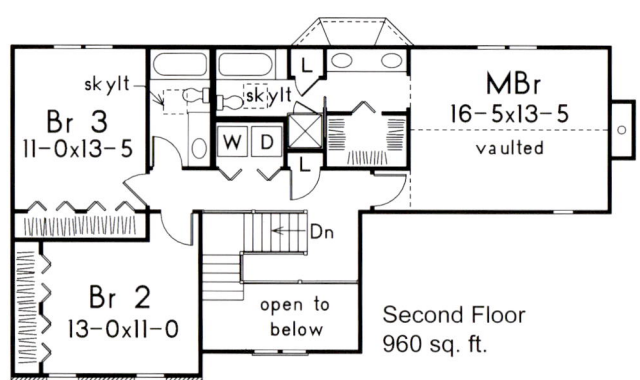

Rear View

Second Floor 960 sq. ft.
- Br 3: 11-0x13-5
- MBr: 16-5x13-5 vaulted
- Br 2: 13-0x11-0

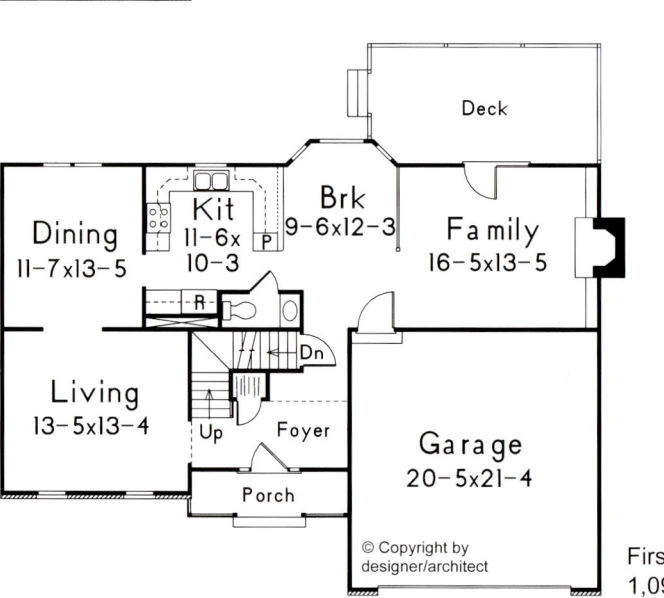

First Floor 1,098 sq. ft.
- Dining: 11-7x13-5
- Kit: 11-6x10-3
- Brk: 9-6x12-3
- Family: 16-5x13-5
- Living: 13-5x13-4
- Garage: 20-5x21-4

© Copyright by designer/architect

To order this plan, visit the Menards Building Materials Desk or visit www.Menards.com

MENARDS

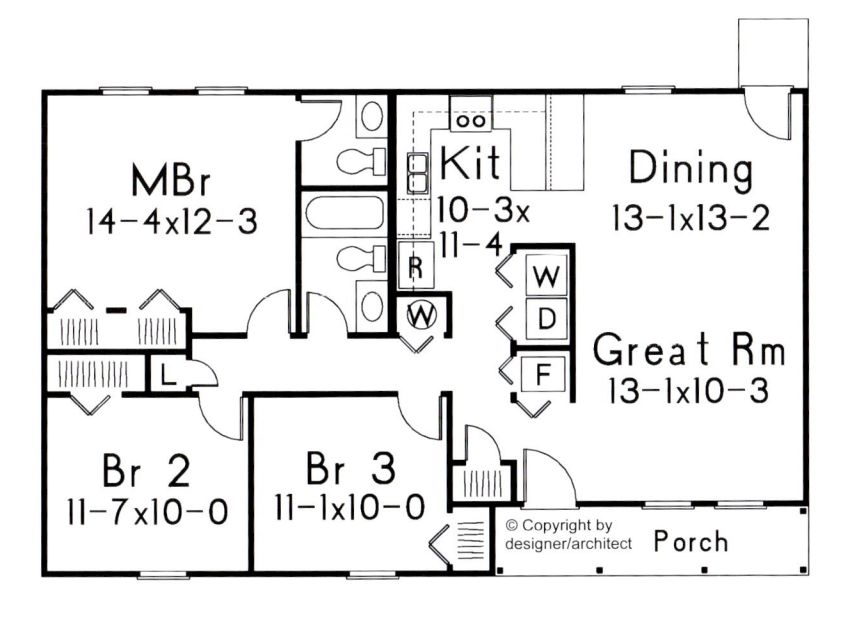

Pinehu...
San Sagu...

Plan #M09-001D-0081

Large Great Room And Dining Area

1,160 total square feet of living area

Width: 44'-0"   Depth: 28'-0"

3 bedrooms, 1 1/2 baths

Crawl space foundation, drawings also include basement and slab foundations

Special features

The U-shaped kitchen includes a breakfast bar and a convenient laundry closet

The master bedroom features a private half bath and a large closet

The dining area has outdoor access

The dining area and great rooms combine to create an open living atmosphere

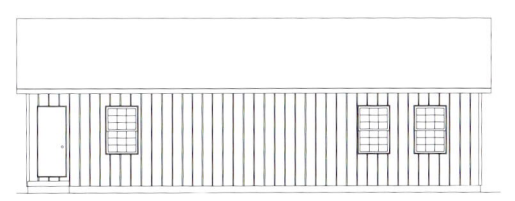

Price Code AA

Rear View

To order this plan, visit the Menards Building Materials Desk or visit www.Menards.com

MENARDS

Plan #M09-007D-0222

Two Patio Home With Courtyard

1,522 total square feet of living area

Width: 43'-0"   Depth: 67'-8"

3 bedrooms, 2 baths

2-car garage

Crawl space foundation, drawings also include slab foundation

Special features

This open floor plan design has 9' ceilings and is perfect for a narrow lot

A cozy covered porch leads to an entry that's open to a large U-shaped kitchen with snack bar, a built-in pantry, abundant cabinets and 26 linear feet of counter space

A walk-in closet, double-entry doors and luxury bath are features of the master bedroom

Price Code A

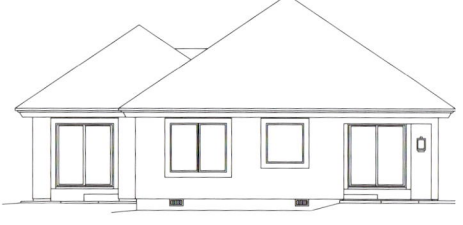

Rear View

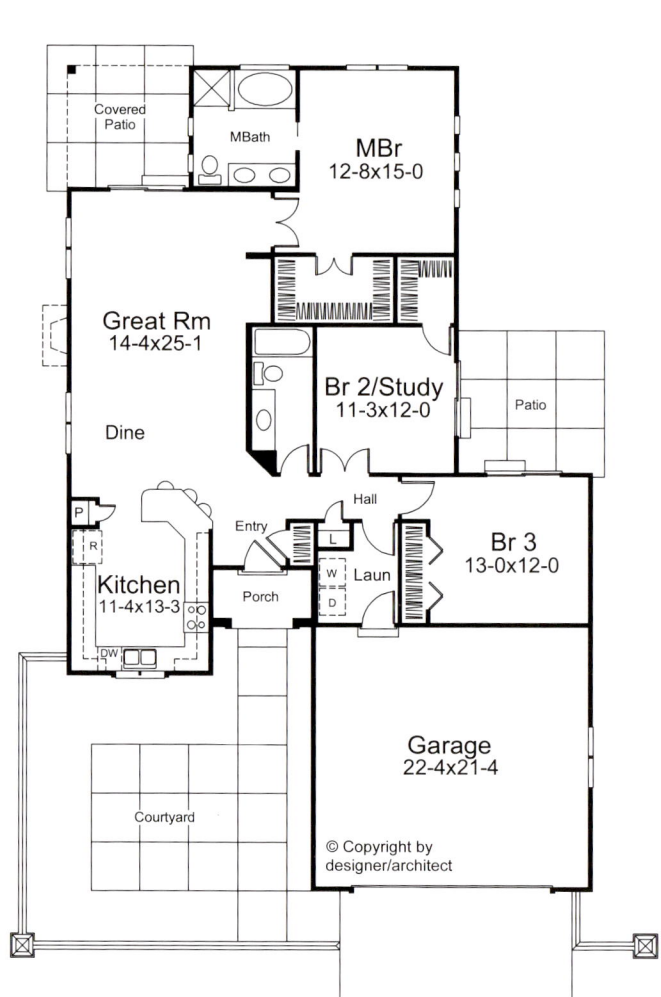

To order this plan, visit the Menards Building Materials Desk or visit www.Menards.com.

MENARDS

Addison

Plan #M09-058D-0032

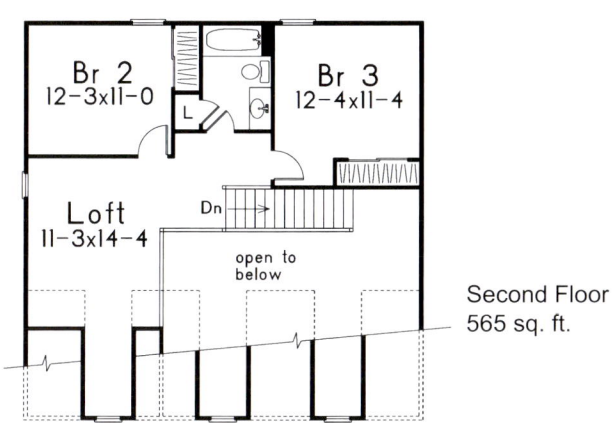

Charming Wrap-Around Porch

1,879 total square feet of living area

Width: 50'-0"   Depth: 42'-0"

3 bedrooms, 2 baths

Crawl space foundation

Special features

An open floor plan on both floors makes this home appear larger than its true size

The loft area overlooks the great room, or can become an optional fourth bedroom

A large storage area in the rear of home has access from the exterior

Price Code C

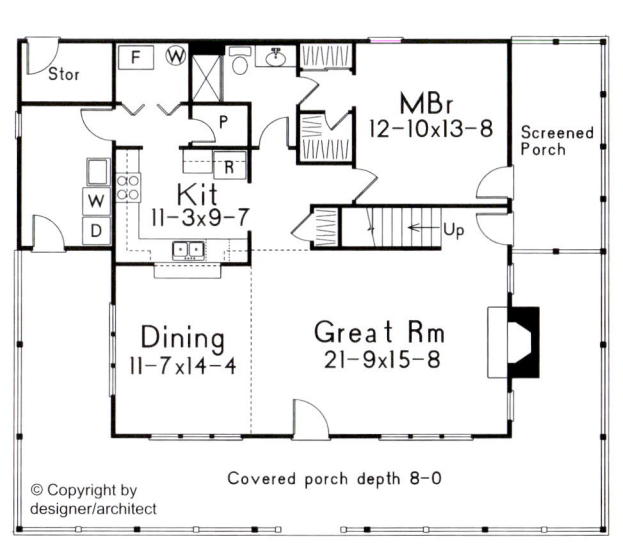

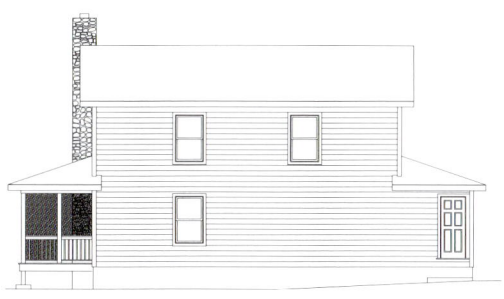

Second Floor 565 sq. ft.
- Br 2: 12-3x11-0
- Br 3: 12-4x11-4
- Loft: 11-3x14-4

First Floor 1,314 sq. ft.
- MBr: 12-10x13-8
- Kit: 11-3x9-7
- Dining: 11-7x14-4
- Great Rm: 21-9x15-8
- Screened Porch
- Covered porch depth 8-0

© Copyright by designer/architect

Rear View

To order this plan, visit the Menards Building Materials Desk or visit www.Menards.com.

53

Milner

MENARDS

Plan #M09-013L-0050

Beautiful Country Porch

2,098 total square feet of living area

Width: 63'-4"   Depth: 86'-6"

3 bedrooms, 2 1/2 baths

3-car side entry detached garage

Crawl space or basement foundation, please specify when ordering

Special features

The covered porch wraps around the entire house, leading to the deck and screened porch in the back

The spacious country kitchen has plenty of cabinet space as well as counterspace

The convenient laundry chute is located near the second floor bathroom

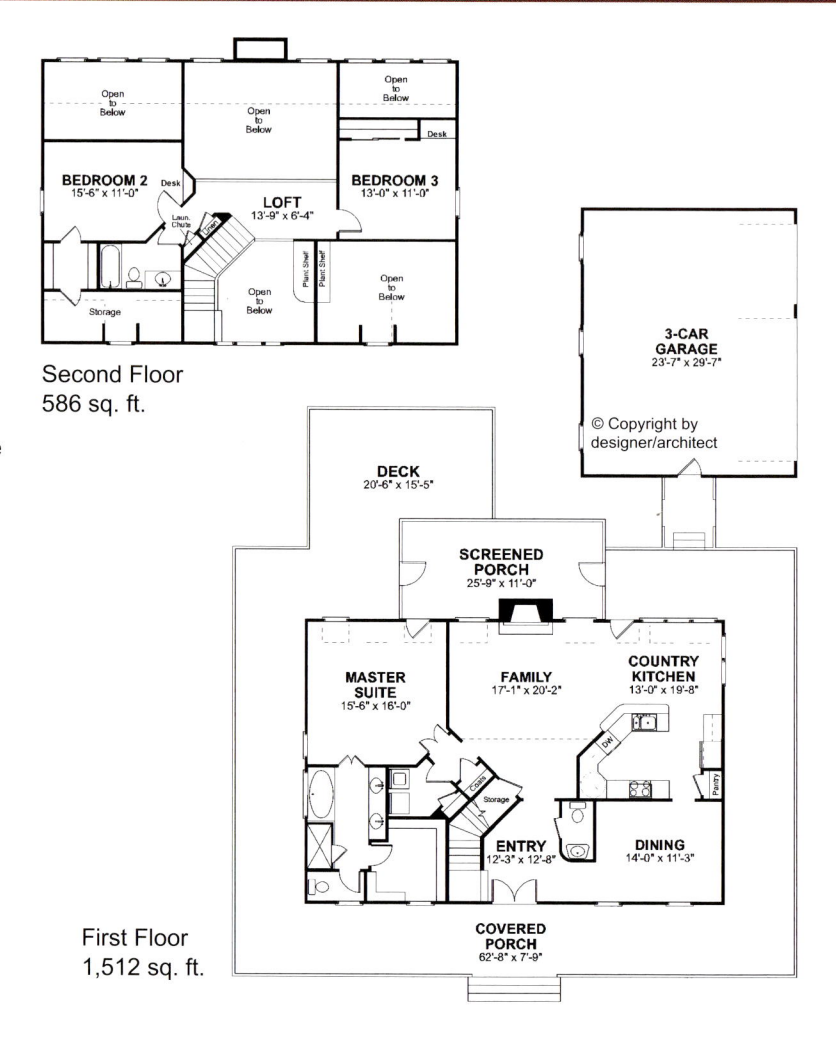

Price Code D

Second Floor 586 sq. ft.

First Floor 1,512 sq. ft.

54   To order this plan, visit the Menards Building Materials Desk or visit www.menards.com

MENARDS

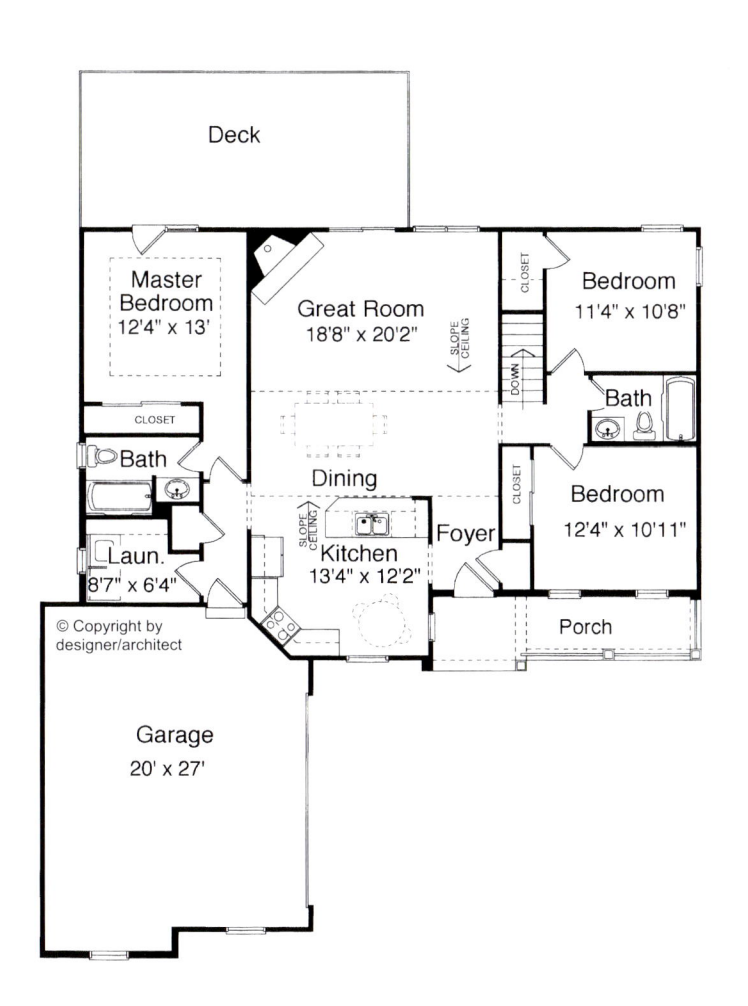

Bozeman

Plan #M09-065L-0062

Stone And Siding Create Charming Exterior

1,390 total square feet of living area

Width: 50'-0"   Depth: 55'-8"

3 bedrooms, 2 baths

2-car side entry garage

Walk-out basement foundation

Special features

The kitchen with snack bar opens to the spacious great room with plenty of space for dining

A corner fireplace warms the adjoining great room and kitchen

The master bedroom is a relaxing retreat with a private bath and direct deck access

The secondary bedrooms are separated from the master bedroom and share a full bath

Price Code A

Floor plan rooms:
- Deck
- Master Bedroom 12'4" x 13'
- Great Room 18'8" x 20'2"
- Bedroom 11'4" x 10'8"
- Bath
- Closet
- Bath
- Dining
- Kitchen 13'4" x 12'2"
- Foyer
- Bedroom 12'4" x 10'11"
- Laun. 8'7" x 6'4"
- Porch
- Garage 20' x 27'

© Copyright by designer/architect

To order this plan, visit the Menards Building Materials Desk or visit www.Menards.com

55

Sherbrooke

MENARDS

Plan #M09-010D-0001

Circle-Top Windows Adorn The Foyer

1,516 total square feet of living area

Width: 53'-0"   Depth: 41'-0"

3 bedrooms, 2 1/2 baths

2-car garage

Basement foundation

Special features

The stairway to the second floor looks out over the living room

The master bedroom enjoys first floor privacy and a luxurious bath

The kitchen has easy access to the deck, laundry closet and garage

Price Code B

Rear View

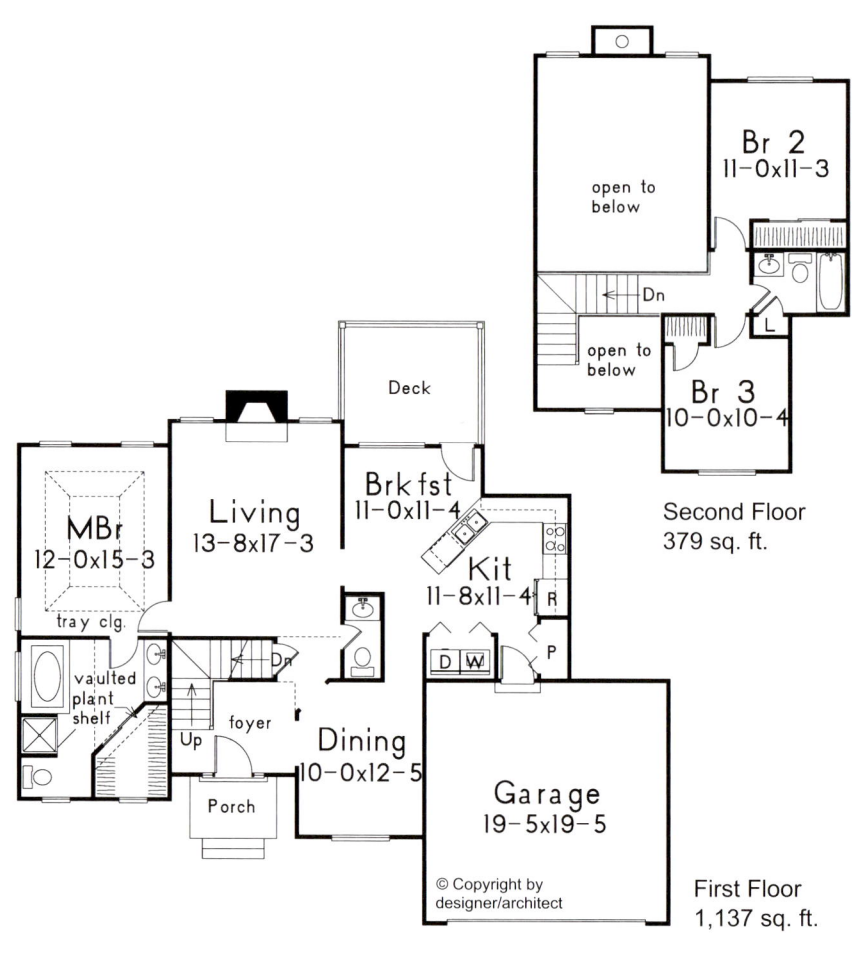

Second Floor
379 sq. ft.

- Br 2 11-0x11-3
- Br 3 10-0x10-4

First Floor
1,137 sq. ft.

- MBr 12-0x15-3 (tray clg.)
- Living 13-8x17-3
- Brkfst 11-0x11-4
- Kit 11-8x11-4
- Dining 10-0x12-5
- Garage 19-5x19-5
- Deck
- Porch
- foyer
- vaulted plant shelf

© Copyright by designer/architect

To order this plan, visit the Menards Building Materials Desk or visit www.Menards.com

MENARDS

Hillbriar

Plan #M09-007D-0061

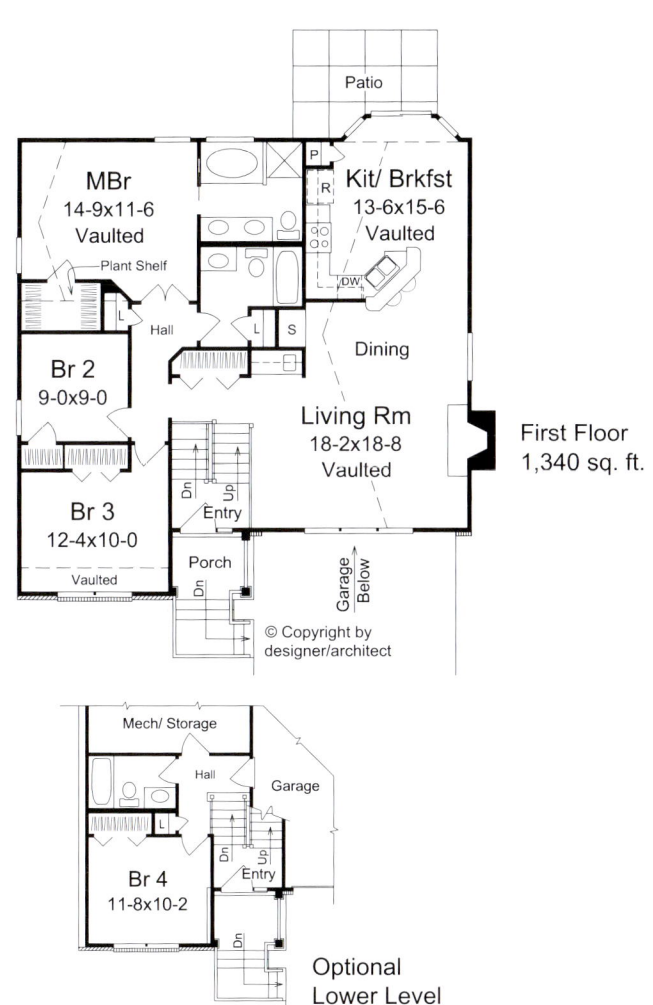

Distinctive Home For Sloping Terrain

1,340 total square feet of living area

Width: 40'-0"   Depth: 40'-8"

3 bedrooms, 2 baths

2-car drive under garage

Basement foundation

Special features

The vaulted living and dining rooms offer a fireplace, a wet bar, and a breakfast counter

The vaulted master bedroom features a double-door entry, a walk-in closet, and a bath

The basement has a huge two-car garage and space for a bedroom/bath expansion

The optional lower level has an additional 636 square feet of living area

Price Code A

Floor Plan — First Floor 1,340 sq. ft.
- MBr 14-9x11-6 Vaulted
- Kit/Brkfst 13-6x15-6 Vaulted
- Br 2 9-0x9-0
- Br 3 12-4x10-0 Vaulted
- Living Rm 18-2x18-8 Vaulted
- Dining
- Patio
- Porch
- Entry
- Garage Below
- Plant Shelf
- Hall

© Copyright by designer/architect

Optional Lower Level
- Mech/Storage
- Garage
- Br 4 11-8x10-2
- Hall
- Entry

Rear View

To order this plan, visit the Menards Building Materials Desk or visit www.Menards.com.

Plan #M09-121D-0010

Vaulted Living Areas For Added Spaciousness

1,281 total square feet of living area

Width: 37'-6"   Depth: 52'-0"

3 bedrooms, 2 baths

2-car garage

Basement foundation

Special features

The functional vaulted kitchen features an angled raised counter for casual dining

The vaulted great room and dining area combine, maximizing the interior for an open, airy feel

The vaulted master bedroom enjoys a walk-in closet and its own private bath

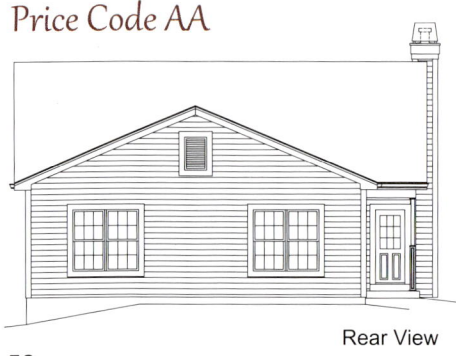

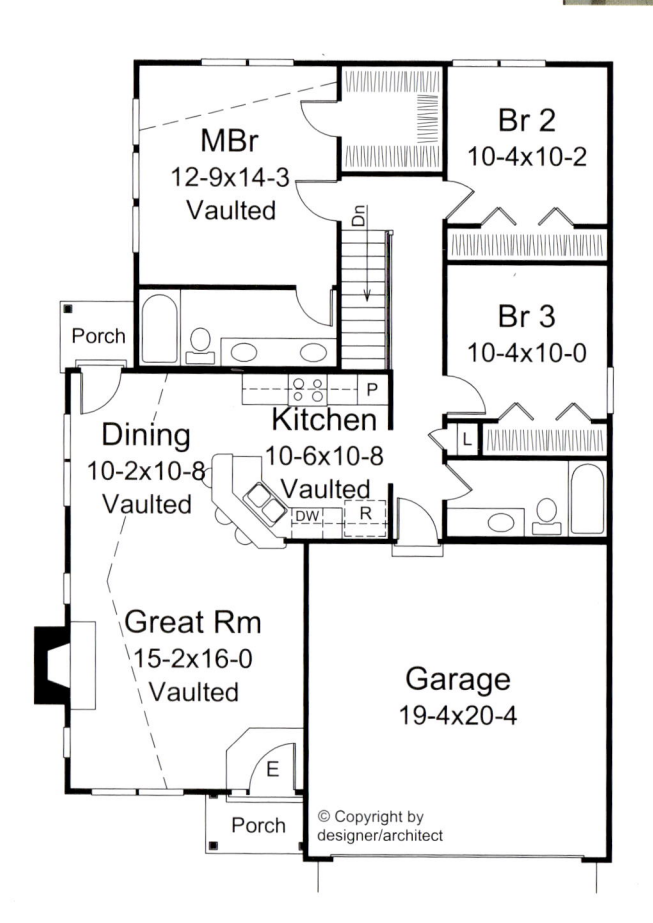

Price Code AA

Rear View

Floor Plan:
- MBr 12-9x14-3 Vaulted
- Br 2 10-4x10-2
- Br 3 10-4x10-0
- Porch
- Dining 10-2x10-8 Vaulted
- Kitchen 10-6x10-8 Vaulted
- Great Rm 15-2x16-0 Vaulted
- Garage 19-4x20-4
- Porch

© Copyright by designer/architect

To order this plan, visit the Menards Building Materials Desk or visit www.Menards.com.

MENARDS

Cumberland

Plan #M09-014D-0005

Economical Ranch For Easy Living

1,314 total square feet of living area

Width: 47'-0"   Depth: 54'-0"

3 bedrooms, 2 baths

2-car garage

Basement foundation

Special features

Energy efficient home with 2" x 6" exterior walls

The covered front porch adds immediate appeal and welcoming charm

The functional kitchen is complete with a pantry and eating bar

The private master bedroom features a large walk-in closet and bath

Price Code A

Rear View

To order this plan, visit the Menards Building Materials Desk or visit www.Menards.com.

Plan #M09-001D-0044

Distinctive Design, Convenient Floor Plan

1,375 total square feet of living area

Width: 57'-4"   Depth: 46'-0"

3 bedrooms, 2 baths

2-car side entry garage

Crawl space foundation, drawings also include basement and slab foundations

Special features

Attractive gables highlight the home's exterior

The master bedroom features patio access, double walk-in closets, and a private bath

The side entry garage includes a handy storage area

2" x 6" exterior walls available for an additional fee, please specify when ordering

Price Code A

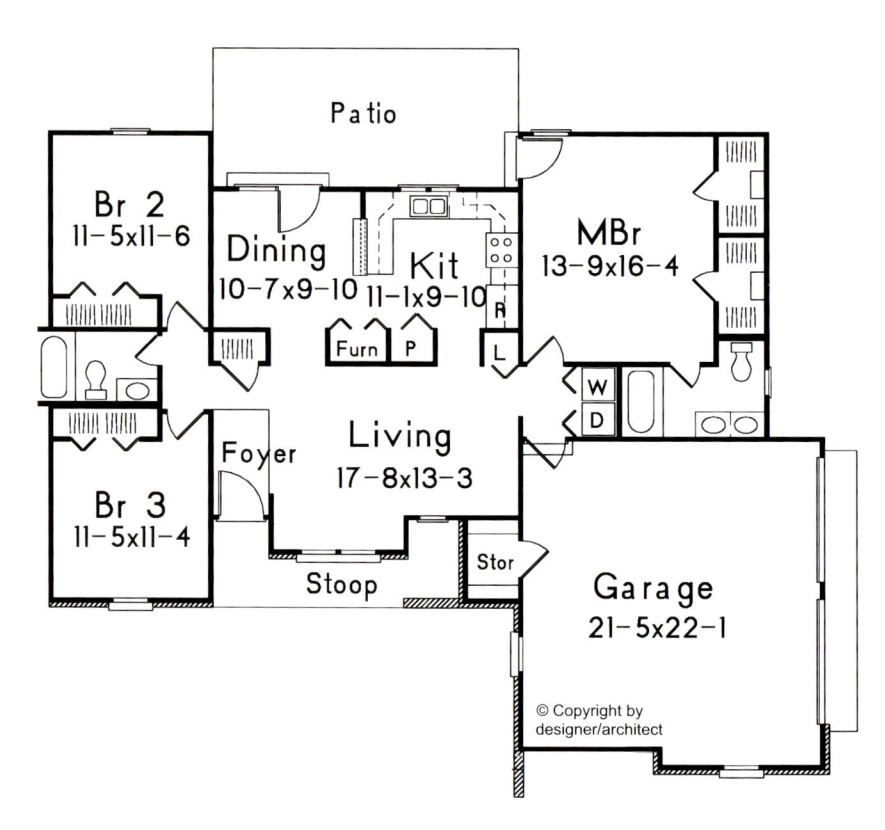

Rear View

To order this plan, visit the Menards Building Materials Desk or visit www.menards.com

MENARDS

Oakbrook

Plan #M09-007D-0123

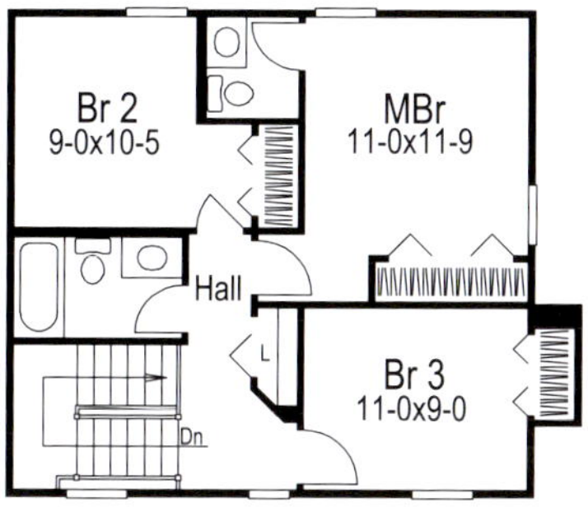

Affordable Two-Story Has It All

1,308 total square feet of living area

Width: 54'-4"   Depth: 31'-0"

3 bedrooms, 1 full bath, 2 half baths

2-car garage

Basement foundation

Special features

The multi-gabled facade and elongated covered front porch create a pleasing country appeal

The large dining room with bay window and view to the rear patio opens to a fully-functional kitchen with snack bar

An attractive U-shaped staircase with hall overlook leads to the second floor

Price Code A

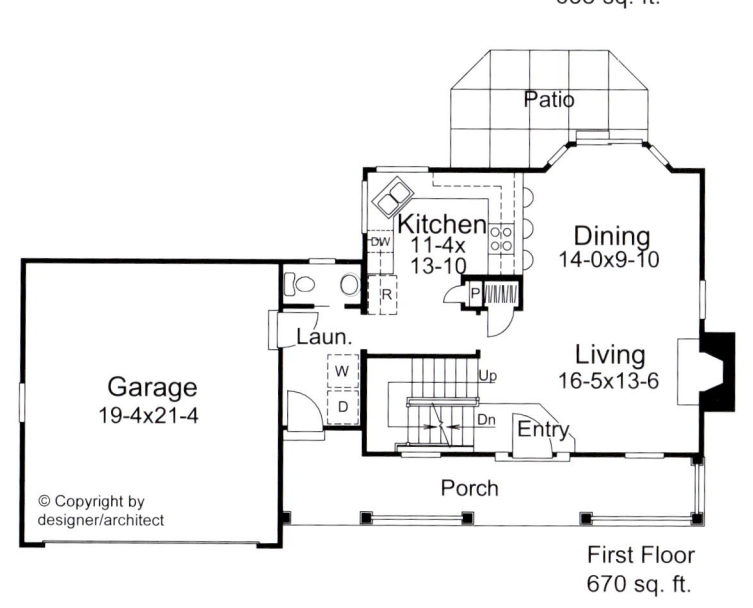

Second Floor 638 sq. ft.

- Br 2: 9-0x10-5
- MBr: 11-0x11-9
- Br 3: 11-0x9-0

First Floor 670 sq. ft.

- Garage: 19-4x21-4
- Kitchen: 11-4x13-10
- Dining: 14-0x9-10
- Living: 16-5x13-6

Rear View

To order this plan, visit the Menards Building Materials Desk or visit www.Menards.com.

61

Westrose

MENARDS

Plan #M09-040D-0026

Cozy Front Porch Welcomes Guests

1,393 total square feet of living area

Width: 42'-0"   Depth: 41'-9"

3 bedrooms, 2 baths

2-car detached garage

Crawl space foundation, drawings also include slab foundation

Special features

The L-shaped kitchen features a walk-in pantry, island cooktop and is convenient to the laundry room and dining area

The master bedroom features a large walk-in closet and private bath with separate tub and shower

A lovely view of the patio can be seen from the dining area

Price Code B

Rear View

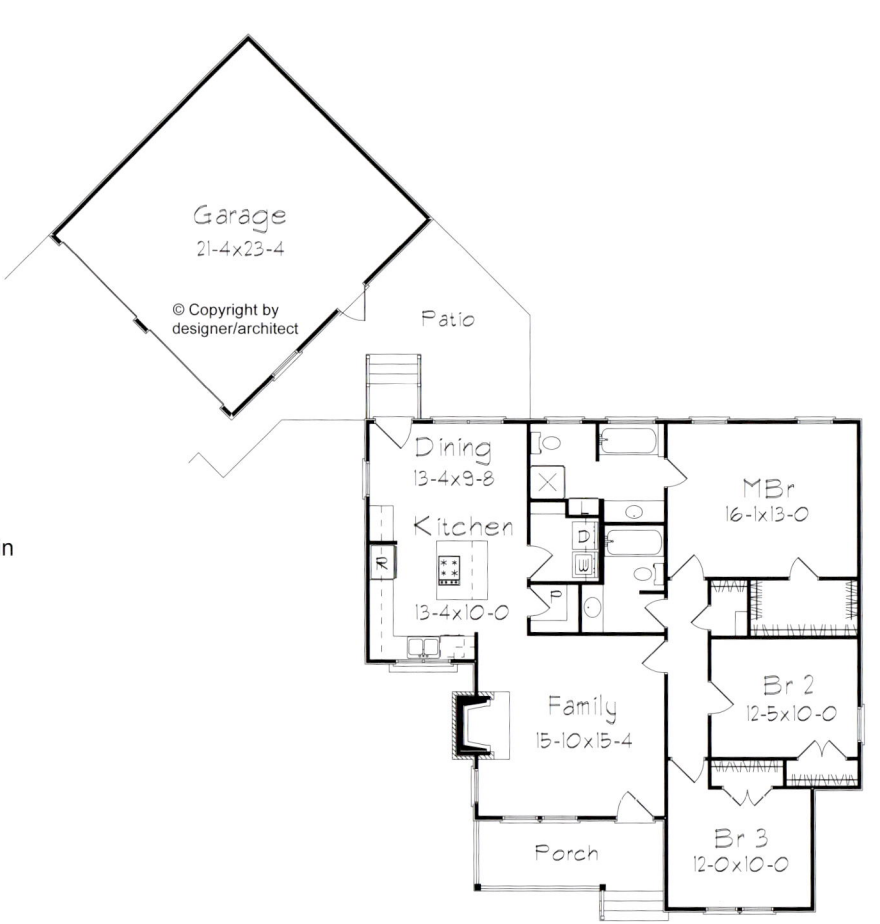

To order this plan, visit the Menards Building Materials Desk or visit www.Menards.com.

MENARDS

Yuma Park

Plan #M09-007D-0233

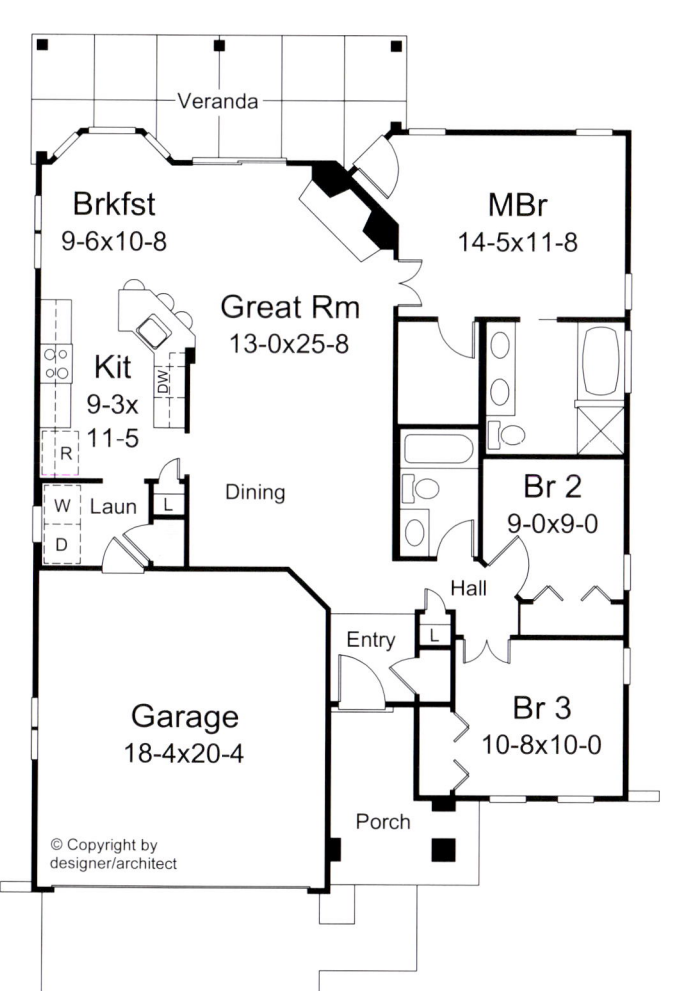

Handsome Home For A Narrow Lot

1,298 total square feet of living area

Width: 38'-0"   Depth: 54'-8"

3 bedrooms, 2 baths

2-car garage

Slab foundation

Special features

Open to the great room is the kitchen with a snack counter, a built-in pantry, and a convenient laundry room with coat closet

The breakfast area enjoys lots of windows including a bay with views of the veranda

A luxury bath, walk-in closet, and a patio door with access to the veranda are the many amenities of the master bedroom

Price Code B

Rear View

To order this plan, visit the Menards Building Materials Desk or visit www.Menards.com.

Ridgeforest

MENARDS

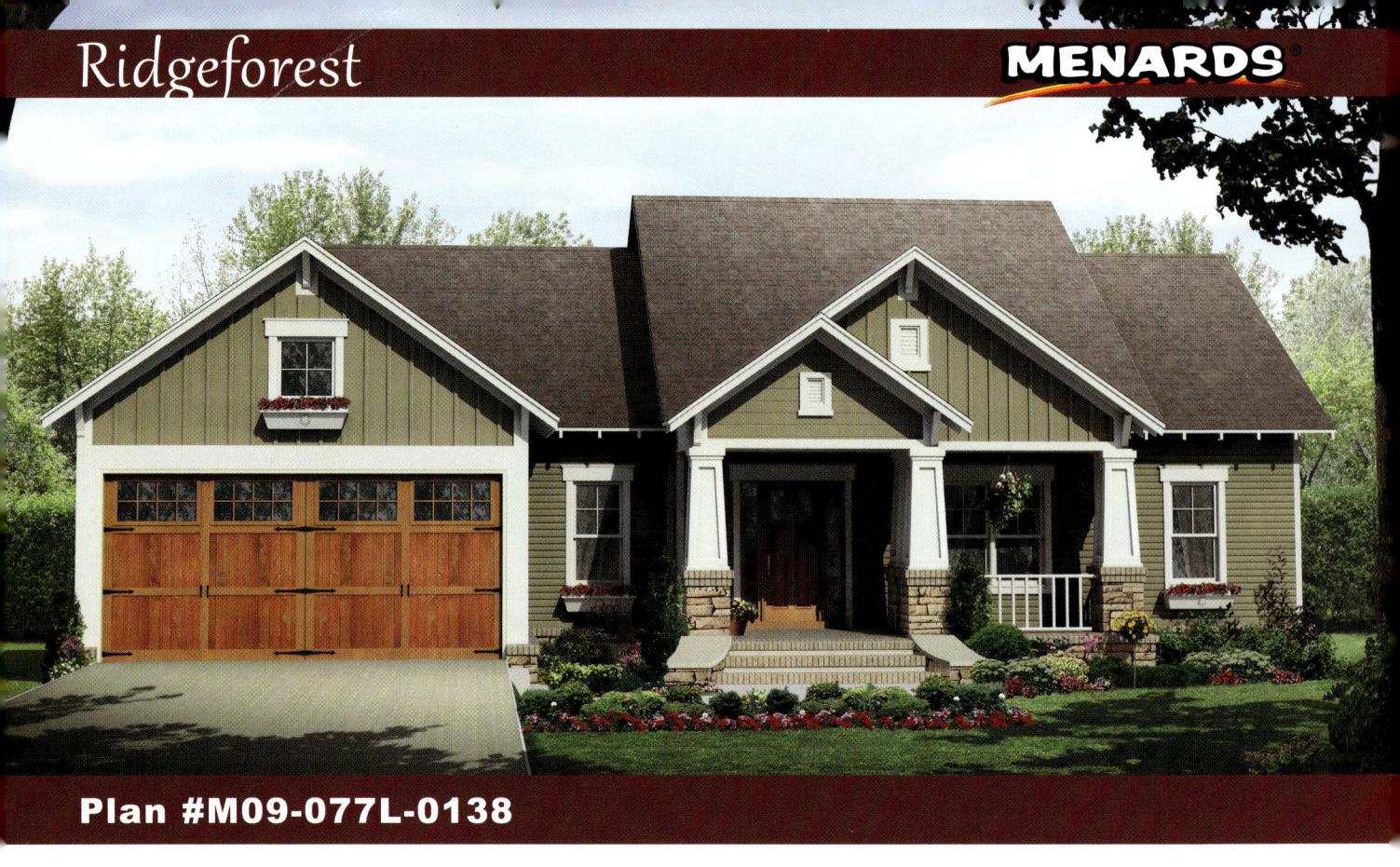

Plan #M09-077L-0138

Delightful Covered Porch

1,509 total square feet of living area

Width: 61'-0"   Depth: 47'-4"

3 bedrooms, 2 baths

2-car garage

Basement, slab or crawl space foundation, please specify when ordering

Special features

A large eating area has covered porch access and is near the kitchen and vaulted great room

Double walk-in closets and a luxury bath complete the master bedroom

Cabinets flank the fireplace in the vaulted great room

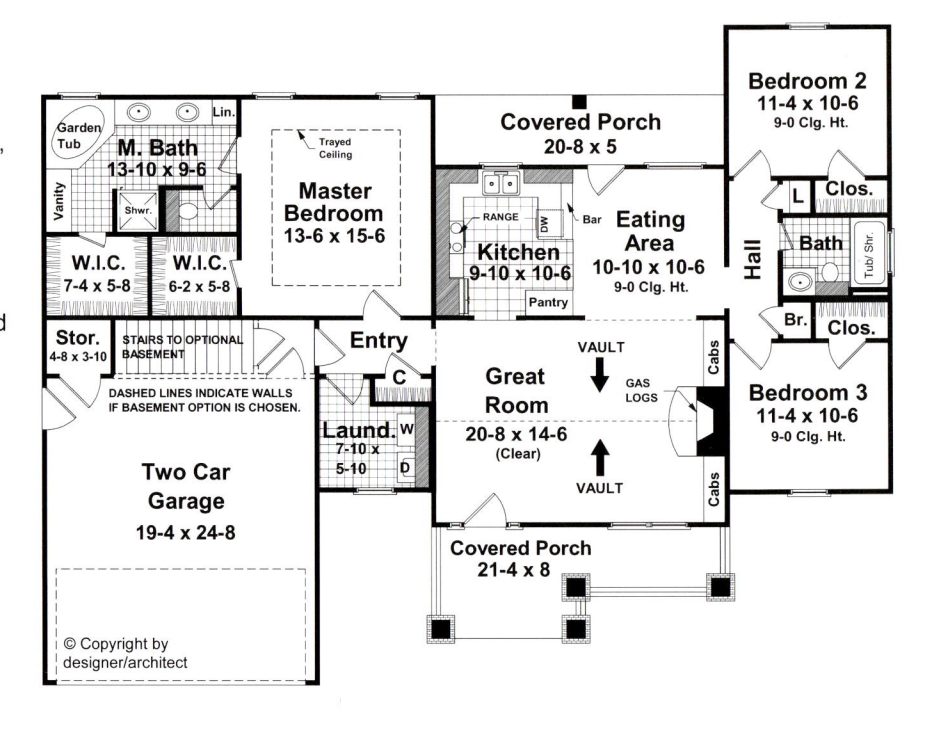

Price Code E

Floor Plan

- Garden Tub
- M. Bath 13-10 x 9-6
- Vanity
- Shwr.
- Lin.
- Master Bedroom 13-6 x 15-6 (Trayed Ceiling)
- W.I.C. 7-4 x 5-8
- W.I.C. 6-2 x 5-8
- Stor. 4-8 x 3-10
- STAIRS TO OPTIONAL BASEMENT
- DASHED LINES INDICATE WALLS IF BASEMENT OPTION IS CHOSEN.
- Two Car Garage 19-4 x 24-8
- Covered Porch 20-8 x 5
- RANGE, DW, Bar
- Kitchen 9-10 x 10-6
- Pantry
- Eating Area 10-10 x 10-6 9-0 Clg. Ht.
- Entry
- Laund. 7-10 x 5-10, W, D
- Great Room 20-8 x 14-6 (Clear) VAULT, GAS LOGS, VAULT
- Cabs
- Covered Porch 21-4 x 8
- Bedroom 2 11-4 x 10-6 9-0 Clg. Ht.
- L, Clos.
- Hall
- Bath, Tub/Shr.
- Br., Clos.
- Bedroom 3 11-4 x 10-6 9-0 Clg. Ht.

© Copyright by designer/architect

To order this plan, visit the Menards Building Materials Desk or visit www.Menards.com

MENARDS

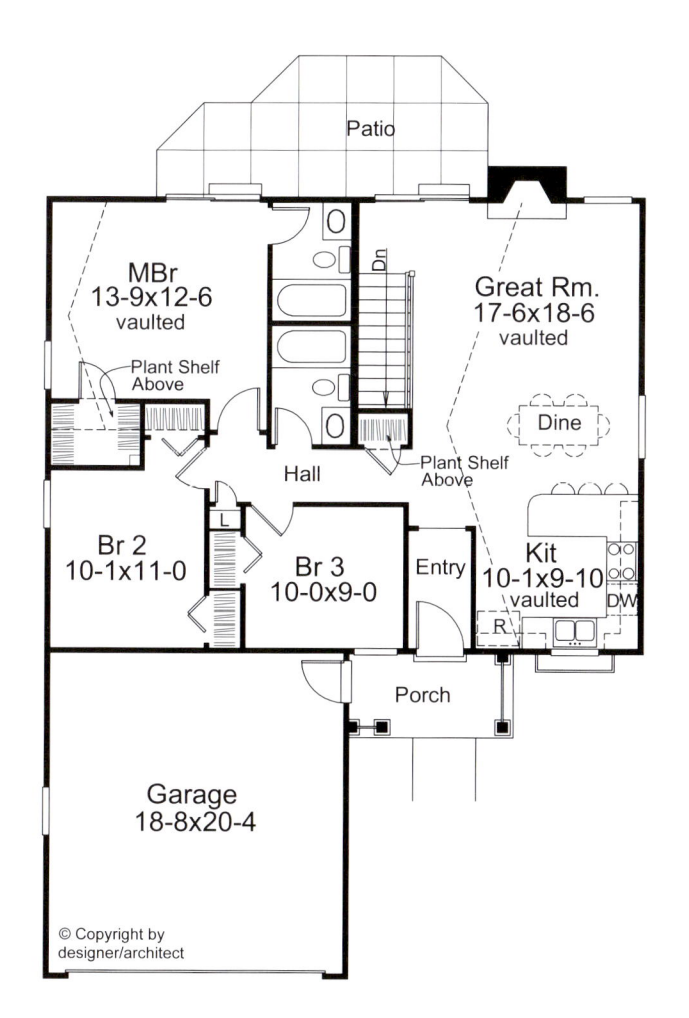

Mapleview Brook

Plan #M09-007D-0177

The Ideal Affordable Home

1,102 total square feet of living area

Width: 38'-0"   Depth: 51'-8"

3 bedrooms, 2 baths

2-car garage

Basement foundation, drawings also include slab and crawl space foundations

Special features

The exterior features a covered front porch, pallidian windows and a planter box

The vaulted great room has a fireplace, view of the rear patio, and a dining area

The U-shaped kitchen includes all of the necessities including a breakfast bar

The master bedroom offers a vaulted ceiling, private bath, and a walk-in closet

Price Code AA

Rear View

To order this plan, visit the Menards Building Materials Desk or visit www.Menards.com.

65

MENARDS

Plan #M09-007D-0088

Country Appeal For A Small Lot

1,299 total square feet of living area

Width: 28'-0"   Depth: 40'-0"

3 bedrooms, 2 1/2 baths

Basement foundation

Special features

The first floor master bedroom has a bay window, a walk-in closet, and a roomy bath

Two generous bedrooms with lots of closet space, a hall bath, linen closet, and balcony overlook comprise the second floor

The large covered front porch is great for relaxing outdoors

Price Code A

Rear View

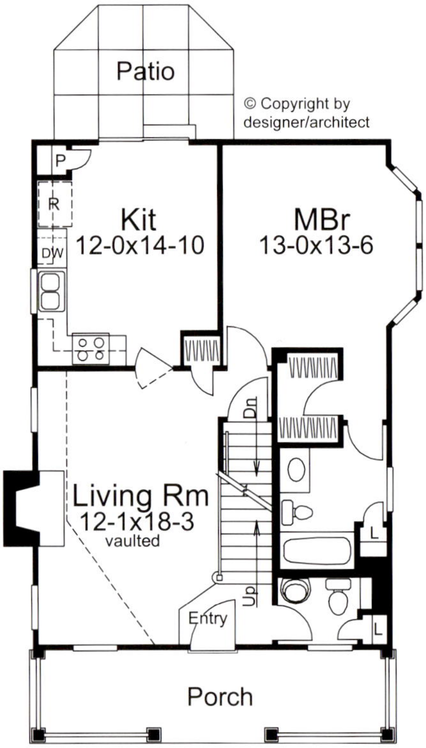

First Floor
834 sq. ft.

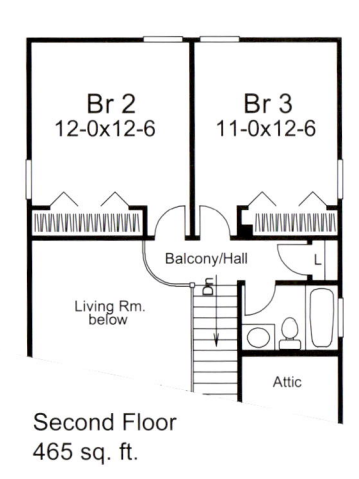

Second Floor
465 sq. ft.

Kit 12-0x14-10
MBr 13-0x13-6
Living Rm 12-1x18-3 vaulted
Br 2 12-0x12-6
Br 3 11-0x12-6

To order this plan, visit the Menards Building Materials Desk or visit www.Menards.com.

MENARDS

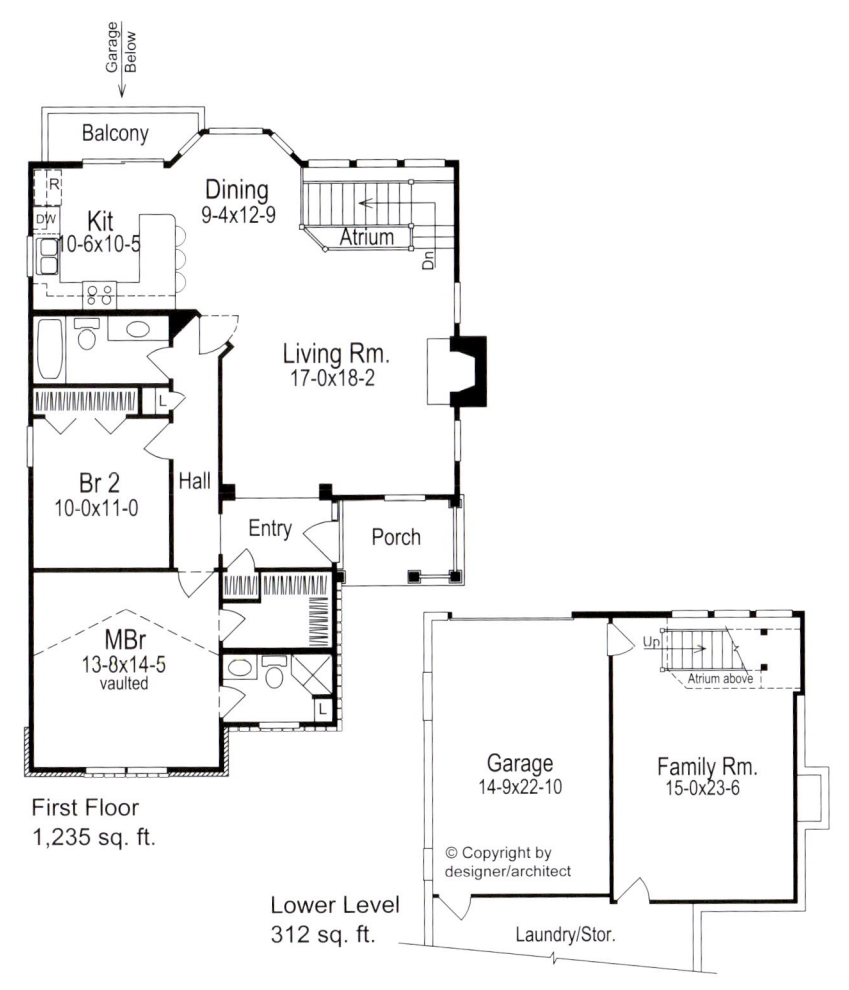

Ashton
Briar

Plan #M09-007D-0103

Atrium Living For Views On A Narrow Lot

1,547 total square feet of living area

Width: 34'-0"   Depth: 48'-10"

2 bedrooms, 2 baths

1-car drive under rear entry garage

Walk-out basement foundation

Special features

Dutch gables and stone accents provide an enchanting appearance

The living room has a fireplace, an atrium window wall, and is open to a dining area

The kitchen has a breakfast counter, cabinet space, and glass sliding doors to a balcony

Price Code A

First Floor 1,235 sq. ft.

- Balcony
- Kit 10-6x10-5
- Dining 9-4x12-9
- Atrium
- Living Rm. 17-0x18-2
- Br 2 10-0x11-0
- Hall
- Entry
- Porch
- MBr 13-8x14-5 vaulted

Lower Level 312 sq. ft.

- Garage 14-9x22-10
- Family Rm. 15-0x23-6
- Atrium above
- Laundry/Stor.

© Copyright by designer/architect

Rear View

To order this plan, visit the Menards Building Materials Desk or visit www.Menards.com.

Plan #M09-013L-0002

Ranch Offers Pleasant Living

1,197 total square feet of living area

Width: 52'-0"   Depth: 42'-0"

3 bedrooms, 2 baths,

2-car garage

Crawl space or slab foundation, please specify when ordering

Special features

The dining area is adjacent to the family room that is ideal for gathering

The private master bath has a vaulted ceiling, a double-bowl vanity, a separate tub, and a shower

A plant shelf in the family room adds charm

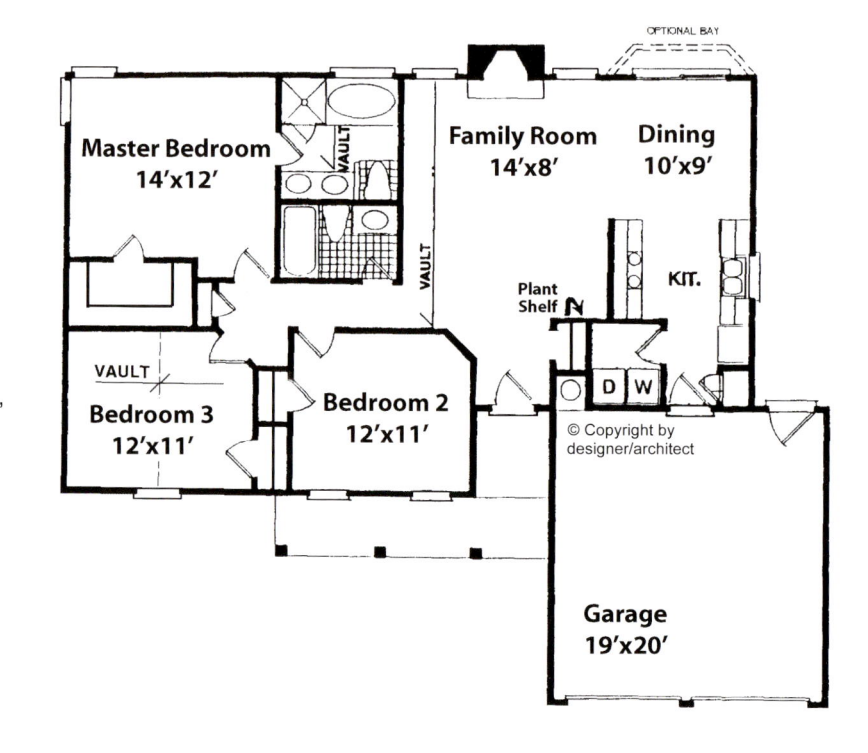

Price Code B

Master Bedroom 14'x12'
Family Room 14'x8'
Dining 10'x9'
Bedroom 3 12'x11'
Bedroom 2 12'x11'
Garage 19'x20'

© Copyright by designer/architect

To order this plan, visit the Menards Building Materials Desk or visit www.Menards.com.

MENARDS

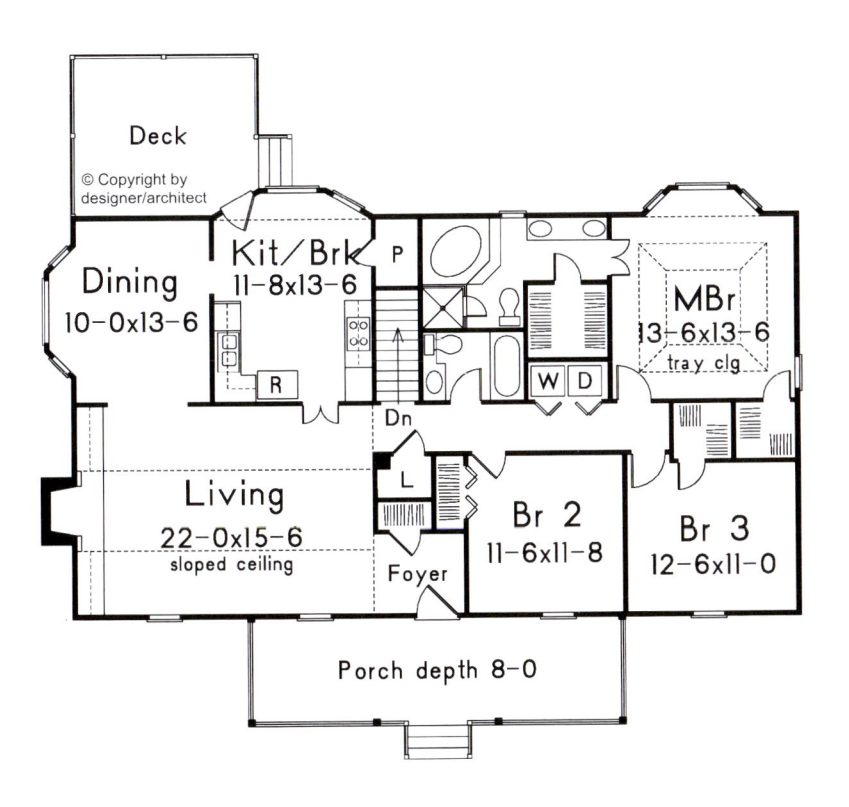

Bay Ranch

Plan #M09-053D-0002

Bay Window Graces Luxury Master Bedroom

1,668 total square feet of living area

Width: 56'-0"   Depth: 40'-0"

3 bedrooms, 2 baths

2-car side entry drive under garage

Walk-out basement foundation

Special features

Large bay windows grace the kitchen/breakfast area, the master bedroom, and dining room

Extensive walk-in closets and storage spaces are located throughout the home

Handy covered entry porch

The large living room has a fireplace, built-in bookshelves, and a sloped ceiling

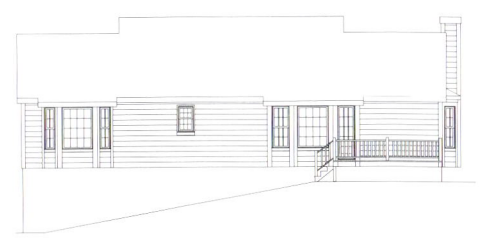

Price Code A

Rear View

Plan #M09-001D-0029

Central Fireplace Warms Family Room

1,260 total square feet of living area

Width: 62'-0"   Depth: 38'-0"

3 bedrooms, 2 baths

2-car garage

Basement foundation, drawings also include crawl space and slab foundations

Special features

The spacious kitchen/dining area features a large pantry, a storage area, and easy access to the garage and laundry room

A pleasant covered front porch adds a practical touch

The master bedroom with a private bath adjoins two other bedrooms, all with plenty of closet space

Price Code A

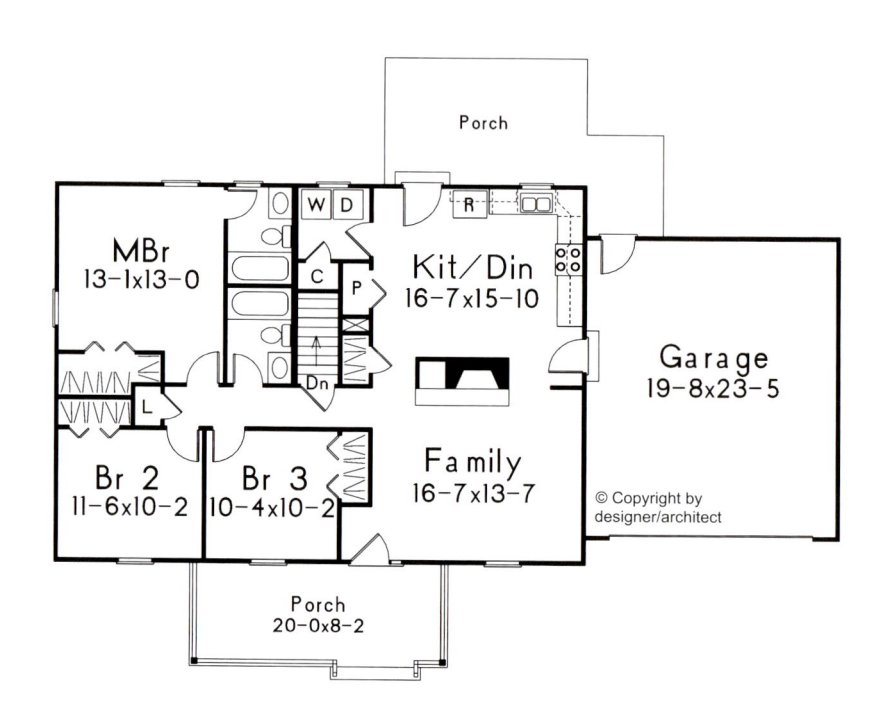

Rear View

To order this plan, visit the Menards Building Materials Desk or visit www.Menards.com

MENARDS

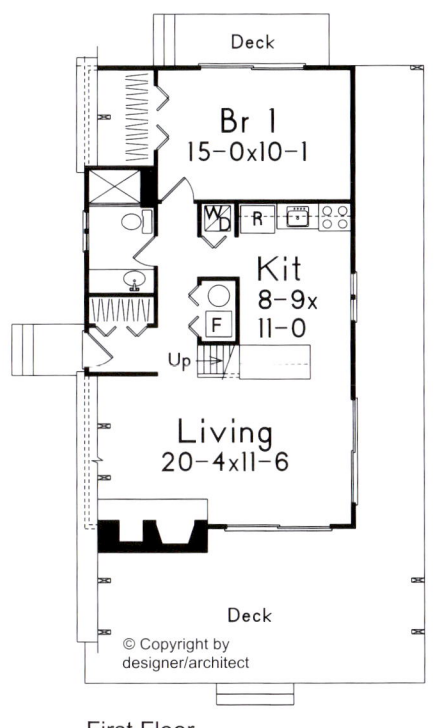

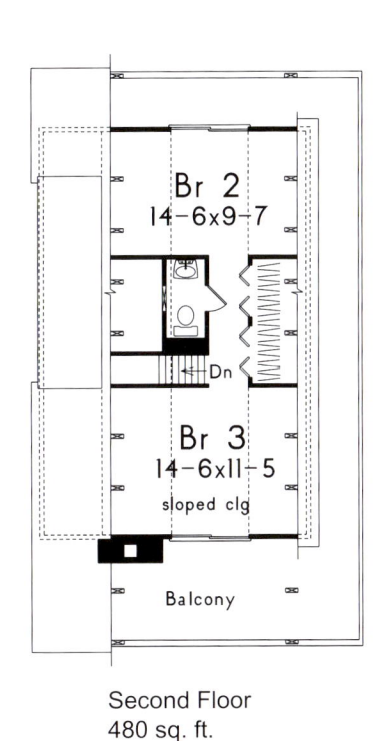

Grantview

Plan #M09-008D-0139

Unique A-Frame Detailing Has Appeal

1,272 total square feet of living area

Width: 26'-4"   Depth: 44'-2"

3 bedrooms, 1 1/2 baths

Crawl space foundation

Special features

A stone fireplace accents the living room

The spacious kitchen includes a snack bar overlooking the living room

The first floor bedroom is roomy and secluded

There is plenty of closet space for the second floor bedrooms plus a generous balcony that wraps around the second floor

Price Code A

First Floor — 792 sq. ft.
- Deck
- Br 1 — 15-0x10-1
- Kit — 8-9x11-0
- Living — 20-4x11-6
- Deck

Second Floor — 480 sq. ft.
- Br 2 — 14-6x9-7
- Br 3 — 14-6x11-5 sloped clg
- Balcony

To order this plan, visit the Menards Building Materials Desk or visit www.Menards.com.

Arcadia

MENARDS

Plan #M09-007D-0200

Especially Designed For A Small Lot

1,137 total square feet of living area

Width: 32'-0"   Depth: 41'-0"

2 bedrooms, 1 1/2 baths

2-car garage

Walk-out basement foundation

Special features

Cleverly designed two-story is disguised as an attractive one-story home

The living room with fireplace is open to the bayed dining area and L-shaped kitchen

The optional finished lower level includes a family room, hall bath and third bedroom and allows for an extra 591 square feet of living area

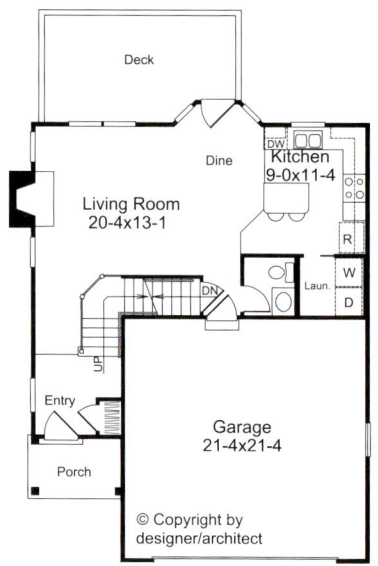

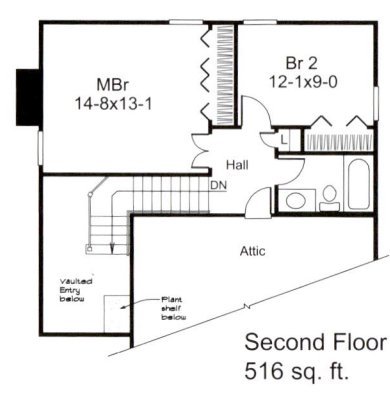

Price Code A

Rear View

First Floor 621 sq. ft.

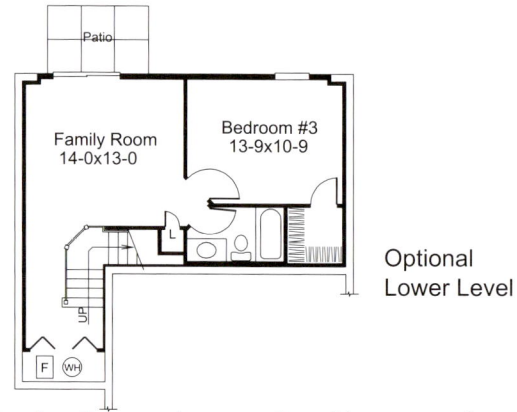

- Deck
- Dine
- Kitchen 9-0x11-4
- Living Room 20-4x13-1
- Laun.
- Entry
- Porch
- Garage 21-4x21-4

© Copyright by designer/architect

Second Floor 516 sq. ft.

- MBr 14-8x13-1
- Br 2 12-1x9-0
- Hall
- Attic
- Vaulted Entry below
- Plant shelf below

Optional Lower Level

- Patio
- Family Room 14-0x13-0
- Bedroom #3 13-9x10-9

To order this plan, visit the Menards Building Materials Desk or visit www.Menards.com

MENARDS

Mapleview

Plan #M09-033D-0013

Second Floor
719 sq. ft.

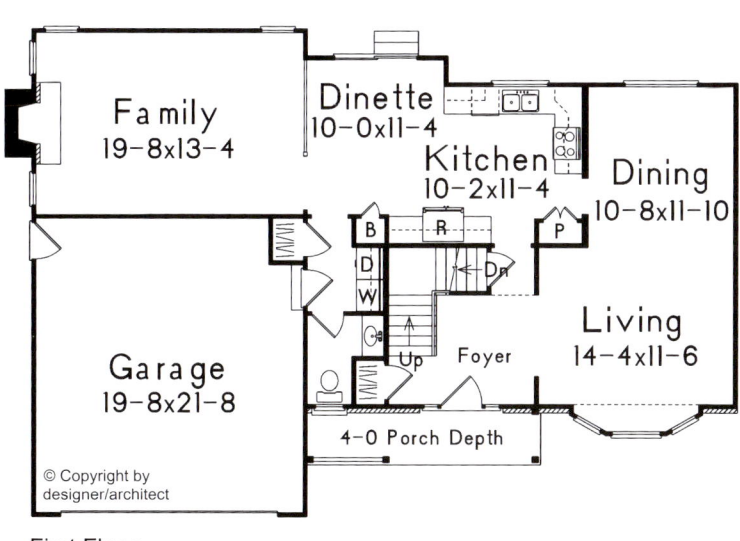

First Floor
1,094 sq. ft.

Great Plan For Formal And Informal Entertaining

1,813 total square feet of living area

Width: 52'-0"   Depth: 36'-0"

3 bedrooms, 2 1/2 baths

2-car garage

Basement foundation

Special features

The bedrooms are located on the second floor for privacy

The living room with large bay window joins the dining room

The family room, dinette and kitchen combine for an impressive living area

The two-story foyer and L-shaped staircase create a dramatic entry

Price Code D

Rear View

To order this plan, visit the Menards Building Materials Desk or visit www.Menards.com.

Rosencrest

MENARDS

Plan #M09-077L-0074

Shutters Add Style To The Exterior

1,502 total square feet of living area

Width: 51'-8"   Depth: 51'-2"

3 bedrooms, 2 baths

2-car side entry garage

Crawl space or slab foundation, please specify when ordering

Special features

The dining area or sunroom is open and airy with windows all around and includes a 9' ceiling and patio access

The kitchen features raised bars facing the dining and living rooms

The gas fireplace makes the living room a warm, friendly place to gather

Price Code E

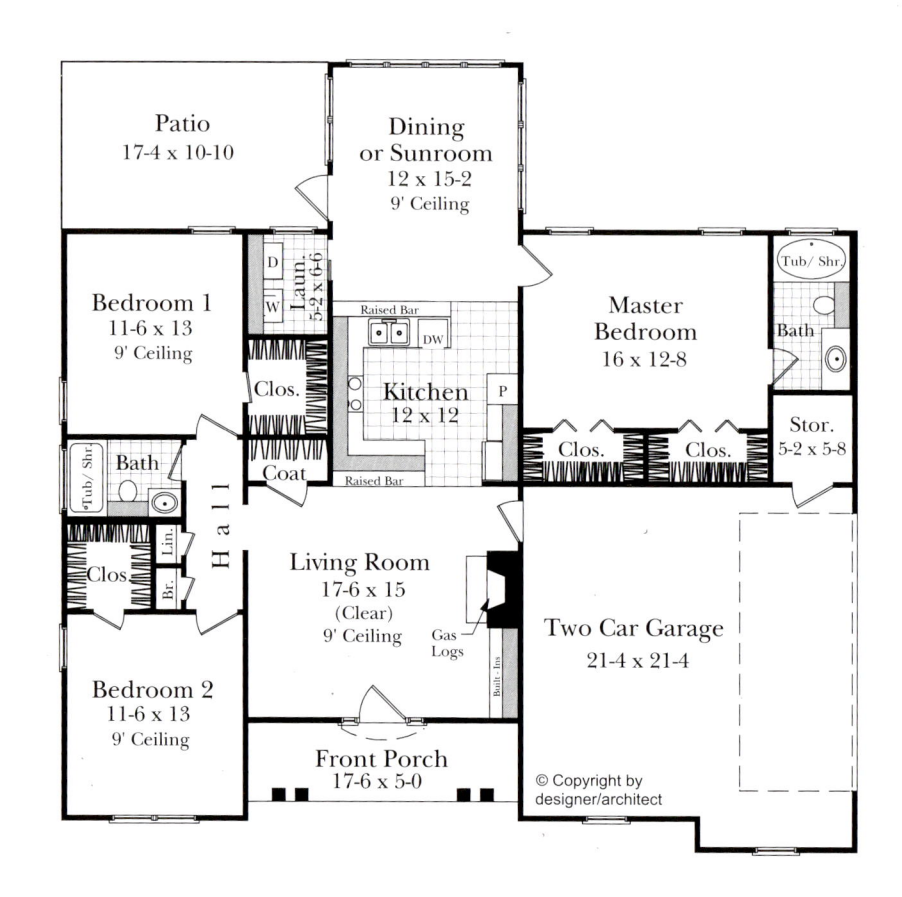

Floor plan rooms:

- Patio 17-4 x 10-10
- Dining or Sunroom 12 x 15-2, 9' Ceiling
- Bedroom 1 11-6 x 13, 9' Ceiling
- Laun. 5-2 x 6-6
- Kitchen 12 x 12
- Master Bedroom 16 x 12-8
- Stor. 5-2 x 5-8
- Bath
- Living Room 17-6 x 15 (Clear) 9' Ceiling
- Two Car Garage 21-4 x 21-4
- Bedroom 2 11-6 x 13, 9' Ceiling
- Front Porch 17-6 x 5-0

© Copyright by designer/architect

To order this plan, visit the Menards Building Materials Desk or visit www.Menards.com

MENARDS

Stillb[...] Sumner

Plan #M09-008D-0153

Great Views From The Covered Deck

792 total square feet of living area

Width: 24'-0"   Depth: 42'-0"

2 bedrooms, 1 bath

Crawl space foundation, drawings also include slab foundation

Special features

The attractive exterior features wood posts and beams, a wrap-around deck with railing, and sliding glass doors with transoms above

The kitchen, living and dining areas enjoy sloped ceilings, a cozy fireplace, and views over the covered deck

Two bedrooms share a bath located just off the hall

Price Code AAA

Floor plan:
- Br 2: 9-1 x 11-1
- Br 1: 11-6 x 11-1
- Kit/Dining: 11-8 x 15-9
- Living: 11-8 x 22-0, vaulted clg
- Covered Deck: 24-0 x 8-0

© Copyright by designer/architect

To order this plan, visit the Menards Building Materials Desk or visit www.Menards.com.

Plan #M09-013L-0028

Casual Farmhouse Appeal

2,239 total square feet of living area

Width: 48'-0"   Depth: 48'-0"

3 bedrooms, 2 1/2 baths

2-car detached garage

Basement or crawl space foundation, please specify when ordering

Special features

Two sets of French doors in the family room lead to a rear covered porch ideal for relaxing

The master bedroom has a spacious bath with an oversized tub placed in a sunny bay window

Both of the second floor bedrooms have storage closets for terrific organizing

Price Code D

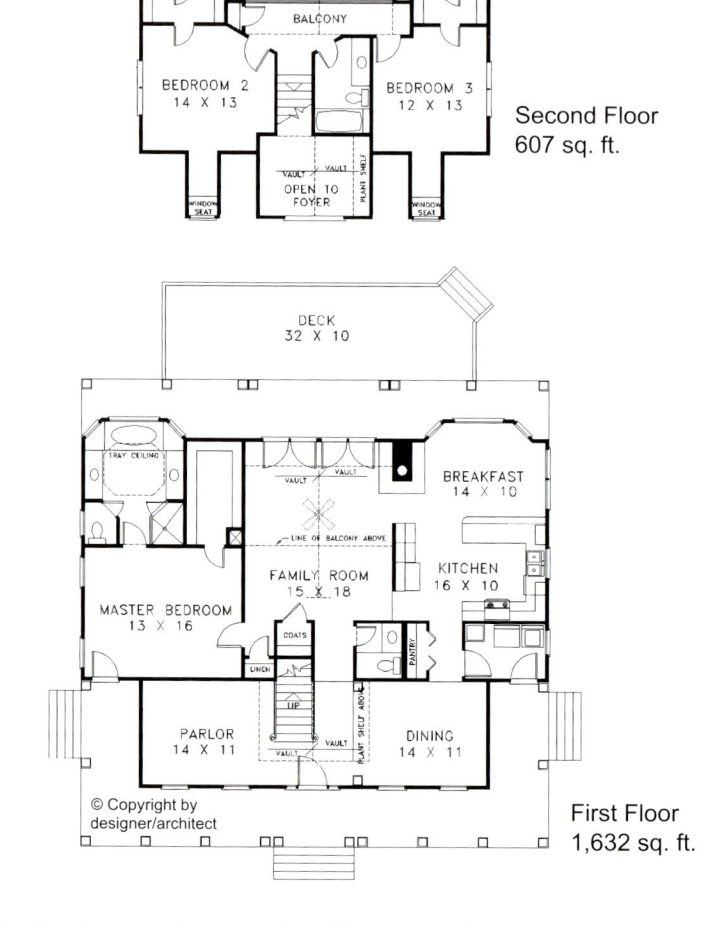

Second Floor 607 sq. ft.

First Floor 1,632 sq. ft.

To order this plan, visit the Menards Building Materials Desk or visit www.menards.com

MENARDS

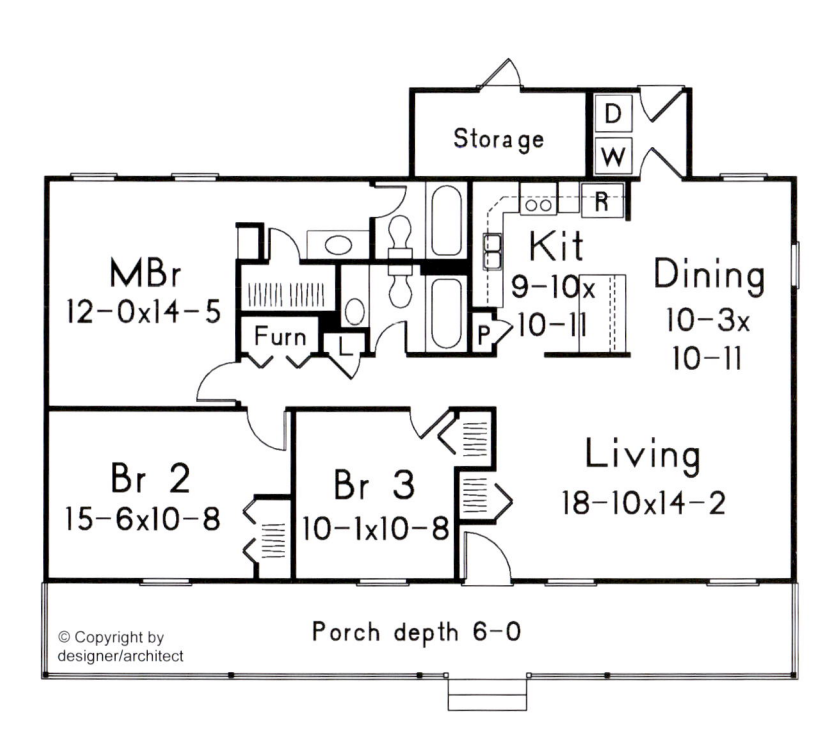

Delta Queen II

Plan #M09-001D-0068

Layout Creates Large Open Living Area

1,285 total square feet of living area

Width: 48'-0"   Depth: 37'-8"

3 bedrooms, 2 baths

Crawl space foundation, drawings also include basement and slab foundations

Special features

A large storage area can be found on the back of the home

The master bedroom includes a dressing area, private bath and built-in bookcase

The kitchen features a pantry, breakfast bar and complete view to the dining room

2" x 6" exterior wall framing available for an additional fee, please specify when ordering

Price Code B

Rear View

Floor plan rooms:
- Storage
- MBr 12-0x14-5
- Kit 9-10x10-11
- Dining 10-3x10-11
- Br 2 15-6x10-8
- Br 3 10-1x10-8
- Living 18-10x14-2
- Porch depth 6-0
- Furn

To order this plan, visit the Menards Building Materials Desk or visit www.Menards.com

Langham

MENARDS

Plan #M09-010D-0007

Large Windows Grace This Split-Level Home

1,427 total square feet of living area

Width: 48'-0"   Depth: 30'-0"

3 bedrooms, 2 baths

2-car drive under garage

Basement foundation

Special features

Practical storage space is situated in the drive under garage

A convenient laundry closet is located on the lower level

The kitchen and dining area both have sliding doors that access the deck

A large expansive space is created by the vaulted living room

Price Code A

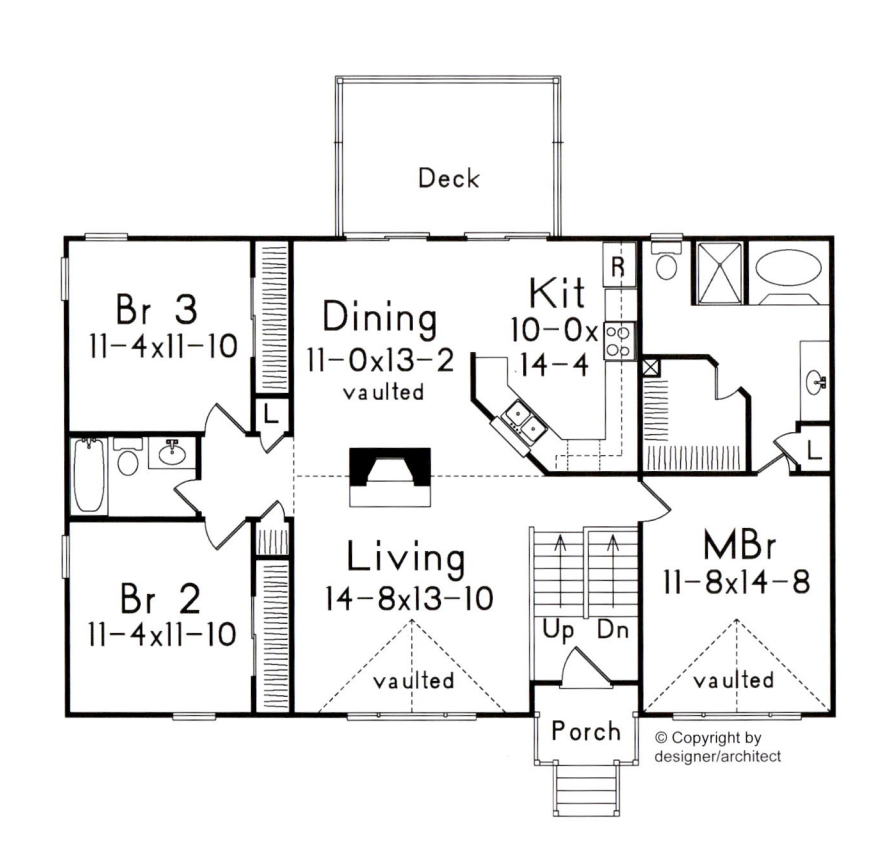

Deck

Br 3
11-4x11-10

Dining
11-0x13-2
vaulted

Kit
10-0x
14-4

Br 2
11-4x11-10

Living
14-8x13-10
vaulted

Up Dn

MBr
11-8x14-8
vaulted

Porch

© Copyright by designer/architect

Rear View

78   To order this plan, visit the Menards Building Materials Desk or visit www.Menards.com.

MENARDS

Hathaway

Plan #M09-007D-0031

Innovative Ranch Has Cozy Corner Patio

1,092 total square feet of living area

Width: 40'-4"   Depth: 42'-0"

3 bedrooms, 1 1/2 baths

1-car garage

Basement foundation, drawings also include slab and crawl space foundations

Special features

A box window and inviting porch with dormers create a charming facade

The eat-in kitchen has a pass-through breakfast bar, corner window wall, pantry, and convenient laundry room with half bath

The master bedroom features a double-door entry and roomy walk-in closet

Price Code AA

Rear View

To order this plan, visit the Menards Building Materials Desk or visit www.Menards.com.

MENARDS

Plan #M09-055L-0105

Welcoming Covered Porch

1,023 total square feet of living area

Width: 45'-0"   Depth: 41'-0"

3 bedrooms, 2 baths

2-car garage

Crawl space or slab foundation, please specify when ordering

Special features

The kitchen includes a snack bar and is open to the great room and breakfast room

The master suite features a private bath

The centrally located laundry area is just steps away from all three bedrooms

Price Code B

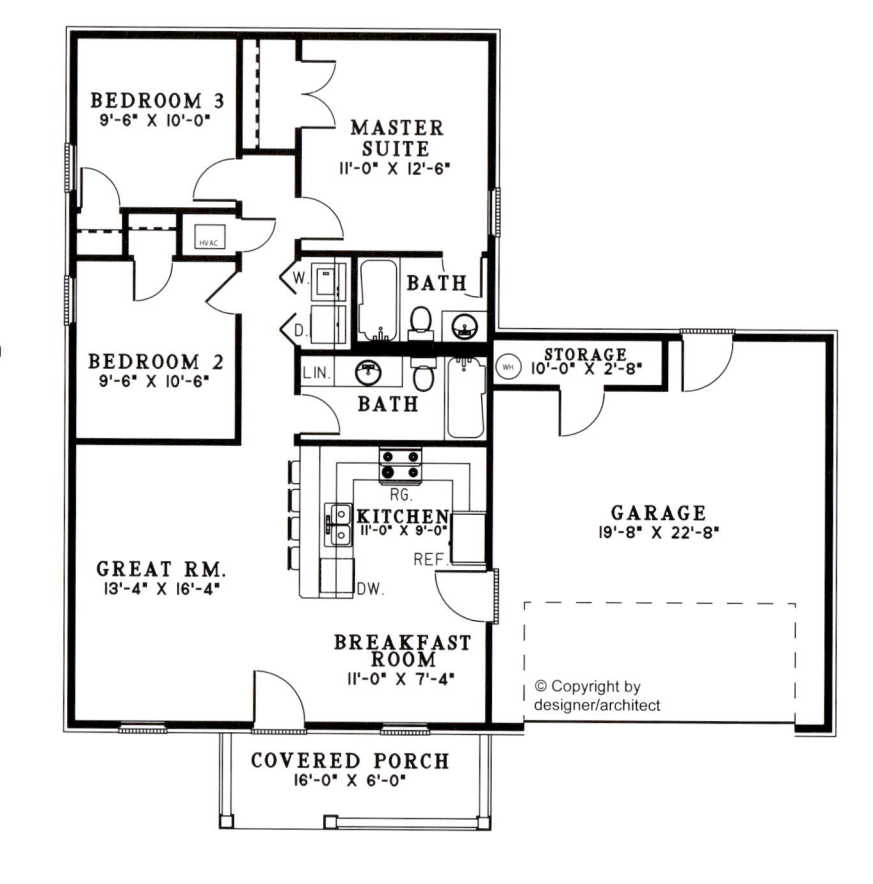

Floor plan:
- BEDROOM 3: 9'-6" X 10'-0"
- MASTER SUITE: 11'-0" X 12'-6"
- BEDROOM 2: 9'-6" X 10'-6"
- BATH
- STORAGE: 10'-0" X 2'-8"
- KITCHEN: 11'-0" X 9'-0"
- GREAT RM.: 13'-4" X 16'-4"
- GARAGE: 19'-8" X 22'-8"
- BREAKFAST ROOM: 11'-0" X 7'-4"
- COVERED PORCH: 16'-0" X 6'-0"

© Copyright by designer/architect

To order this plan, visit the Menards Building Materials Desk or visit www.Menards.com

MENARDS

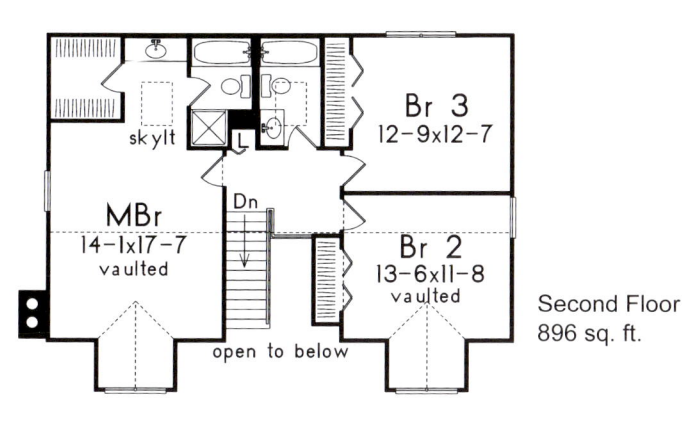

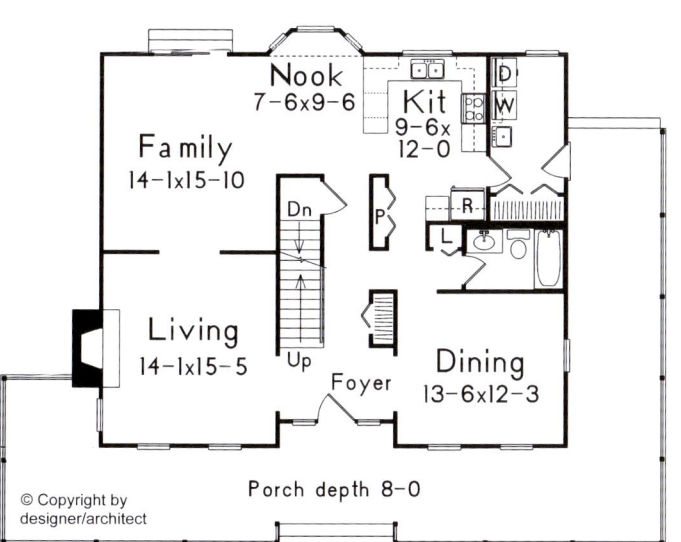

Kingsmill

Plan #M09-008D-0085

Attractive Dormers Enhance Facade

2,112 total square feet of living area

Width: 54'-0"   Depth: 42'-2"

3 bedrooms, 3 baths

Basement foundation, drawings also include crawl space foundation

Special features

The kitchen efficiently connects to the formal dining area

A bayed nook is located between the family room and kitchen creating an ideal breakfast area

The vaulted master bedroom features a skylight, walk-in closet and private bath

Price Code C

Second Floor 896 sq. ft.

- MBr 14-1x17-7 vaulted
- Br 3 12-9x12-7
- Br 2 13-6x11-8 vaulted
- skylt

First Floor 1,216 sq. ft.

- Nook 7-6x9-6
- Kit 9-6x12-0
- Family 14-1x15-10
- Living 14-1x15-5
- Dining 13-6x12-3
- Foyer
- Porch depth 8-0

© Copyright by designer/architect

To order this plan, visit the Menards Building Materials Desk or visit www.Menards.com.

Ferguson

MENARDS

Plan #M09-040D-0006

Well-Sculptured Design, Inside And Out

1,759 total square feet of living area

Width: 46'-0"   Depth: 45'-4"

3 bedrooms, 2 1/2 baths

2-car garage

Basement foundation

Special features

The striking entry is created by a unique staircase layout, and a open high ceiling

The second floor bedrooms share a private dressing area and bath

The bonus area over the garage, that is included in the square footage, could easily convert to a fourth bedroom or activity center

Price Code AA

Rear View

Second Floor
631 sq. ft.

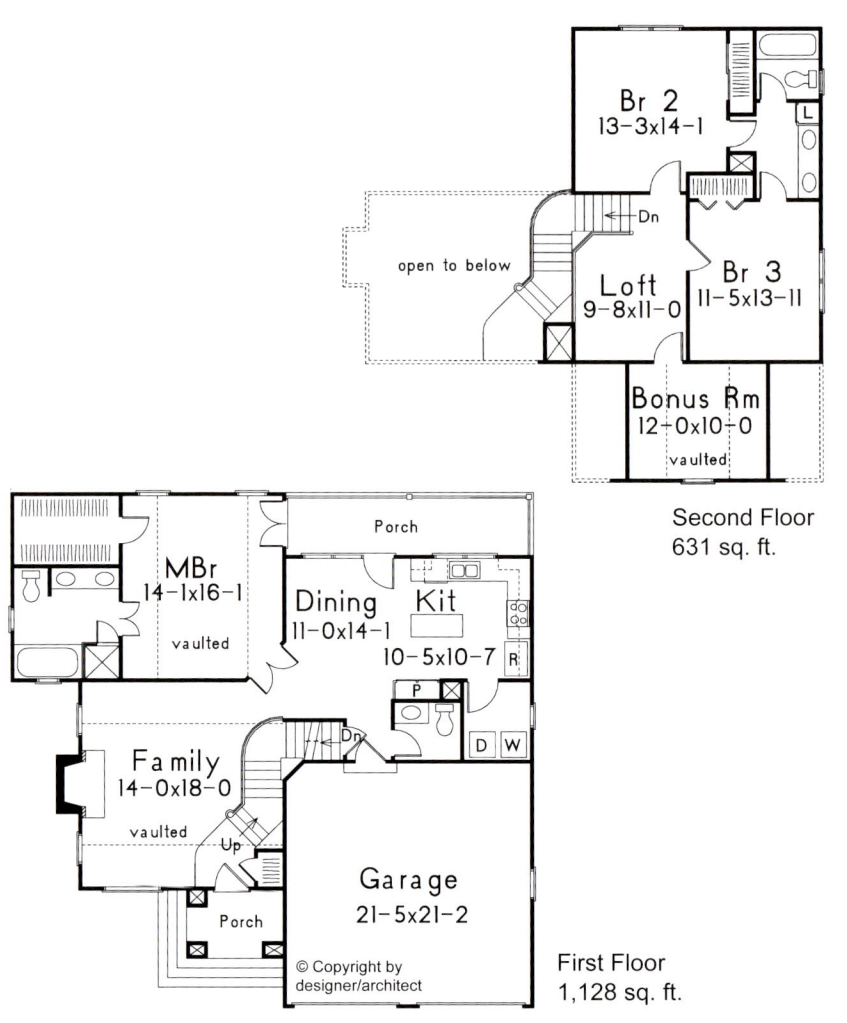

- Br 2: 13-3x14-1
- Loft: 9-8x11-0
- Br 3: 11-5x13-11
- Bonus Rm: 12-0x10-0 vaulted
- open to below

First Floor
1,128 sq. ft.

- MBr: 14-1x16-1 vaulted
- Dining: 11-0x14-1
- Kit: 10-5x10-7
- Family: 14-0x18-0 vaulted
- Garage: 21-5x21-2
- Porch

© Copyright by designer/architect

To order this plan, visit the Menards Building Materials Desk or visit www.Menards.com.

MENARDS

Mona Park

Plan #M09-055L-0188

Bayed Dining Room

1,525 total square feet of living area

Width: 51'-6"   Depth: 49'-10"

3 bedrooms, 2 baths

2-car garage

Slab, crawl space or basement foundation, please specify when ordering; walk-out basement foundation available for an additional fee

Special features

The kitchen is enhanced with an open bar that connects to the great room

A corner gas fireplace warms the entire great room and beyond

The master suite features a whirlpool tub flanked by walk-in closets

Price Code C

To order this plan, visit the Menards Building Materials Desk or visit www.Menards.com.

Ivy Place

MENARDS

Plan #M09-017D-0002

Farmhouse Style Offers Great Privacy

1,805 total square feet of living area

Width: 60'-0"   Depth: 38'-6"

3 bedrooms, 2 1/2 baths

2-car side entry garage

Basement foundation, drawings also include slab foundation

Special features

Energy efficient home with 2" x 6" exterior walls

The master bedroom forms its own wing

The second floor bedrooms share a hall bath

The large great room with fireplace blends into the formal dining room

Price Code D

Rear View

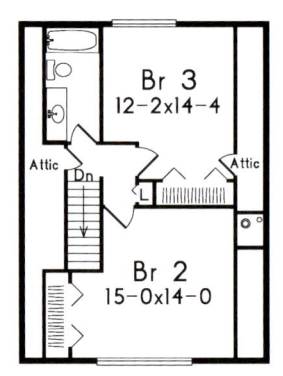

Second Floor
560 sq. ft.

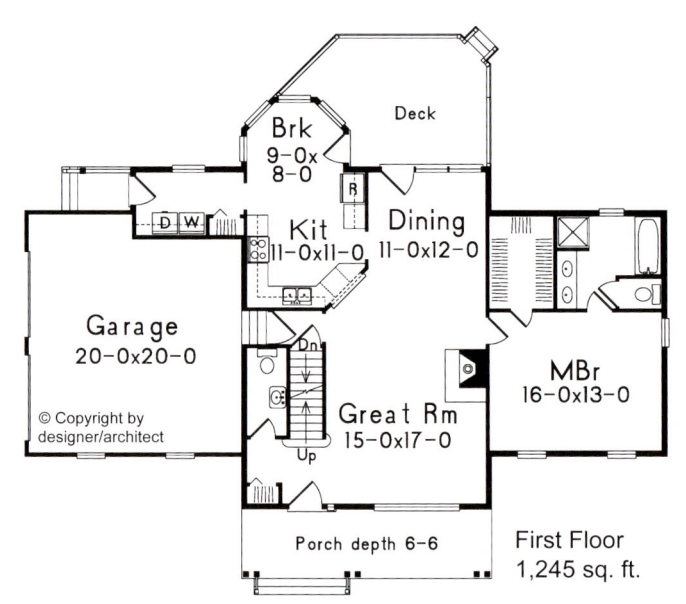

- Br 3: 12-2x14-4
- Br 2: 15-0x14-0
- Attic

First Floor
1,245 sq. ft.

- Brk: 9-0x8-0
- Kit: 11-0x11-0
- Dining: 11-0x12-0
- Garage: 20-0x20-0
- Great Rm: 15-0x17-0
- MBr: 16-0x13-0
- Deck
- Porch depth 6-6

© Copyright by designer/architect

To order this plan, visit the Menards Building Materials Desk or visit www.menards.com

MENARDS

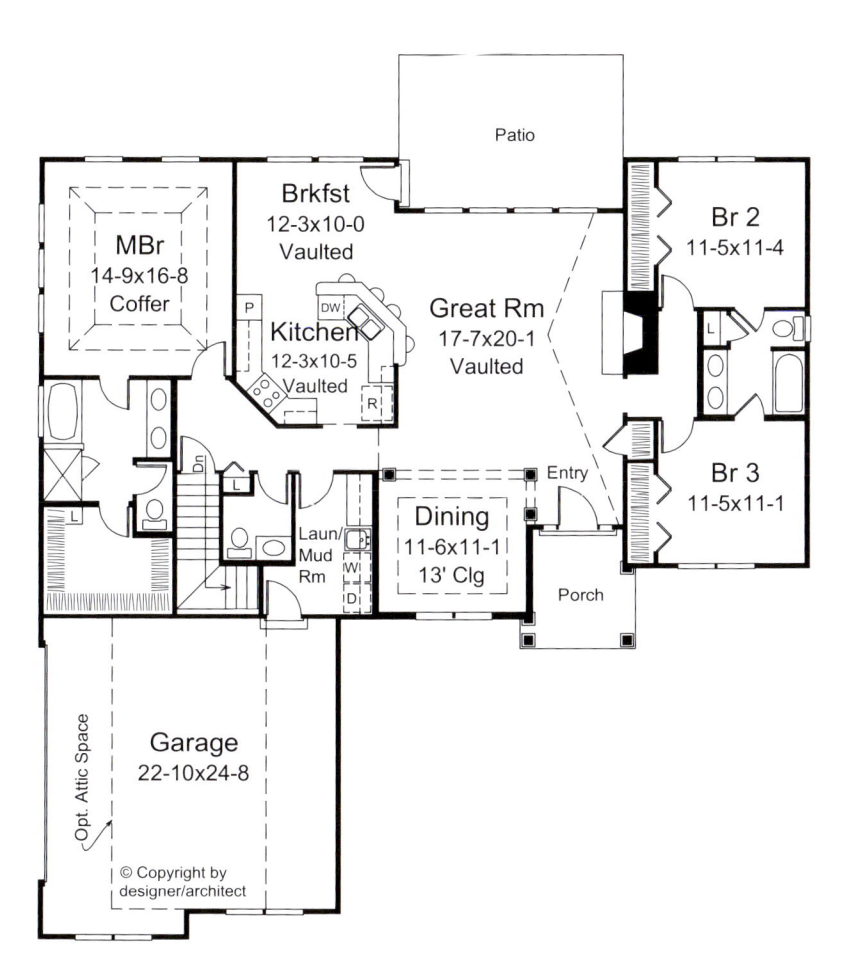

Rebecca

Plan #M09-121D-0015

Welcoming Covered Front Porch

1,983 total square feet of living area

Width: 60'-0"   Depth: 61'-0"

3 bedrooms, 2 1/2 baths

2-car side entry garage

Basement foundation

Special features

The vaulted great room offers a fireplace and a wall of windows to brighten the space

The master bath has a separate toilet room, a double-bowl vanity, and a large walk-in closet

Bedrooms #2 and #3 share a bath

The optional attic space above the garage has an additional 273 square feet of living area

Price Code B

Rear View

To order this plan, visit the Menards Building Materials Desk or visit www.Menards.com.

Floor plan rooms:
- MBr 14-9x16-8 Coffer
- Brkfst 12-3x10-0 Vaulted
- Kitchen 12-3x10-5 Vaulted
- Great Rm 17-7x20-1 Vaulted
- Br 2 11-5x11-4
- Br 3 11-5x11-1
- Dining 11-6x11-1 13' Clg
- Laun/Mud Rm
- Garage 22-10x24-8
- Patio
- Porch
- Entry
- Opt. Attic Space

© Copyright by designer/architect

Carmel Valley

MENARDS

Plan #M09-039L-0027

Wonderful Two-Story Home

1,612 total square feet of living area

Width: 58'-8"   Depth: 42'-0"

3 bedrooms, 2 1/2 baths

2-car garage

Basement foundation

Special features

A private master bedroom offers all of the essentials for luxurious everyday living

A delightful family room with fireplace is ideally suited for casual family gatherings

This well-planned design enjoys a center island in the kitchen

Price Code C

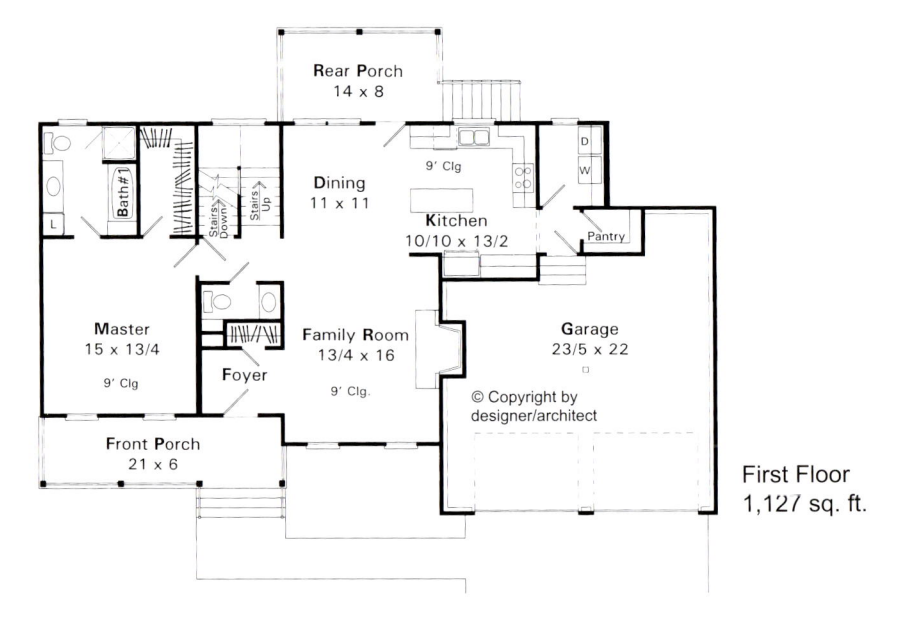

Second Floor 485 sq. ft.
- Bedroom #3: 11 x 11, 8' Clg.
- Bath #2
- Bedroom #2: 13/4 x 12, 8' Clg.

First Floor 1,127 sq. ft.
- Rear Porch: 14 x 8
- Dining: 11 x 11
- Kitchen: 10/10 x 13/2, 9' Clg
- Bath #1
- Master: 15 x 13/4, 9' Clg
- Foyer
- Family Room: 13/4 x 16, 9' Clg.
- Garage: 23/5 x 22
- Front Porch: 21 x 6

© Copyright by designer/architect

To order this plan, visit the Menards Building Materials Desk or visit www.Menards.com

MENARDS

Rutherford

Plan #M09-008D-0178

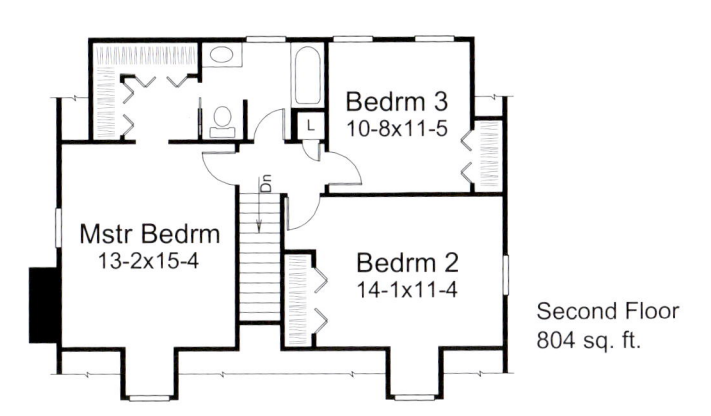

Second Floor
804 sq. ft.

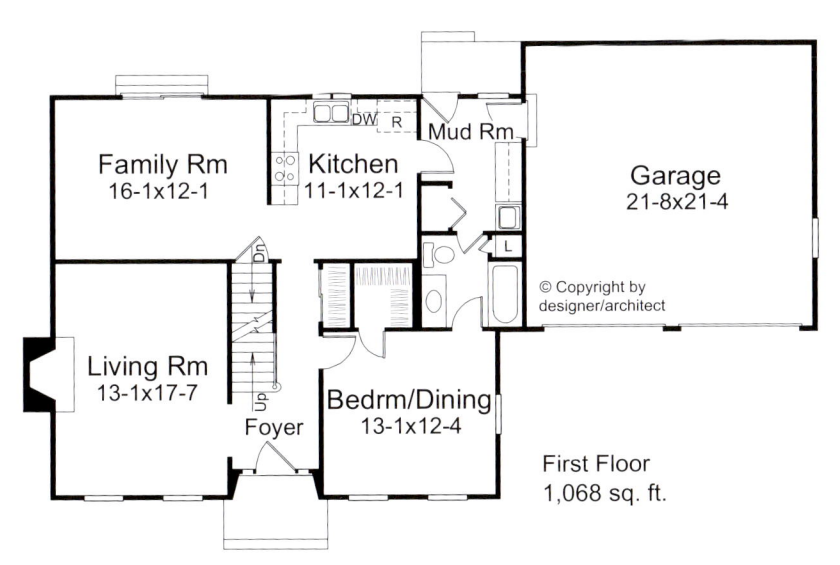

- Mstr Bedrm 13-2x15-4
- Bedrm 3 10-8x11-5
- Bedrm 2 14-1x11-4

First Floor
1,068 sq. ft.

- Family Rm 16-1x12-1
- Kitchen 11-1x12-1
- Mud Rm
- Garage 21-8x21-4
- Living Rm 13-1x17-7
- Bedrm/Dining 13-1x12-4
- Foyer

© Copyright by designer/architect

Design Has Traditional Elegance

1,872 total square feet of living area

Width: 60'-0"   Depth: 30'-8"

4 bedrooms, 2 baths

2-car garage

Basement foundation, drawings also include crawl space and slab foundations

Special features

The recessed porch has an entry door with sidelights and roof dormers adding charm

The foyer with handcrafted staircase adjoins the living room with fireplace

The first floor bedroom/dining has access to the bath and laundry room making it perfect for a live-in parent retreat

The master bedroom on the second floor enjoys double closets and private access to the hall bath

Price Code C

To order this plan, visit the Menards Building Materials Desk or visit www.Menards.com.

Harrison Glen

MENARDS

Plan #M09-013L-0045

Efficiently Designed Two-Story

1,695 total square feet of living area

Width: 50'-0" Depth: 48'-8"

3 bedrooms, 3 baths

2-car garage

Basement foundation

Special features

The large family room with fireplace makes a spacious, yet cozy gathering place

The garage has a convenient workshop space in the back

The screened porch offers protection from the sun and insects and connects to the open deck

The bonus room above the garage has an additional 290 square feet of living area

Price Code C

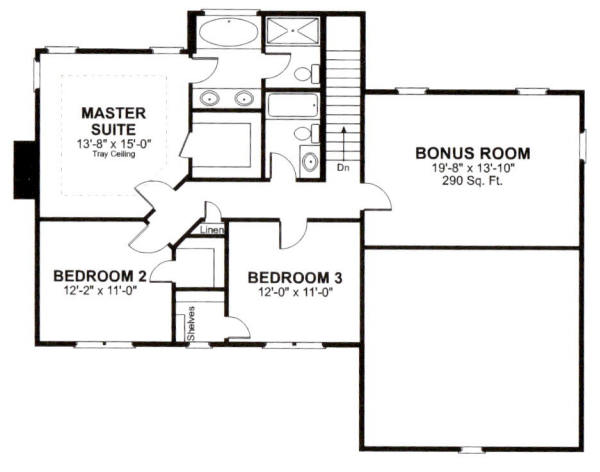

Second Floor
816 sq. ft.

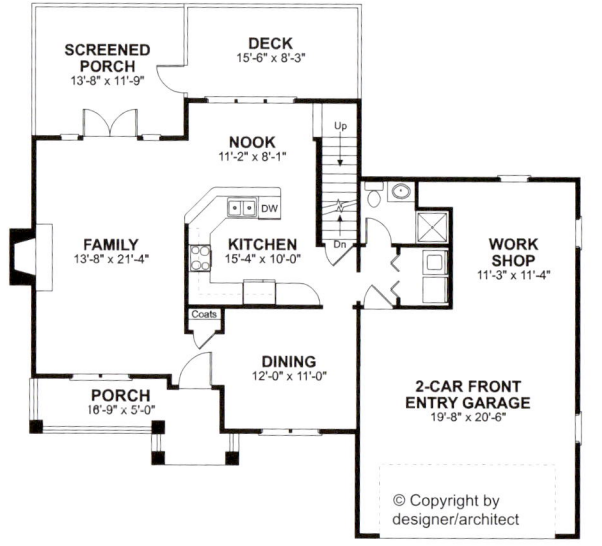

- MASTER SUITE 13'-8" x 15'-0" Tray Ceiling
- BONUS ROOM 19'-8" x 13'-10" 290 Sq. Ft.
- BEDROOM 2 12'-2" x 11'-0"
- BEDROOM 3 12'-0" x 11'-0"

First Floor
879 sq. ft.

- SCREENED PORCH 13'-8" x 11'-9"
- DECK 15'-6" x 8'-3"
- NOOK 11'-2" x 8'-1"
- FAMILY 13'-8" x 21'-4"
- KITCHEN 15'-4" x 10'-0"
- WORK SHOP 11'-3" x 11'-4"
- DINING 12'-0" x 11'-0"
- PORCH 16'-9" x 5'-0"
- 2-CAR FRONT ENTRY GARAGE 19'-8" x 20'-6"

© Copyright by designer/architect

To order this plan, visit the Menards Building Materials Desk or visit www.Menards.com.

MENARDS

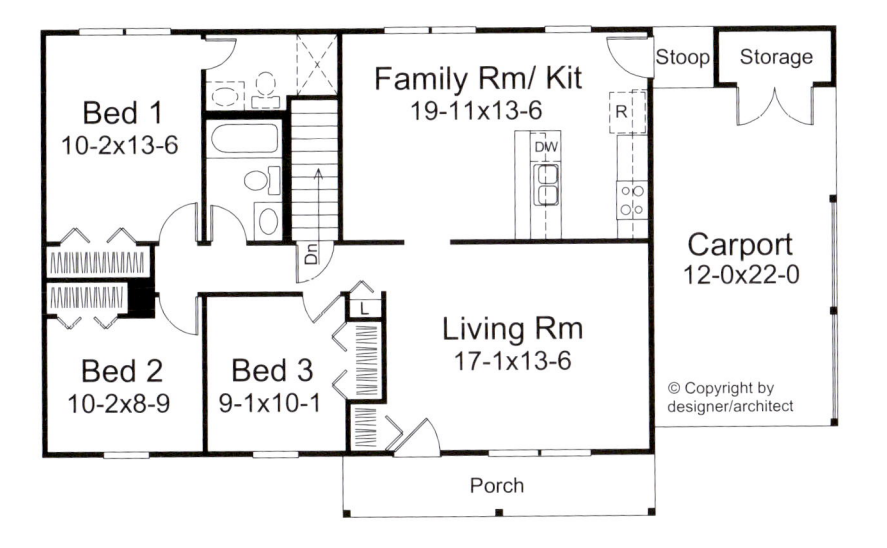

Jonesb[oro]

Newcast[le]

Plan #M09-008D-0026

Lovely Inviting Covered Porch

1,120 total square feet of living area

Width: 52'-0"   Depth: 32'-0"

3 bedrooms, 1 bath

1-car carport

Basement foundation, drawings also include crawl space and slab foundations

Special features

The family room/kitchen creates a useful spacious area

The rustic, colonial design is perfect for many surroundings

An oversized living room is ideal for entertaining

The carport includes a functional storage area

The optional master bath can be converted to a closet for extra storage

Price Code AA

Floor plan:
- Bed 1: 10-2x13-6
- Bed 2: 10-2x8-9
- Bed 3: 9-1x10-1
- Family Rm/Kit: 19-11x13-6
- Living Rm: 17-1x13-6
- Carport: 12-0x22-0
- Stoop
- Storage
- Porch
- © Copyright by designer/architect

To order this plan, visit the Menards Building Materials Desk or visit www.Menards.com.

...te Falls

MENARDS

Plan #M09-013L-0006

Anything But Basic Ranch

1,414 total square feet of living area

Width: 53'-0"   Depth: 46'-8"

3 bedrooms, 2 baths

2-car garage

Basement, crawl space or slab foundation, please specify when ordering

Special features

The dining area has double-doors situated in a sunny bay window

There's a nicely appointed private bath in the master bedroom

The oversized eat-in kitchen has plenty of space for a casual dining table

Price Code B

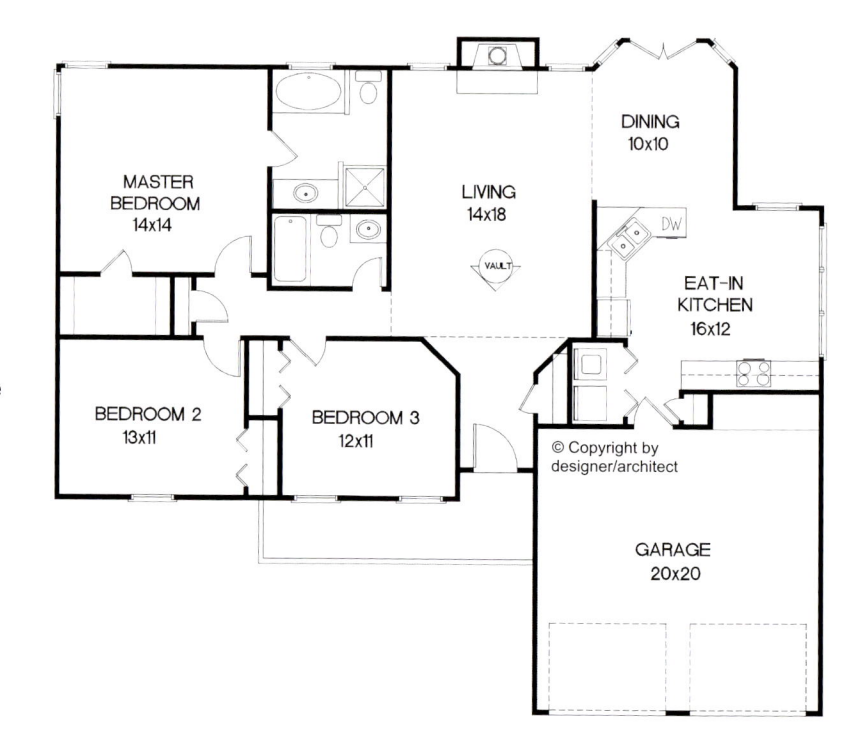

To order this plan, visit the Menards Building Materials Desk or visit www.Menards.com

MENARDS

Loraine

Plan #M09-121D-0048

Refreshing Open Floor Plan

1,615 total square feet of living area

Width: 44'-0"   Depth: 53'-4"

2 bedrooms, 2 baths

2-car garage

Basement foundation

Special features

The large great room has a fireplace with shelves, and a wonderful wall of windows

The kitchen enjoys a corner walk-in pantry, and a wrap-around counter with space for up to five people

The master bedroom is cheerful thanks to five windows, and it includes an spacious private bath with a corner whirlpool tub

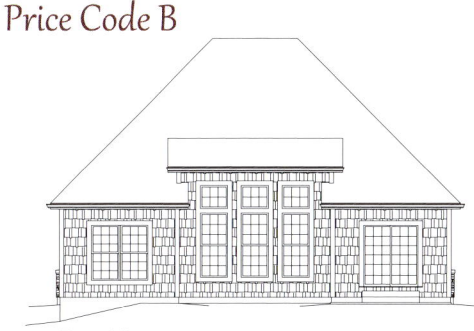

Price Code B

Rear View

Patio

Brkfst/ Dining
12-8x14-11

Great Rm
16-9x21-11
12' Clg

MBr
12-8x14-6
Coffer Clg

Kitchen
12-8x12-9

Garage
22-8x24-0

Foyer

Br 2
12-8x11-0

Porch

© Copyright by designer/architect

To order this plan, visit the Menards Building Materials Desk or visit www.Menards.com.

Kirkland Hollow

MENARDS®

Plan #M09-055L-0350

Photo, above - Gracious and warm, the den provides an inviting atmosphere full of warmth and casual country comfort.

Photo, left - Plenty of cabinetry and counterspace line the U-shaped kitchen offering an abundance of storage, while also keeping everything efficiently within reach when cooking and preparing meals.

Photo, above - The fireplace commands full attention in the comfortable surroundings of the den. No doubt its warmth will be felt throughout the interior of the first floor of this home and especially the adjacent dining room.

Photo, right - Simple country style living is perfectly displayed in this modest bedroom.

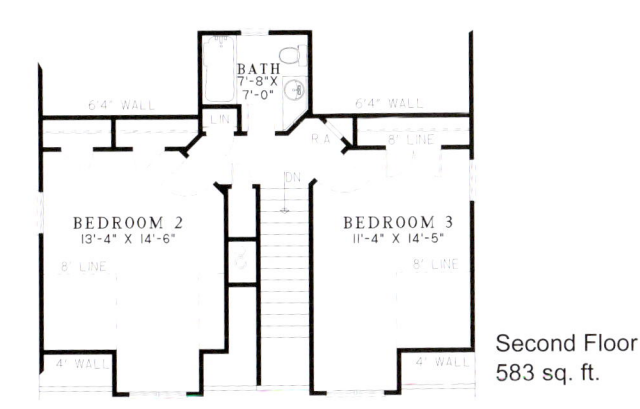

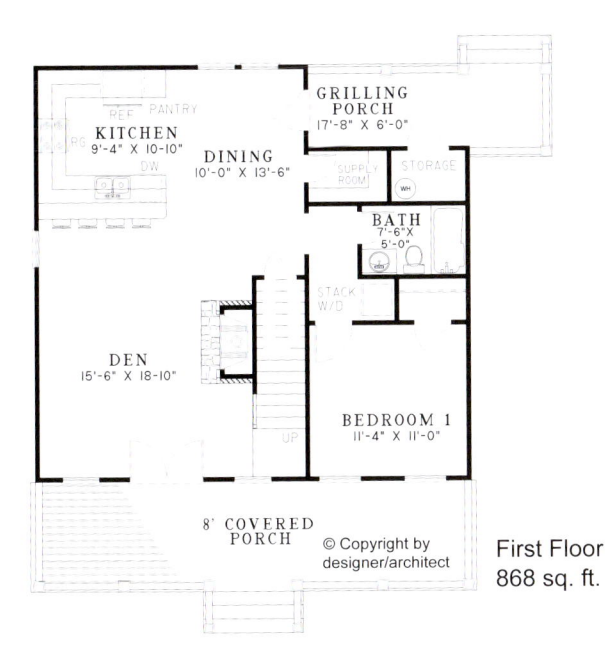

Plan #M09-055L-0350

Country Cottage For A Narrow Lot

1,451 total square feet of living area

Width: 37'-8"   Depth: 38'-4"

3 bedrooms, 2 baths

Slab or crawl space foundation, please specify when ordering; basement or walk-out basement foundations available for an additional fee

Special features

A cozy atmosphere is achieved in the den with a prominent stone fireplace

An 8' deep covered front porch encourages outdoor relaxation and enjoyment

Two secondary bedrooms with dormers share a full bath

Price Code B

Second Floor 583 sq. ft.

First Floor 868 sq. ft.

To order this plan, visit the Menards Building Materials Desk.

MENARDS

Plan #M09-007D-0029

A Cottage With Class

576 total square feet of living area

Width: 24'-0"   Depth: 30'-0"

1 bedroom, 1 bath

Crawl space foundation

Special features

This perfect country retreat features a vaulted living room and entry with skylights and a plant shelf above

The bedroom boasts a double-door entry, vaulted ceiling, a spacious closet, and bath access

The kitchen offers generous storage and a pass-through breakfast bar

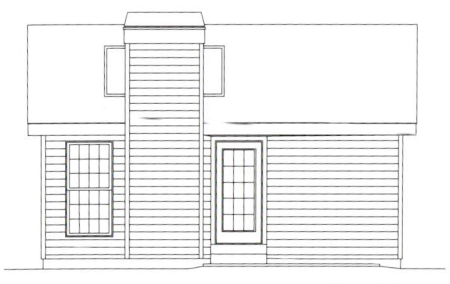

Price Code AAA

Rear View

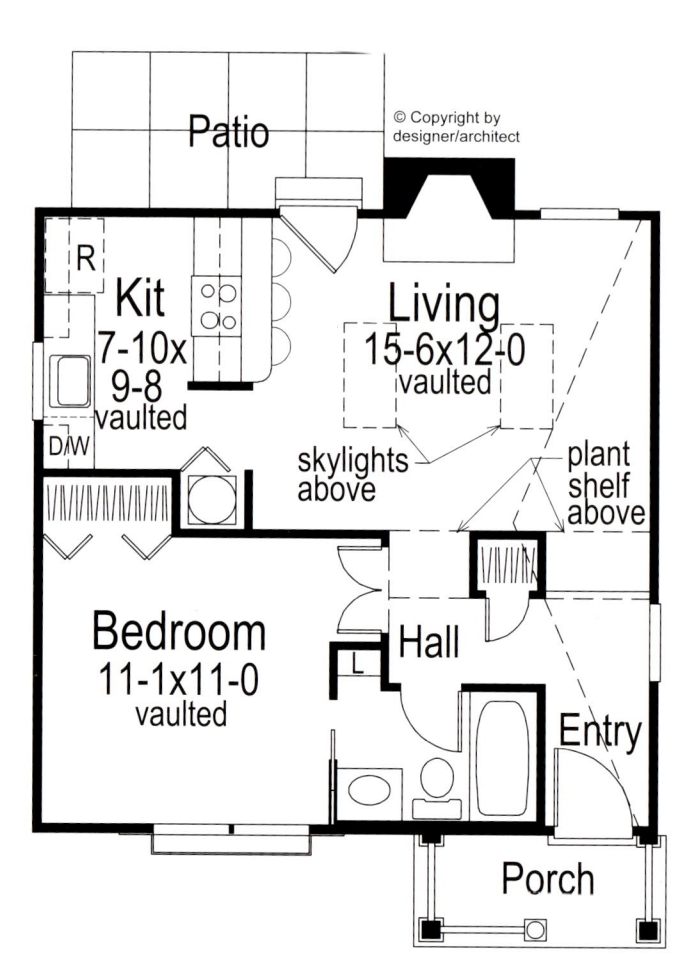

To order this plan, visit the Menards Building Materials Desk or visit www.menards.com

MENARDS

Waverly / Haverhill

Plan #M09-001D-0036

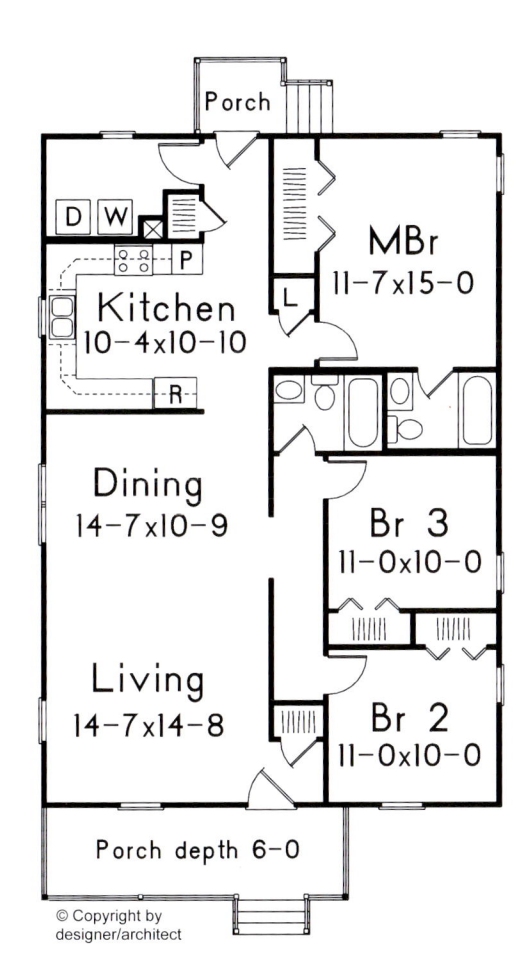

Gabled, Covered Front Porch

1,320 total square feet of living area

Width: 30'-0"   Depth: 50'-0"

3 bedrooms, 2 baths

Crawl space foundation

Special features

A functional U-shaped kitchen has a pantry

Large living and dining areas join to create an open atmosphere

The secluded master bedroom includes a private full bath

The covered front porch opens into a large living area with a convenient coat closet

The utility/laundry room is located near the kitchen

Price Code A

Floor plan dimensions:
- Porch
- Kitchen 10-4 x 10-10
- MBr 11-7 x 15-0
- Dining 14-7 x 10-9
- Br 3 11-0 x 10-0
- Living 14-7 x 14-8
- Br 2 11-0 x 10-0
- Porch depth 6-0

© Copyright by designer/architect

Rear View

To order this plan, visit the Menards Building Materials Desk or visit www.Menards.com.

Plan #M09-040D-0028

Cottage Style Is Appealing And Cozy

828 total square feet of living area

Width: 28'-0"   Depth: 31'-6"

2 bedrooms, 1 bath

Crawl space foundation

Special features

The vaulted ceiling in the family room enhances space

The convenient laundry room is located near the rear entry

There is efficient storage space under the stairs

A covered entry porch provides a cozy sitting area and plenty of shade

Price Code AAA

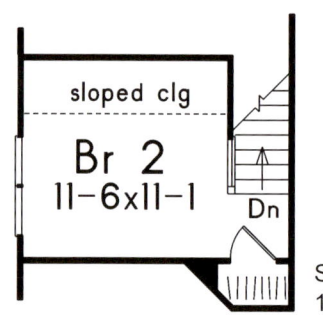

Rear View

Second Floor
168 sq. ft.

Br 2 11-6x11-1
sloped clg

First Floor
660 sq. ft.

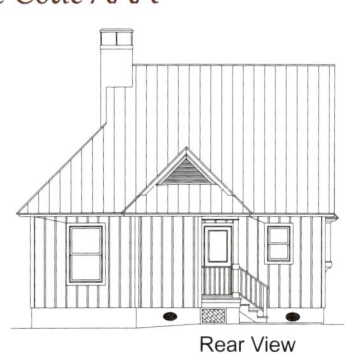

Br 1 12-2x10-2
Kitchen 11-6x11-1
Family 15-5x12-7 vaulted
Porch depth 7-4

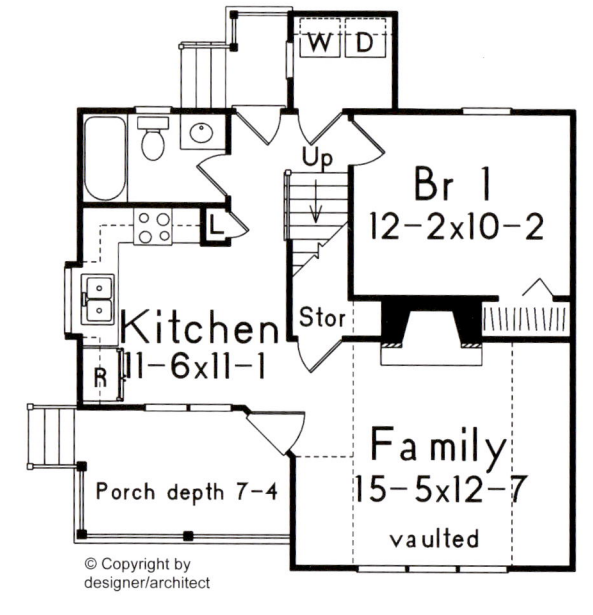

© Copyright by designer/architect

To order this plan, visit the Menards Building Materials Desk or visit www.menards.com.

MENARDS

Hampt[on]

Plan #M09-007D-0013

Home For Narrow Lot Offers Wide Open Spaces

1,492 total square feet of living area

Width: 37'-0"   Depth: 47'-8"

3 bedrooms, 2 1/2 baths

2-car garage

Basement foundation

Special features

Stucco and dutch-hipped roofs add warmth and charm to the facade

An angled entry spills into the living and dining rooms that shares warmth from the fireplace flanked by arched windows

The master bedroom has a walk-in closet, and a private bath with a shower and tub

Price Code A

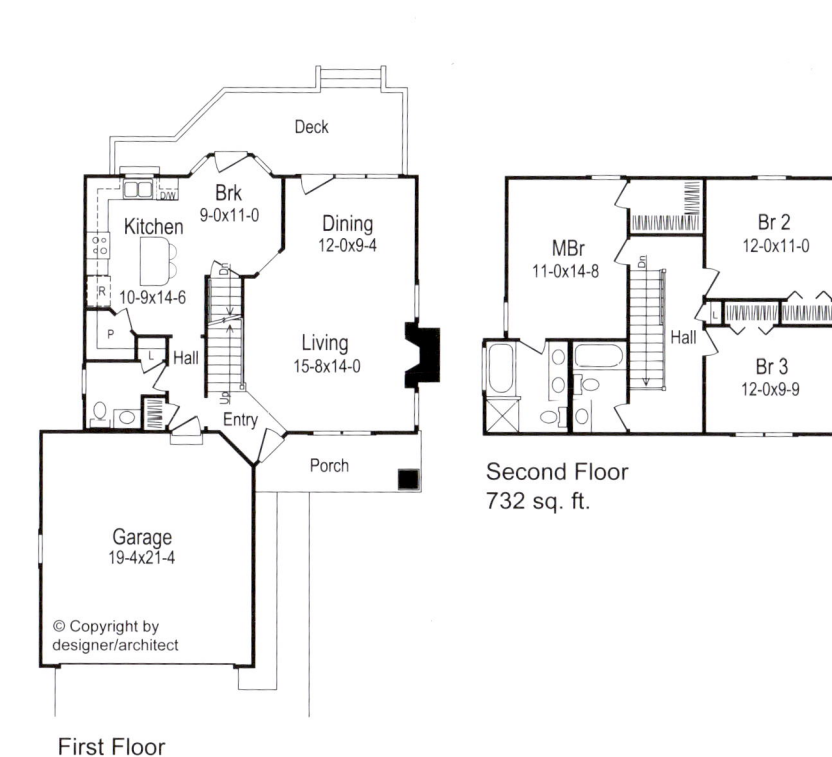

First Floor
760 sq. ft.

Second Floor
732 sq. ft.

Rear View

To order this plan, visit the Menards Building Materials Desk or visit www.Menards.com.

Plan #M09-007D-0105

Stylish Retreat For A Narrow Lot

1,084 total square feet of living area

Width: 35'-0"   Depth: 40'-8"

2 bedrooms, 2 baths

Basement foundation

Special features

The living room has a front feature window, a fireplace and a dining area with a patio

The U-shaped kitchen features lots of cabinets and a bayed breakfast room

Both of the bedrooms have walk-in closets and access to their own bath

Price Code AA

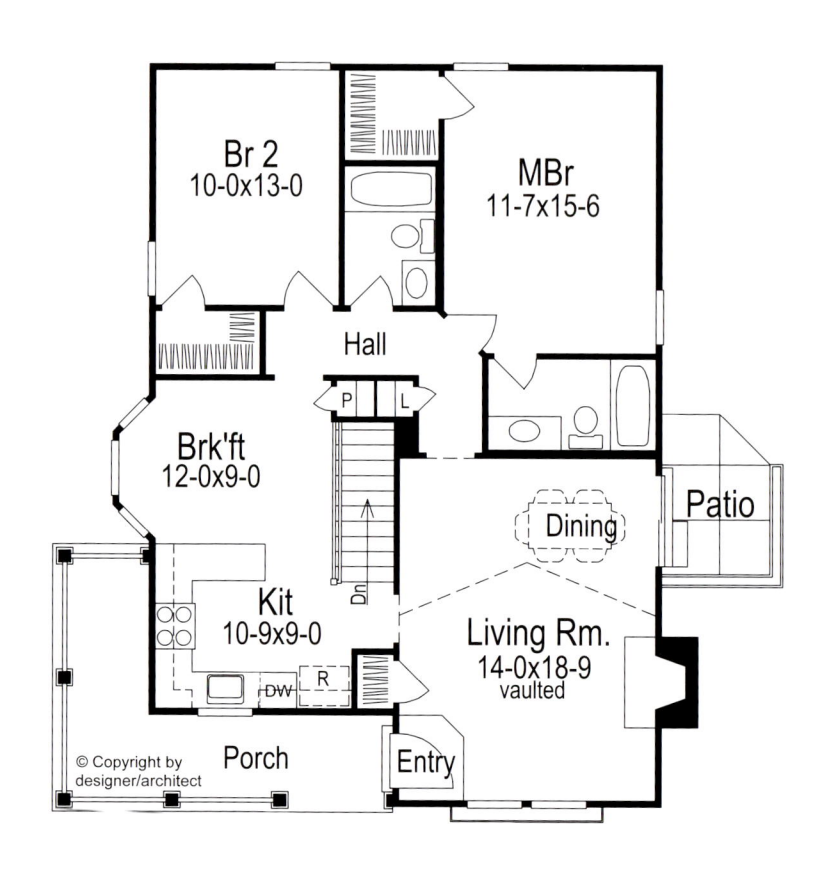

Rear View

To order this plan, visit the Menards Building Materials Desk or visit www.Menards.com

MENARDS

Woodsmill

Plan #M09-007D-0042

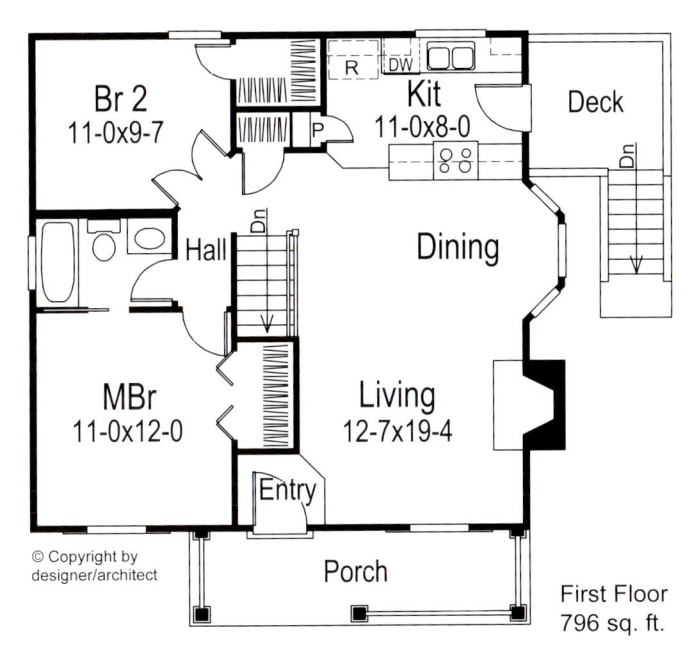

Br 2 11-0x9-7
Kit 11-0x8-0
Deck
Hall
Dining
MBr 11-0x12-0
Living 12-7x19-4
Entry
Porch

© Copyright by designer/architect

First Floor 796 sq. ft.

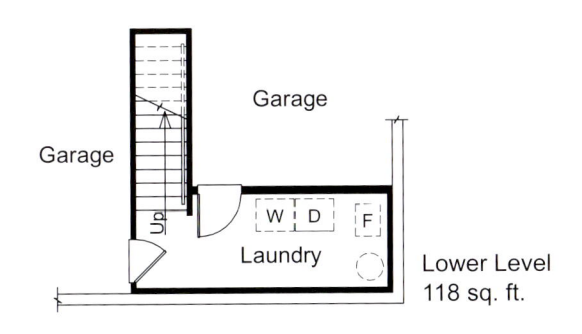

Garage
Garage
Laundry

Lower Level 118 sq. ft.

Small Home Is Remarkably Spacious

914 total square feet of living area

Width: 30'-0"   Depth: 33'-0"

2 bedrooms, 1 bath

2-car drive under rear entry garage

Basement foundation

Special features

This home has a lovely large covered front porch for leisurely evenings

The dining area with bay, an open staircase, and a pass-through kitchen create openness

The basement has a storage area, and a finished laundry and mechanical room

Price Code AA

Rear View

To order this plan, visit the Menards Building Materials Desk or visit www.Menards.com.

Plan #M09-058D-0004

Country Cottage Offers A Large Vaulted Living Space

962 total square feet of living area

Width: 36'-0"   Depth: 36'-0"

2 bedrooms, 1 bath

Crawl space foundation

Special features

Both the kitchen and the family room share warmth from the fireplace

The charming facade features a covered porch on one side, a screened porch on the other, and attractive planter boxes

An L-shaped kitchen boasts a convenient pantry

Price Code AA

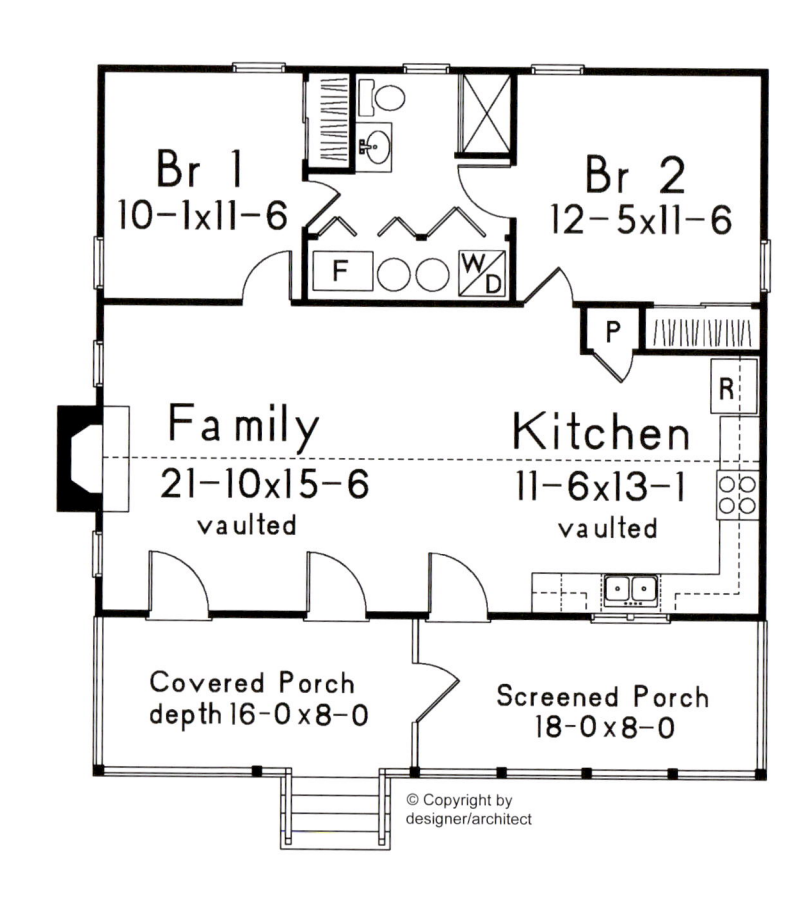

Rear View

Br 1
10-1x11-6

Br 2
12-5x11-6

Family
21-10x15-6
vaulted

Kitchen
11-6x13-1
vaulted

Covered Porch
depth 16-0 x 8-0

Screened Porch
18-0 x 8-0

© Copyright by designer/architect

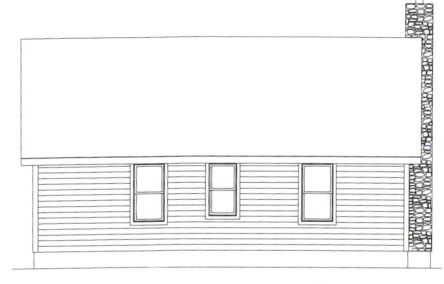

To order this plan, visit the Menards Building Materials Desk or visit www.Menards.com.

MENARDS

Baldwin

Plan #M09-013L-0132

Cheerful Narrow Lot Home

2,296 total square feet of living area

Width: 40'-0" Depth: 68'-0"

3 bedrooms, 3 1/2 baths

2-car garage

Crawl space foundation

Special features

The highly functional kitchen offers double snack bars, a pantry, and an adjacent breakfast nook

Located off the breakfast nook is an oversized laundry room with plenty of space for a washer and dryer as well as a laundry sink and upright freezer

The spacious master bedroom, with its bowed window, tray ceiling, sitting area, luxurious bath and abundant closet, is truly an owner's retreat

The second floor features two secondary bedroom suites, each featuring a walk-in closet and private bath

Price Code F

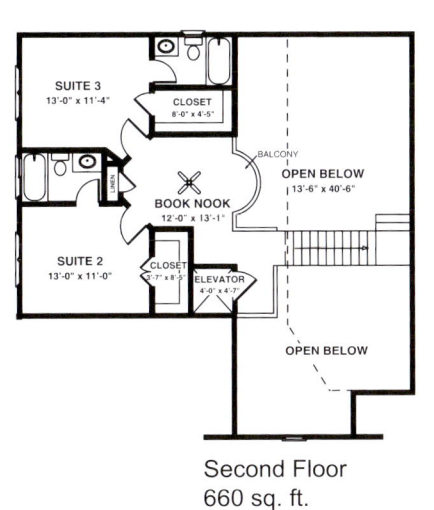

First Floor
1,636 sq. ft.

Second Floor
660 sq. ft.

To order this plan, visit the Menards Building Materials Desk or visit www.Menards.com.

Galanti

MENARDS

Plan #M09-072L-0058

Craftsman Style Cottage

1,800 total square feet of living area

Width: 34'-4"   Depth: 84'-4"

3 bedrooms, 2 baths

2-car rear entry garage

Basement foundation

Special features

Suited for a narrow lot, this bungalow offers tremendous curb appeal and a stylish interior

An entire wall of windows adds a generous amount of sunlight to the family room

The master bedroom is separated from the other bedrooms and also enjoys a private bath with a shower and a whirlpool tub

Price Code D

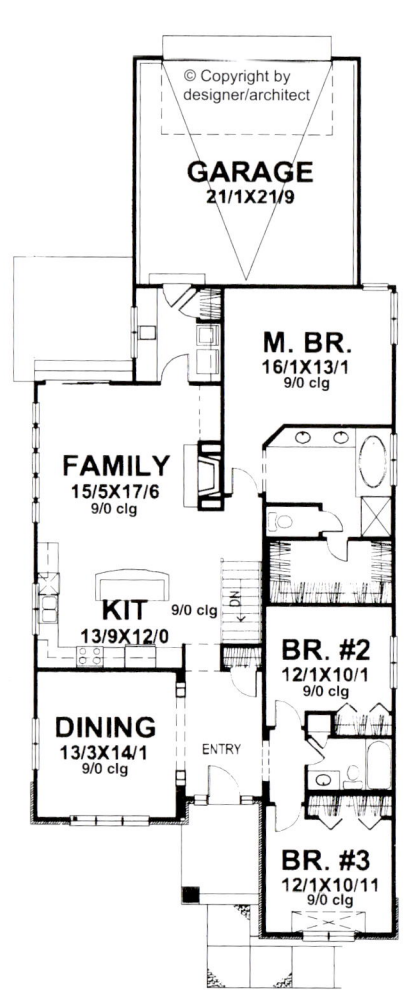

GARAGE 21/1X21/9

M. BR. 16/1X13/1 9/0 clg

FAMILY 15/5X17/6 9/0 clg

KIT 13/9X12/0 9/0 clg

BR. #2 12/1X10/1 9/0 clg

DINING 13/3X14/1 9/0 clg

ENTRY

BR. #3 12/1X10/11 9/0 clg

To order this plan, visit the Menards Building Materials Desk or visit www.Menards.com

MENARDS

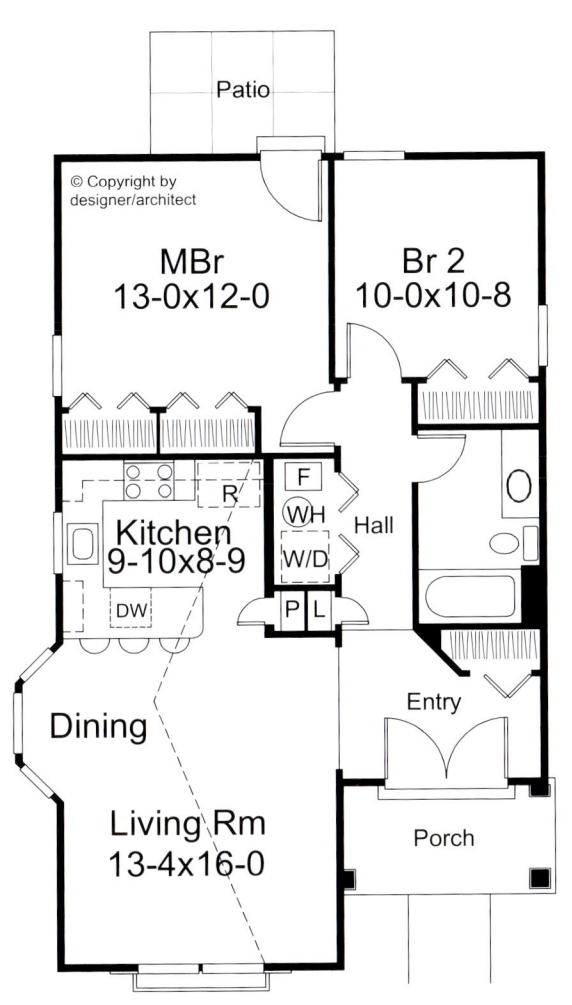

Shadybend Fair

Plan #M09-007D-0175

Stylish Cottage Home

882 total square feet of living area

Width: 26'-0" Depth: 40'-0"

2 bedrooms, 1 bath

Crawl space foundation, drawings also include slab and basement foundations

Special features

An inviting porch and entry lure the owners and guests into this warm and cozy home

The living room features a vaulted ceiling, a bayed dining area, and is open to a well-equipped U-shaped kitchen

The master bedroom has two separate closets and patio access

Price Code AAA

Rear View

To order this plan, visit the Menards Building Materials Desk or visit www.Menards.com.

MENARDS

Plan #M09-007D-0102

Four Bedroom Home For A Narrow Lot

1,452 total square feet of living area

Width: 32'-0"   Depth: 51'-0"

4 bedrooms, 2 baths

Basement foundation

Special features

The large living room features a cozy corner fireplace, bayed dining area, and access from the entry with guest closet

The forward-facing master bedroom enjoys having its own bath and linen closet

Three additional bedrooms share a bath

2" x 6" exterior wall framing available for an additional fee, please specify when ordering

Price Code A

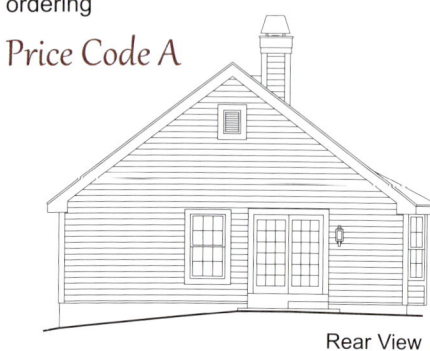

Rear View

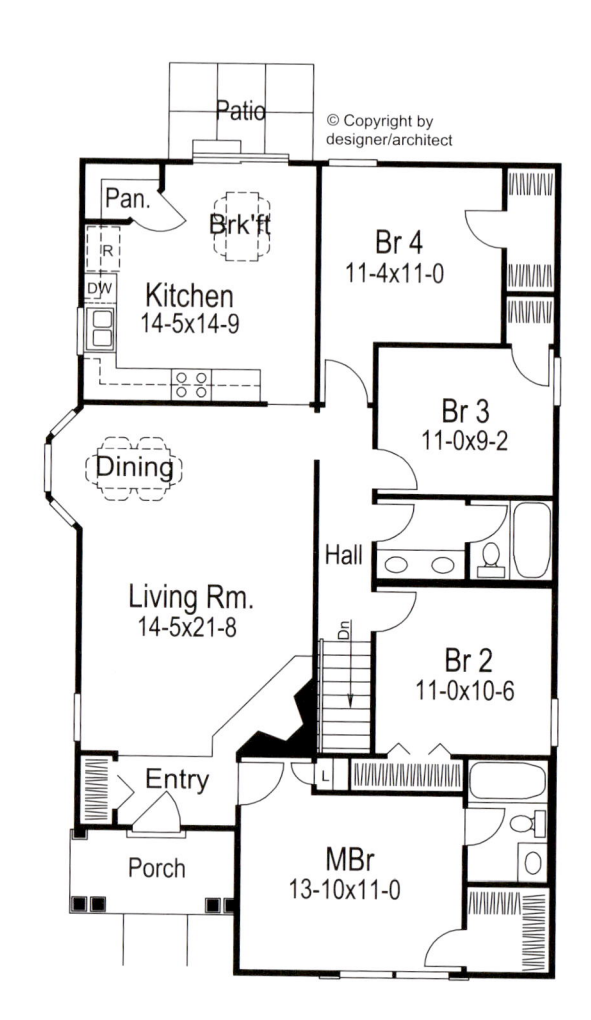

To order this plan, visit the Menards Building Materials Desk or visit www.Menards.com

MENARDS

Rivers

Plan #M09-055L-0063

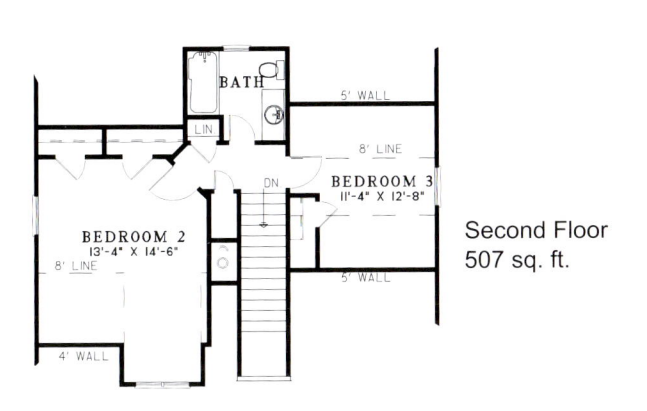

Sportsman's Paradise Cabin

1,397 total square feet of living area

Width: 31'-8"   Depth: 38'-4"

3 bedrooms, 2 baths

Crawl space or slab foundation, please specify when ordering

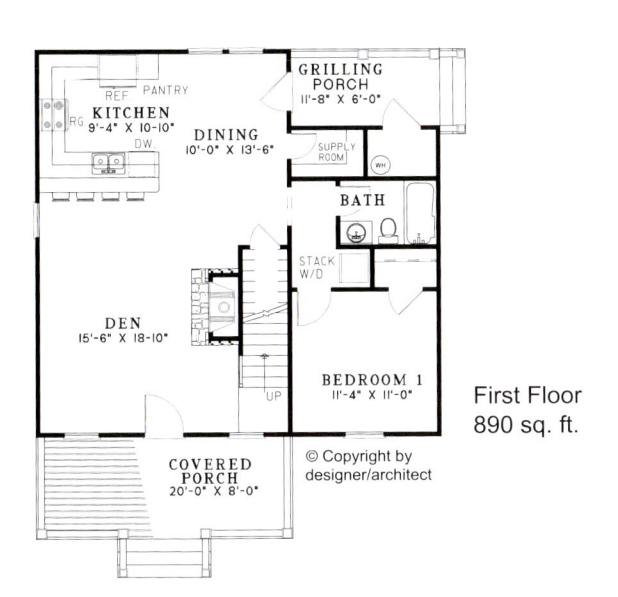

Special features

The den with rock hearth fireplace opens to the dining area and the kitchen

The kitchen and dining area have an eat-in bar with access to a rear grilling porch

The second floor bedrooms have unique ceilings and lots of closet space

Price Code B

Second Floor 507 sq. ft.

- BATH
- 5' WALL
- LIN
- 8' LINE
- BEDROOM 3 11'-4" X 12'-8"
- DN
- BEDROOM 2 13'-4" X 14'-6"
- 8' LINE
- 5' WALL
- 4' WALL

First Floor 890 sq. ft.

- REF PANTRY
- KITCHEN 9'-4" X 10'-10"
- RG
- DW
- DINING 10'-0" X 13'-6"
- GRILLING PORCH 11'-8" X 6'-0"
- SUPPLY ROOM
- WH
- BATH
- STACK W/D
- DEN 15'-6" X 18'-10"
- BEDROOM 1 11'-4" X 11'-0"
- UP
- COVERED PORCH 20'-0" X 8'-0"

© Copyright by designer/architect

To order this plan, visit the Menards Building Materials Desk or visit www.Menards.com.

MENARDS

Plan #M09-121D-0028

Country-Style Cottage

1,433 total square feet of living area

Width: 36'-0"   Depth: 54'-0"

2 bedrooms, 2 baths

2-car garage

Basement foundation

Special features

The vaulted dining area enjoys access to the rear patio

The kitchen boasts a corner island and flows into the vaulted great room

There are many amenities in the master bedroom including a private bath and a walk-in closet

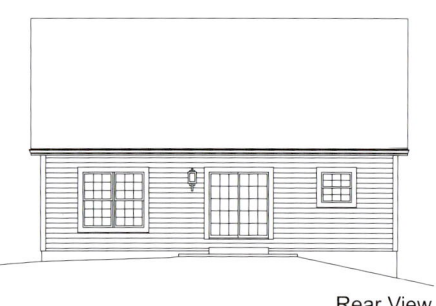

Price Code AA

Rear View

Patio

Kit
10-4x11-8
Vaulted

Dining
10-4x11-8
Vaulted

MBr
14-0x16-0
Vaulted
Opt Coffer

Great Rm
17-8x16-3
Vaulted

Plant Shelf Above

Dn

Br 2
11-4x10-0

Entry

Porch

Garage
19-4x21-0

© Copyright by designer/architect

To order this plan, visit the Menards Building Materials Desk or visit www.Menards.com

MENARDS

Driftwood Spring

Plan #M09-013L-0012

Compact And Simple

1,647 total square feet of living area

Width: 28'-0"   Depth: 46'-0"

2 bedrooms, 1 bath

Slab foundation

Special features

The enormous great room boasts a vaulted ceiling

Located in the great room is an open kitchen with an island and a breakfast bar

The stunning loft overlooks the great room below

Price Code C

First Floor
1,288 sq. ft.

- Bedroom 1: 11'-10" x 10'-0"
- Bedroom 2: 11'-4" x 10'-0"
- Great Room: 27'-4" x 29'-5" (20' high ceiling)
- Deck/Patio: 11'-6" x 18'-8"
- Porch: 24'-4" x 7'-6"
- Deck: 7'-6" x 36'-0"

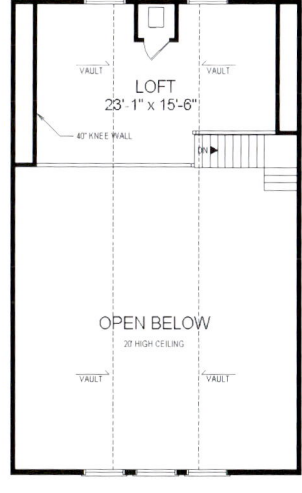

Second Floor
359 sq. ft.

- Loft: 23'-1" x 15'-6" (40" knee wall)
- Open Below (20' high ceiling)

To order this plan, visit the Menards Building Materials Desk or visit www.Menards.com.

107

Dogwood

MENARDS

Plan #M09-058D-0010

Small And Cozy Cabin

676 total square feet of living area

Width: 26'-0"   Depth: 32'-0"

1 bedroom, 1 bath

Crawl space foundation

Special features

A see-through fireplace between the bedroom and living area adds character

The dining and living areas are open

The full-length front covered porch is perfect for enjoying the outdoors

2" x 6" exterior wall framing available for an additional fee, please specify when ordering

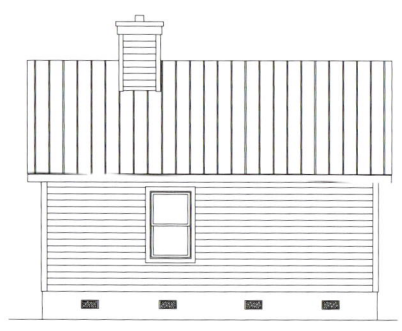

Price Code AAA

Rear View

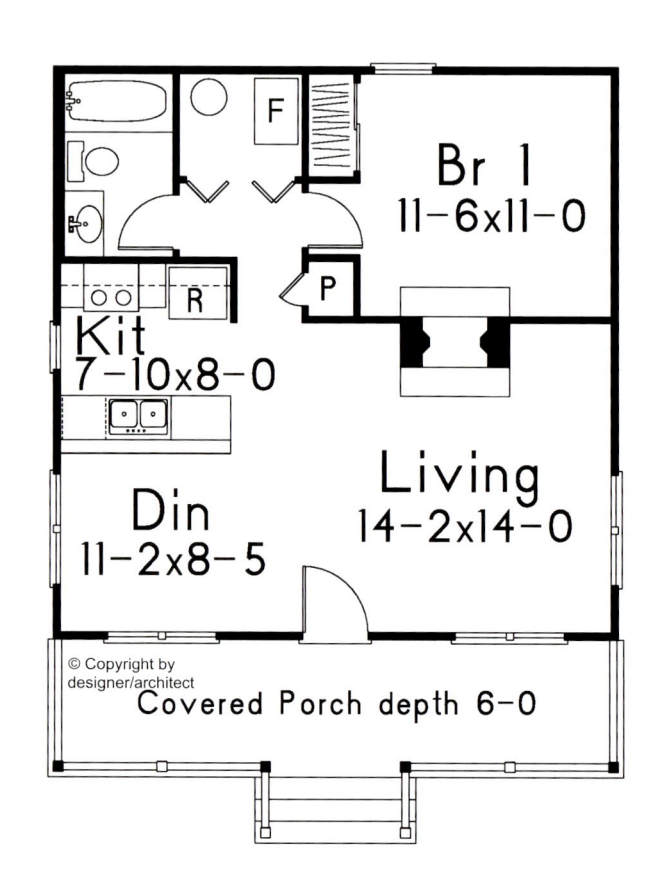

Br 1
11-6x11-0

Kit
7-10x8-0

Din
11-2x8-5

Living
14-2x14-0

© Copyright by designer/architect

Covered Porch depth 6-0

To order this plan, visit the Menards Building Materials Desk or visit www.Menards.com

MENARDS

River Elderberry

Plan #M09-007D-0142

Cozy Retreat For Weekends

480 total square feet of living area

Width: 38'-0"   Depth: 30'-0"

1 bedroom, 1 bath

1-car garage

Slab foundation

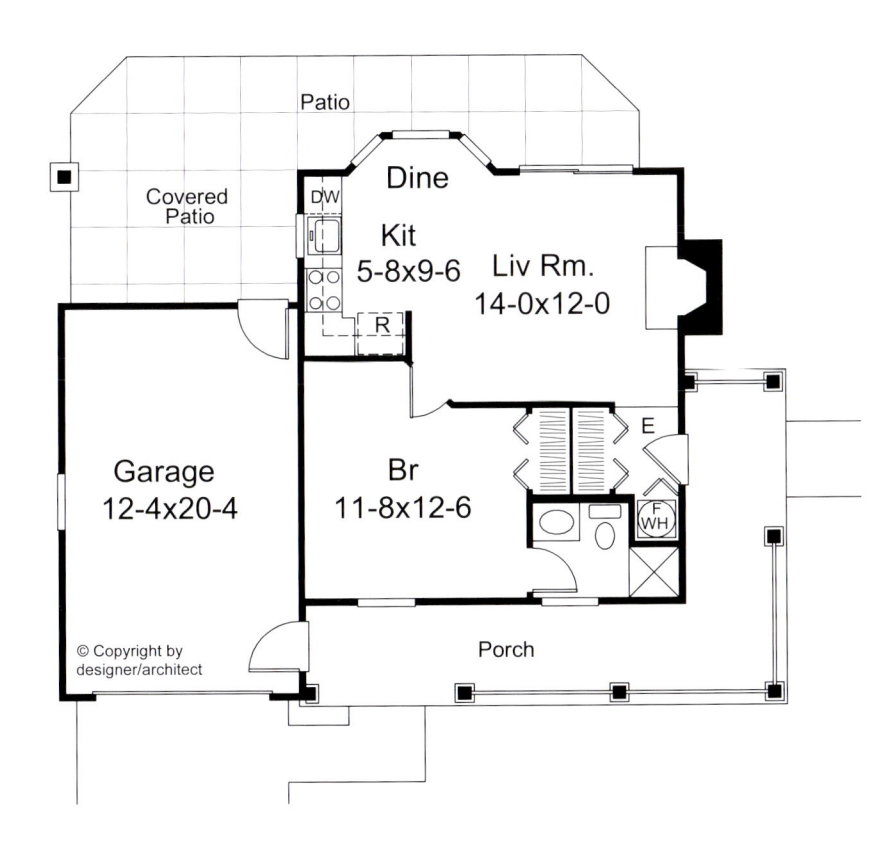

Special features

An inviting wrap-around porch and rear covered patio are perfect for summer evenings

The living room features a fireplace, a separate entry foyer with coat closet, and sliding doors to a rear patio

The compact, but complete kitchen has a bayed dining area and a window at the sink

Price Code AAA

Floor plan labels:
- Patio
- Covered Patio
- Dine
- Kit 5-8x9-6
- Liv Rm. 14-0x12-0
- Garage 12-4x20-4
- Br 11-8x12-6
- Porch
- © Copyright by designer/architect

Rear View

To order this plan, visit the Menards Building Materials Desk or visit www.Menards.com

MENARDS

Plan #M09-055L-0069

Cozy Cabin With Open Floor Plan

1,400 total square feet of living area

Width: 32'-0"   Depth: 42'-0"

2 bedrooms, 2 baths

Crawl space or slab foundation; basement and walk-out basement foundations available for an additional fee, please specify when ordering

Special features

A front covered porch leads into the vaulted great room

The great room features a layout that's entirely open to the dining area and kitchen for added spaciousness

The rear grilling porch includes a practical and convenient supply room

Price Code B

First Floor
948 sq. ft.

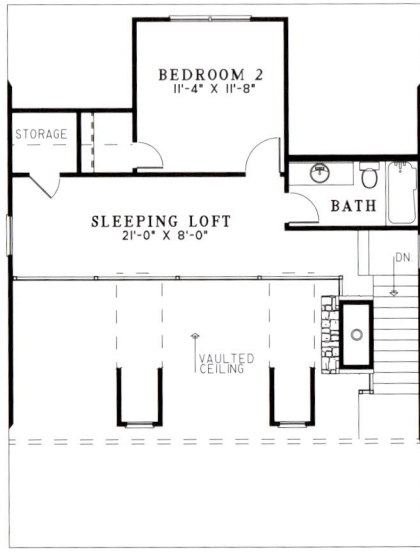

Second Floor
452 sq. ft.

To order this plan, visit the Menards Building Materials Desk or visit www.Menards.com

MENARDS

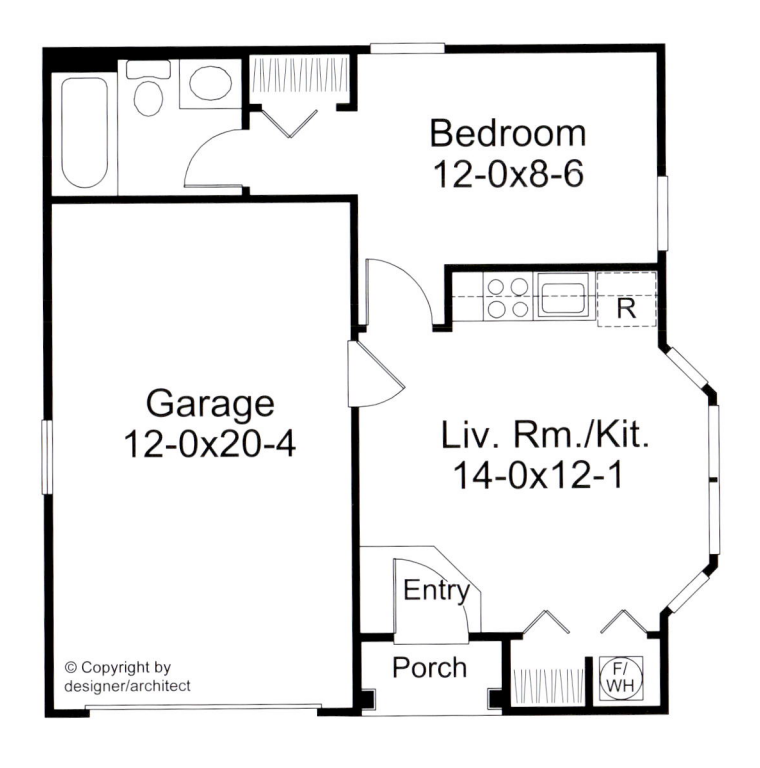

Corina

Plan #M09-007D-0196

Comfortable And Cozy Cottage

421 total square feet of living area

Width: 27'-0"   Depth: 27'-0"

1 bedroom, 1 bath

1-car garage

Slab foundation

Special features

A recessed porch for protection from inclement weather adds charm to the exterior

The living room features a large bay window, a convenient kitchenette, and an entry area with a guest closet

A full size bath and closet are provided for the bedroom

Price Code AAA

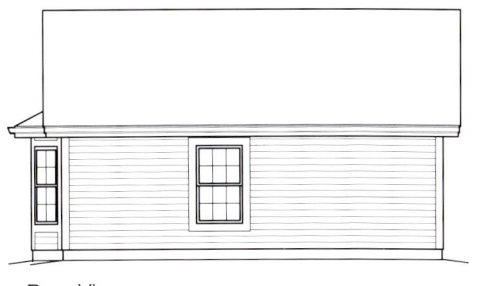

Floor plan:
- Bedroom 12-0x8-6
- Garage 12-0x20-4
- Liv. Rm./Kit. 14-0x12-1
- Entry
- Porch
- © Copyright by designer/architect

Rear View

To order this plan, visit the Menards Building Materials Desk or visit www.Menards.com

...ngton Forest

MENARDS

Plan #M09-007D-0238

Narrow Lot Old World Charm

2,250 total square feet of living area

Width: 45'-0"   Depth: 52'-8"

3 bedrooms, 2 1/2 baths

2-car garage

Basement foundation

Special features

The living room with fireplace enjoys an adjacent entry foyer, a guest closet, and a large separate dining area with patio access

A snack bar, a center island, and a walk-in pantry are a few amenities of the kitchen

The breakfast area has an interesting curved wall and glass sliding doors to the rear patio

The finished closet space on the lower level is 134 square feet and is included in the total square footage

Price Code E

Rear View

Br 2 11-4x15-1
MBr 17-4x14-3 Vaulted
Br 3 13-1x11-7
Balcony

Second Floor 1,036 sq. ft.

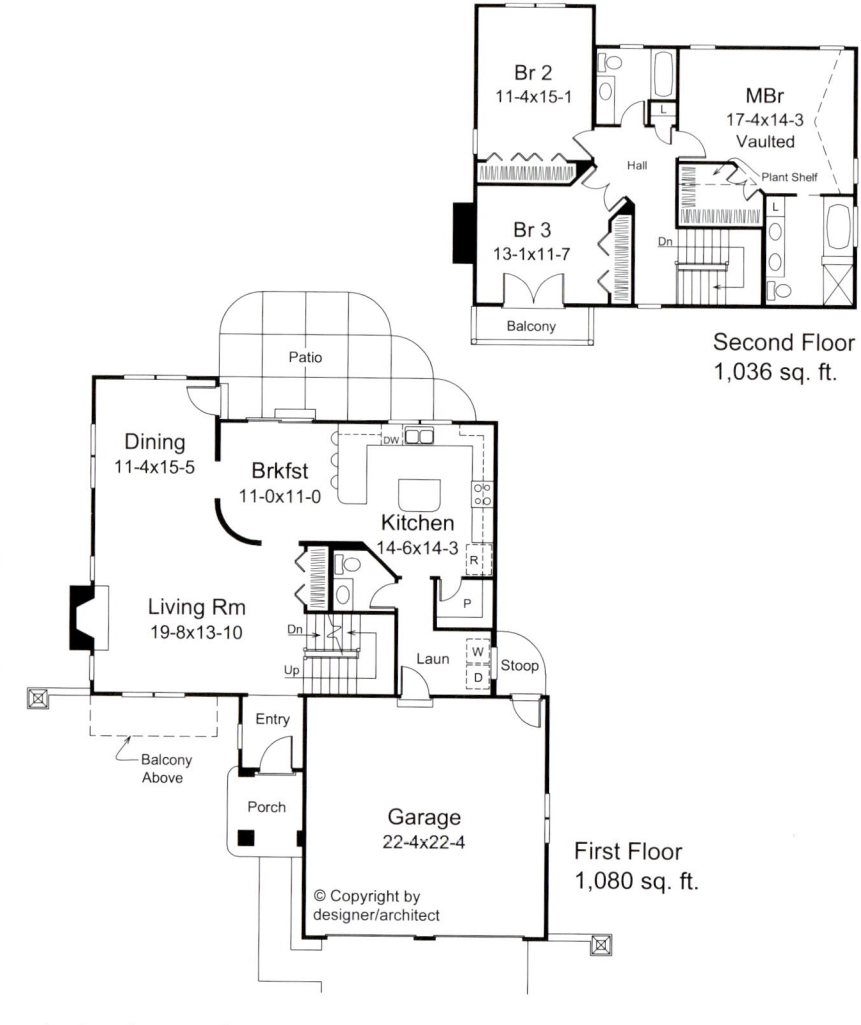

Patio
Dining 11-4x15-5
Brkfst 11-0x11-0
Kitchen 14-6x14-3
Living Rm 19-8x13-10
Laun
Stoop
Balcony Above
Entry
Porch
Garage 22-4x22-4

© Copyright by designer/architect

First Floor 1,080 sq. ft.

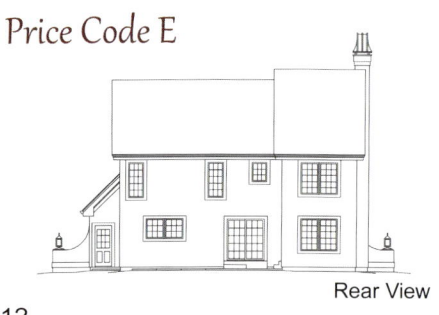

112   To order this plan, visit the Menards Building Materials Desk or visit www.Menards.com

MENARDS

Verden

Plan #M09-055L-0070

Second Floor
409 sq. ft.

First Floor
1,016 sq. ft.

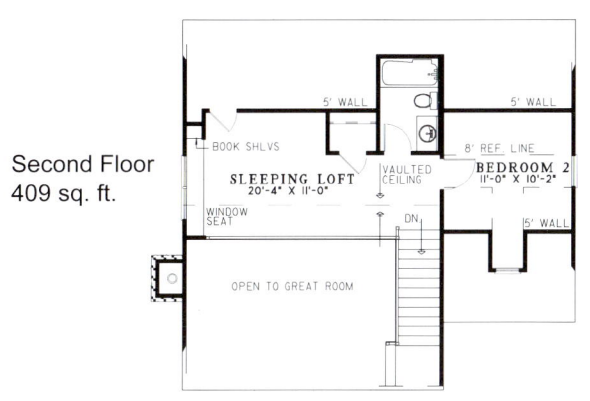

Unique Cabin With Sleeping Loft

1,425 total square feet of living area

Width: 36'-2"   Depth: 48'-0"

2 bedrooms, 2 baths

Crawl space or slab foundation, please specify when ordering

Special features

The great room features a vaulted ceiling and a cozy fireplace

The sleeping loft boasts a vaulted ceiling, a window seat, and bookshelves

A unique built-in window seat graces the breakfast room

The rear covered grilling porch includes a cleaning table with a built-in sink which is perfect for cleaning game or fish

Price Code B

To order this plan, visit the Menards Building Materials Desk or visit www.Menards.com.

Wilshire Terrace

MENARDS

Plan #M09-055L-0067

Comfortable Sports Cabin

1,472 total square feet of living area

Width: 44'-2"   Depth: 39'-0"

3 bedrooms, 2 baths

Crawl space or slab foundation, please specify when ordering

Special features

The 8' wrap-around porch entry is inviting and creates an outdoor living area

The great room has a rock hearth fireplace and is open to the second floor above

The side grilling porch has a cleaning sink for fish or game

The optional bonus room on the second floor has an additional 199 square feet of living area

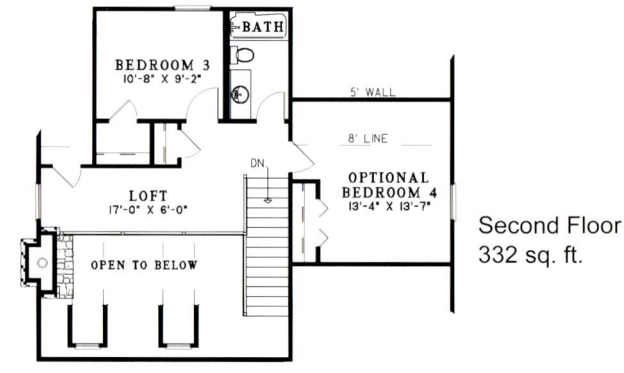

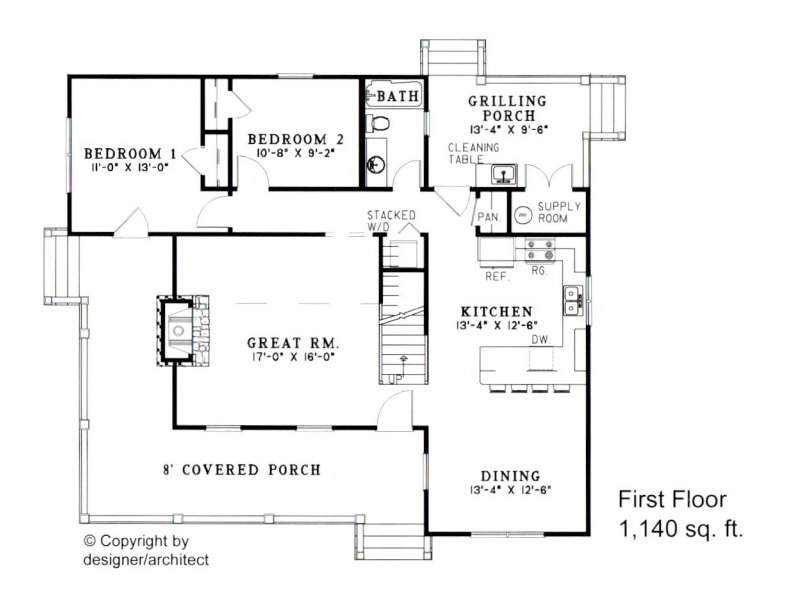

Price Code B

Second Floor 332 sq. ft.

- Bedroom 3: 10'-8" X 9'-2"
- Loft: 17'-0" X 6'-0"
- Optional Bedroom 4: 13'-4" X 13'-7"

First Floor 1,140 sq. ft.

- Bedroom 1: 11'-0" X 13'-0"
- Bedroom 2: 10'-8" X 9'-2"
- Grilling Porch: 13'-4" X 9'-6"
- Great Rm.: 17'-0" X 16'-0"
- Kitchen: 13'-4" X 12'-6"
- Dining: 13'-4" X 12'-6"
- 8' Covered Porch

© Copyright by designer/architect

To order this plan, visit the Menards Building Materials Desk or visit www.Menards.com

MENARDS

Summerledge

Plan #M09-007D-0128

Cottage With Screened Porch, Garage And Shop

1,072 total square feet of living area

Width: 52'-0"   Depth: 40'-8"

2 bedrooms, 2 baths

2-car side entry garage

Basement foundation

Special features

Integrated open and screened front porches guarantee comfortable summer enjoyment

The oversized garage includes an area for a shop and miscellaneous storage

The U-shaped kitchen and breakfast nook are adjacent to the living room

An additional 345 square feet of optional living area on the lower level includes a third bedroom and a bath

Price Code AA

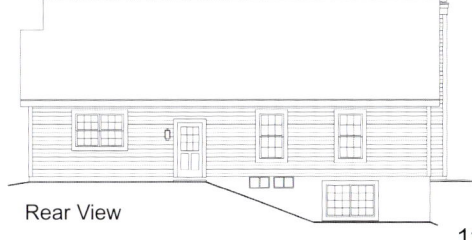

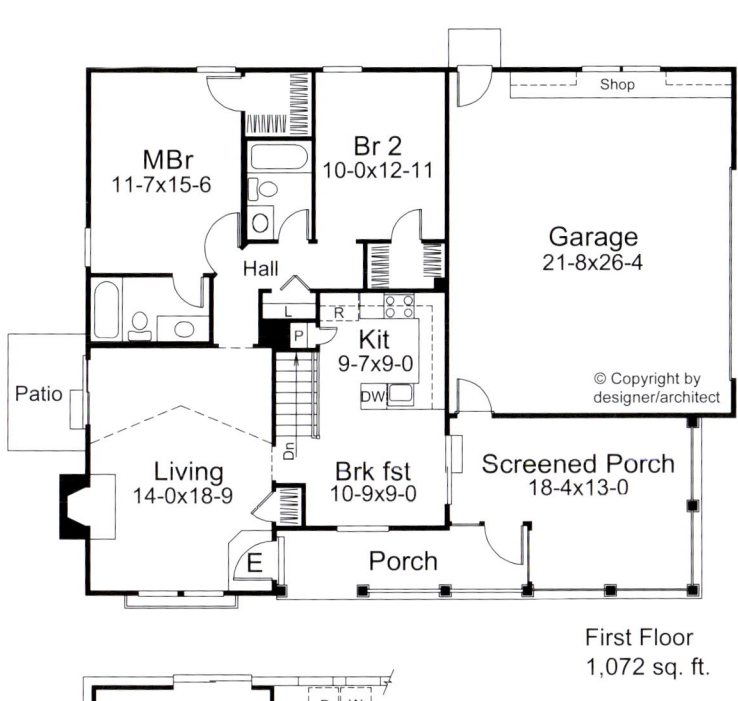

First Floor 1,072 sq. ft.

- MBr 11-7x15-6
- Br 2 10-0x12-11
- Garage 21-8x26-4
- Shop
- Kit 9-7x9-0
- Living 14-0x18-9
- Brk fst 10-9x9-0
- Screened Porch 18-4x13-0
- Patio
- Porch
- Hall

© Copyright by designer/architect

Optional Lower Level

- Br 3 13-4x12-3
- Basement
- Hall

Rear View

To order this plan, visit the Menards Building Materials Desk or visit www.Menards.com

Cadwell

MENARDS

Plan #M09-013L-0044

Abundance Of Closet Space

1,420 total square feet of living area

Width: 50'-0"   Depth: 57'-4"

3 bedrooms, 2 baths

Crawl space or slab foundation, please specify when ordering

Special features

A windowed wall in the master suite lets in plenty of light and creates an open atmosphere

A high ceiling connects the family room and dining area into a large, airy room

The large corner counter in the kitchen provides an easy place for quick meals

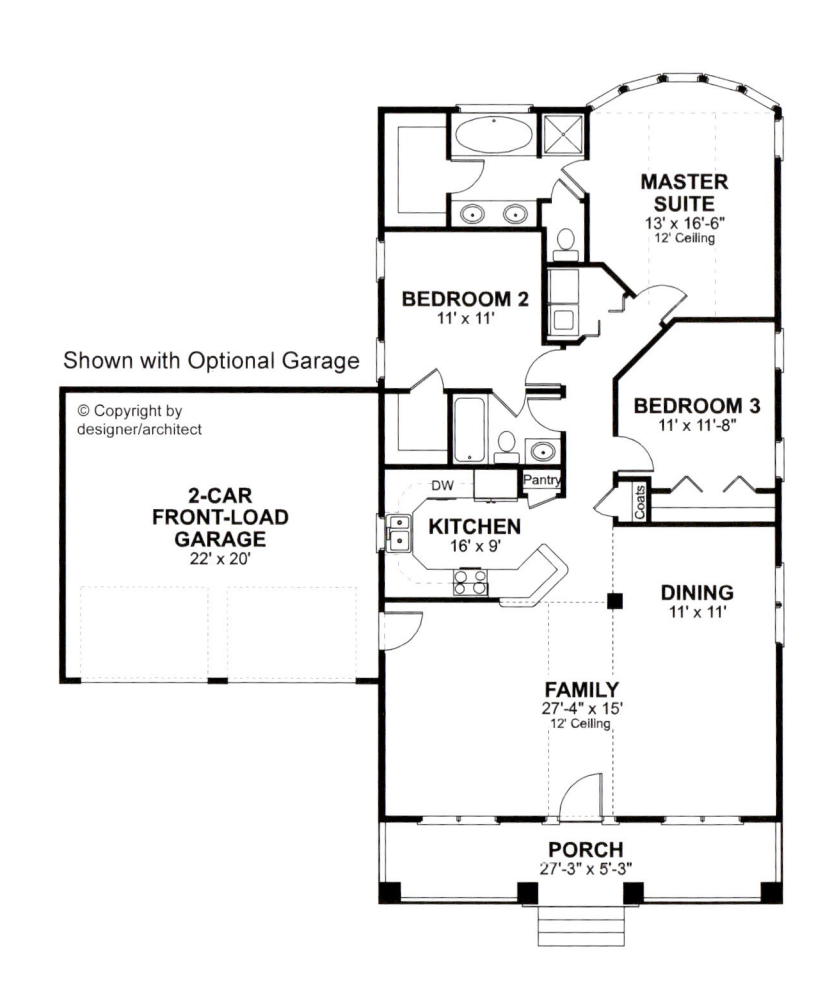

Price Code B

Shown with Optional Garage

© Copyright by designer/architect

- MASTER SUITE 13' x 16'-6" 12' Ceiling
- BEDROOM 2 11' x 11'
- BEDROOM 3 11' x 11'-8"
- 2-CAR FRONT-LOAD GARAGE 22' x 20'
- KITCHEN 16' x 9'
- DINING 11' x 11'
- FAMILY 27'-4" x 15' 12' Ceiling
- PORCH 27'-3" x 5'-3"

To order this plan, visit the Menards Building Materials Desk or visit www.Menards.com

MENARDS

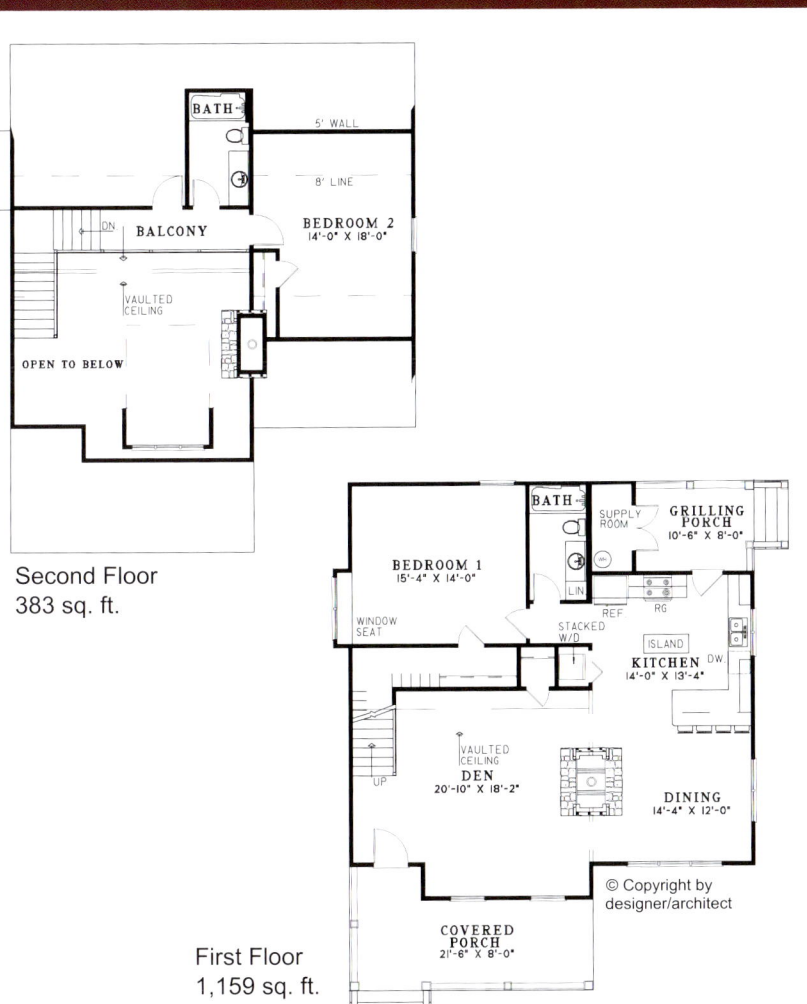

Mesa Mountain

Plan #M09-055L-0071

This Cabin Will Provide Fond Memories

1,542 total square feet of living area

Width: 37'-2"   Depth: 45'-0"

2 bedrooms, 2 baths

Crawl space or slab foundation, please specify when ordering

Special features

The den has a vaulted ceiling and a free-standing walk-around fireplace

The kitchen features an eating bar and an island work area

The rear covered grilling porch with supply room and kitchen access is a convenient feature

Price Code C

Second Floor 383 sq. ft.

- BATH
- 5' WALL
- 8' LINE
- BEDROOM 2 14'-0" X 18'-0"
- BALCONY
- VAULTED CEILING
- OPEN TO BELOW

First Floor 1,159 sq. ft.

- BATH
- GRILLING PORCH 10'-6" X 8'-0"
- SUPPLY ROOM
- BEDROOM 1 15'-4" X 14'-0"
- WINDOW SEAT
- STACKED W/D
- LIN
- REF
- RG
- ISLAND
- KITCHEN 14'-0" X 13'-4"
- DW
- VAULTED CEILING
- DEN 20'-10" X 18'-2"
- DINING 14'-4" X 12'-0"
- UP
- COVERED PORCH 21'-6" X 8'-0"

© Copyright by designer/architect

To order this plan, visit the Menards Building Materials Desk or visit www.Menards.com.

117

Fernberry

MENARDS

Plan #M09-013L-0133

Delightful Country Cabin

953 total square feet of living area

Width: 36'-0"   Depth: 42'-4"

2 bedrooms, 1 1/2 baths

Crawl space foundation

Special features

Relax on the covered porches that are perfectly suited for charming rocking chairs

With two large bedrooms that feature oversized closets, a spacious kitchen, and a family room with a fireplace, this home has everything you need to enjoy a vacation getaway

The kitchen has a sunny corner double sink, a roomy center island/snack bar, and it shares a vaulted ceiling with the family room

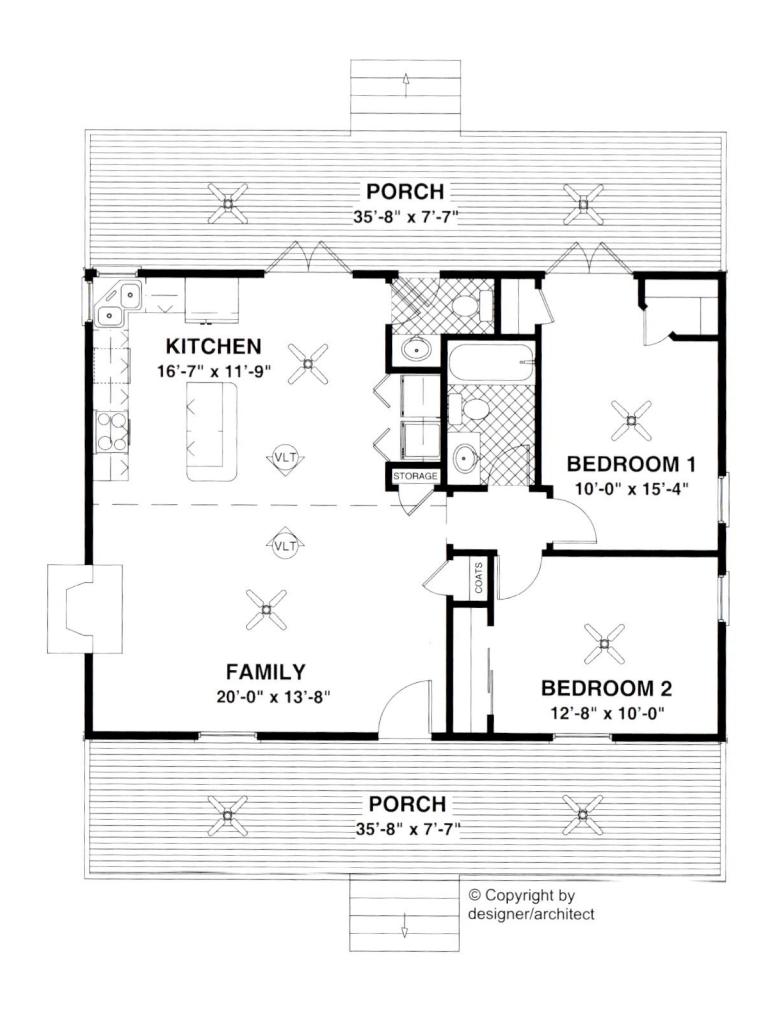

Price Code A

PORCH 35'-8" x 7'-7"

KITCHEN 16'-7" x 11'-9"

BEDROOM 1 10'-0" x 15'-4"

STORAGE

COATS

FAMILY 20'-0" x 13'-8"

BEDROOM 2 12'-8" x 10'-0"

PORCH 35'-8" x 7'-7"

© Copyright by designer/architect

118   To order this plan, visit the Menards Building Materials Desk or visit www.Menards.com

MENARDS

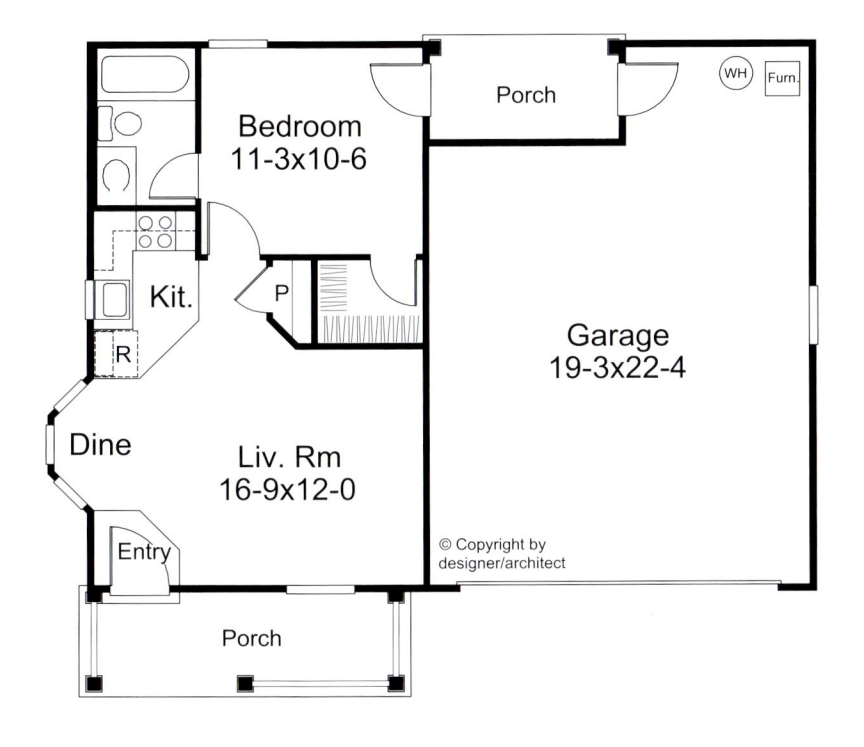

Briaridge

Plan #M09-007D-0199

Ideal Cottage For Leisure Living

496 total square feet of living area

Width: 39'-0"   Depth: 33'-0"

1 bedroom, 1 bath

2-car garage

Slab foundation

Special features

The traditional front exterior and rear both enjoy shady porches for relaxing evenings

The living room with bayed dining area is open to a functional L-shaped kitchen with a convenient pantry

A full bath, a large walk-in closet, and access to both the rear porch and the garage enhance the spacious bedroom

Price Code AAA

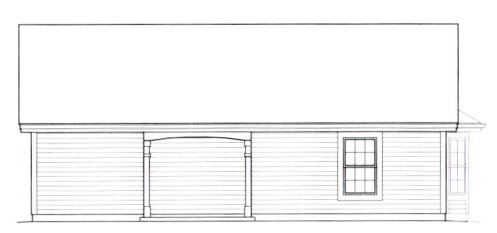

Rear View

To order this plan, visit the Menards Building Materials Desk or visit www.Menards.com

MacKenzie

MENARDS

Plan #M09-121D-0040

Amenity-Filled Master Bedroom And Bath

1,863 total square feet of living area

Width: 58'-0"   Depth: 58'-0"

3 bedrooms, 2 1/2 baths

2-car side entry garage

Basement foundation

Special features

The vaulted ceiling spans from the foyer to the great room, creating an open atmosphere

The centrally located kitchen easily serves both the formal dining room as well as the more casual breakfast area

An angled eating bar in the kitchen is a handy spot for quick meals anytime of the day

The beautiful master bedroom promises privacy and enjoys its own well appointed bath and a walk-in closet

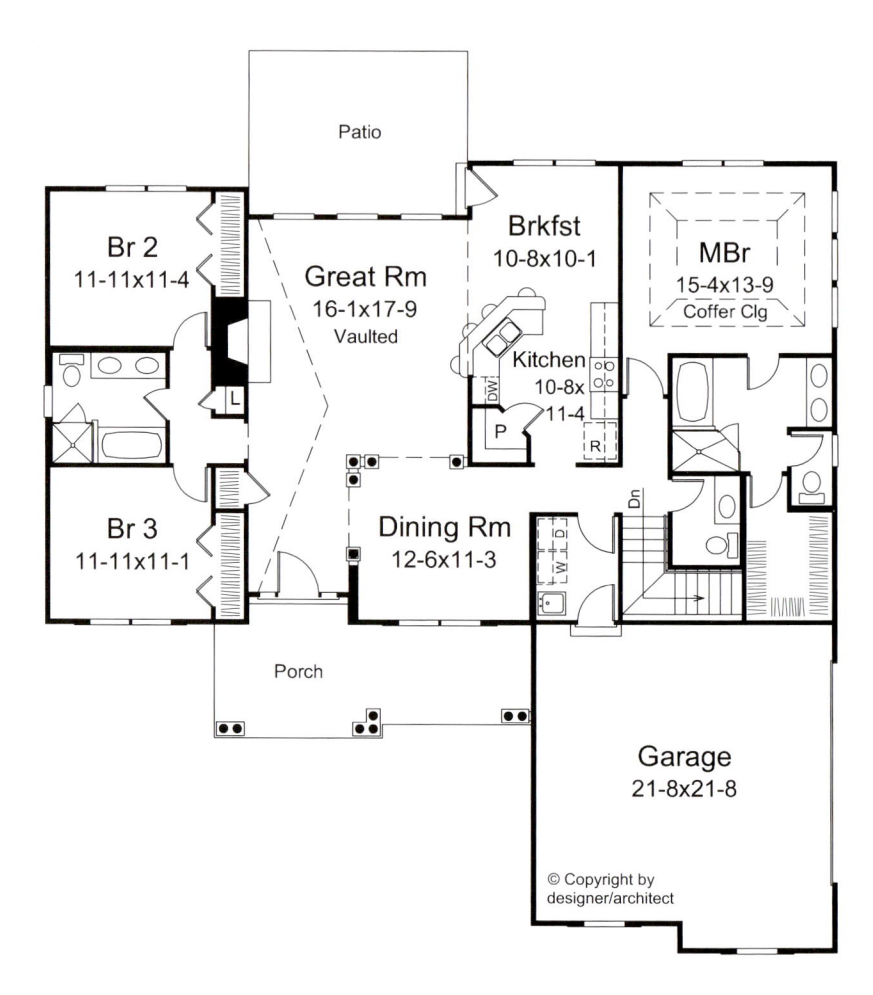

Price Code B

Floor plan rooms:
- Patio
- Br 2: 11-11x11-4
- Great Rm: 16-1x17-9 Vaulted
- Brkfst: 10-8x10-1
- MBr: 15-4x13-9 Coffer Clg
- Kitchen: 10-8x11-4
- Br 3: 11-11x11-1
- Dining Rm: 12-6x11-3
- Porch
- Garage: 21-8x21-8

© Copyright by designer/architect

To order this plan, visit the Menards Building Materials Desk or visit www.Menards.com

MENARDS

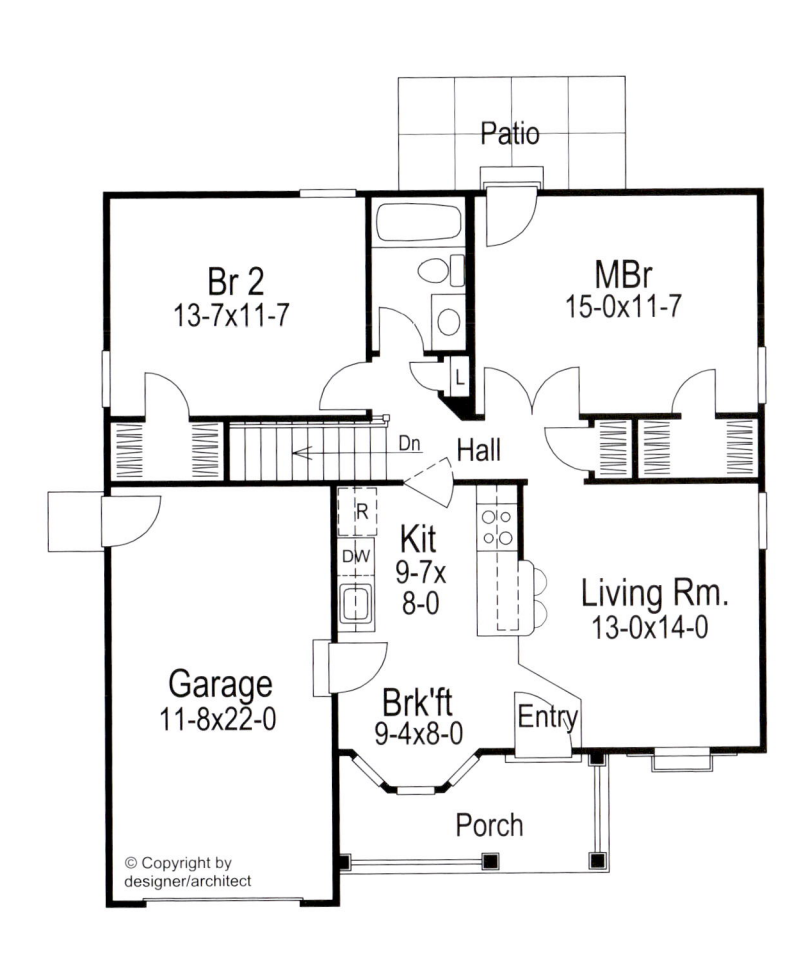

Rosepo... Lanaw...

Plan #M09-007D-0109

Elegance In A Starter Or Retirement Home

888 total square feet of living area

Width: 35'-0"   Depth: 38'-0"

2 bedrooms, 1 bath

1-car garage

Basement foundation

Special features

This home features an eye-catching exterior and has a spacious covered porch

The bayed breakfast room is open to the living room and adjoins the kitchen

The roomy bedrooms feature walk-in closets

The master bedroom has patio access

Price Code AAA

Rear View

To order this plan, visit the Menards Building Materials Desk or visit www.Menards.com.

MENARDS

Plan #M09-077L-0008

Quaint Cottage

600 total square feet of living area

Width: 31'-8"   Depth: 26'-0"

1 bedroom, 1 bath

Slab, basement, or crawl space foundation, please specify when ordering

Special features

This small home features a spacious living room that connects to the efficient kitchen with a raised snack bar

The kitchen and bedroom access the rear porch and covered or screened porch that offers exceptional outdoor living space

A bonus room is provided for a hobby room or second bedroom and is included in the square footage

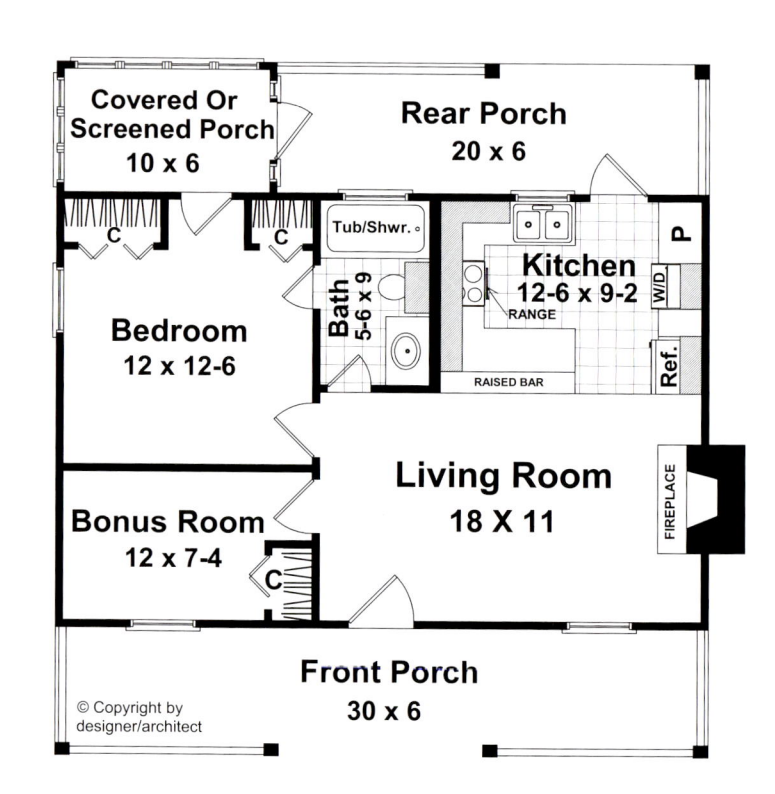

Price Code B

Covered Or Screened Porch 10 x 6

Rear Porch 20 x 6

Bath 5-6 x 9

Kitchen 12-6 x 9-2

Bedroom 12 x 12-6

Bonus Room 12 x 7-4

Living Room 18 X 11

Front Porch 30 x 6

© Copyright by designer/architect

122   To order this plan, visit the Menards Building Materials Desk or visit www.Menards.com

MENARDS

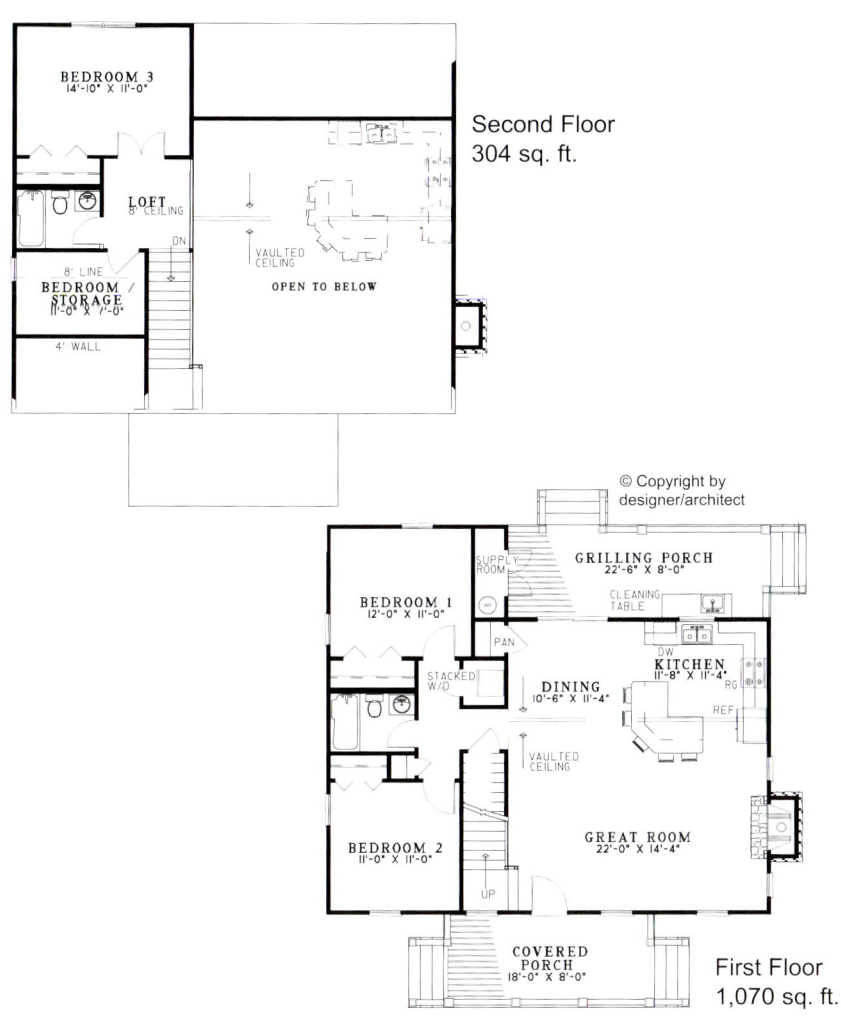

Foxton

Plan #M09-055L-0068

Two-Story Living Spaces Enlarge This Home

1,374 total square feet of living area

Width: 40'-4"   Depth: 41'-6"

3 bedrooms, 2 baths

Crawl space or slab foundation, please specify when ordering

Special features

The L-shaped counterspace in the kitchen seats five people

The spacious covered grilling porch is accessible from the dining room for convenience and also features a cleaning table and preparation area

There is a versatile bedroom/storage area on the second floor

Price Code B

Second Floor 304 sq. ft.

First Floor 1,070 sq. ft.

To order this plan, visit the Menards Building Materials Desk or visit www.Menards.com.

123

Edelton

MENARDS®

Plan #M09-055L-0064

Cabin Cottage With French Door Entry

1,544 total square feet of living area

Width: 34'-4"   Depth: 48'-4"

3 bedrooms, 2 baths

Crawl space or slab foundation, please specify when ordering

Special features

The great room has a vaulted ceiling and a cozy fireplace

The 32' x 8' covered grilling porch in the rear also features a supply room and a cleaning table with a sink

The kitchen features a center island with seating for five people offering great function

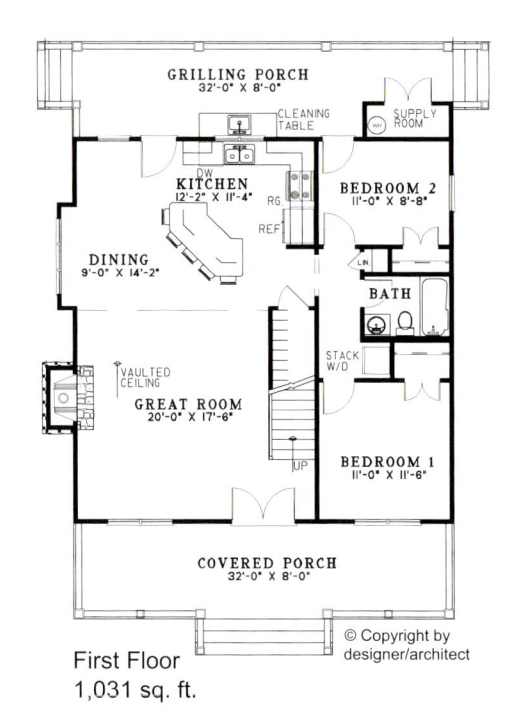

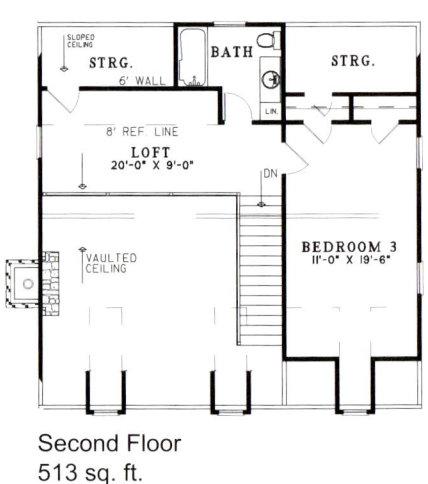

Price Code C

First Floor
1,031 sq. ft.

Second Floor
513 sq. ft.

© Copyright by designer/architect

MENARDS

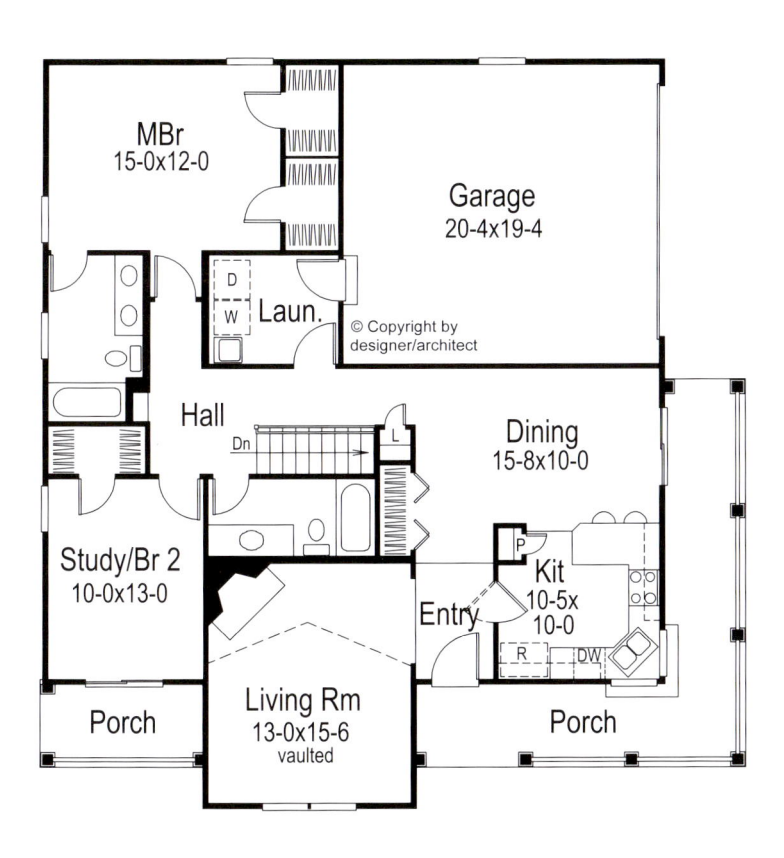

Springhill

Plan #M09-007D-0133

Porches Enhance Small Retirement Or Starter Home

1,316 total square feet of living area

Width: 45'-0"   Depth: 48'-4"

2 bedrooms, 2 baths

2-car side entry garage

Basement foundation, drawings also include crawl space and slab foundations

Special features

Porches are accessible from the entry, the dining room, and the study/bedroom #2

The kitchen has corner windows, an outdoor plant shelf, a snack bar, a built-in pantry, and opens to a large dining room

The roomy bedrooms feature walk-in closets and have easy access to oversized baths

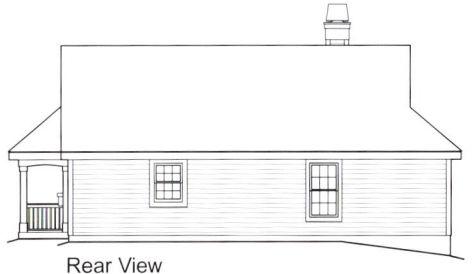

Price Code A

Floor plan rooms:
- MBr 15-0x12-0
- Garage 20-4x19-4
- Laun.
- Hall
- Dining 15-8x10-0
- Study/Br 2 10-0x13-0
- Entry
- Kit 10-5x10-0
- Living Rm 13-0x15-6 vaulted
- Porch (x2)

Rear View

To order this plan, visit the Menards Building Materials Desk or visit www.Menards.com.

125

Evelyn

MENARDS

Plan #M09-121D-0013

Charming Home With Atrium

2,100 total square feet of living area

Width: 56'-8"   Depth: 59'-0"

3 bedrooms, 2 baths

2-car garage

Walk-out basement foundation

Special features

The spacious vaulted great room has a fireplace, and a staircase to the atrium below

The efficient kitchen has seating for quick and easy meals next to the sunny bayed breakfast area

A bay window, a private bath, and a walk-in closet are some of the amenities of the master bedroom

Price Code B

Rear View

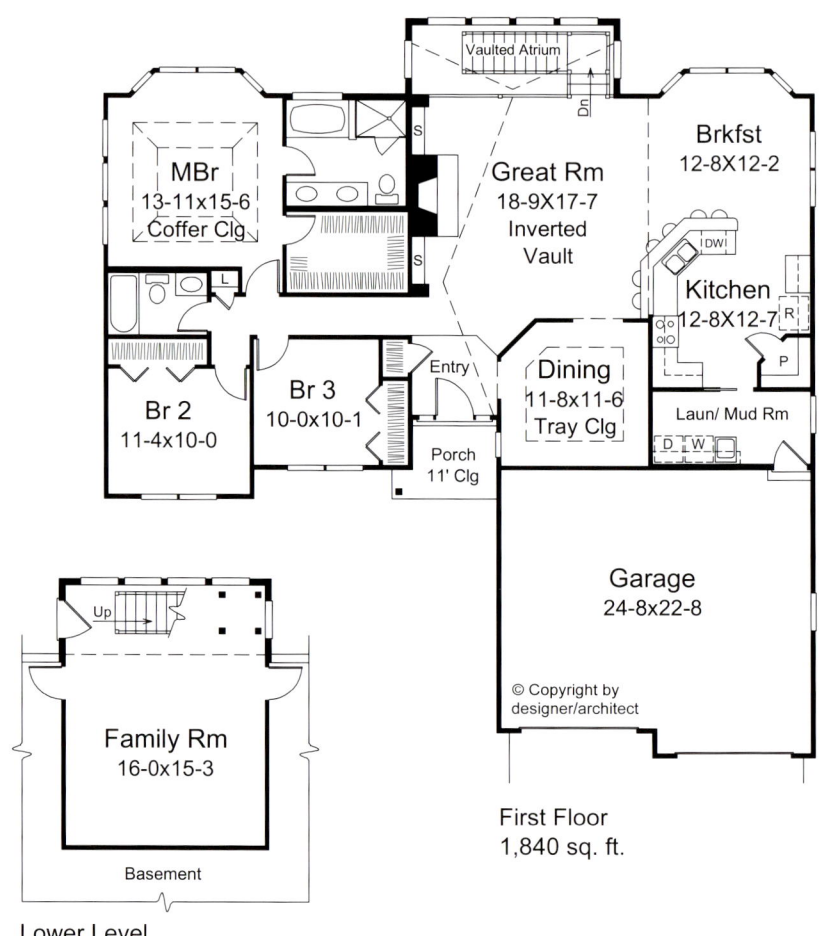

Vaulted Atrium

MBr 13-11x15-6 Coffer Clg

Great Rm 18-9X17-7 Inverted Vault

Brkfst 12-8X12-2

Kitchen 12-8X12-7

Br 2 11-4x10-0

Br 3 10-0x10-1

Entry

Dining 11-8x11-6 Tray Clg

Laun/ Mud Rm

Porch 11' Clg

Garage 24-8x22-8

© Copyright by designer/architect

Family Rm 16-0x15-3

Basement

Lower Level 260 sq. ft.

First Floor 1,840 sq. ft.

126   To order this plan, visit the Menards Building Materials Desk or visit www.Menards.com

MENARDS

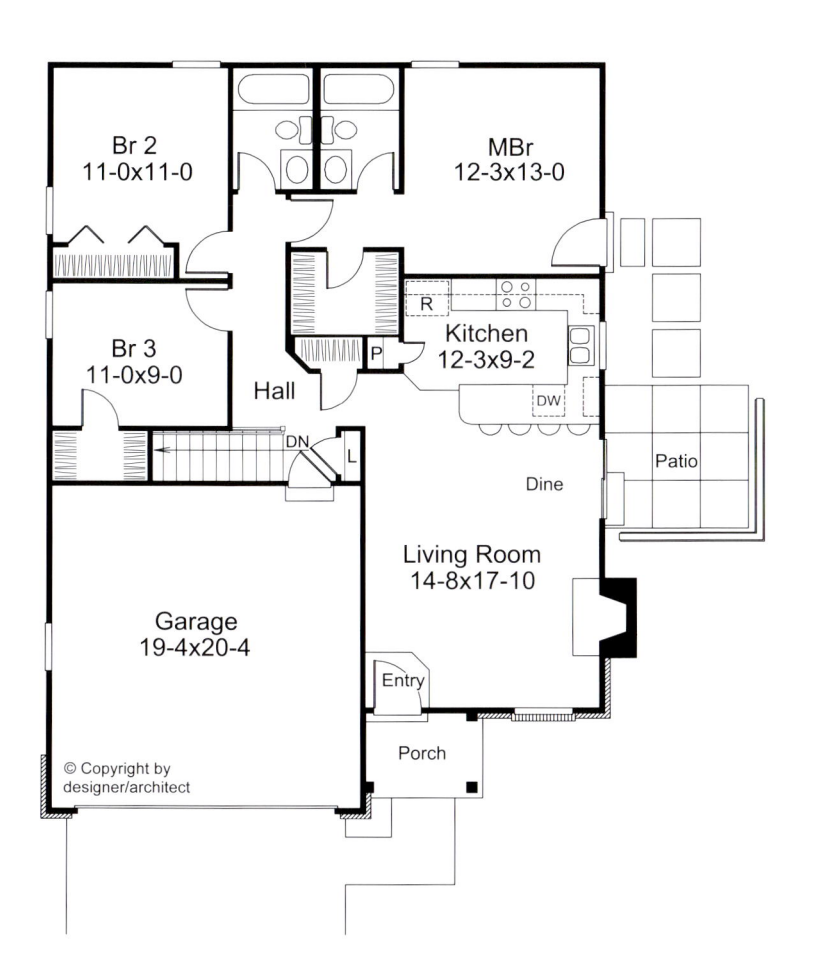

Jenny Manor

Plan #M09-007D-0201

Functional Design For Compact Lot

1,153 total square feet of living area

Width: 37'-4"   Depth: 47'-8"

3 bedrooms, 2 baths

2-car garage

Basement foundation

Special features

An arched window, detailed brickwork, and a roof dormer combine for a stylish exterior

A fireplace, U-shaped kitchen with a built-in pantry, and a dining area with a view to the patio are the many features of the living room

The master bedroom includes a private bath, a walk-in closet, and access to the patio

Price Code A

Rear View

To order this plan, visit the Menards Building Materials Desk or visit www.Menards.com.

Oakford

MENARDS

Plan #M09-007D-0173

Inviting Spacious Home

2,121 total square feet of living area

Width: 47'-0"   Depth: 42'-0"

4 bedrooms, 3 1/2 baths

2-car garage

Basement foundation, drawings also include slab and crawl space foundations

Special features

The spacious great room includes a corner fireplace, a bayed dining area, and glass sliding doors to the rear patio

A huge center island with seating for six, a built-in pantry, and 26' of counterspace are just a few amenities in the awesome kitchen

Price Code C

Rear View

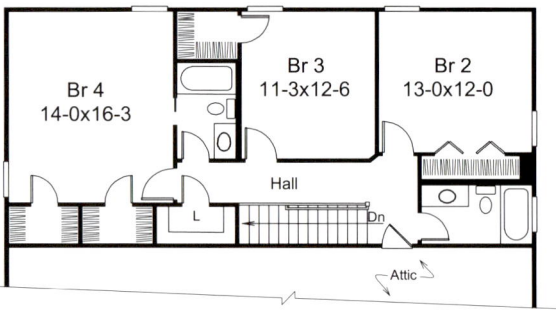

Second Floor
915 sq. ft.

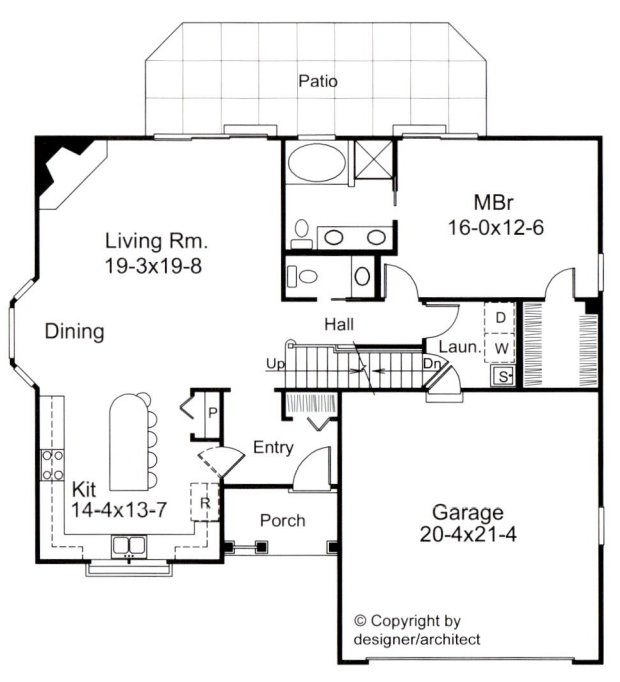

- Br 4: 14-0x16-3
- Br 3: 11-3x12-6
- Br 2: 13-0x12-0

First Floor
1,206 sq. ft.

- Living Rm.: 19-3x19-8
- MBr: 16-0x12-6
- Kit: 14-4x13-7
- Garage: 20-4x21-4

© Copyright by designer/architect

To order this plan, visit the Menards Building Materials Desk or visit www.menards.com

MENARDS

Sapelo

Plan #M09-013L-0129

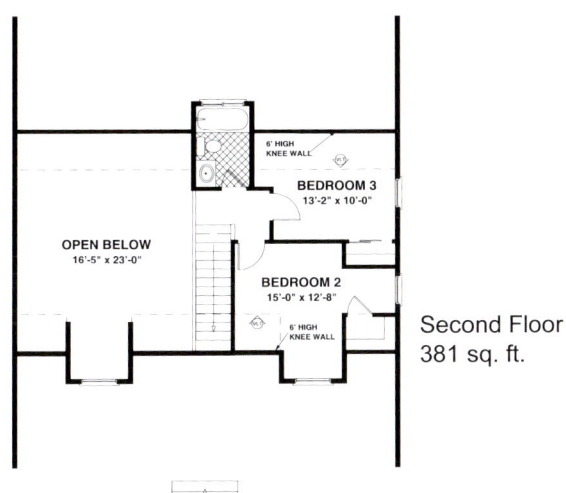

Open Floor Plan

1,334 total square feet of living area

Width: 36'-0"   Depth: 42'-4"

3 bedrooms, 2 1/2 baths

Crawl space foundation, basement foundation available for an additional fee

Special features

This welcoming design is ideal for a vacation, starter or empty-nester home

Relax on the cozy front and rear covered porches that are large enough for rocking chairs

The spacious first floor master suite features a walk-in closet, a sitting area, and a private bath

The second floor features two bedrooms that share a full bath

Price Code D

Second Floor 381 sq. ft.

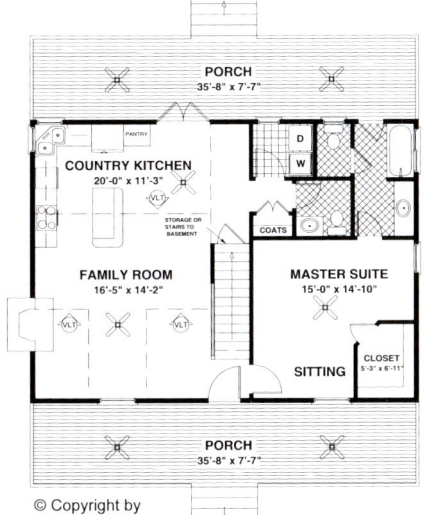

- Bedroom 3: 13'-2" x 10'-0"
- Open Below: 16'-5" x 23'-0"
- Bedroom 2: 15'-0" x 12'-8"
- 6' High Knee Wall

First Floor 953 sq. ft.

- Porch: 35'-8" x 7'-7"
- Country Kitchen: 20'-0" x 11'-3"
- Family Room: 16'-5" x 14'-2"
- Master Suite: 15'-0" x 14'-10"
- Sitting
- Closet: 5'-3" x 6'-11"
- Porch: 35'-8" x 7'-7"

© Copyright by designer/architect

To order this plan, visit the Menards Building Materials Desk or visit www.Menards.com.

129

Simmons

MENARDS

Plan #M09-077L-0178

Charming Curb Appeal

1,900 total square feet of living area

Width: 69'-0"   Depth: 57'-0"

3 bedrooms, 2 1/2 baths

2-car side entry garage

Slab or crawl space foundation, please specify when ordering

Special features

The breakfast area enjoys the view of the large fireplace located in the great room

The master bedroom is separated from the other bedrooms for privacy and features a luxury bath and two walk-in closets

The dining/office is a versatile space that can adapt to your needs

The bonus room above the garage has an additional 348 square feet of living area

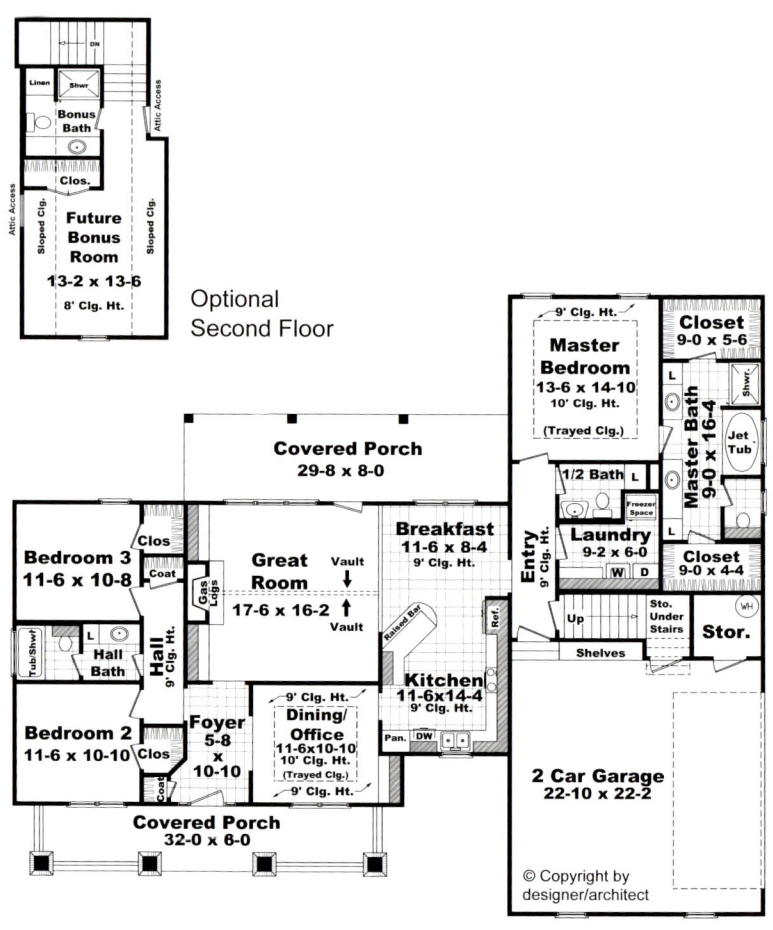

Price Code E

Optional Second Floor

Future Bonus Room 13-2 x 13-6, 8' Clg. Ht.
Bonus Bath

First Floor 1,900 sq. ft.

- Master Bedroom 13-6 x 14-10, 10' Clg. Ht. (Trayed Clg.)
- Master Bath 9-0 x 16-4
- Closet 9-0 x 5-6
- Closet 9-0 x 4-4
- 1/2 Bath
- Laundry 9-2 x 6-0
- Covered Porch 29-8 x 8-0
- Breakfast 11-6 x 8-4, 9' Clg. Ht.
- Great Room 17-6 x 16-2, Vault
- Kitchen 11-6 x 14-4, 9' Clg. Ht.
- Bedroom 3 11-6 x 10-8
- Bedroom 2 11-6 x 10-10
- Hall Bath
- Foyer 5-8 x 10-10
- Dining/Office 11-6 x 10-10, 10' Clg. Ht. (Trayed Clg.)
- 2 Car Garage 22-10 x 22-2
- Covered Porch 32-0 x 6-0

© Copyright by designer/architect

MENARDS

Greeley Cove

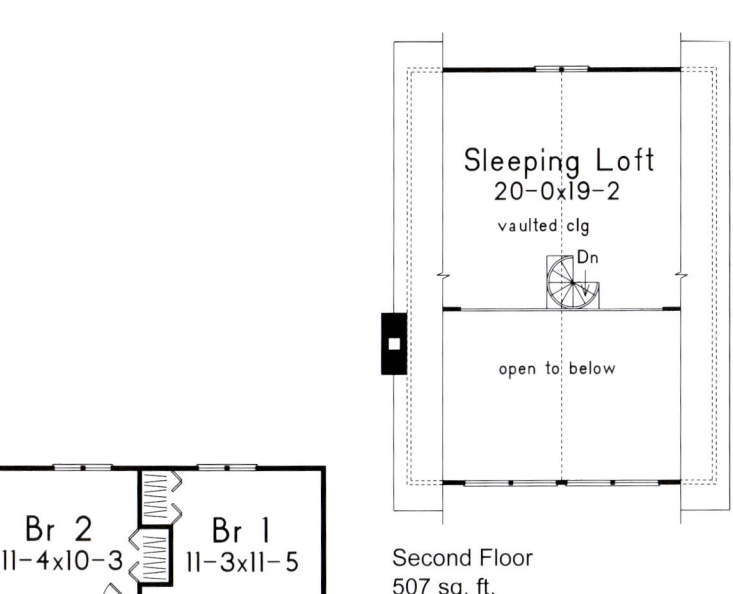

Plan #M09-008D-0140

Cozy Vacation Retreat

1,391 total square feet of living area

Width: 28'-2"   Depth: 34'-0"

2 bedrooms, 1 bath

Pier foundation, drawings also include crawl space foundation

Special features

The large living room with masonry fireplace features a soaring vaulted ceiling

A spiral staircase in the hall leads to a huge second floor sleeping loft overlooking the living room below

Two first floor bedrooms share a convenient full bath

Price Code A

Sleeping Loft 20-0x19-2 vaulted clg
open to below

Second Floor 507 sq. ft.

Br 2 11-4x10-3
Br 1 11-3x11-5
Kit 9-1x7-9
Living 25-4x13-8
Deck

© Copyright by designer/architect

First Floor 884 sq. ft.

To order this plan, visit the Menards Building Materials Desk or visit www.Menards.com.

Canton Crest

MENARDS

Plan #M09-013L-0154

Great Porch Opportunities

953 total square feet of living area

Width: 36'-0"   Depth: 42'-4"

2 bedrooms, 1 1/2 baths

Crawl space foundation

Special features

Covered front and rear porches feature ceiling fans to keep you comfortable in warmer weather

Two generous bedrooms, each with a walk-in closet, share a spacious bathroom

A dramatic vaulted ceiling crowns the open family room and kitchen

Price Code A

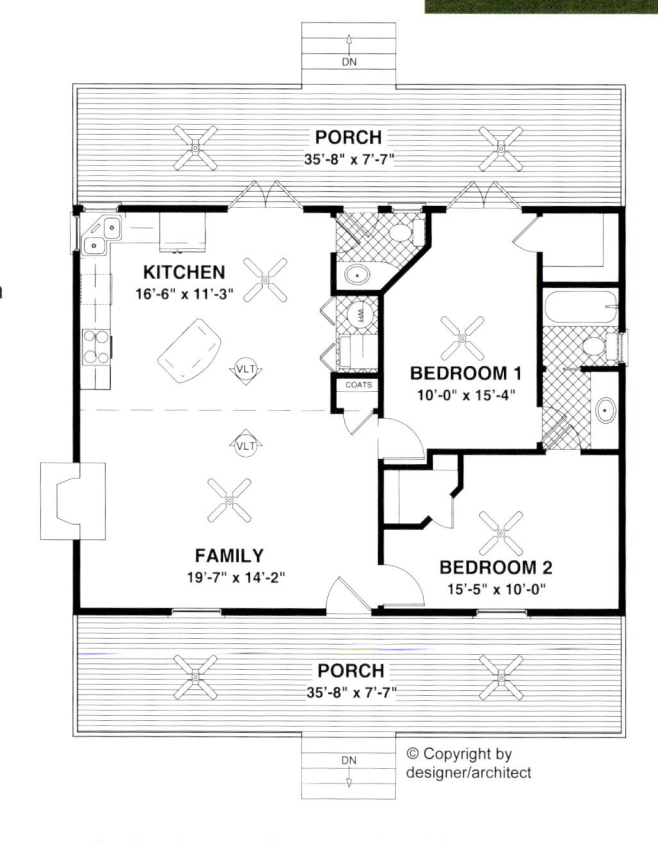

PORCH
35'-8" x 7'-7"

KITCHEN
16'-6" x 11'-3"

BEDROOM 1
10'-0" x 15'-4"

FAMILY
19'-7" x 14'-2"

BEDROOM 2
15'-5" x 10'-0"

PORCH
35'-8" x 7'-7"

© Copyright by designer/architect

To order this plan, visit the Menards Building Materials Desk or visit www.Menards.com.

MENARDS

Greenbay

Plan #M09-007D-0181

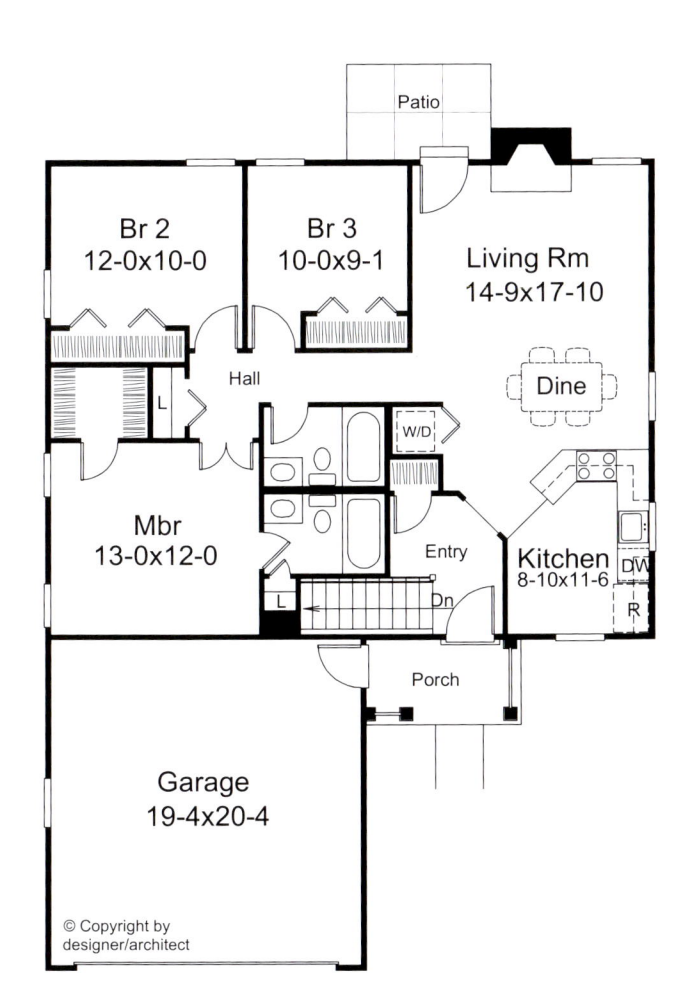

Charming Three-Bedroom Home

1,140 total square feet of living area

Width: 38'-0"   Depth: 52'-8"

3 bedrooms, 2 baths

2-car garage

Basement foundation, drawings also include slab and crawl space foundations

Special features

The entry, with a convenient staircase to the basement, leads to spacious living and dining rooms open to the adjacent kitchen

The master bedroom enjoys a double-door entry, walk-in closet, and a private bath with its own linen closet

Price Code AA

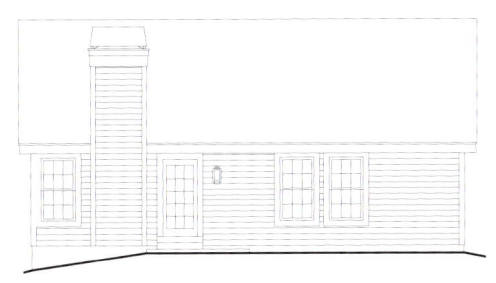

Rear View

Floor plan rooms:
- Patio
- Br 2: 12-0x10-0
- Br 3: 10-0x9-1
- Living Rm: 14-9x17-10
- Hall
- Dine
- Mbr: 13-0x12-0
- Entry
- Kitchen: 8-10x11-6
- Porch
- Garage: 19-4x20-4

© Copyright by designer/architect

To order this plan, visit the Menards Building Materials Desk or visit www.Menards.com.

Barnesville

MENARDS

Plan #M09-013L-0019

Elegant Arched Front Porch Attracts Attention

1,992 total square feet of living area

Width: 63'-0"   Depth: 57'-2"

3 bedrooms, 2 1/2 baths

3-car side entry garage

Basement, crawl space or slab foundation, please specify when ordering

Special features

The bayed breakfast room overlooks the outdoor deck and connects to the screened porch

The private formal living room in the front of the home could easily be converted to a home office or study

A compact, yet efficient kitchen is conveniently situated between the breakfast and dining rooms

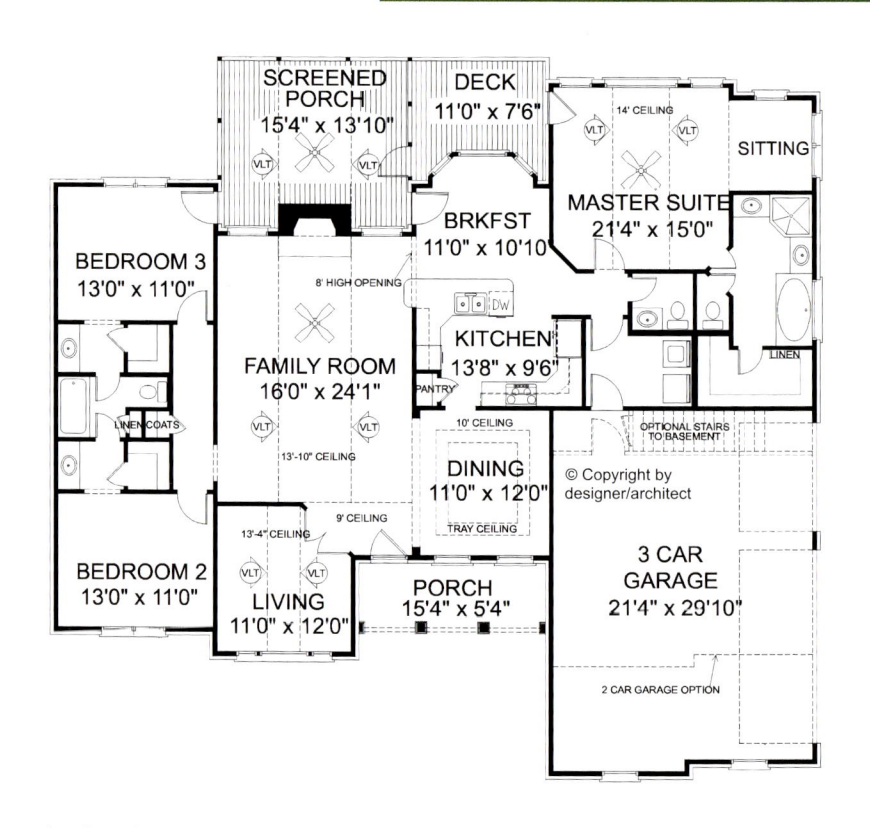

Price Code C

Floor Plan:

- SCREENED PORCH 15'4" x 13'10"
- DECK 11'0" x 7'6"
- BEDROOM 3 13'0" x 11'0"
- BRKFST 11'0" x 10'10"
- MASTER SUITE 21'4" x 15'0" (14' CEILING, SITTING)
- FAMILY ROOM 16'0" x 24'1" (13'-10" CEILING, 8' HIGH OPENING)
- KITCHEN 13'8" x 9'6"
- DINING 11'0" x 12'0" (10' CEILING, TRAY CEILING)
- BEDROOM 2 13'0" x 11'0" (13'-4" CEILING)
- LIVING 11'0" x 12'0" (9' CEILING)
- PORCH 15'4" x 5'4"
- 3 CAR GARAGE 21'4" x 29'10"
- 2 CAR GARAGE OPTION
- OPTIONAL STAIRS TO BASEMENT

© Copyright by designer/architect

To order this plan, visit the Menards Building Materials Desk or visit www.Menards.com.

MENARDS

Brisba[n]

Plan #M09-055L-0026

Bayed Dining Room

1,538 total square feet of living area

Width: 50'-0"   Depth: 56'-0"

3 bedrooms, 2 baths

2-car garage

Slab, walk-out basement, basement, or crawl space foundation, please specify when ordering

Special features

Energy efficient home with 2" x 6" exterior walls

The dining and great rooms are highlighted in this design

The master suite has many amenities including double walk-in closets in the private bath

This Traditional ranch facade looks great in any neighborhood

Price Code C

Floor plan:

- MASTER SUITE 16'-10" X 11'-6" 9' PAN CEILING
- M. BATH 10'-6" X 6'-0" SKL
- GREAT RM. 20'-0" X 15'-6" 9' BOXED CEILING
- DINING 10'-6" X 11'-10"
- KITCHEN 10'-0" X 10'-0"
- FOYER
- BEDROOM 3 11'-10" X 11'-0"
- BATH
- BEDROOM 2 11'-10" X 11'-0" VAULTED CEILING
- LAU.
- STORAGE
- COVERED PORCH
- GARAGE 21'-0" X 21'-0"

© Copyright by designer/architect

To order this plan, visit the Menards Building Materials Desk or visit www.Menards.com.

MENARDS

Plan #M09-121D-0017

Handsome Two Bedroom Ranch

1,379 total square feet of living area

Width: 40'-0"   Depth: 52'-0"

2 bedrooms, 1 bath

2-car garage

Basement foundation

Special features

The kitchen shares the center island and eating bar with the open great room for easy meals

Both of the bedrooms have ample closet space and enjoy bay windows

The vaulted breakfast area boasts a bay window with access to the rear patio

Price Code AA

Rear View

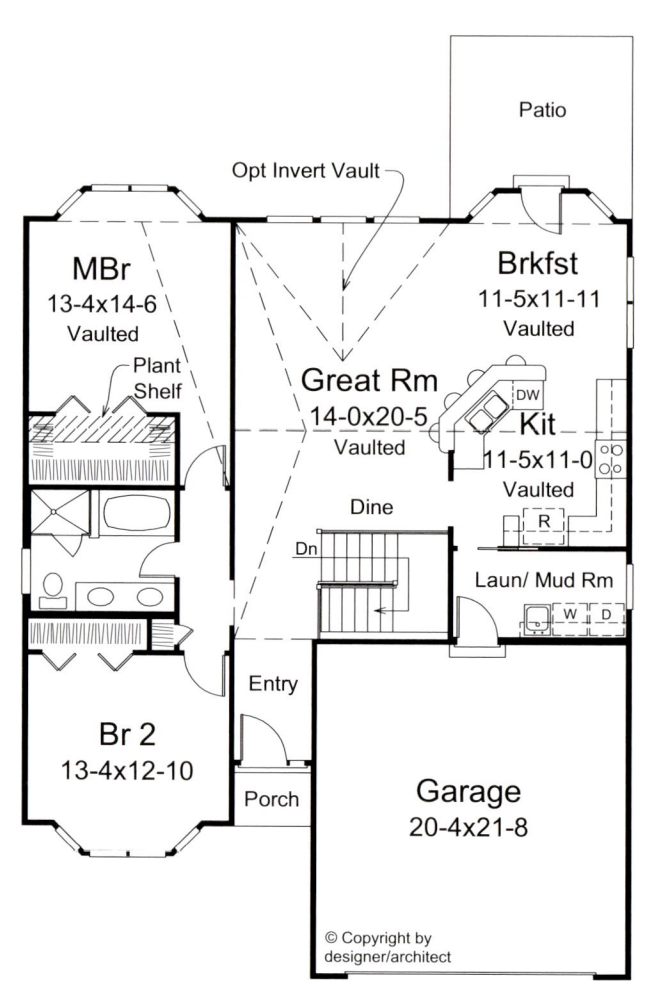

Patio

MBr 13-4x14-6 Vaulted

Plant Shelf

Opt Invert Vault

Brkfst 11-5x11-11 Vaulted

Great Rm 14-0x20-5 Vaulted

Kit 11-5x11-0 Vaulted

Dine

Dn

Laun/ Mud Rm

Entry

Br 2 13-4x12-10

Porch

Garage 20-4x21-8

© Copyright by designer/architect

To order this plan, visit the Menards Building Materials Desk or visit www.Menards.com

MENARDS

Ridgewood

Plan #M09-007D-0112

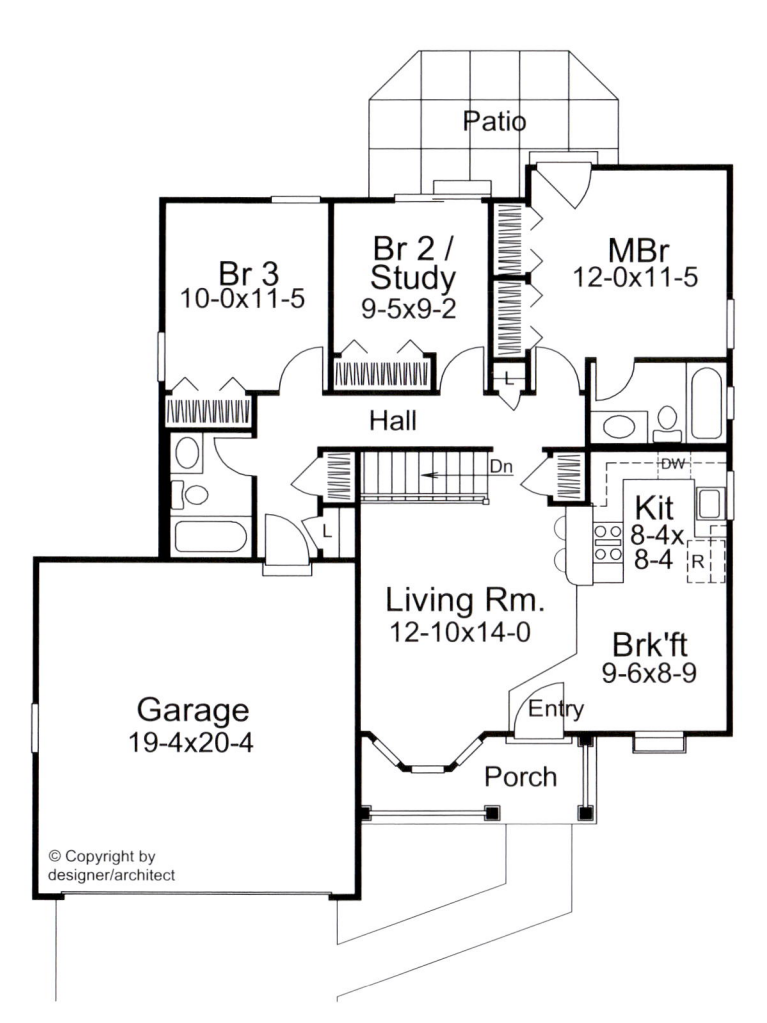

Excellent Home For A Small Family

1,062 total square feet of living area

Width: 42'-8"   Depth: 45'-0"

3 bedrooms, 2 baths

2-car garage

Basement foundation

Special features

Handsome curb appeal is created by the triple-gable facade

The efficient U-shaped kitchen features a snack bar, a breakfast area, and is open to the bayed living room

Both the master bedroom, with its own private bath, and bedroom #2/study enjoy access to the rear patio

Price Code AA

Rear View

To order this plan, visit the Menards Building Materials Desk or visit www.Menards.com

137

Welsberg

MENARDS

Plan #M09-055L-0213

Grand Covered Porch Is Inviting

1,921 total square feet of living area

Width: 84'-0"   Depth: 55'-6"

3 bedrooms, 2 baths

2-car side entry garage

Slab or crawl space foundation; walk-out basement and basement foundations are available for an additional fee, please specify when ordering

Special features

- The secondary bedrooms share a Jack and Jill bath
- A massive living room is warmed by a fireplace and includes a built-in media center
- The wrap-around kitchen counter with seating opens to the dining/hearth room
- The optional second floor has an additional 812 square feet of living space

Price Code C

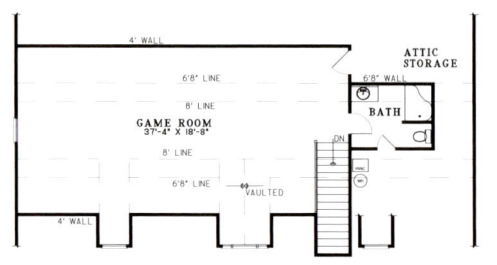

Optional Second Floor

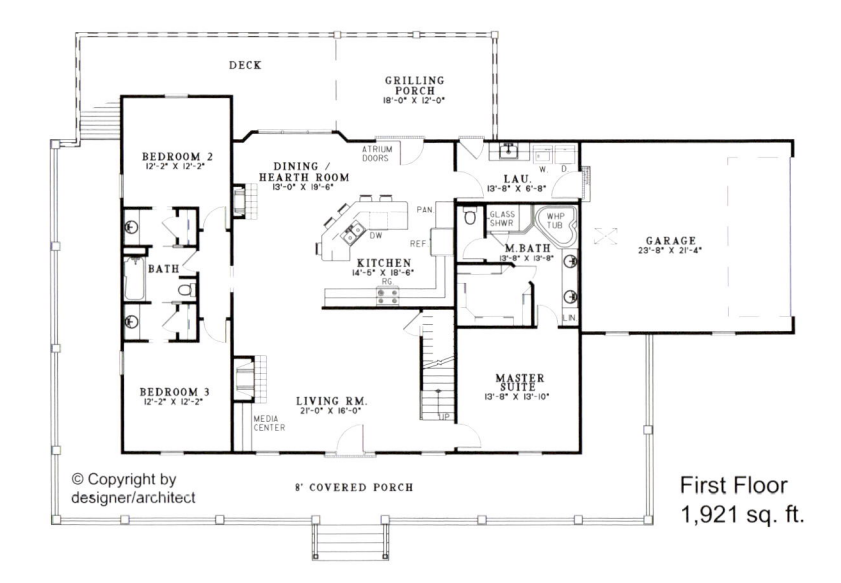

First Floor
1,921 sq. ft.

To order this plan, visit the Menards Building Materials Desk or visit www.Menards.com

MENARDS

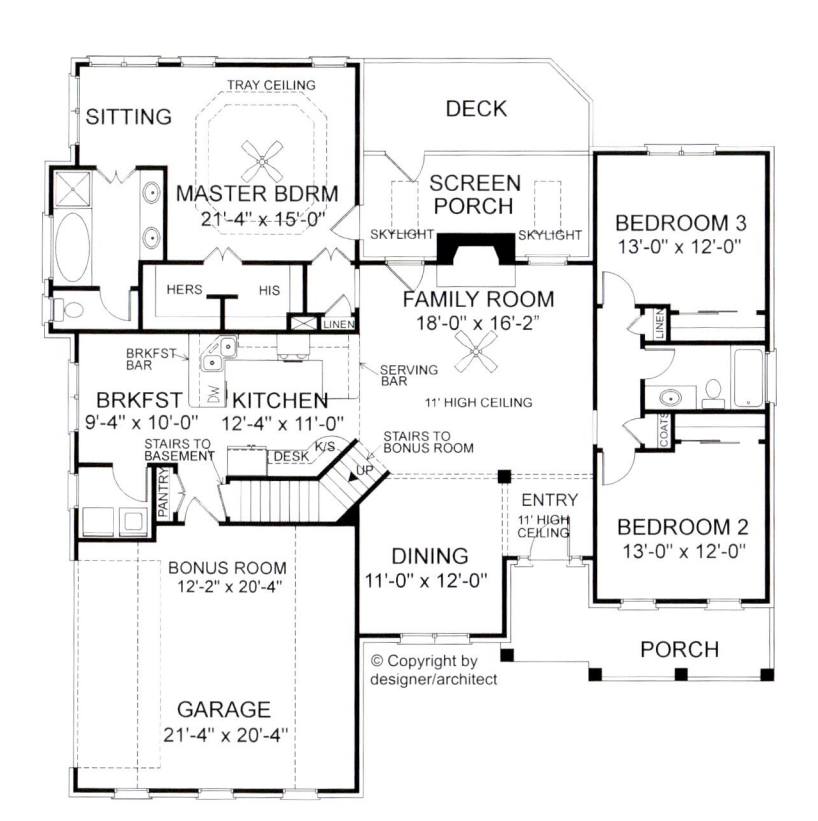

Ellisport

Plan #M09-013L-0015

Uncommonly Styled Ranch

1,787 total square feet of living area

Width: 55'-8"   Depth: 56'-6"

3 bedrooms, 2 baths

2-car side entry garage

Basement, crawl space or slab foundation, please specify when ordering

Special features

Skylights brighten the screen porch that connects to the family room, master bedroom and the deck outdoors

The master bedroom features a comfortable sitting area, a large private bath, and a his and hers walk-in closet

The kitchen has a serving bar that extends dining into the family room

The bonus room above the garage has an additional 263 square feet of living area

Price Code B

To order this plan, visit the Menards Building Materials Desk or visit www.Menards.com.

Marina Bay

Plan #M09-007D-0244

Atrium Home With Sunbelt Style

1,605 total square feet of living area

Width: 59'-0"   Depth: 52'-0"

2 bedrooms, 2 baths

2-car side entry garage

Walk-out basement foundation

Special features

Stucco, a wrap-around porch, and palladian windows with custom grilles are a few of this home's unique design features

The great room offers a bay window, fireplace, access to the rear deck and a dining balcony

The two-story atrium is 168 square feet and is included in the total square footage

Double-entry doors lead you into the master bedroom that enjoys an awesome luxury bath and walk-in closet

Price Code C

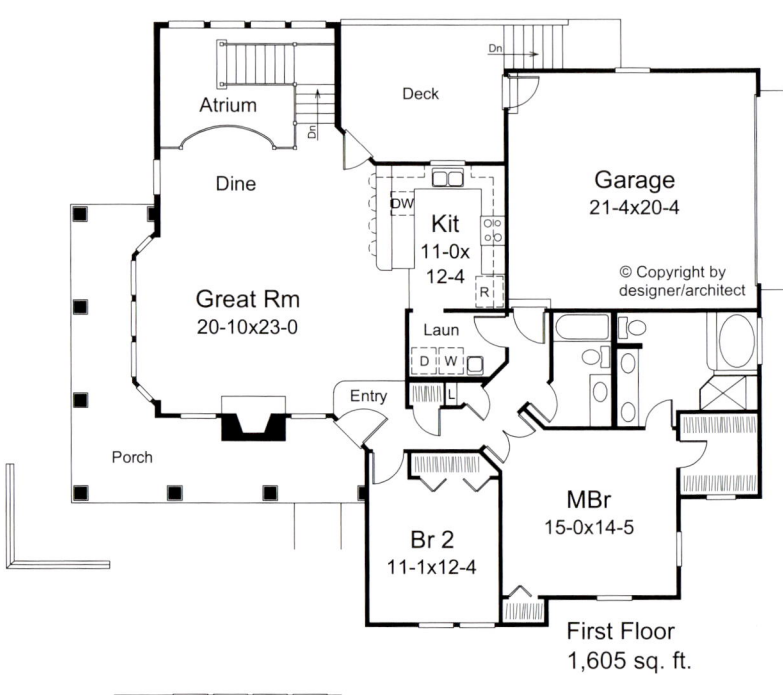

Rear View

First Floor 1,605 sq. ft.

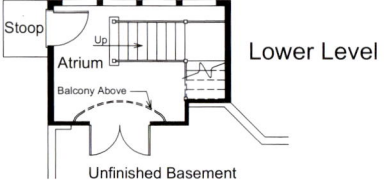

Lower Level

140 To order this plan, visit the Menards Building Materials Desk or visit www.Menards.com

MENARDS

Berrybrook

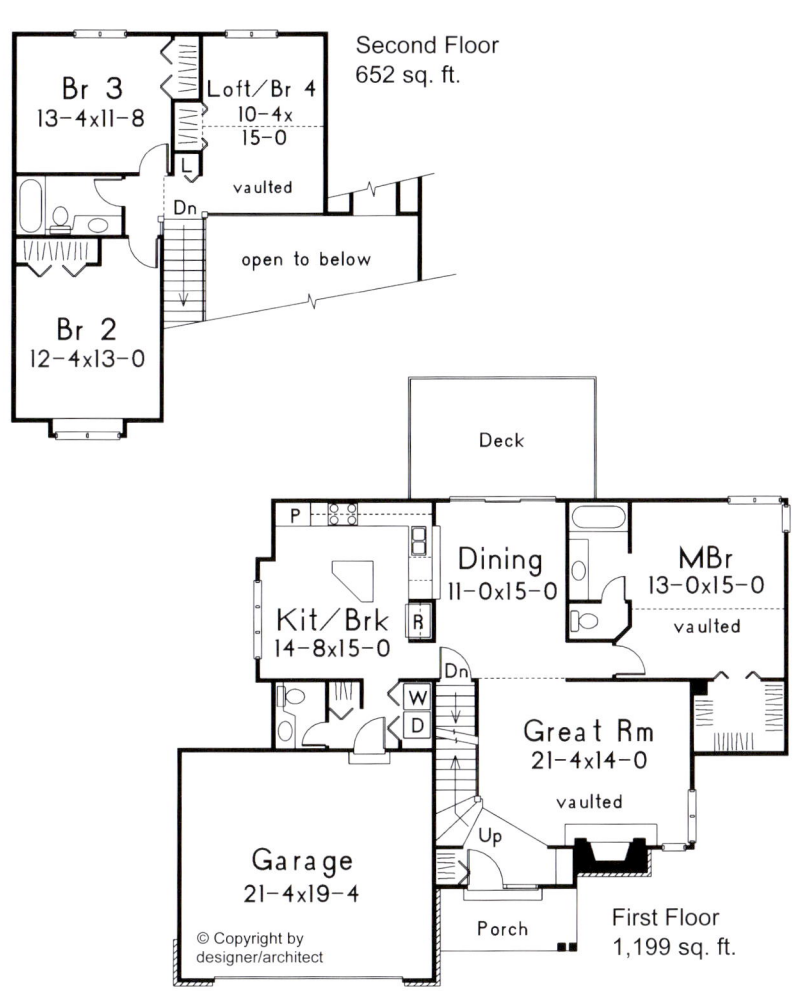

Plan #M09-022D-0009

Second Floor 652 sq. ft.

- Br 3 — 13-4x11-8
- Loft/Br 4 — 10-4x15-0 vaulted
- Br 2 — 12-4x13-0
- open to below

First Floor 1,199 sq. ft.

- Deck
- Kit/Brk — 14-8x15-0
- Dining — 11-0x15-0
- MBr — 13-0x15-0 vaulted
- Great Rm — 21-4x14-0 vaulted
- Garage — 21-4x19-4
- Porch

© Copyright by designer/architect

Vaulted Great Room With Open Entrance

1,851 total square feet of living area

Width: 52'-0"   Depth: 41'-4"

4 bedrooms, 2 1/2 baths

2-car garage

Basement foundation

Special features

The high-impact entrance to the great room also leads directly to the second floor

The first floor master bedroom suite features a corner window and a walk-in closet

The kitchen/breakfast room has a center work island and a pass-through to the dining room

The second floor bedrooms share a bath

Price Code D

Rear View

To order this plan, visit the Menards Building Materials Desk or visit www.Menards.com

Woodbine

Plan #M09-008D-0078

Wonderful Victorian Styling

1,971 total square feet of living area

Width: 51'-11"   Depth: 46'-8"

3 bedrooms, 2 1/2 baths

2-car garage

Basement foundation

Special features

The great room, kitchen and the breakfast area unite to provide a central living space

The unique parlor offers a place for nice conversation near the dining area

The deluxe master bedroom has a walk-in closet and a sunny master bath

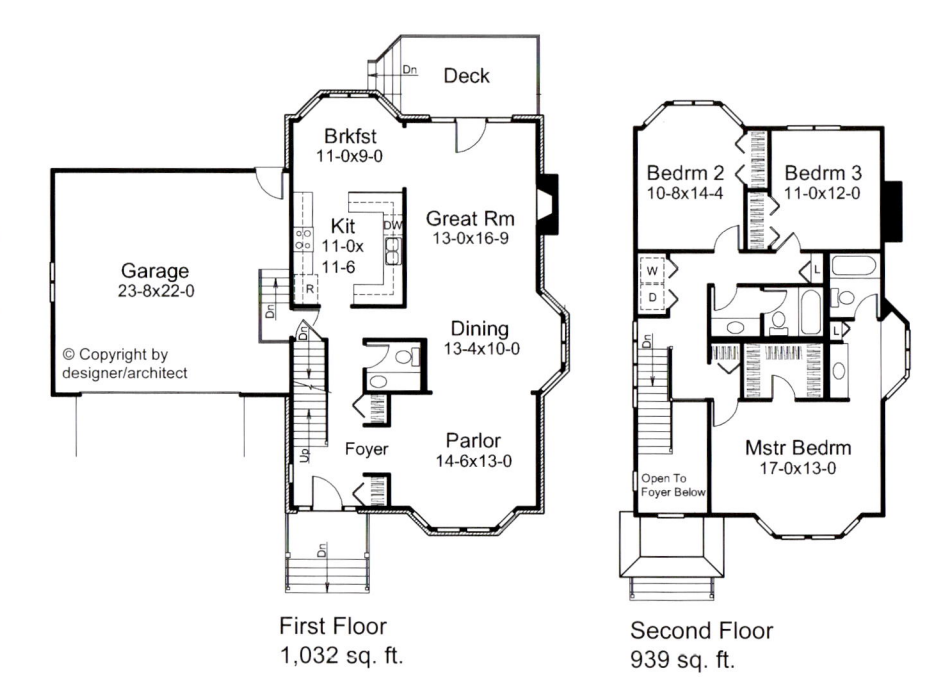

Price Code C

First Floor
1,032 sq. ft.

Second Floor
939 sq. ft.

To order this plan, visit the Menards Building Materials Desk or visit www.Menards.com.

MENARDS

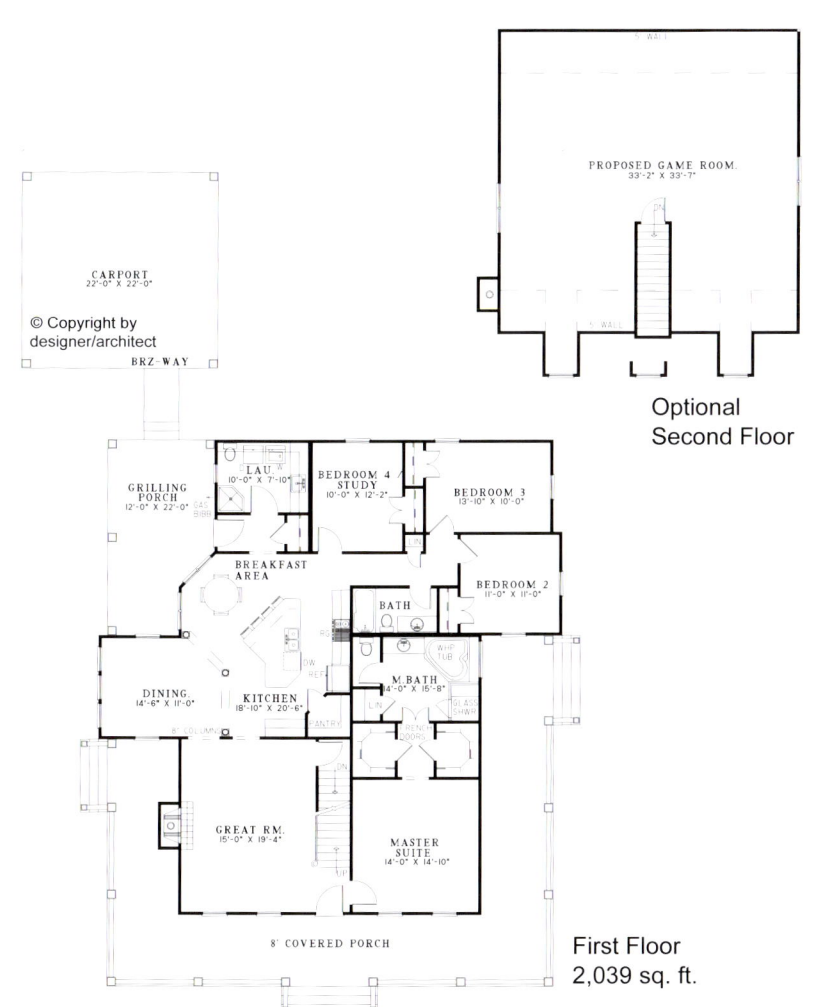

Casalone Ridge

Plan #M09-055L-0196

Rear Grilling Porch

2,039 total square feet of living area

Width: 60'-6"   Depth: 91'-4"

4 bedrooms, 3 baths

2-car side entry detached carport

Slab or crawl space foundation, please specify when ordering

Special features

A walk-in pantry and an extra-large island add convenience to the open kitchen

Columns define the formal dining room, while adding elegance

The luxurious master suite features two walk-in closets and French doors leading to the relaxing master bath

The optional second floor has an additional 1,155 square feet of living space

Price Code D

Optional Second Floor

First Floor
2,039 sq. ft.

To order this plan, visit the Menards Building Materials Desk or visit www.Menards.com.

Mayberry Cove

MENARDS

Plan #M09-058D-0014

Year-Round Hideaway

416 total square feet of living area

Width: 26'-0"   Depth: 22'-0"

Sleeping area, 1 bath

Slab foundation

Special features

The open floor plan of this home creates a spacious feeling

The covered front porch has rustic appeal

The kitchen offers plenty of cabinets and workspace

A large linen closet is centrally located and close to the full bath

2" x 6" exterior wall framing available for an additional fee, please specify when ordering

Price Code AAA

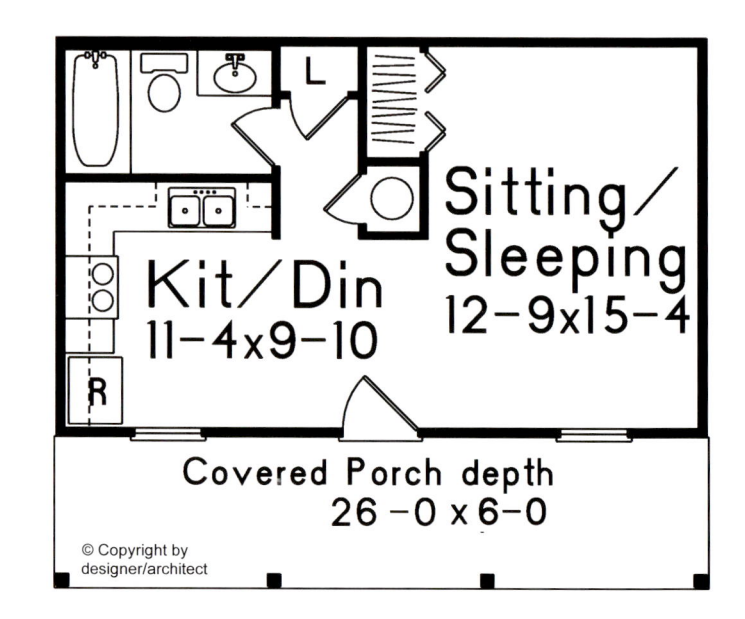

Kit/Din 11-4 x 9-10

Sitting/Sleeping 12-9 x 15-4

Covered Porch depth 26-0 x 6-0

© Copyright by designer/architect

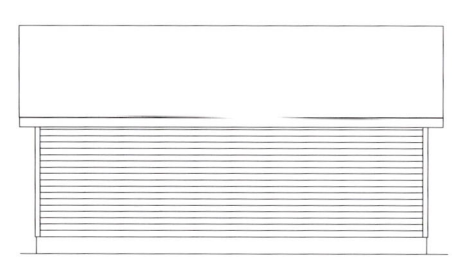

Rear View

To order this plan, visit the Menards Building Materials Desk or visit www.Menards.com.

MENARDS

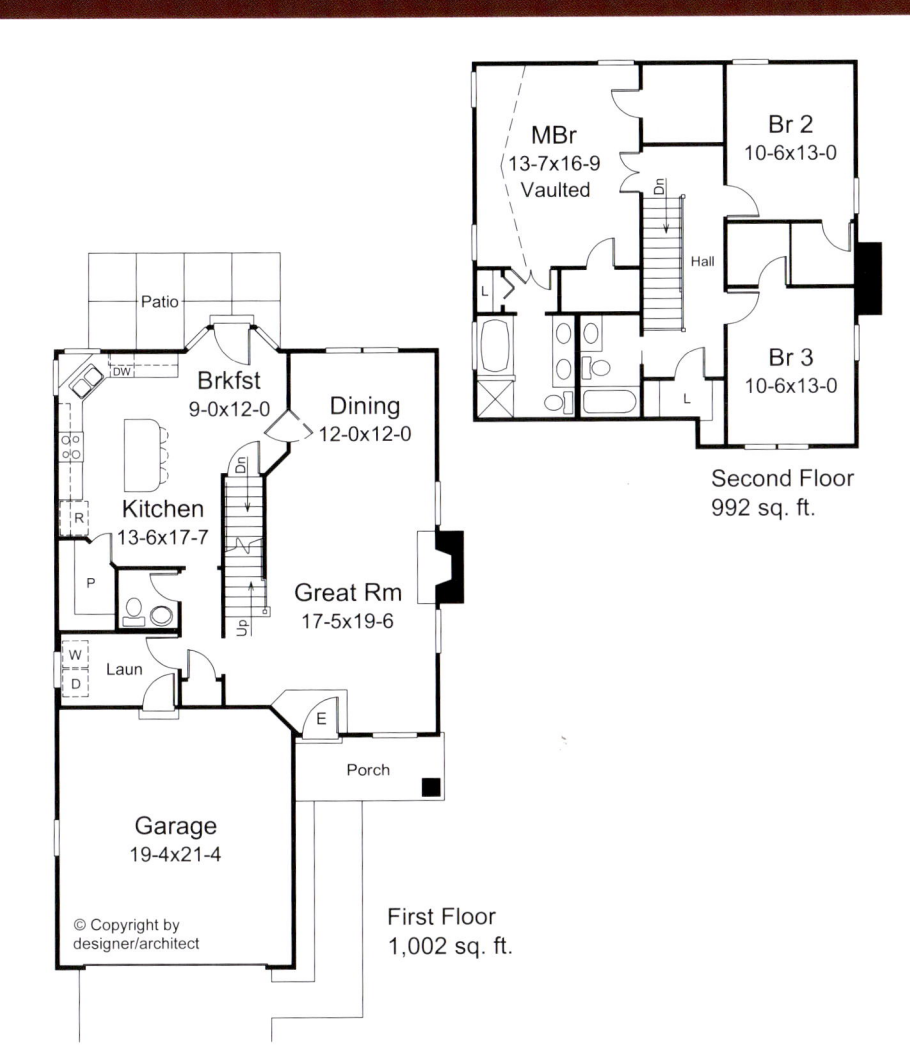

Wiseman Park

Plan #M09-007D-0237

Striking Two-Story Home

1,994 total square feet of living area

Width: 34'-0"   Depth: 53'-8"

3 bedrooms, 2 1/2 baths

2-car garage

Basement, crawl space or slab foundation, please specify when ordering

Special features

A double sink with corner windows, a snack bar island, a walk-in pantry, and a bayed breakfast area are all features of the kitchen

The vaulted master bedroom has a luxury bath with linen closet

The large great room enjoys a fireplace

Price Code B

First Floor 1,002 sq. ft.

- Patio
- Brkfst
- Dining 12-0x12-0
- Kitchen 13-6x17-7
- Great Rm 17-5x19-6
- Laun
- Porch
- Garage 19-4x21-4

© Copyright by designer/architect

Second Floor 992 sq. ft.

- MBr 13-7x16-9 Vaulted
- Br 2 10-6x13-0
- Hall
- Br 3 10-6x13-0

Rear View

To order this plan, visit the Menards Building Materials Desk or visit www.Menards.com

145

Goodwin

MENARDS

Plan #M09-014D-0009

Vaulted Ceilings Throughout Create Dramatic Interior

1,428 total square feet of living area

Width: 54'-0"   Depth: 46'-6"

3 bedrooms, 2 baths

2-car garage

Basement foundation, drawings also include crawl space foundation

Special features

Energy efficient home with 2" x 6" exterior walls

10' ceilings in the entry and hallway

The kitchen is loaded with amenities including an island with a salad sink and pantry

The vaulted master bedroom includes a large walk-in closet and private master bath

Price Code A

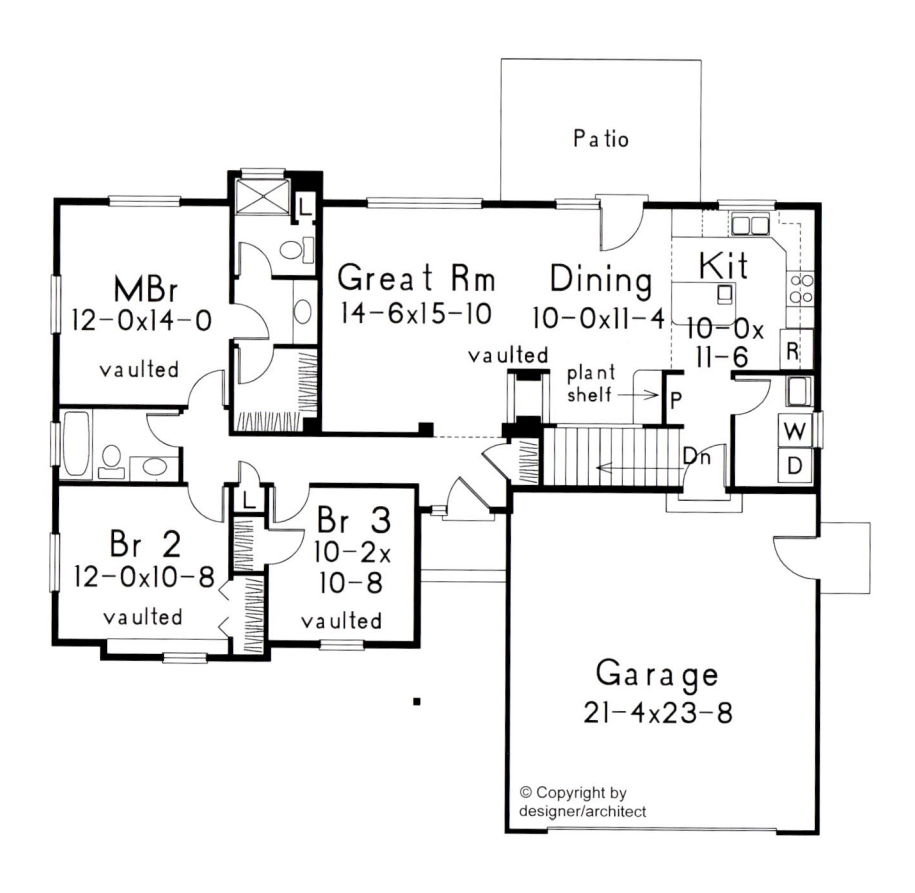

Rear View

146   To order this plan, visit the Menards Building Materials Desk or visit www.Menards.com

MBr 12-0x14-0 vaulted
Great Rm 14-6x15-10 vaulted
Dining 10-0x11-4 vaulted
Kit 10-0x11-6
Patio
Br 2 12-0x10-8 vaulted
Br 3 10-2x10-8 vaulted
Garage 21-4x23-8

© Copyright by designer/architect

MENARDS

Mayland

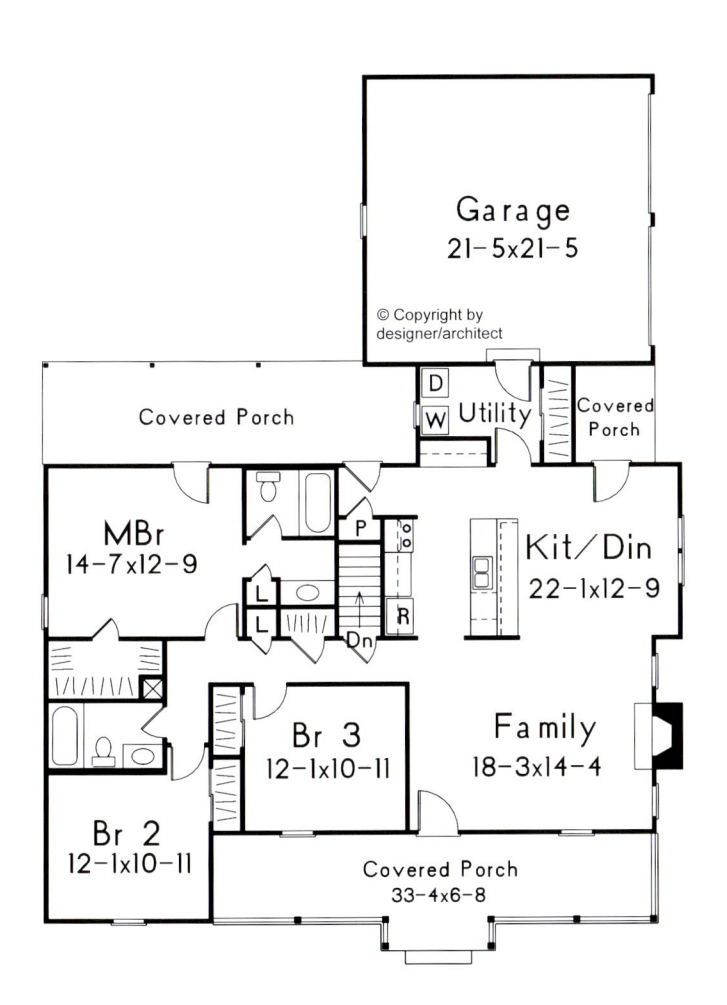

Plan #M09-001D-0031

Country-Style Home With Large Front Porch

1,501 total square feet of living area

Width: 48'-0"   Depth: 66'-0"

3 bedrooms, 2 baths

2-car side entry garage

Basement foundation, drawings also include crawl space and slab foundations

Special features

The spacious kitchen/dining area is open to the covered porch

A convenient utility room is adjacent to the garage

The master bedroom features a private bath, a dressing area, and access to the large covered porch

Price Code B

Rear View

To order this plan, visit the Menards Building Materials Desk or visit www.Menards.com.

Edison Park

MENARDS

Plan #M09-057D-0012

Perfect Design For A Narrow Lot

1,112 total square feet of living area

Width: 28'-0"   Depth: 42'-0"

3 bedrooms, 1 bath

Basement foundation

Special features

Energy efficient home with 2" x 6" exterior walls

Brick, an arched window, and a planter box decorate the facade of this lovely ranch home

The eat-in kitchen offers an abundance of counterspace and enjoys access to the outdoors

Three bedrooms are situated together for easy family living

Price Code AA

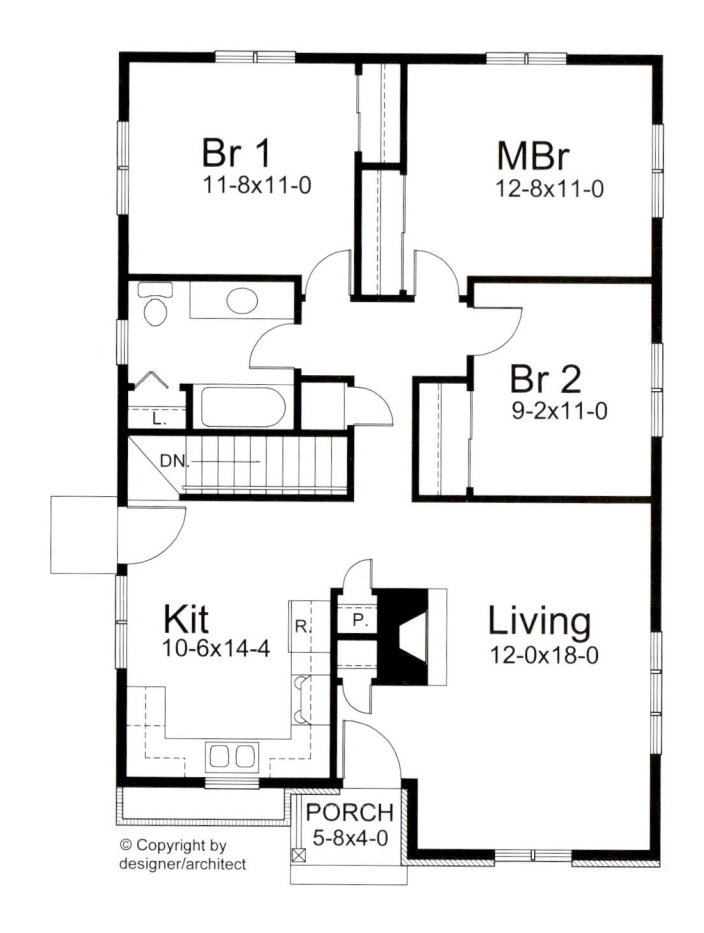

Br 1
11-8x11-0

MBr
12-8x11-0

Br 2
9-2x11-0

Kit
10-6x14-4

Living
12-0x18-0

PORCH
5-8x4-0

© Copyright by designer/architect

148

To order this plan, visit the Menards Building Materials Desk or visit www.Menards.com

MENARDS

Chloe

Plan #M09-121D-0007

Detached Garage
23-4x23-4

© Copyright by designer/architect

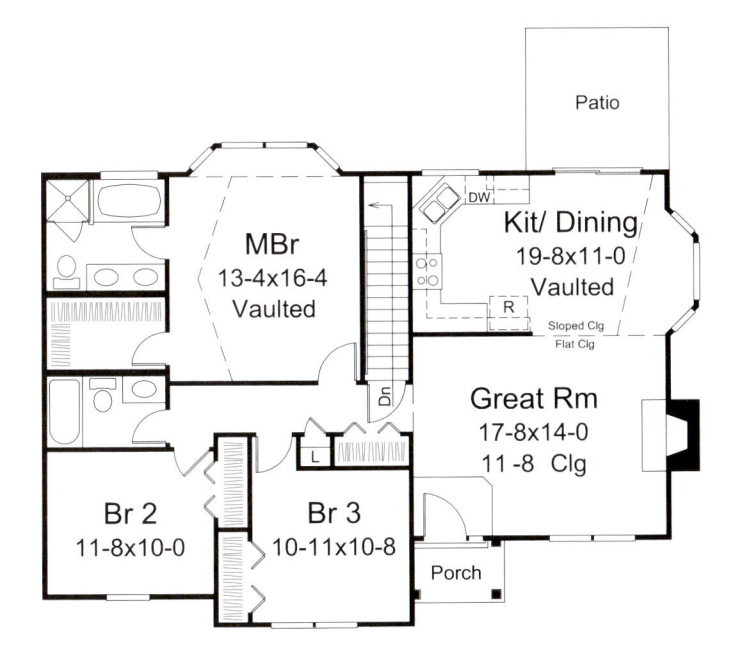

Patio

MBr
13-4x16-4
Vaulted

Kit/ Dining
19-8x11-0
Vaulted

Sloped Clg
Flat Clg

Great Rm
17-8x14-0
11-8 Clg

Br 2
11-8x10-0

Br 3
10-11x10-8

Porch

Spacious Great Room

1,308 total square feet of living area

Width: 46'-0"   Depth: 34'-0"

3 bedrooms, 2 baths

2-car detached garage

Basement foundation

Special features

A lovely bay window and access to the rear patio are some of the features of the vaulted kitchen/dining area

A tall ceiling and warming fireplace in the great room appeal to every homeowner

The vaulted master bedroom showcases a large walk-in closet, bay window and private bath

Price Code AA

Rear View

To order this plan, visit the Menards Building Materials Desk or visit www.Menards.com.

149

Forestville

MENARDS

Plan #M09-040D-0015

Covered Porch Adds Charm To The Entrance

1,655 total square feet of living area

Width: 81'-0" Depth: 50'-8"

3 bedrooms, 2 baths

2-car garage

Crawl space foundation

Special features

The master bedroom features a 9' ceiling, walk-in closet and bath with a dressing area

The oversized family room includes a 10' ceiling and a masonry see-through fireplace

The island kitchen has convenient access to the laundry room

The handy covered walkway from the garage leads to the kitchen and dining area

Price Code B

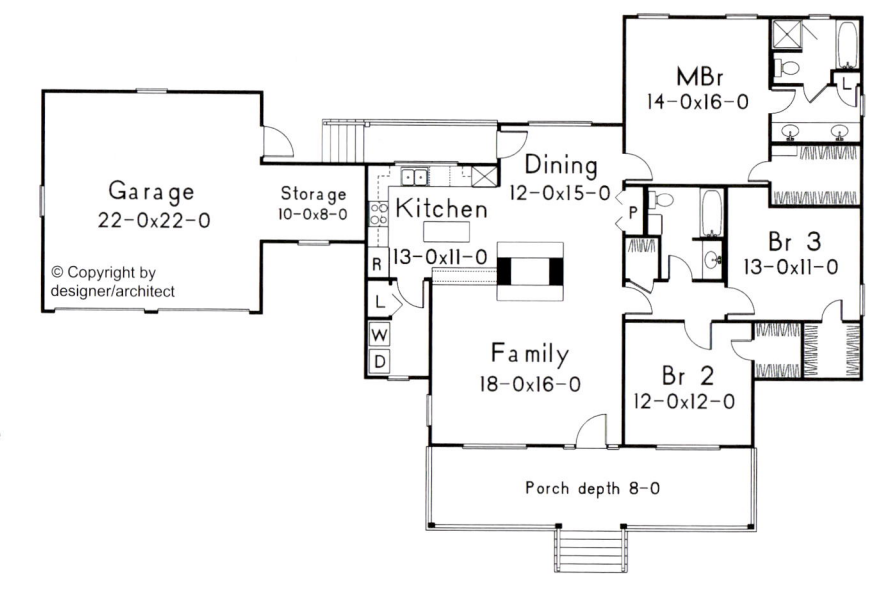

Rear View

150

To order this plan, visit the Menards Building Materials Desk or visit www.Menards.com

MENARDS

Grass Roots II

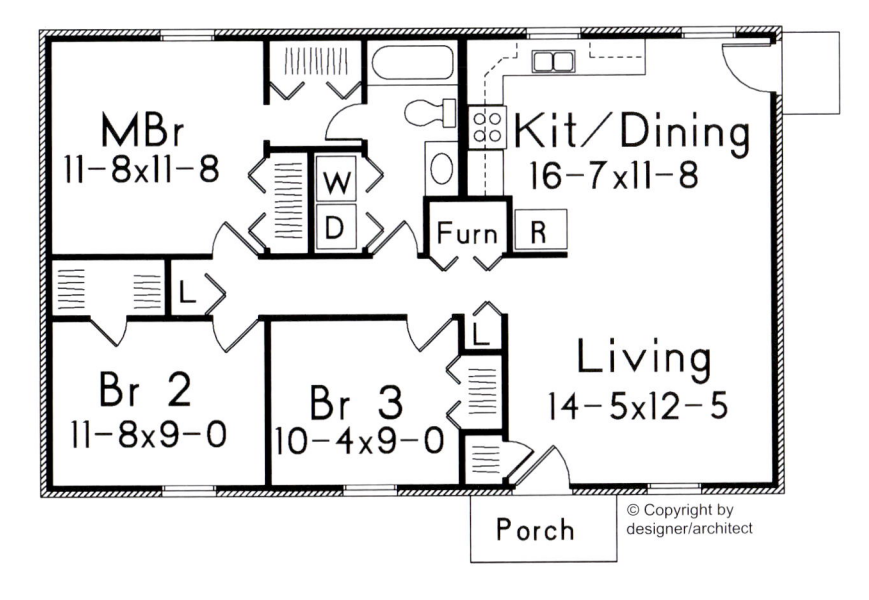

Plan #M09-001D-0042

Open Living Space Creates Comfortable Atmosphere

1,000 total square feet of living area

Width: 40'-0" Depth: 25'-0"

3 bedrooms, 1 bath

Crawl space foundation, drawings also include basement and slab foundations

Special features

The full bath includes a convenient hide-away laundry closet large enough for a separate washer and dryer

The master bedroom includes double closets and private access to the bath

The foyer features a handy coat closet

The kitchen features an L-shaped design and easy access outdoors

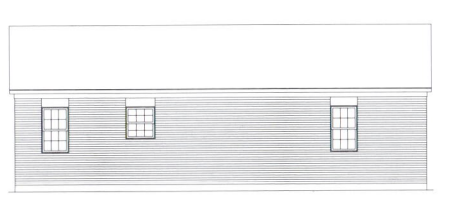

Price Code AA

MBr 11-8x11-8

Kit/Dining 16-7x11-8

Br 2 11-8x9-0

Br 3 10-4x9-0

Living 14-5x12-5

Porch

© Copyright by designer/architect

Rear View

To order this plan, visit the Menards Building Materials Desk or visit www.Menards.com

Lexburg

MENARDS

Plan #M09-045D-0012

Open Layout Ensures Easy Living

976 total square feet of living area

Width: 20'-0"   Depth: 26'-0"

3 bedrooms, 1 1/2 baths

Basement foundation

Special features

The cozy front porch opens into the large living area

All of the the bedrooms in this home are located on the second floor for privacy

The dining room has access to the outdoors

Price Code AA

First Floor
488 sq. ft.

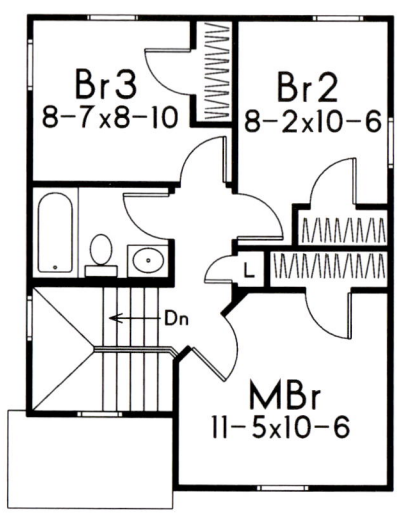

Kit 10-0x7-10
Dining 11-5x8-0
Living 11-5x17-6
Porch Depth 4-0

© Copyright by designer/architect

Second Floor
488 sq. ft.

Br3 8-7x8-10
Br2 8-2x10-6
MBr 11-5x10-6

Rear View

152

To order this plan, visit the Menards Building Materials Desk or visit www.Menards.com

MENARDS

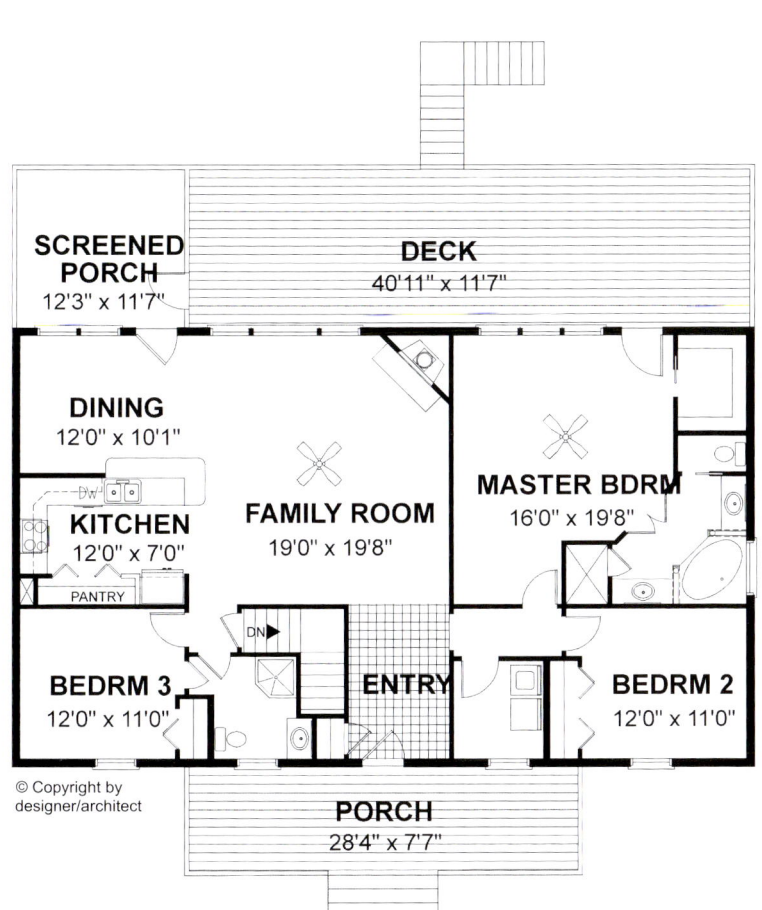

Evergreen Point

Plan #M09-013L-0014

A Rustic Drive Under Ranch

1,728 total square feet of living area

Width: 54'-0"   Depth: 32'-0"

3 bedrooms, 2 baths

2-car drive under side entry garage

Basement or crawl space foundation, please specify when ordering

Special features

The large entry leads to the family room featuring a corner fireplace and a window wall overlooking an enormous deck

The master bedroom is adorned with a dramatic bath featuring an angled entry and a corner whirlpool tub

A built-in eating bar extends off of the kitchen counter and overlooks the nearby family and dining rooms

Price Code C

Floor plan rooms:
- SCREENED PORCH 12'3" x 11'7"
- DECK 40'11" x 11'7"
- DINING 12'0" x 10'1"
- KITCHEN 12'0" x 7'0" (PANTRY)
- FAMILY ROOM 19'0" x 19'8"
- MASTER BDRM 16'0" x 19'8"
- BEDRM 3 12'0" x 11'0"
- ENTRY
- BEDRM 2 12'0" x 11'0"
- PORCH 28'4" x 7'7"

© Copyright by designer/architect

To order this plan, visit the Menards Building Materials Desk or visit www.Menards.com.

Cornwall

MENARDS

Plan #M09-008D-0088

Embracing The Sun With Skylights

1,850 total square feet of living area

Width: 60'-0" Depth: 33'-4"

3 bedrooms, 2 1/2 baths

2-car garage

Basement foundation

Special features

The large living room with fireplace is illuminated by three second story skylights

The living and dining rooms are separated by a low wall, while the dining room and kitchen are separated by a snack bar creating a spacious atmosphere

The master bedroom has a huge bath with a double-bowl vanity and a large walk-in closet

Two second floor bedrooms share a uniquely designed bath

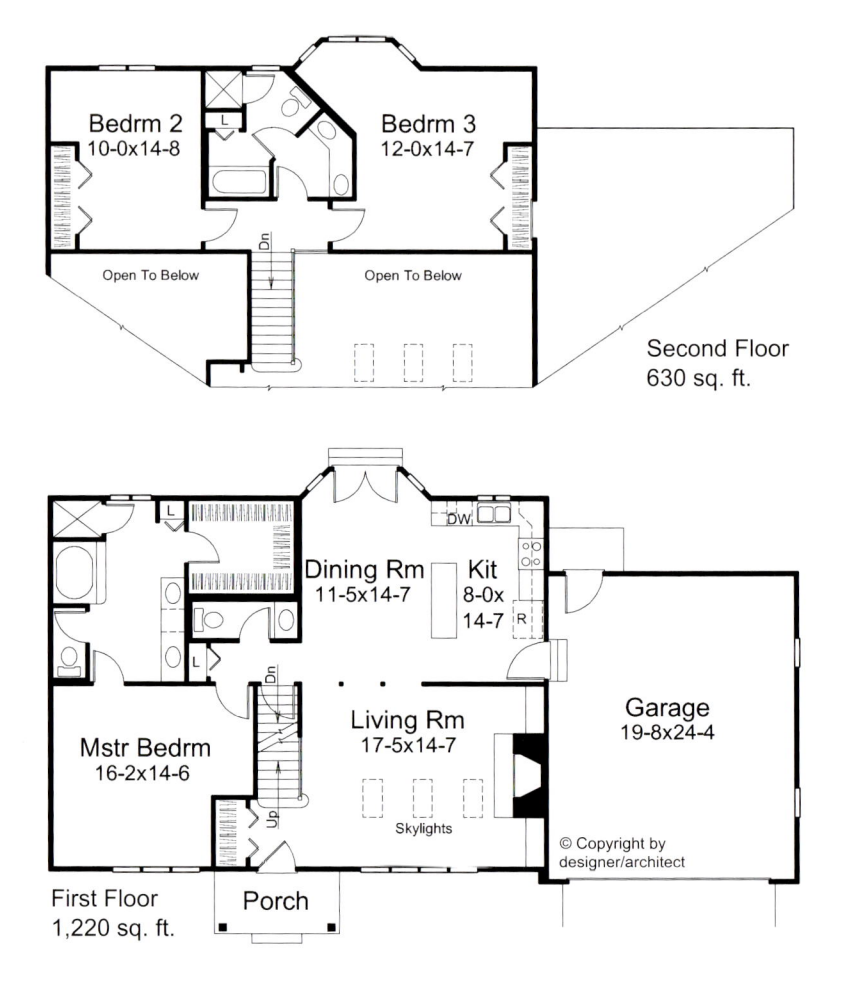

Price Code C

Bedrm 2
10-0x14-8

Bedrm 3
12-0x14-7

Open To Below

Open To Below

Second Floor
630 sq. ft.

Dining Rm
11-5x14-7

Kit
8-0x14-7

Mstr Bedrm
16-2x14-6

Living Rm
17-5x14-7

Skylights

Garage
19-8x24-4

© Copyright by designer/architect

First Floor
1,220 sq. ft.

Porch

154 To order this plan, visit the Menards Building Materials Desk or visit www.Menards.com

MENARDS

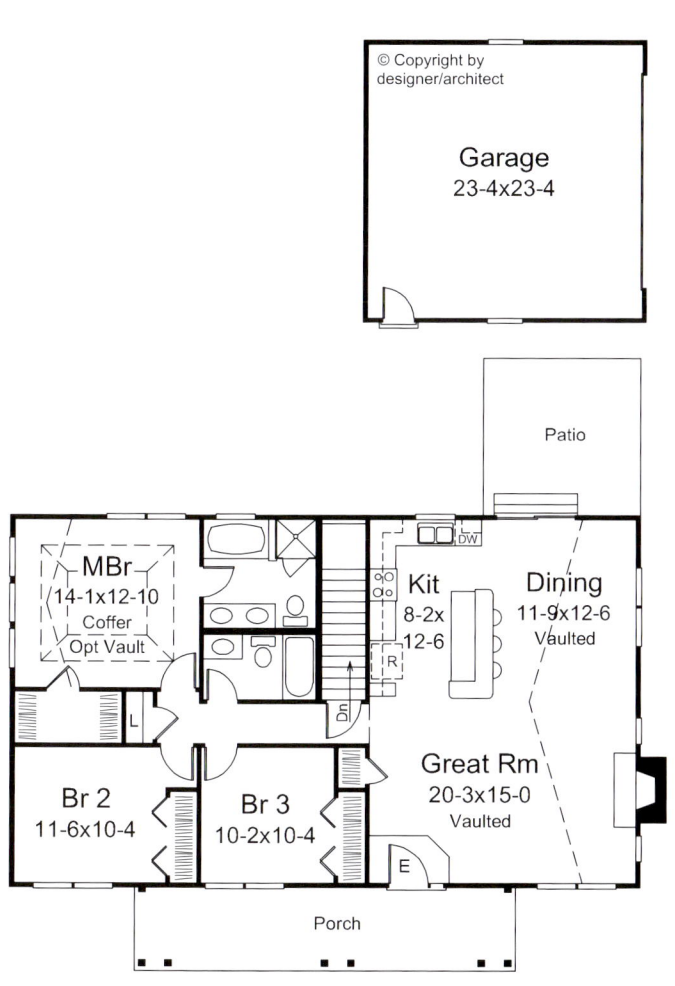

Sydney

Plan #M09-121D-0025

Beautiful Country Ranch Home

1,368 total square feet of living area

Width: 50'-0"   Depth: 34'-6"

3 bedrooms, 2 baths

2-car detached garage

Basement foundation

Special features

The vaulted great room and dining area boast a fireplace and sliding door access to the rear patio

The efficiently designed kitchen enjoys an island with a breakfast bar perfect for casual meals

Multiple windows brighten the master bedroom that has a walk-in closet and private bath

Price Code AA

To order this plan, visit the Menards Building Materials Desk or visit www.Menards.com.

...tmoore

MENARDS®

Plan #M09-001D-0024

Functional Layout For Comfortable Living

1,360 total square feet of living area

Width: 68'-0"   Depth: 38'-0"

3 bedrooms, 2 baths

2-car side entry garage

Basement foundation, drawings also include crawl space and slab foundations

Special features

The kitchen/dining room features an island workspace and plenty of dining area

The master bedroom has a large walk-in closet and a private bath

The laundry room is adjacent to the kitchen for easy access

The large closets in the secondary bedrooms maintain organization

Price Code A

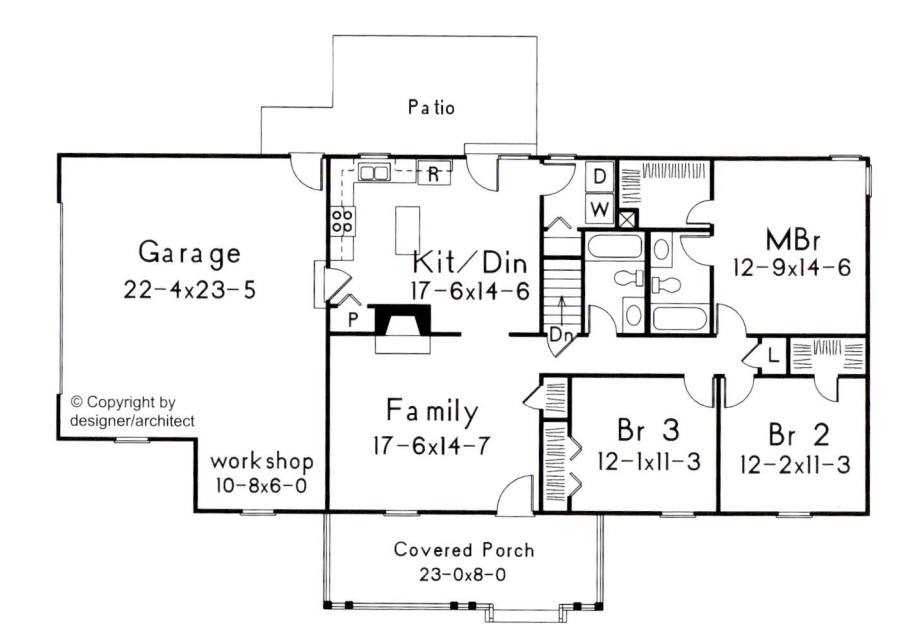

Patio

Garage 22-4x23-5

Kit/Din 17-6x14-6

MBr 12-9x14-6

Family 17-6x14-7

Br 3 12-1x11-3

Br 2 12-2x11-3

workshop 10-8x6-0

Covered Porch 23-0x8-0

© Copyright by designer/architect

Rear View

To order this plan, visit the Menards Building Materials Desk or visit www.Menards.com

MENARDS

Forest Ridge

Plan #M09-007D-0210

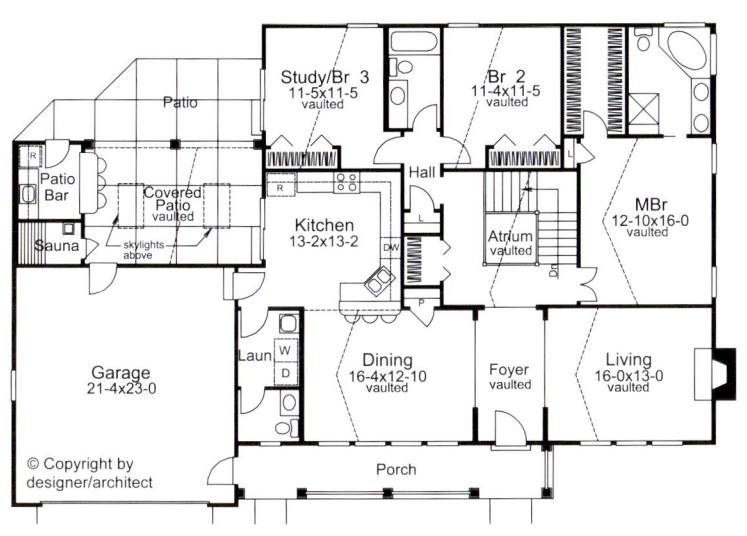

Clerestory Windows Brighten Atrium Staircase

1,942 total square feet of living area

Width: 70'-4"   Depth: 47'-0"

3 bedrooms, 2 1/2 baths

2-car garage

Walk-out basement foundation

Special features

An elongated porch and classy foyer leads into a central atrium with a winding staircase to the lower level

The kitchen is open to the dining area and has views of the covered patio

The lower level features an additional 708 square feet with an optional spacious family room and fourth bedroom with bath

Price Code B

First Floor 1,852 sq. ft.

- Patio
- Patio Bar
- Sauna
- Covered Patio vaulted
- skylights above
- Garage 21-4x23-0
- Laun
- Study/Br 3 11-5x11-5 vaulted
- Kitchen 13-2x13-2
- Hall
- Br 2 11-4x11-5 vaulted
- Atrium vaulted
- MBr 12-10x16-0 vaulted
- Dining 16-4x12-10 vaulted
- Foyer vaulted
- Living 16-0x13-0 vaulted
- Porch

© Copyright by designer/architect

Lower Level 90 sq. ft.

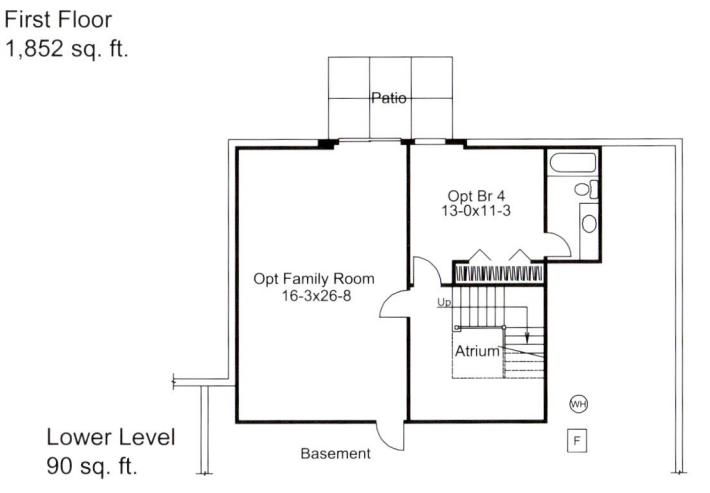

- Patio
- Opt Br 4 13-0x11-3
- Opt Family Room 16-3x26-8
- Atrium
- Basement

Rear View

To order this plan, visit the Menards Building Materials Desk or visit www.Menards.com.

El Dorado

MENARDS

Plan #M09-022D-0002

Floor-To-Ceiling Window Expands Compact Two-Story

1,246 total square feet of living area

Width: 36'-8"   Depth: 38'-8"

3 bedrooms, 2 baths

2-car garage

Basement foundation

Special features

The corner living room window adds openness

The out-of-the-way kitchen with dining area accesses the outdoors

The private first floor master bedroom has interesting corner windows

A large walk-in closet is located in bedroom #3

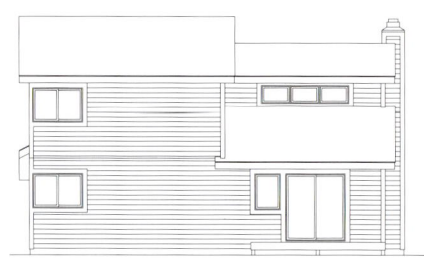

Price Code A

Rear View

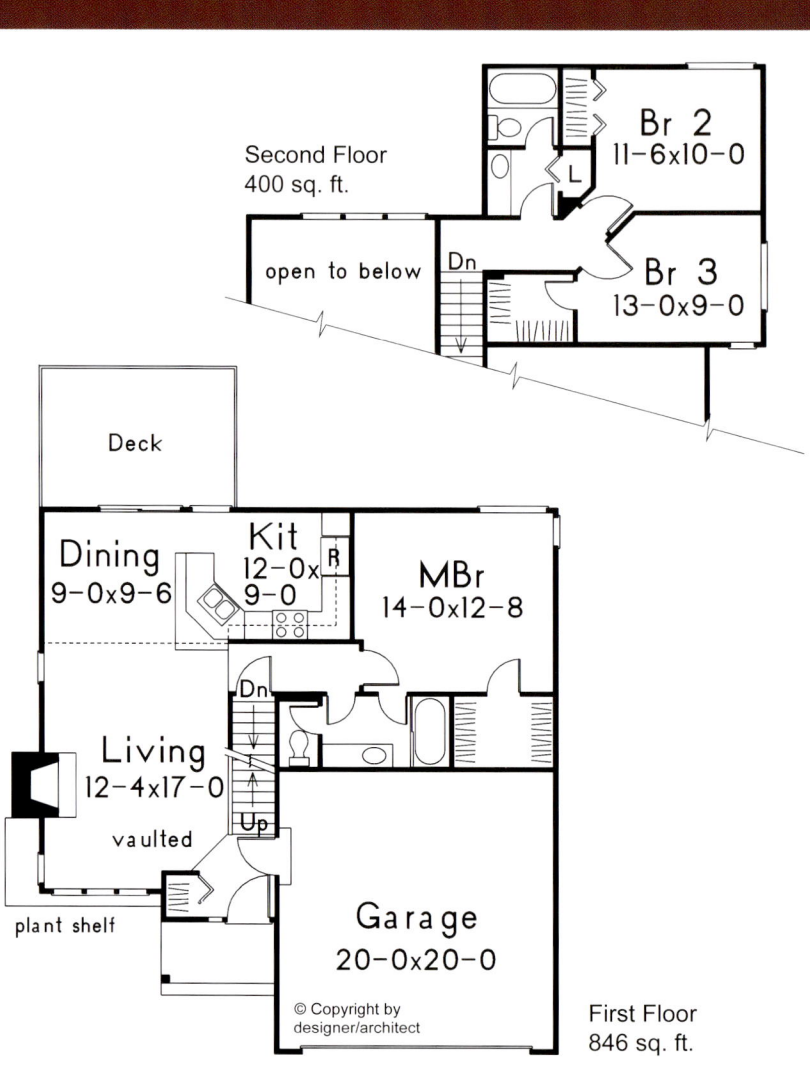

Second Floor 400 sq. ft.
- Br 2: 11-6x10-0
- Br 3: 13-0x9-0
- open to below

First Floor 846 sq. ft.
- Deck
- Dining: 9-0x9-6
- Kit: 12-0x9-0
- MBr: 14-0x12-8
- Living: 12-4x17-0 vaulted
- Garage: 20-0x20-0
- plant shelf

© Copyright by designer/architect

To order this plan, visit the Menards Building Materials Desk or visit www.Menards.com

MENARDS

Provider 11

Plan #M09-001D-0040

Perfect Home For A Small Family

864 total square feet of living area

Width: 36'-0"   Depth: 28'-0"

2 bedrooms, 1 bath

Crawl space foundation, drawings also include basement and slab foundations

Special features

An L-shaped kitchen with a convenient pantry is adjacent to the dining area

This home has easy access to the laundry, linen, and storage closets

Both of the bedrooms include ample closet space

Price Code AAA

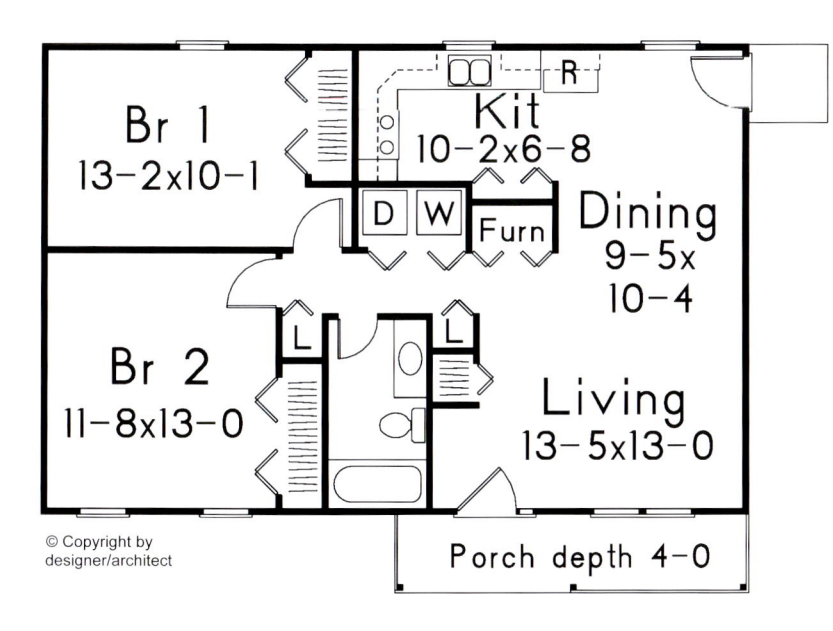

Floor plan:
- Br 1: 13-2 x 10-1
- Br 2: 11-8 x 13-0
- Kit: 10-2 x 6-8
- Dining: 9-5 x 10-4
- Living: 13-5 x 13-0
- Porch depth 4-0

© Copyright by designer/architect

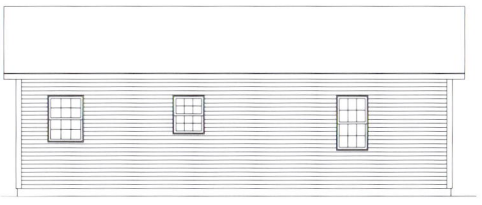

Rear View

To order this plan, visit the Menards Building Materials Desk or visit www.Menards.com.

Brookwood

MENARDS

Plan #M09-008D-0147

Unique, Yet Functional Design

1,316 total square feet of living area

Width: 26'-0"   Depth: 40'-0"

3 bedrooms, 1 bath

Crawl space foundation

Special features

The massive vaulted family/living room is accented with a fireplace and views to the outdoors through sliding glass doors

The galley-style kitchen is centrally located and overlooks the family/living room

The unique separate shower room near the bath doubles as a convenient mud room

Price Code A

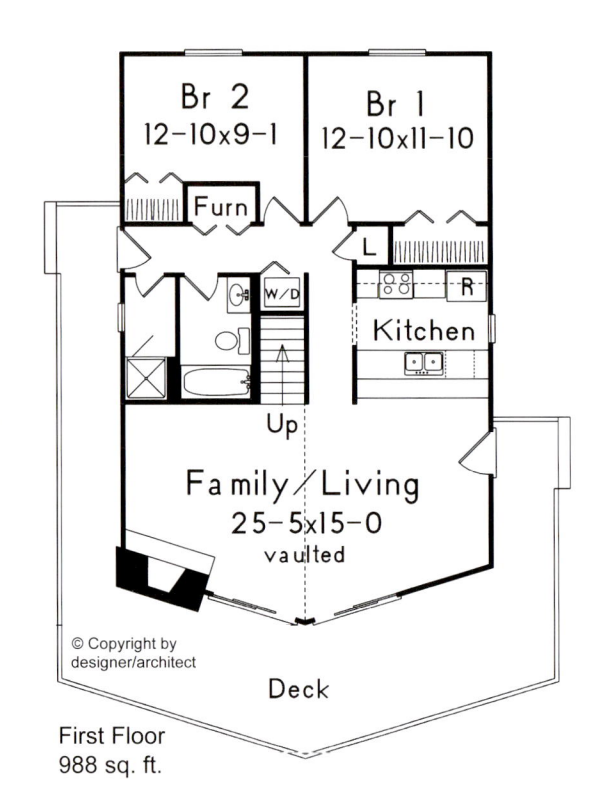

Br 2 12-10x9-1
Br 1 12-10x11-10
Br 3 13-8x10-1
Family/Living 25-5x15-0 vaulted

First Floor 988 sq. ft. 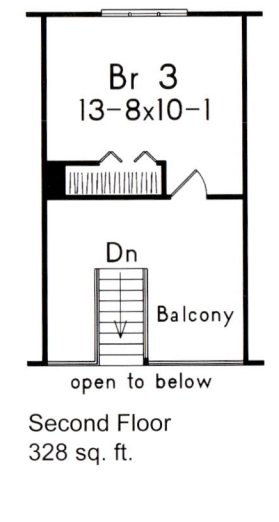
Second Floor 328 sq. ft.

160

To order this plan, visit the Menards Building Materials Desk or visit www.Menards.com

MENARDS

Crosswood

Plan #M09-001D-0088

Ideal For A Starter Home

800 total square feet of living area

Width: 32'-0"   Depth: 25'-0"

2 bedrooms, 1 bath

Crawl space foundation, drawings also include basement foundation

Special features

The master bedroom has a walk-in closet and private access to the bath

The large living room features a handy coat closet at the front entry

The kitchen/dining area includes a side entrance, a convenient coat closet, and a washer and dryer closeted area

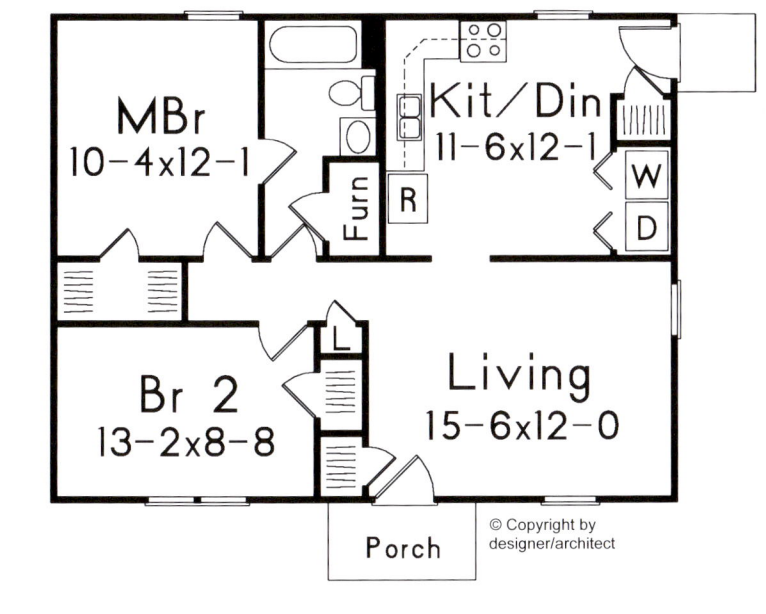

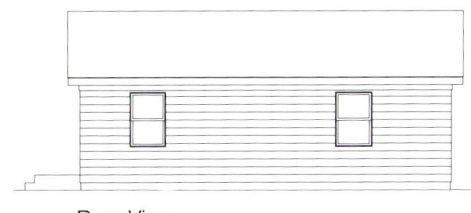

Price Code AAA

MBr 10-4x12-1

Kit/Din 11-6x12-1

Br 2 13-2x8-8

Living 15-6x12-0

Porch

© Copyright by designer/architect

Rear View

To order this plan, visit the Menards Building Materials Desk or visit www.Menards.com.

Mount Berry

Plan #M09-013L-0159

Great Porch Opportunities

1,992 total square feet of living area

Width: 63'-0"   Depth: 57'-2"

3 bedrooms, 2 1/2 baths

3-car side entry garage

Slab, basement or crawl space foundation, please specify when ordering

Special features

Enter double doors off the foyer and discover a secluded living room that could also be converted to a home office

The spacious master suite enjoys its own sunny sitting area, pampering bath, and walk-in closet

The kitchen is positioned perfectly between the bayed breakfast area and the formal dining room with tray ceiling

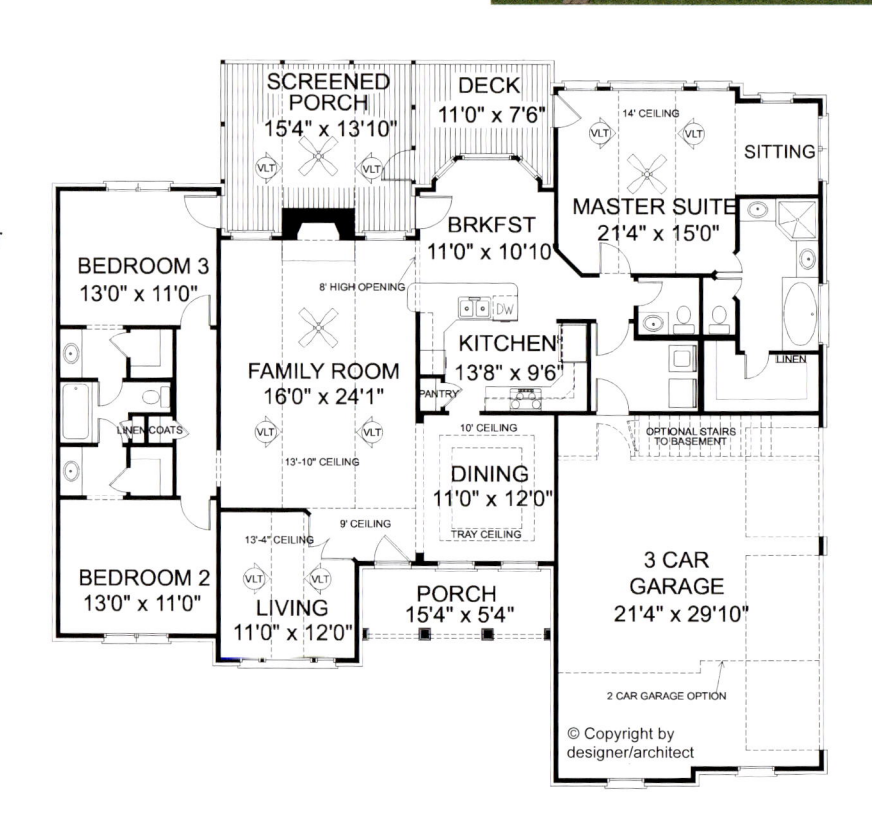

Price Code B

To order this plan, visit the Menards Building Materials Desk or visit www.Menards.com

MENARDS

Hailey

Plan #M09-121D-0020

Vaulted Ceilings Add Charisma

2,037 total square feet of living area

Width: 70'-8"   Depth: 47'-0"

3 bedrooms, 2 1/2 baths

2-car garage

Basement foundation

Special features

The vaulted kitchen/breakfast area enjoys a walk-in pantry and a sunny bay window with access to the rear patio

The storage area in the garage has access to the outdoors

Two spacious walk-in closets and a private bath are some of the amenities of the master bedroom

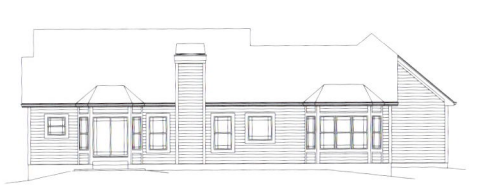

Price Code B

Rear View

To order this plan, visit the Menards Building Materials Desk or visit www.Menards.com.

Glenwood

MENARDS

Plan #M09-007D-0040

Apartment Garage With Surprising Interior

632 total square feet of living area

Width: 28'-0"   Depth: 26'-0"

1 bedroom, 1 bath
2-car garage
Slab foundation

Special features

The porch leads to the vaulted entry and staircase with a feature window and closet

The vaulted living room has a fireplace, large palladian window, and kitchen access

A garden tub with arched window is part of a very roomy bath

Price Code AAA

Rear View

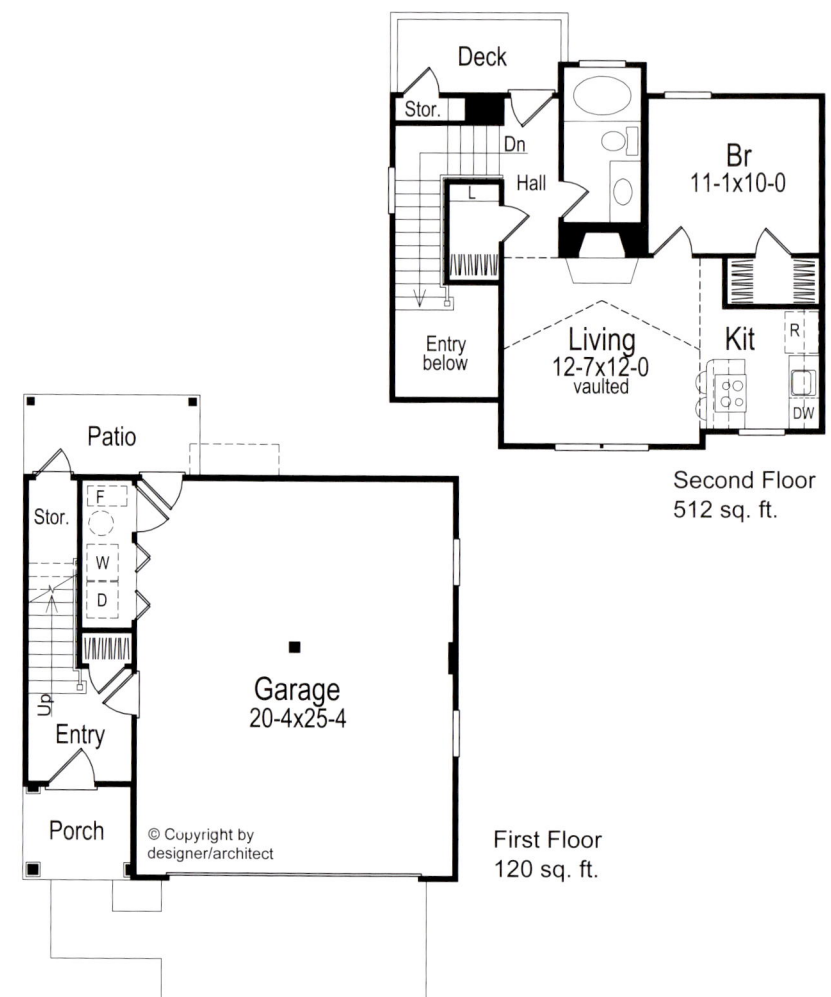

Second Floor
512 sq. ft.

First Floor
120 sq. ft.

164

To order this plan, visit the Menards Building Materials Desk or visit www.Menards.com.

MENARDS

Delta Queen 1

Plan #M09-001D-0067

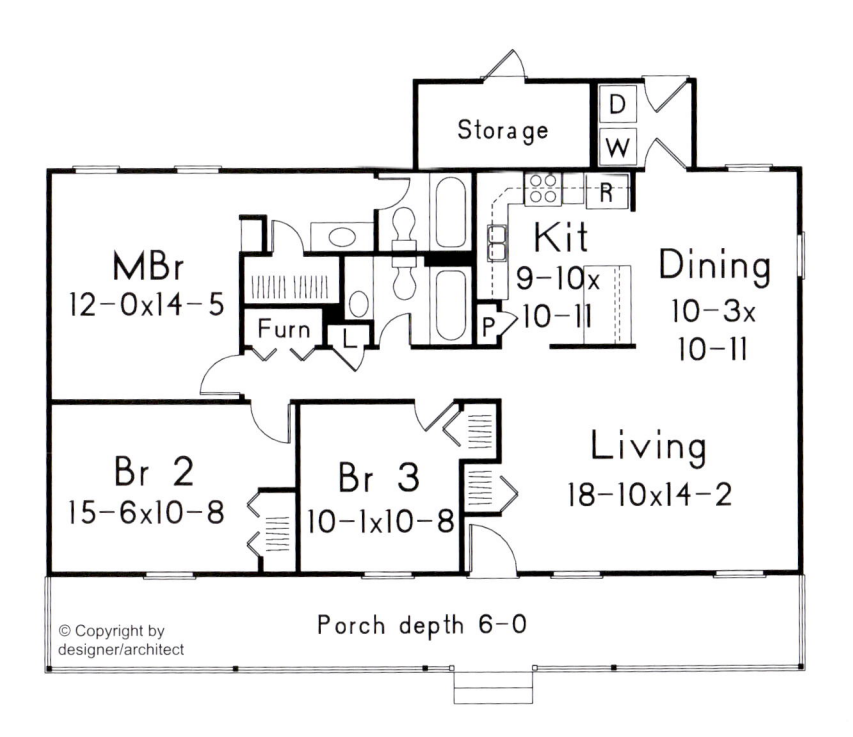

Layout Creates Large Open Living Area

1,285 total square feet of living area

Width: 48'-0"   Depth: 37'-8"

3 bedrooms, 2 baths

Crawl space foundation, drawings also include basement and slab foundations

Special features

This home has a country-style covered porch

The large storage area on the back of the home is a handy feature

The master bedroom includes a dressing area, private bath and built-in bookcase

The kitchen features a pantry, breakfast bar and complete view to the dining area

2" x 6" exterior wall framing available for an additional fee, please specify when ordering

Price Code B

Floor plan rooms:
- Storage
- MBr 12-0x14-5
- Kit 9-10x10-11
- Dining 10-3x10-11
- Br 2 15-6x10-8
- Br 3 10-1x10-8
- Living 18-10x14-2
- Furn
- Porch depth 6-0

© Copyright by designer/architect

Rear View

To order this plan, visit the Menards Building Materials Desk or visit www.Menards.com.

Summerview

MENARDS

Plan #M09-007D-0068

Tranquility Of An Atrium Cottage

1,922 total square feet of living area

Width: 55'-8"   Depth: 46'-4"

2 bedrooms, 2 baths

1-car side entry garage

Walk-out basement foundation

Special features

The wrap-around country porch is perfect for peaceful evenings

The vaulted great room enjoys a large bay window, stone fireplace, pass-through kitchen and awesome rear views through an atrium window wall

The master bedroom features a double-door entry, walk-in closet and a fabulous bath

Price Code B

First Floor 1,415 sq. ft.

- Atrium
- Dining Area
- Kit 10-2x11-9
- Garage 22-0x11-9
- Great Rm 18-0x21-8 vaulted
- © Copyright by designer/architect
- Laun.
- Entry
- Hall
- Porch
- Br 2 11-4x12-6
- MBr 12-8x15-0
- Shelves
- Vaulted

Lower Level 507 sq. ft.

- Patio
- Family Rm 25-0x21-4
- Unexcavated
- Unfinished Basement

Rear View

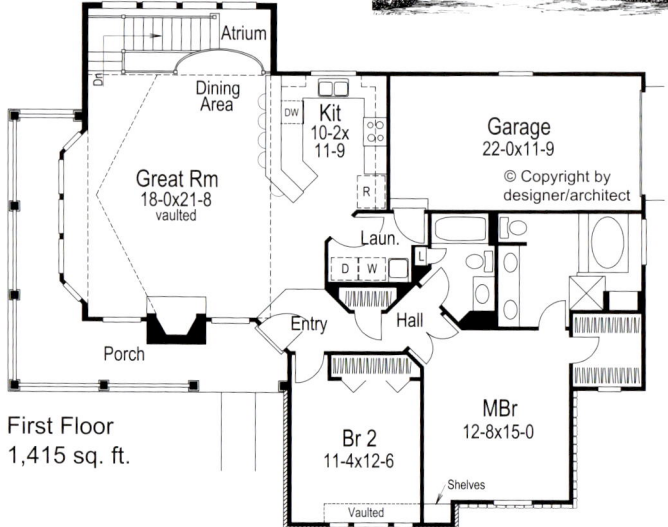

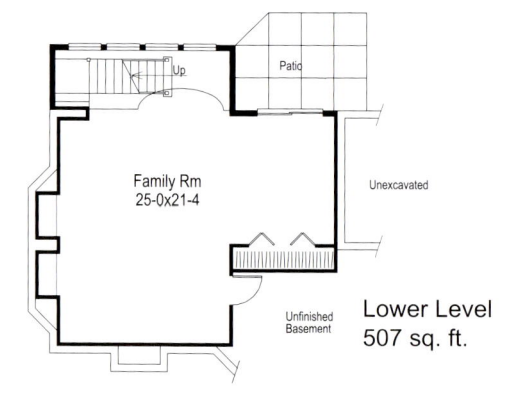

166   To order this plan, visit the Menards Building Materials Desk or visit www.Menards.com.

MENARDS

Breezewood

Plan #M09-008D-0134

Rustic Haven

1,275 total square feet of living area

Width: 28'-0"   Depth: 32'-0"

4 bedrooms, 2 baths

Basement foundation, drawings also include crawl space and slab foundations

Special features

Wall shingles and a stone veneer fireplace all fashion an irresistible rustic appeal

The living area features a fireplace and opens to an efficient kitchen

Two bedrooms on the second floor share a full bath

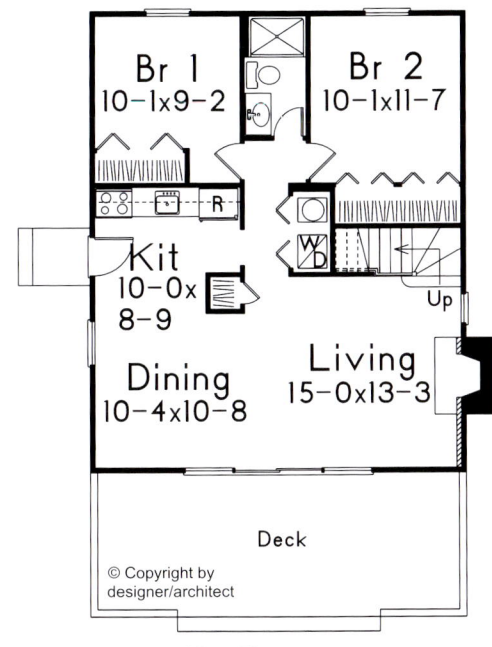

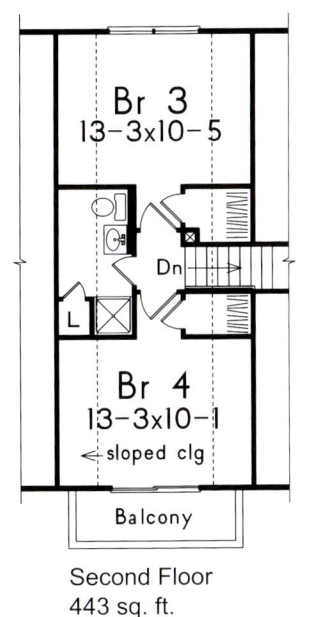

Price Code A

First Floor
832 sq. ft.

- Br 1: 10-1x9-2
- Br 2: 10-1x11-7
- Kit: 10-0x8-9
- Dining: 10-4x10-8
- Living: 15-0x13-3
- Deck

© Copyright by designer/architect

Second Floor
443 sq. ft.

- Br 3: 13-3x10-5
- Br 4: 13-3x10-1 ←sloped clg
- Balcony

To order this plan, visit the Menards Building Materials Desk or visit www.Menards.com.

Carroll

MENARDS

Plan #M09-013L-0049

Brick And Planter Boxes Decorate Front

1,944 total square feet of living area

Width: 52'-0"   Depth: 40'-4"

4 bedrooms, 3 baths

3-car side entry garage

Basement foundation

Special features

The kitchen opens to the nook and dining room for easy meal access

The combined pantry and laundry room connect the home to the garage and the workshop

The large master suite has a spacious closet with plenty of room to hang clothes as well as store linens

The sunny guest bedroom with large closet and full bath creates a welcoming room for visitors

Price Code C

Second Floor 925 sq. ft.
- MASTER SUITE 20'-0" x 15'-0" Tray Ceiling
- BONUS PLAYROOM/MEDIA ROOM 21'-3" x 11'-6" 263 Sq. Ft.
- BEDROOM 3 11'-0" x 13'-0"
- BEDROOM 2 14'-0" x 11'-0"

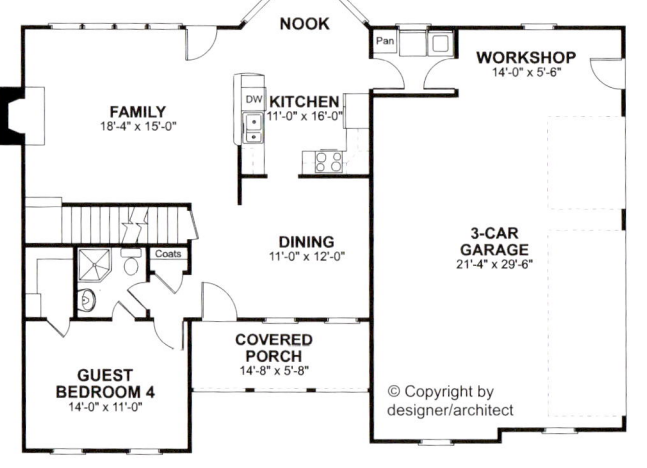

First Floor 1,019 sq. ft.
- NOOK
- FAMILY 18'-4" x 15'-0"
- KITCHEN 11'-0" x 16'-0"
- WORKSHOP 14'-0" x 5'-6"
- DINING 11'-0" x 12'-0"
- 3-CAR GARAGE 21'-4" x 29'-6"
- COVERED PORCH 14'-8" x 5'-8"
- GUEST BEDROOM 4 14'-0" x 11'-0"

© Copyright by designer/architect

To order this plan, visit the Menards Building Materials Desk or visit www.Menards.com

MENARDS

Siminridge

Plan #M09-007D-0087

Compact Home For Sloping Lot

1,332 total square feet of living area

Width: 30'-6"   Depth: 40'-0"

3 bedrooms, 2 baths

4-car tandem drive under garage

Walk-out basement foundation

Special features

This home offers both basement and first floor entry locations

The living room features a vaulted ceiling, fireplace, exterior balcony and dining area

An L-shaped kitchen offers cabinetry, a bayed breakfast area, and patio access

2" x 6" exterior wall framing available for an additional fee, please specify when ordering

Price Code A

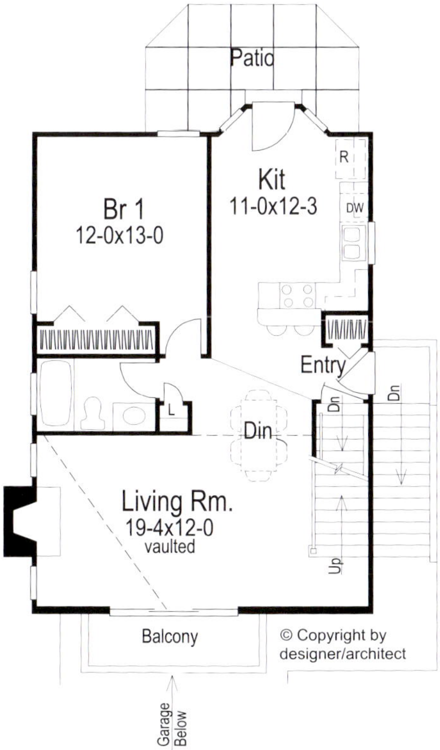

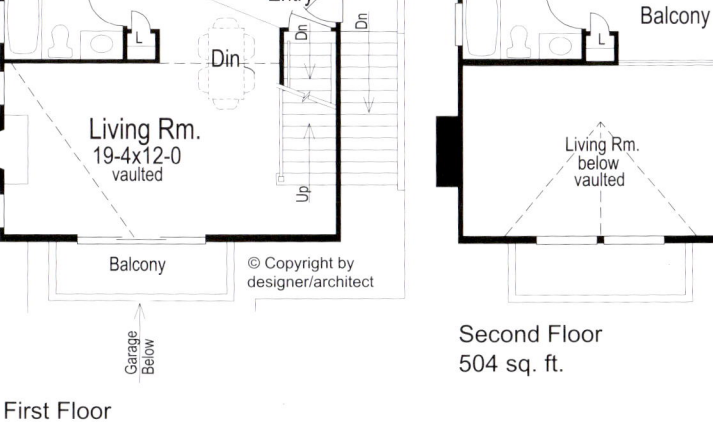

First Floor
828 sq. ft.

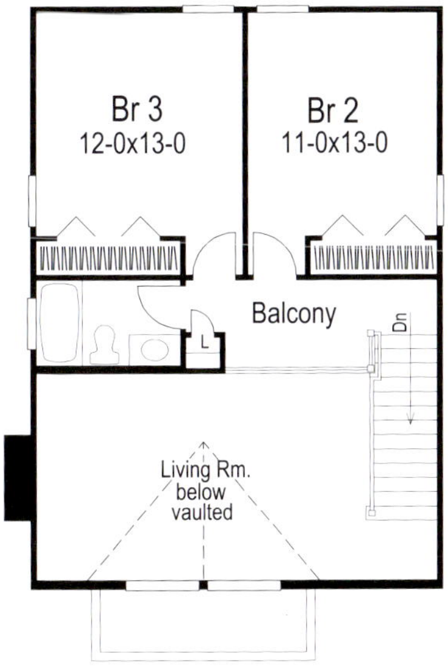

Second Floor
504 sq. ft.

Rear View

To order this plan, visit the Menards Building Materials Desk or visit www.Menards.com.

Skyliner

MENARDS

Plan #M09-008D-0151

A Home Designed For Hillside Views

1,806 total square feet of living area

Width: 28'-0"   Depth: 40'-0"

3 bedrooms, 2 baths

Walk-out basement foundation

Special features

The wrap-around deck, great for entertaining, enhances this home's appearance

The side entry foyer accesses two rear bedrooms, a hall bath, and the living and dining areas

The L-shaped kitchen is open to the dining area

Lots of living area is provided on the lower level, including a spacious family room with a fireplace, and sliding doors to the patio under the deck

The future room on the lower level has an additional 322 square feet of living area

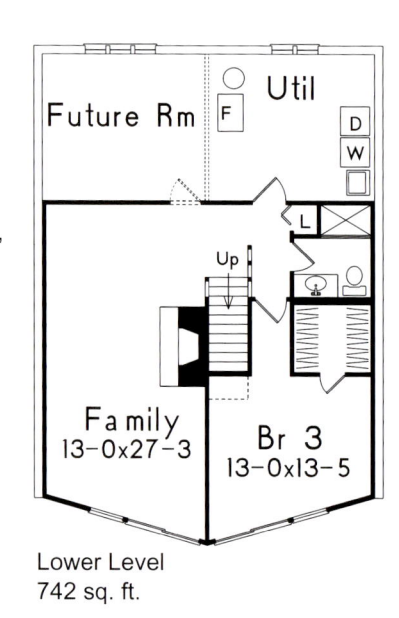

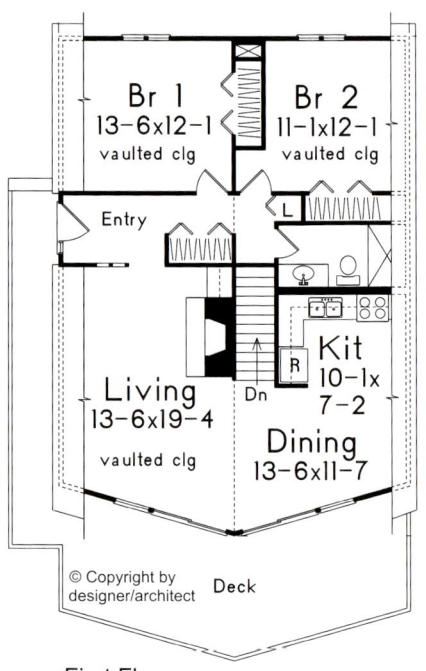

Price Code C

Lower Level
742 sq. ft.

- Future Rm
- Util
- Family 13-0x27-3
- Br 3 13-0x13-5

First Floor
1,064 sq. ft.

- Br 1 13-6x12-1 vaulted clg
- Br 2 11-1x12-1 vaulted clg
- Entry
- Living 13-6x19-4 vaulted clg
- Kit 10-1x 7-2
- Dining 13-6x11-7
- Deck

© Copyright by designer/architect

170

To order this plan, visit the Menards Building Materials Desk or visit www.menards.com.

MENARDS

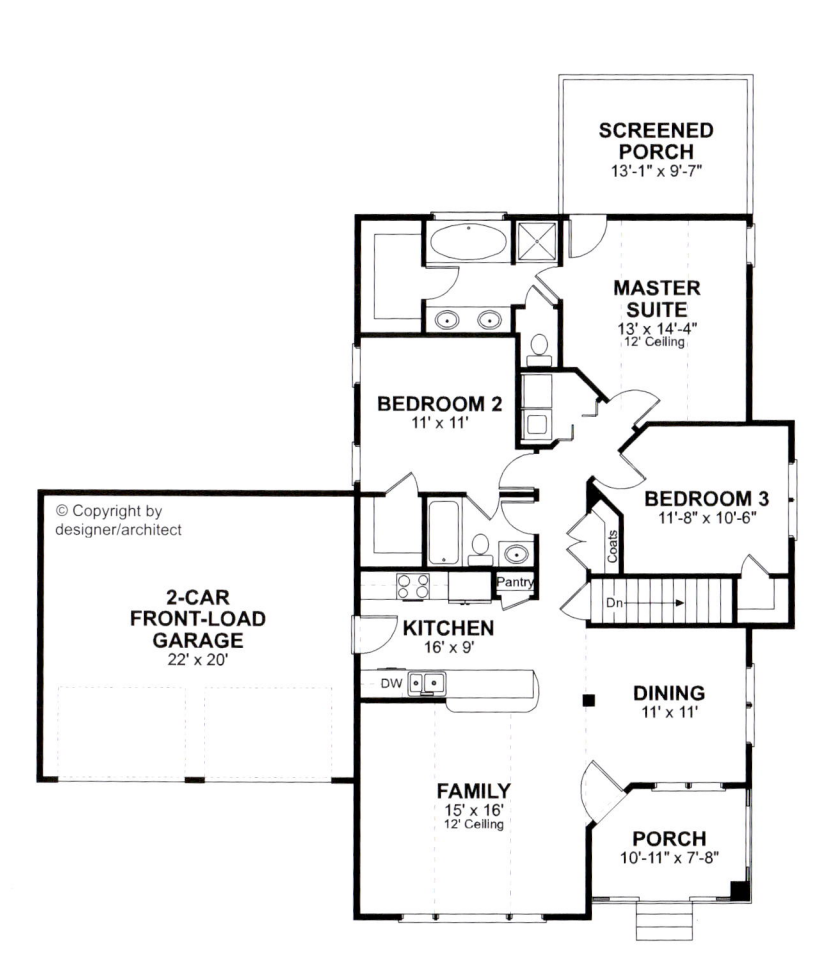

Newton

Plan #M09-013L-0043

A Lovely Layout For Casual Family Living

1,343 total square feet of living area

Width: 50'-0"   Depth: 60'-0"

3 bedrooms, 2 baths

2-car garage

Basement or slab foundation, please specify when ordering

Special features

A large front window and a high ceiling create an open family room

The kitchen has plenty of counterspace for dining and preparing food

A screened porch is connected to the master suite for an open air feel

The laundry room is centrally located between all of the bedrooms

Price Code B

SCREENED PORCH 13'-1" x 9'-7"

MASTER SUITE 13' x 14'-4" 12' Ceiling

BEDROOM 2 11' x 11'

© Copyright by designer/architect

2-CAR FRONT-LOAD GARAGE 22' x 20'

BEDROOM 3 11'-8" x 10'-6"

KITCHEN 16' x 9'

DINING 11' x 11'

FAMILY 15' x 16' 12' Ceiling

PORCH 10'-11" x 7'-8"

To order this plan, visit the Menards Building Materials Desk or visit www.Menards.com.

Stonetrail

MENARDS

Plan #M09-007D-0189

Apartment Garage Plus RV Storage

713 total square feet of living area

Width: 38'-8"   Depth: 42'-4"

1 bedroom, 1 1/2 baths

2-car garage, RV garage

Slab foundation

Special features

The living room features a bayed dining area and a separate entry with access to the garage, and staircase to the second floor

An efficient L-shaped kitchen has a view to the rear yard and a built-in pantry

The second floor offers a large bedroom with alcove for a desk, walk-in closet and a private bath off the hall

Price Code AAA

Rear View

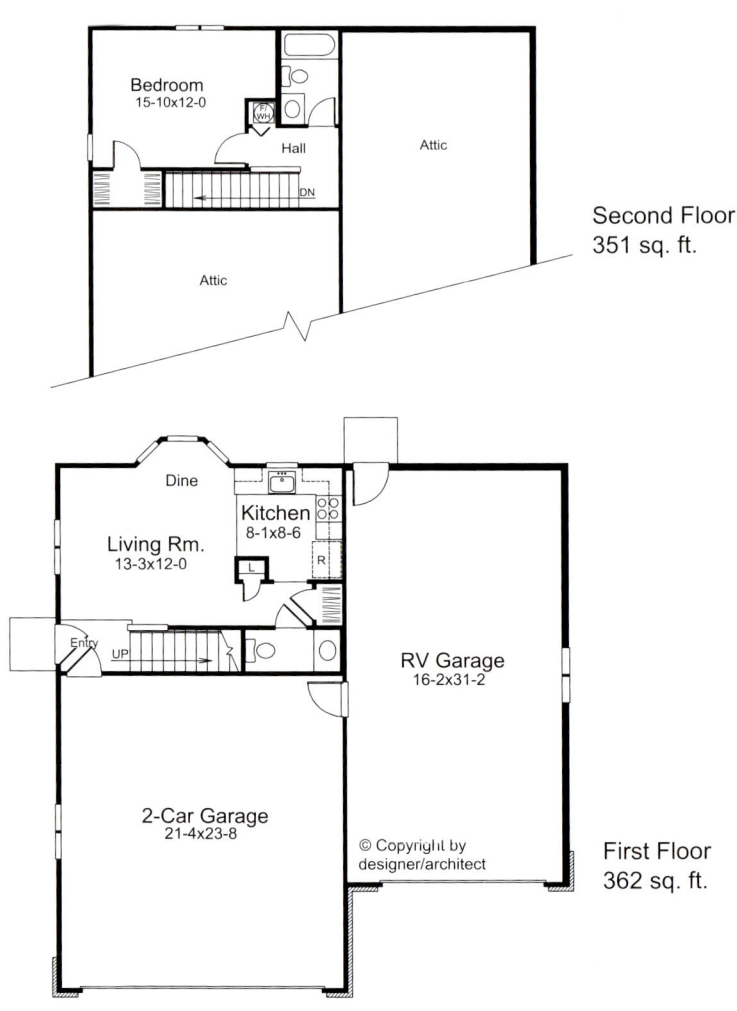

Bedroom 15-10x12-0
Hall
Attic
Attic
Second Floor 351 sq. ft.

Dine
Kitchen 8-1x8-6
Living Rm. 13-3x12-0
Entry
UP
RV Garage 16-2x31-2
2-Car Garage 21-4x23-8
© Copyright by designer/architect
First Floor 362 sq. ft.

To order this plan, visit the Menards Building Materials Desk or visit www.Menards.com

MENARDS

Hatteras 1

Plan #M09-001D-0055

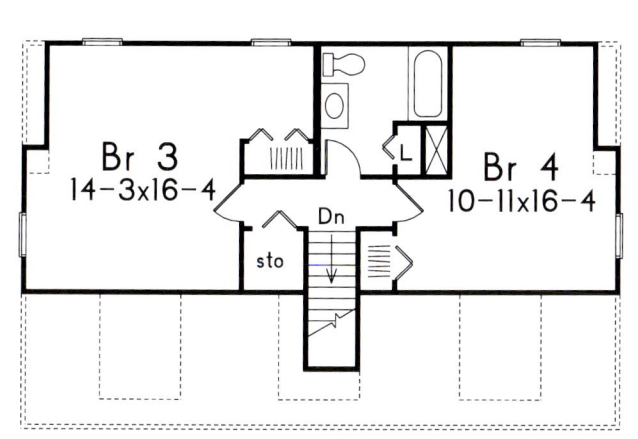

Second Floor
665 sq. ft.

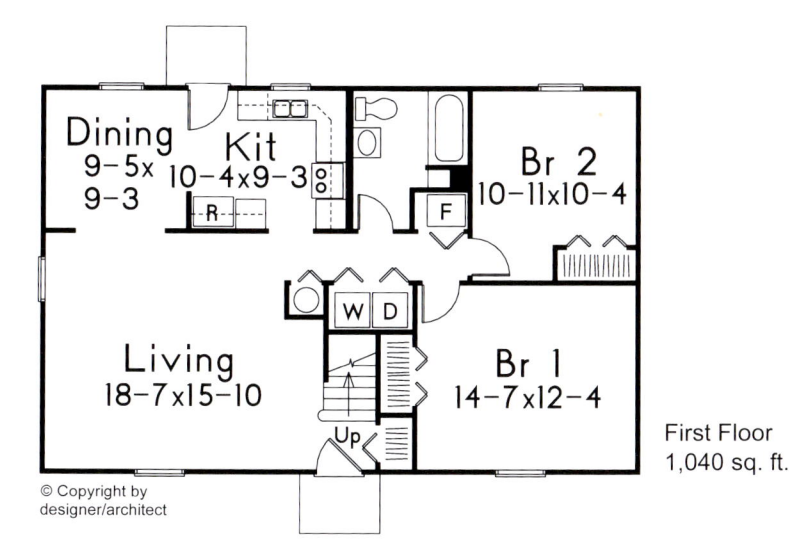

First Floor
1,040 sq. ft.

Br 3
14-3x16-4

Br 4
10-11x16-4

Dining
9-5x 9-3

Kit
10-4x9-3

Br 2
10-11x10-4

Living
18-7x15-10

Br 1
14-7x12-4

© Copyright by designer/architect

Plenty Of Room For A Growing Family

1,705 total square feet of living area

Width: 40'-0"   Depth: 26'-0"

4 bedrooms, 2 baths

Crawl space foundation, drawings also include basement and slab foundations

Special features

There are two bedrooms on the first floor for convenience and two bedrooms on the second floor for privacy

The L-shaped kitchen is adjacent to the dining room

2" x 6" exterior wall framing available for an additional fee, please specify when ordering

Price Code B

Rear View

To order this plan, visit the Menards Building Materials Desk or visit www.Menards.com.

Barrett Hill

MENARDS

Plan #M09-058D-0013

Comfortable Vacation Retreat

1,073 total square feet of living area

Width: 43'-0"   Depth: 34'-0"

2 bedrooms, 1 bath

Crawl space foundation

Special features

This home includes a lovely covered front porch and a screened porch off the dining area

An attractive box window brightens the kitchen

Space for an efficiency washer and dryer is located conveniently between the bedrooms

The family room includes a fireplace with flanking bookshelves and a spacious vaulted ceiling

Price Code AA

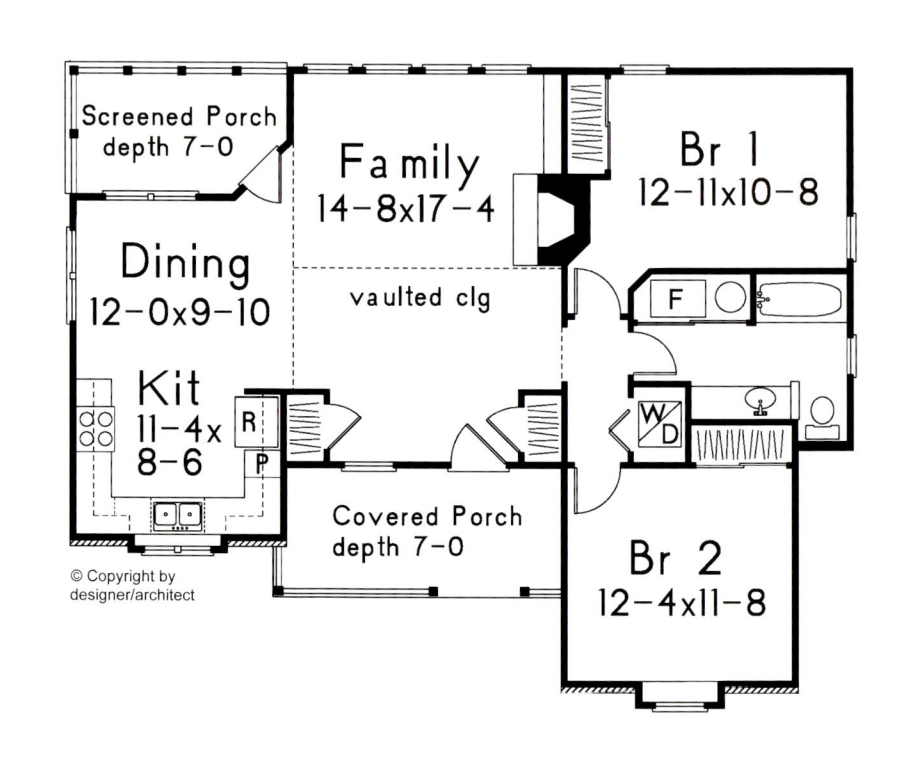

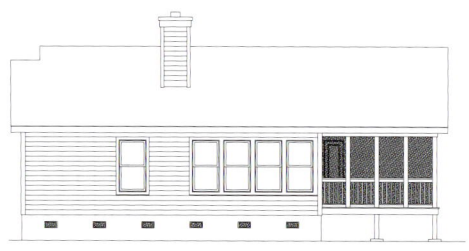

Rear View

174   To order this plan, visit the Menards Building Materials Desk or visit www.Menards.com

MENARDS

Pineview

Plan #M09-001D-0018

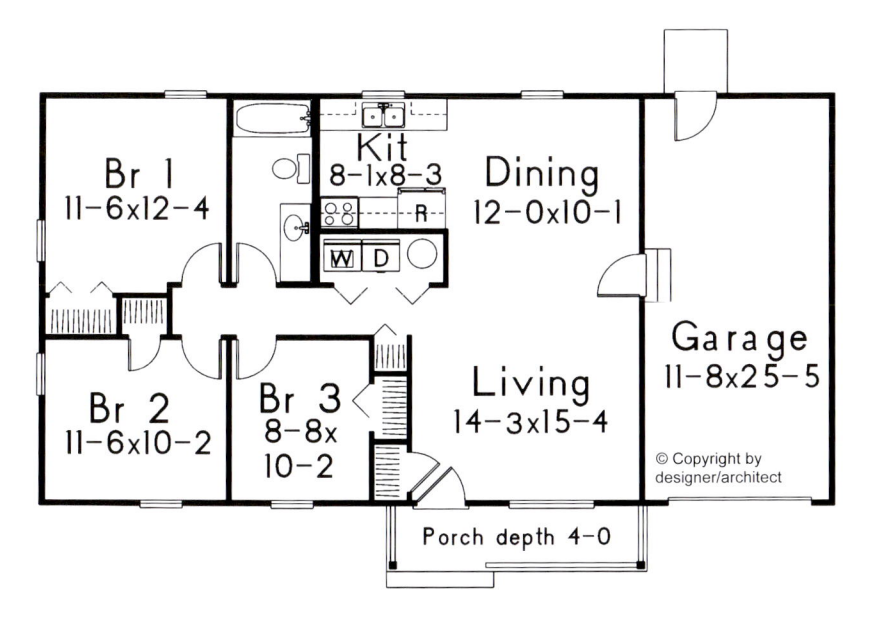

Front Porch And Center Gable Add Style To This Ranch

988 total square feet of living area

Width: 50'-0"   Depth: 30'-0"

3 bedrooms, 1 bath

1-car garage

Basement foundation, drawings also include crawl space foundation

Special features

This home has a pleasant covered front porch entry

The kitchen, living and dining areas are combined to maximize space

The entry has a convenient coat closet

The laundry closet is located adjacent to the bedrooms for convenience

Price Code AA

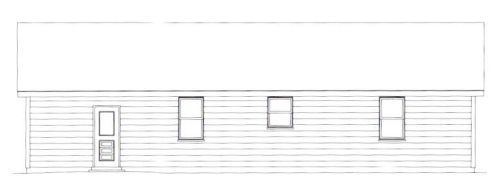

Br 1 11-6x12-4
Kit 8-1x8-3
Dining 12-0x10-1
Br 2 11-6x10-2
Br 3 8-8x10-2
Living 14-3x15-4
Garage 11-8x25-5
Porch depth 4-0

© Copyright by designer/architect

Rear View

To order this plan, visit the Menards Building Materials Desk or visit www.Menards.com.

Sabrina

MENARDS

Plan #M09-017D-0007

Pillared Front Porch Generates Charm And Warmth

1,567 total square feet of living area

Width: 67'-6"   Depth: 46'-8"

3 bedrooms, 2 baths

2-car side entry garage

Partial basement/crawl space foundation, drawings also include slab foundation

Special features

Energy efficient home with 2" x 6" exterior walls

The cheerful, windowed dining area has terrace access

The master bedroom is separated for privacy

The future area available on the second floor has an additional 338 square feet of living area

Price Code C

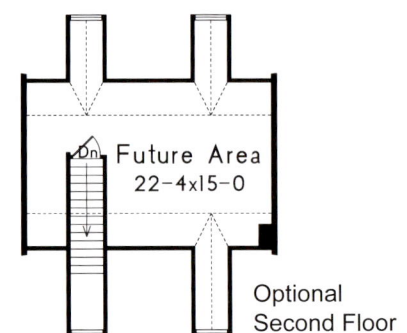

Rear View

Future Area 22-4x15-0

Optional Second Floor

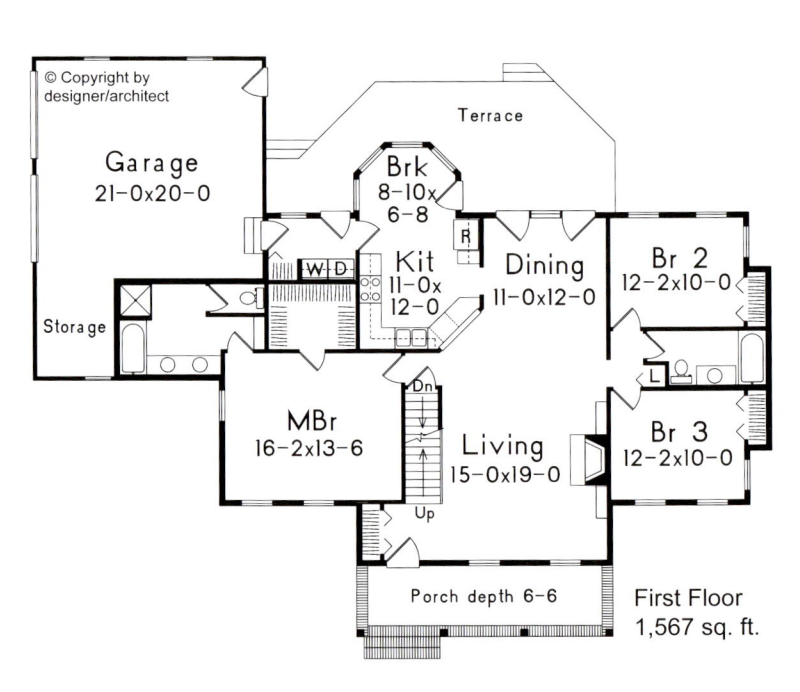

© Copyright by designer/architect

Terrace

Garage 21-0x20-0

Brk 8-10x 6-8

Kit 11-0x 12-0

Dining 11-0x12-0

Br 2 12-2x10-0

Storage

MBr 16-2x13-6

Living 15-0x19-0

Br 3 12-2x10-0

Porch depth 6-6

First Floor 1,567 sq. ft.

To order this plan, visit the Menards Building Materials Desk or visit www.Menards.com

MENARDS

Stonegate Manor

Plan #M09-007D-0137

Country Lodge With Screened Porch And Fireplace

1,568 total square feet of living area

Width: 72'-8" Depth: 44'-4"

2 bedrooms, 2 baths

3-car side entry garage

Crawl space foundation

Special features

The lodge-like vaulted great room features a stone fireplace, a step-up entrance foyer, and opens to a huge screened porch

The kitchen has an island and peninsula, a convenient laundry area, and adjoins a spacious dining area that leads to a screened porch and rear patio

The master bedroom has two walk-in closets, a luxury bath and access to the screened porch and patio

Price Code B

Rear View

To order this plan, visit the Menards Building Materials Desk or visit www.Menards.com.

WAKEFIELD Forest

MENARDS

Plan #M09-077L-0001

Gables Add Warmth To Exterior

1,638 total square feet of living area

Width: 72'-10"   Depth: 41'-0"

3 bedrooms, 2 baths

2-car side entry garage

Basement, crawl space or slab foundation, please specify when ordering

Special features

The great room features a fireplace with flanking doors that access the covered porch

The centrally located kitchen serves the breakfast and dining areas with ease

There is plenty of storage space located in the garage

Price Code E

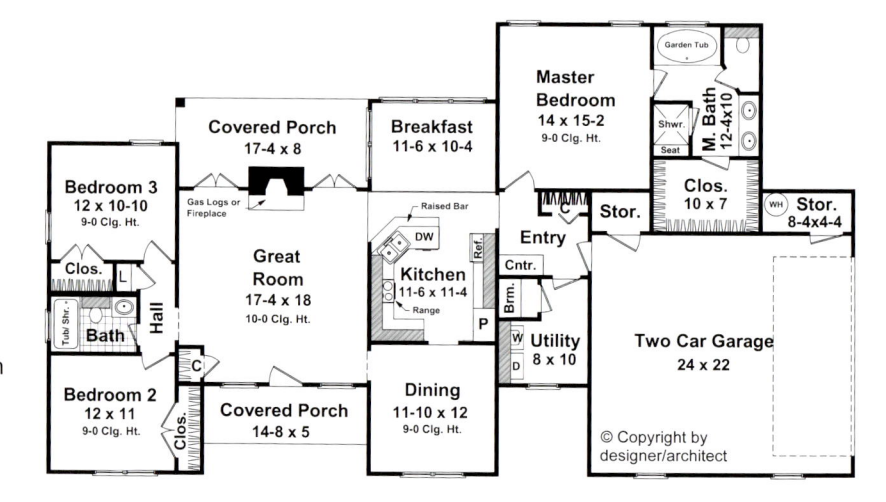

Master Bedroom 14 x 15-2, 9-0 Clg. Ht.
M. Bath 12-4x10, Garden Tub, Shwr. Seat
Clos. 10 x 7
Stor. 8-4x4-4
Covered Porch 17-4 x 8, Gas Logs or Fireplace
Breakfast 11-6 x 10-4
Bedroom 3 12 x 10-10, 9-0 Clg. Ht.
Great Room 17-4 x 18, 10-0 Clg. Ht.
Kitchen 11-6 x 11-4, Raised Bar
Entry
Utility 8 x 10
Two Car Garage 24 x 22
Bedroom 2 12 x 11, 9-0 Clg. Ht.
Covered Porch 14-8 x 5
Dining 11-10 x 12, 9-0 Clg. Ht.

© Copyright by designer/architect

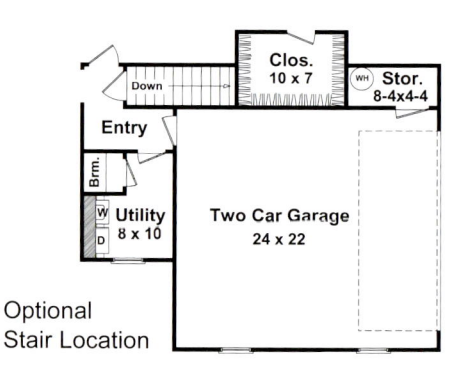

Optional Stair Location
Clos. 10 x 7
Stor. 8-4x4-4
Entry
Utility 8 x 10
Two Car Garage 24 x 22

To order this plan, visit the Menards Building Materials Desk or visit www.Menards.com

MENARDS

Burlington 1

Plan #M09-001D-0072

Peaceful Shaded Front Porch

1,288 total square feet of living area

Width: 46'-0"   Depth: 32'-0"

3 bedrooms, 2 baths

Crawl space foundation, drawings also include basement and slab foundations

Special features

The kitchen, dining area, and great room join to create an open living space

The master bedroom includes a private bath

The secondary bedrooms enjoy ample closet space

The hall bath features a convenient laundry closet

The dining room accesses the outdoors, perfect when grilling

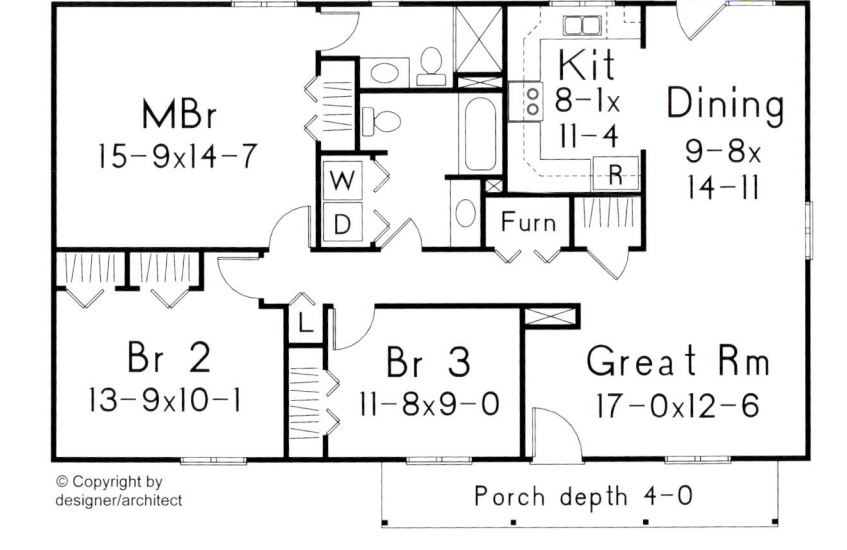

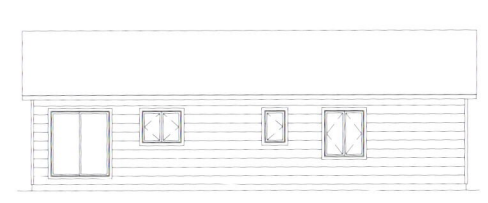

Price Code A

MBr 15-9x14-7

Kit 8-1x 11-4

Dining 9-8x 14-11

Br 2 13-9x10-1

Br 3 11-8x9-0

Great Rm 17-0x12-6

Porch depth 4-0

© Copyright by designer/architect

Rear View

To order this plan, visit the Menards Building Materials Desk or visit www.Menards.com.

Paige

MENARDS

Plan #M09-121D-0016

Charming Country Cottage

1,582 total square feet of living area

Width: 42'-4"   Depth: 54'-0"

3 bedrooms, 2 baths

2-car detached garage

Basement foundation

Special features

The wrap-around covered front porch is perfect for relaxing and enjoying the outdoors

Vaulted ceilings throughout this home provide an open and airy atmosphere

The kitchen boasts a large walk-in pantry and ample counterspace with an eating bar for convenient meals

Price Code A

Detached Garage
23-4x23-4

© Copyright by designer/architect

Patio

MBr
13-8x15-0
Std Coffer
Opt Vault

Dining/ Brkfst
13-6x13-4
Vaulted

Kit
10-7x13-4
Vaulted

Br 2
10-0x10-6

Great Rm
17-8x17-8
Vaulted

Entry

Br 3
13-8x11-8

Porch

Rear View

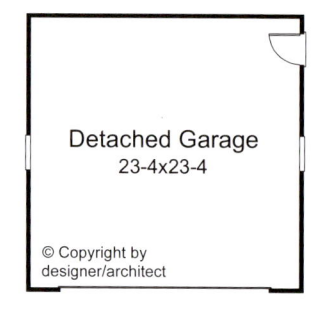

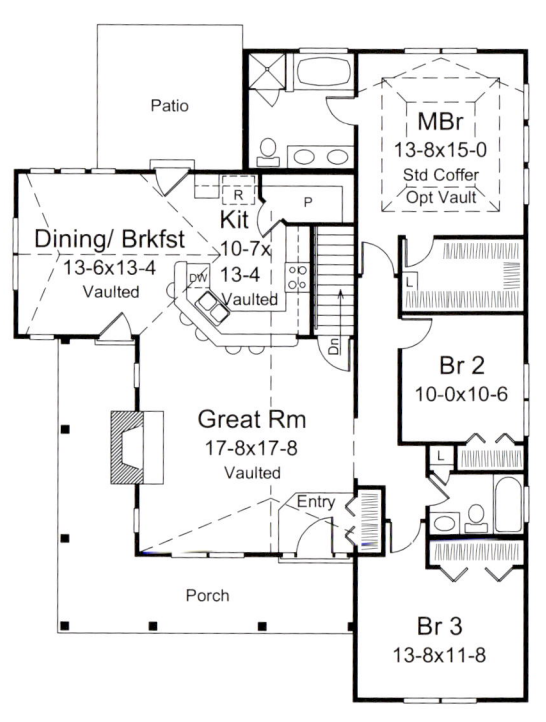

To order this plan, visit the Menards Building Materials Desk or visit www.Menards.com

MENARDS

Albert

Plan #M09-053D-0058

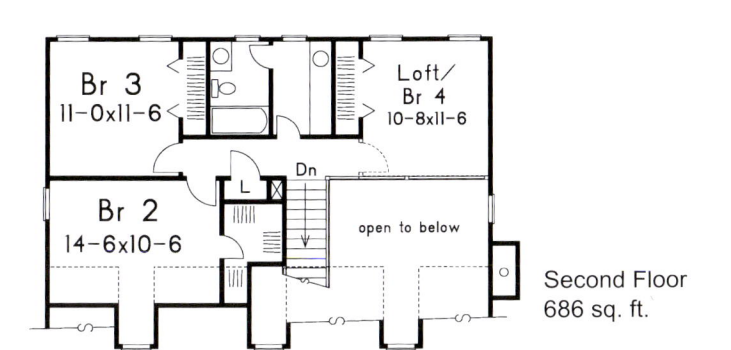

Lovely Country Home

1,818 total square feet of living area

Width: 38'-0"   Depth: 32'-0"

4 bedrooms, 2 1/2 baths

2-car drive under side entry garage

Walk-out basement foundation

Special features

The breakfast room is tucked behind the kitchen and has a laundry closet

The vaulted living room features a fireplace

The master bedroom has two closets, and a bath with a double-bowl vanity and a tub

The lower level has an additional 599 square feet of living area

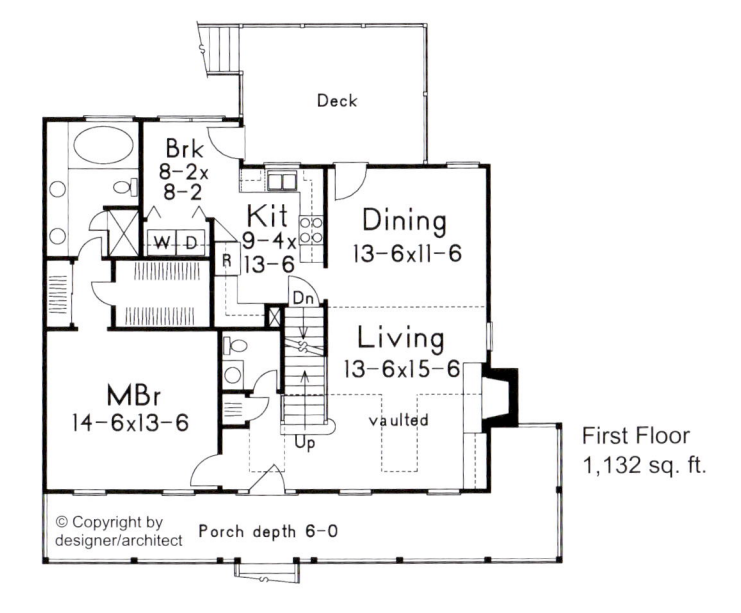

Price Code A

Second Floor 686 sq. ft.

- Br 3: 11-0x11-6
- Br 2: 14-6x10-6
- Loft/Br 4: 10-8x11-6

First Floor 1,132 sq. ft.

- Brk: 8-2x8-2
- Kit: 9-4x13-6
- Dining: 13-6x11-6
- Living: 13-6x15-6 vaulted
- MBr: 14-6x13-6

Porch depth 6-0

© Copyright by designer/architect

Rear View

To order this plan, visit the Menards Building Materials Desk or visit www.Menards.com.

Bogart

MENARDS

Plan #M09-013L-0156

Angled Master Bedroom Suite Adds Interest

1,800 total square feet of living area

Width: 63'-0"   Depth: 73'-0"

3 bedrooms, 3 baths

3-car side entry garage

Crawl space foundation; slab and basement foundations available for an additional fee

Special features

Many lovely window accents are found throughout the home providing a warm glow and plenty of natural light

Highly functional ceiling fans are located in the screen porch, angled master bedroom suite, and the family room

Bedrooms #2 and #3 each contain ample closet space and immediate access to a full bath

The bonus room above the garage has an additional 503 square feet of living space

Price Code B

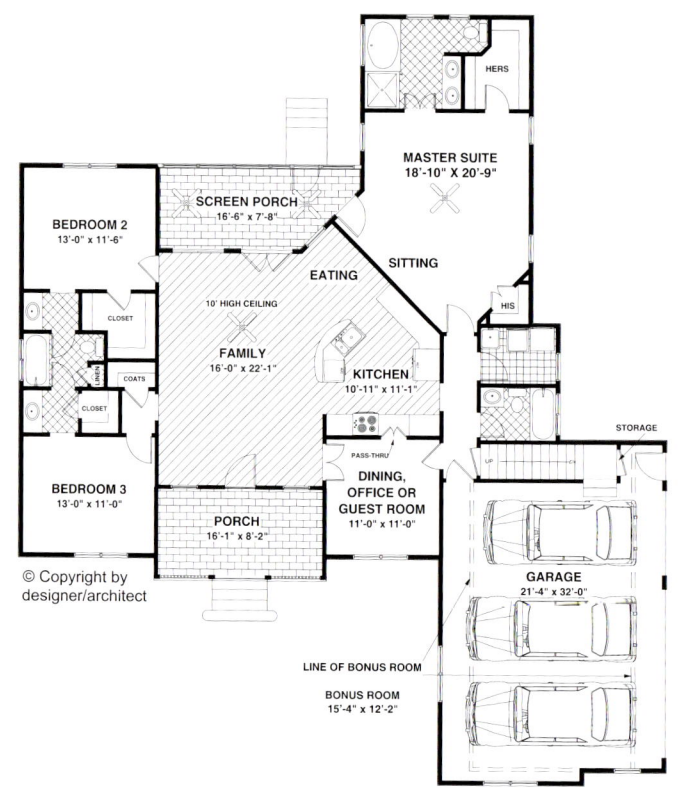

To order this plan, visit the Menards Building Materials Desk or visit www.Menards.com

MENARDS

Caroline

Plan #M09-068D-0006

Second Floor 667 sq. ft.

- Br 2: 10-0x10-0 vaulted clg
- Br 3: 10-2x10-0 vaulted clg
- MBr: 17-5x15-1 vaulted clg
- Sitting

First Floor 732 sq. ft.

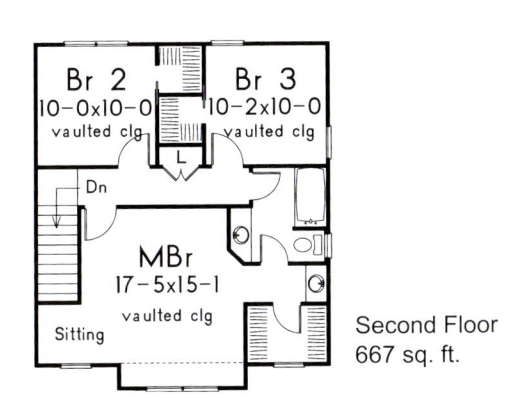

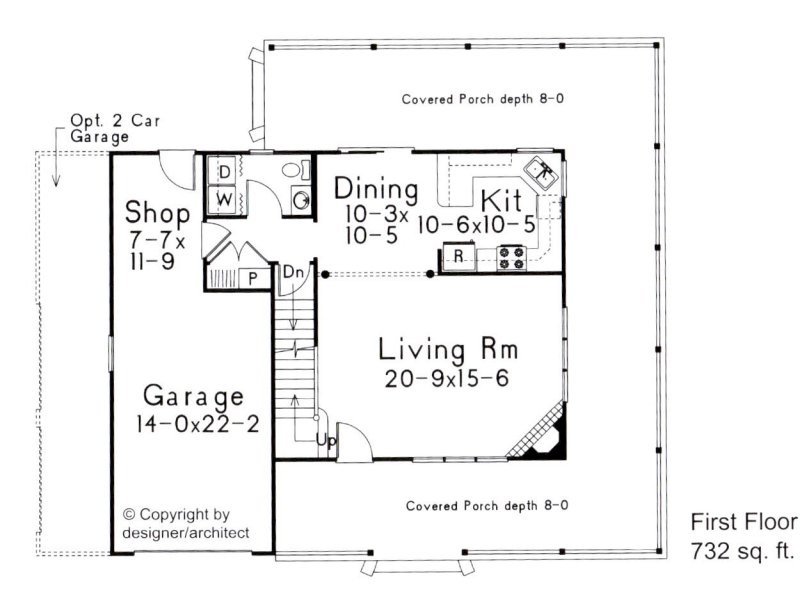

- Opt. 2 Car Garage
- Covered Porch depth 8-0
- Shop: 7-7x11-9
- Dining: 10-3x10-5
- Kit: 10-6x10-5
- Living Rm: 20-9x15-6
- Garage: 14-0x22-2
- Covered Porch depth 8-0

© Copyright by designer/architect

Covered Porch Surrounds Home

1,399 total square feet of living area

Width: 46'-9"   Depth: 43'-6"

3 bedrooms, 1 1/2 baths

1-car garage

Basement foundation, drawings also include crawl space and slab foundations

Special features

The living room overlooks the dining area through arched columns

The laundry room contains a handy half bath

The spacious master bedroom includes a sitting area, a walk-in closet, and plenty of sunlight

Price Code A

Rear View

To order this plan, visit the Menards Building Materials Desk or visit www.Menards.com.

Alpine

MENARDS

Plan #M09-007D-0027

Apartment Garage With Imagination

654 total square feet of living area

Width: 29'-0"   Depth: 27'-6"

1 bedroom, 1 bath

2-car garage

Floating slab foundation

Special features

The two-story vaulted entry has a balcony overlook and large cheerful windows

The vaulted living room is open to a pass-through kitchen and breakfast bar and has access onto an outdoor balcony

The vaulted bedroom has a private bath and walk-in closet

Price Code AAA

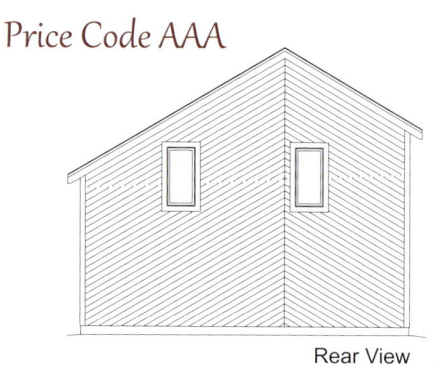

Rear View

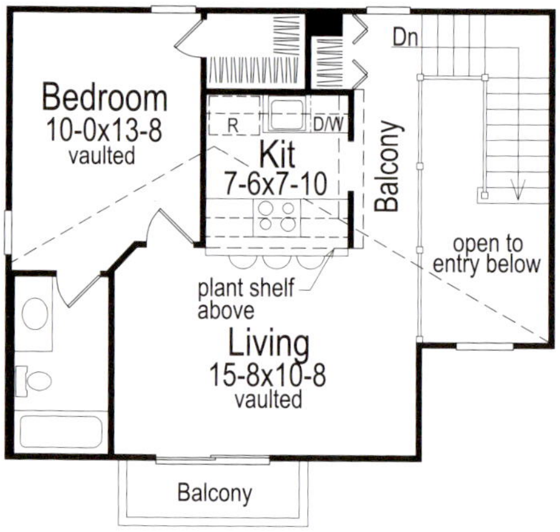

Second Floor 528 sq. ft.
- Bedroom 10-0x13-8 vaulted
- Kit 7-6x7-10
- Living 15-8x10-8 vaulted
- Balcony
- plant shelf above
- open to entry below

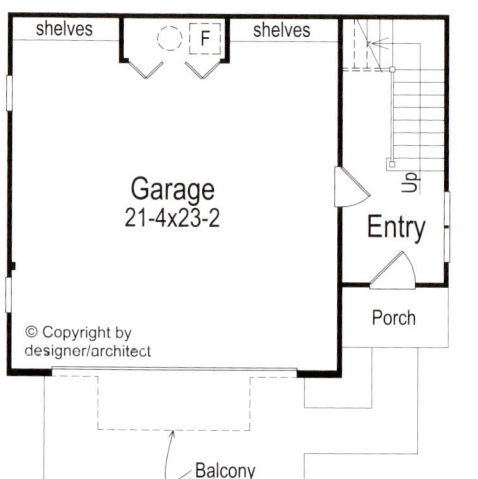

First Floor 126 sq. ft.
- Garage 21-4x23-2
- Entry
- Porch
- Balcony
- © Copyright by designer/architect

To order this plan, visit the Menards Building Materials Desk or visit www.Menards.com.

MENARDS

Highlander

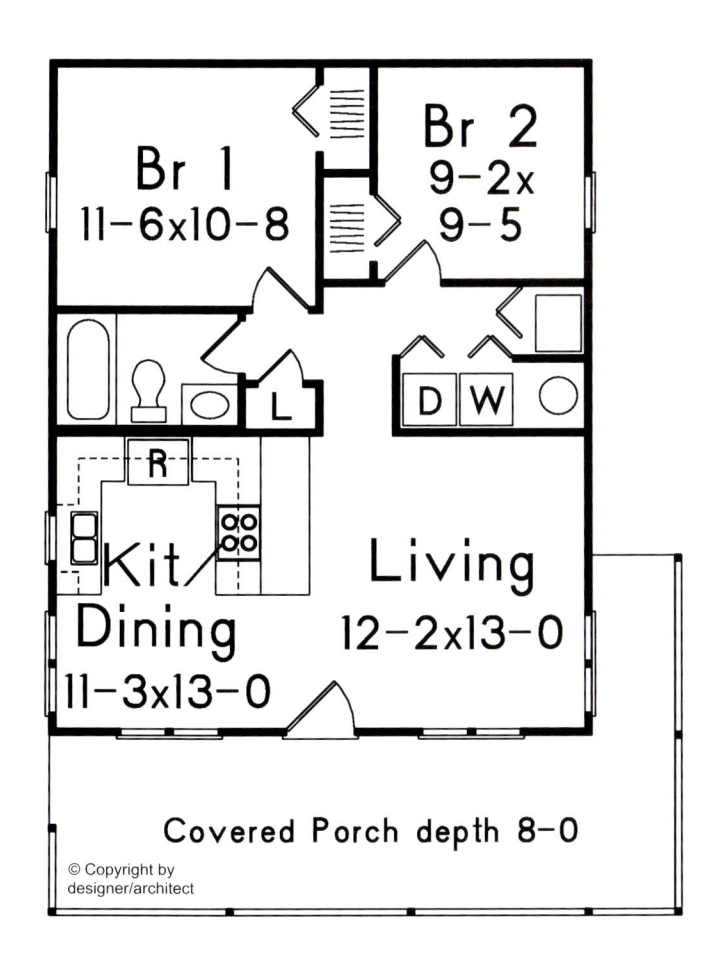

Plan #M09-001D-0085

Designed For Comfort And Utility

720 total square feet of living area

Width: 28'-0"   Depth: 38'-0"

2 bedrooms, 1 bath

Crawl space foundation, drawings also include slab foundation

Special features

Abundant windows in the living and dining rooms provide generous sunlight

The secluded laundry area has a handy storage closet

The U-shaped kitchen with large breakfast bar opens into the living area

The large covered porch offers plenty of outdoor living space

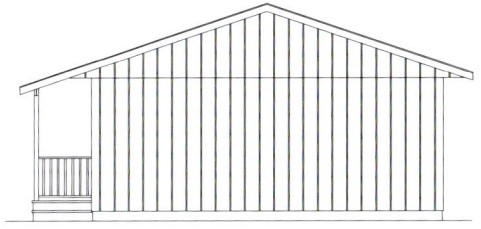

Price Code AAA

Floor plan:
- Br 1: 11-6 x 10-8
- Br 2: 9-2 x 9-5
- Kit/Dining: 11-3 x 13-0
- Living: 12-2 x 13-0
- Covered Porch depth 8-0

© Copyright by designer/architect

Rear View

To order this plan, visit the Menards Building Materials Desk or visit www.Menards.com.

Coburg Manor

MENARDS

Plan #M09-065L-0173

Exciting Two-Story

1,969 total square feet of living area

Width: 58'-0"   Depth: 44'-4"

3 bedrooms, 2 1/2 baths

2-car garage

Basement foundation

Special features

An octagon-shaped tower, a covered porch, arched trim, and a boxed window decorate the exterior

The great room with fireplace, high windows and rear yard access provides an excellent atmosphere for family activities

The dramatic views into the great room and foyer are offered at the second floor balcony where there is ample room for a computer area or reading loft

The second floor bonus room has an additional 268 square feet of living space

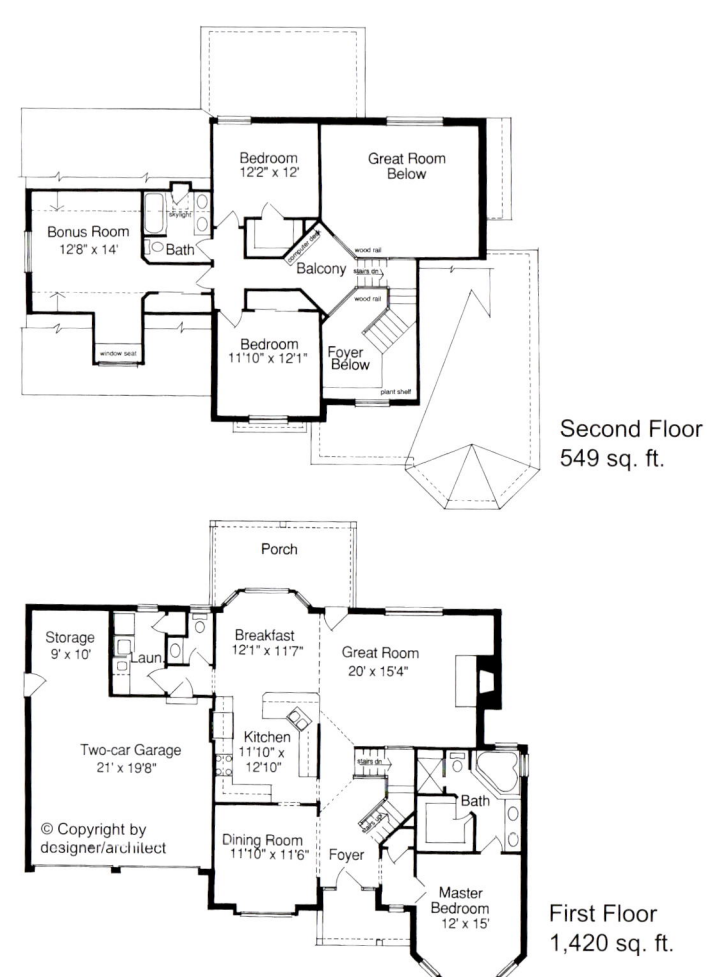

Price Code C

Second Floor 549 sq. ft.

First Floor 1,420 sq. ft.

186 To order this plan, visit the Menards Building Materials Desk or visit www.Menards.com

MENARDS

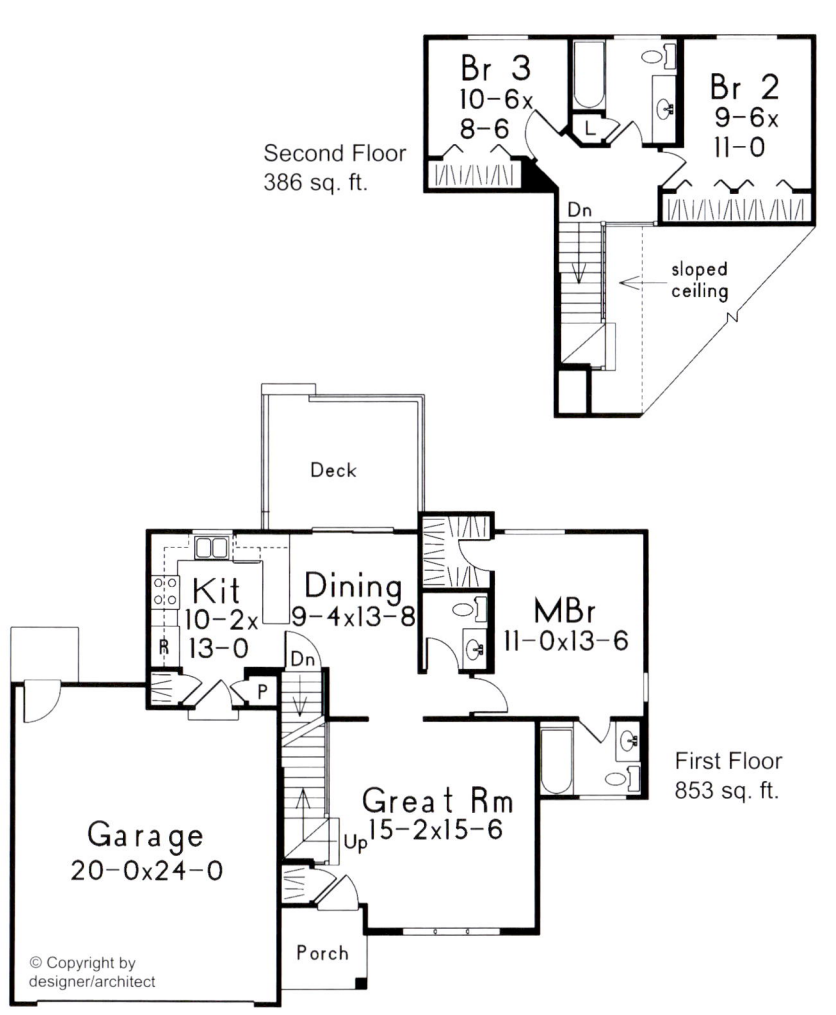

Dover

Plan #M09-041D-0005

Gables Accent This Home

1,239 total square feet of living area

Width: 47'-0"   Depth: 36'-8"

3 bedrooms, 2 1/2 baths

2-car garage

Basement foundation

Special features

The master bedroom has a private bath and a roomy walk-in closet

A convenient coat closet and pantry are located near the garage entrance

The dining area accesses the deck

The stairway with sloped ceiling creates an open atmosphere in the great room

Price Code A

Second Floor 386 sq. ft.

- Br 3 10-6x8-6
- Br 2 9-6x11-0

First Floor 853 sq. ft.

- Kit 10-2x13-0
- Dining 9-4x13-8
- MBr 11-0x13-6
- Great Rm 15-2x15-6
- Garage 20-0x24-0

Rear View

To order this plan, visit the Menards Building Materials Desk or visit www.Menards.com.

Grass Roots 1

MENARDS®

Plan #M09-001D-0041

Open Living Space Creates Comfortable Atmosphere

1,000 total square feet of living area

Width: 40'-0"   Depth: 25'-0"

3 bedrooms, 1 bath

Crawl space foundation, drawings also include basement and slab foundations

Special features

The bathroom includes a convenient closeted laundry area

The master bedroom includes double closets and private access to the bath

The foyer features a handy coat closet

The kitchen/dining area provides easy access outdoors

Price Code AA

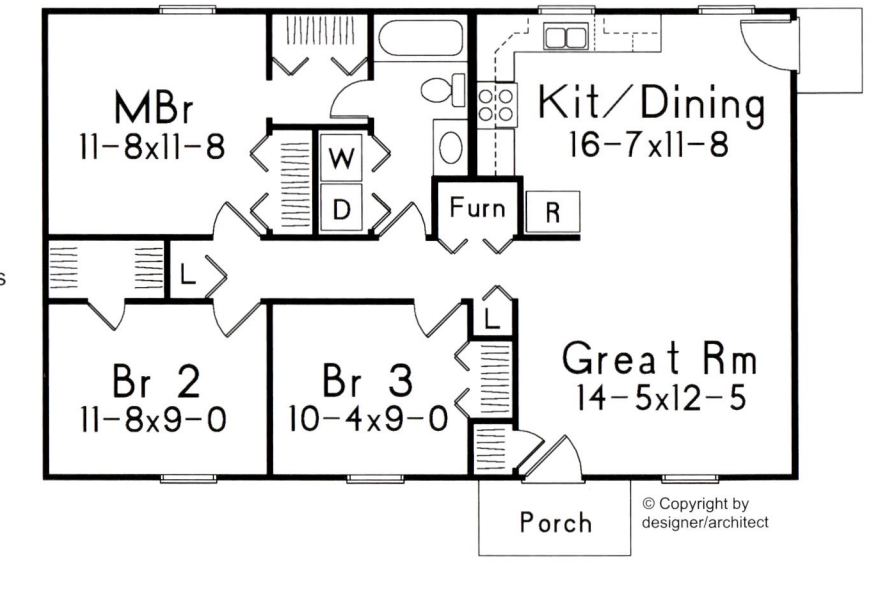

Floor plan:
- MBr 11-8x11-8
- Kit/Dining 16-7x11-8
- Br 2 11-8x9-0
- Br 3 10-4x9-0
- Great Rm 14-5x12-5
- Porch
- Furn
- W/D

© Copyright by designer/architect

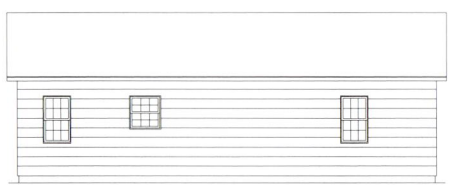

Rear View

188 To order this plan, visit the Menards Building Materials Desk or visit www.Menards.com.

MENARDS

Plan #M09-013L-0001

Open Living Spaces

1,050 total square feet of living area

Width: 36'-0"   Depth: 42'-0"

3 bedrooms, 2 baths

1-car garage

Basement or slab foundation, please specify when ordering

Special features

The master bedroom has its own private bath and access to the outdoors onto a private patio

Vaulted ceilings in the living and dining areas create a feeling of spaciousness

The laundry closet is convenient to all of the bedrooms

An efficient U-shaped kitchen opens to the living and dining areas

Price Code B

To order this plan, visit the Menards Building Materials Desk or visit www.Menards.com

Plan #M09-058D-0058

Window Brightens Living Room

1,865 total square feet of living area

Width: 38'-0"   Depth: 42'-0"

3 bedrooms, 2 1/2 baths

2-car garage

Basement foundation

Special features

The family room, breakfast area and kitchen combine forming a large open area

A double-door entry leads to the grand master bedroom that includes two walk-in closets and a private bath

Bedrooms #2 and #3 enjoy walk-in closets and share a bath

Price Code C

Second Floor 962 sq. ft.

- Br 2: 12-2x12-1
- MBr: 17-5x13-11
- Br 3: 12-1x12-2

First Floor 903 sq. ft.

- Family: 12-1x15-0
- Breakfast: 11-7x14-10
- Kitchen: 11-7x12-10
- Living: 12-1x14-0
- Covered Porch: 16-0x4-0
- Garage: 19-4x19-8

© Copyright by designer/architect

Rear View

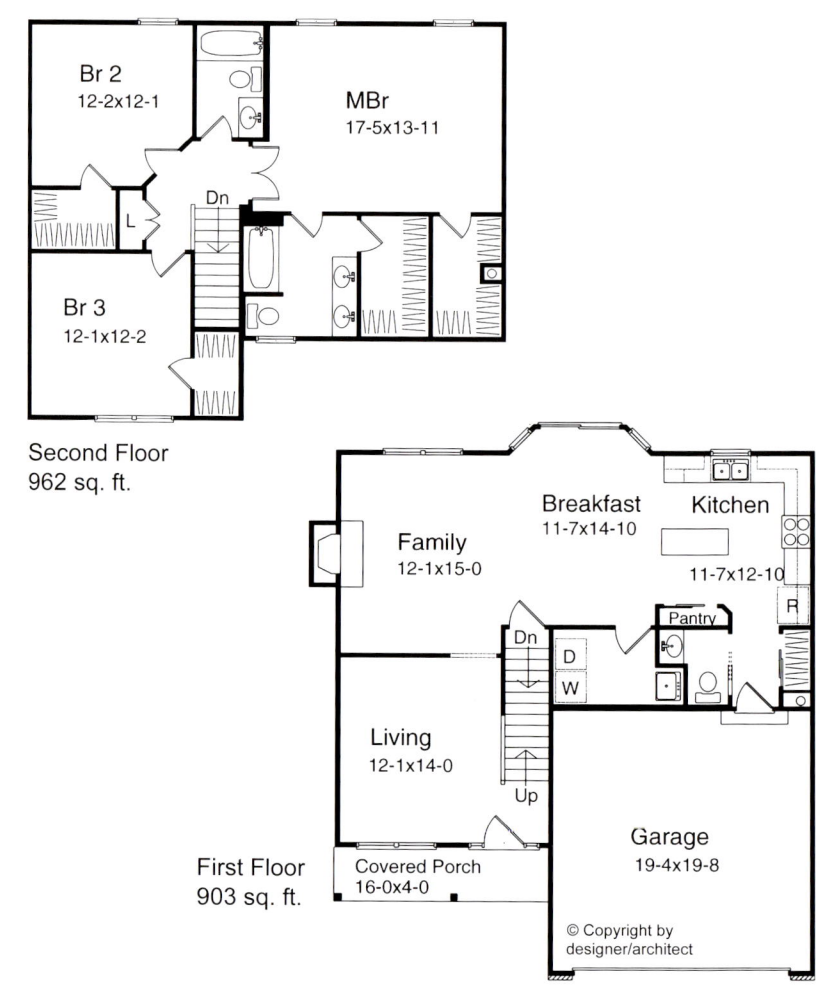

To order this plan, visit the Menards Building Materials Desk or visit www.Menards.com.

MENARDS

Winford

Plan #M09-037D-0012

Sheltered Entrance Opens To Stylish Features

1,661 total square feet of living area

Width: 52'-0"   Depth: 58'-4"

3 bedrooms, 2 baths

2-car garage

Slab foundation

Special features

The large open foyer with angled wall and high ceiling adds to the spacious living room

The kitchen and dining area have impressive cathedral ceilings and a French door allowing access to the rear porch

The secluded master bedroom has a large walk-in closet, unique brick wall arrangement and 10' ceiling

Price Code B

Rear View

To order this plan, visit the Menards Building Materials Desk or visit www.Menards.com.

Hatteras II

Plan #M09-001D-0056

Front Dormers Add Light And Space

1,705 total square feet of living area

Width: 40'-0" Depth: 26'-0"

4 bedrooms, 2 baths

Crawl space foundation, drawings also include basement and slab foundations

Special features

This cozy design includes two bedrooms on the first floor and two bedrooms on the second floor for added privacy

The L-shaped kitchen provides easy access to the dining room and the outdoors

2" x 6" exterior wall framing available for an additional fee, please specify when ordering

Price Code B

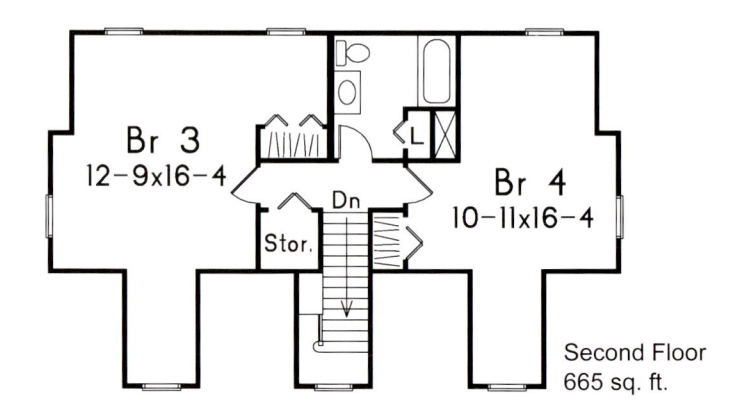

Rear View

Br 3
12-9x16-4

Br 4
10-11x16-4

Stor.

Second Floor
665 sq. ft.

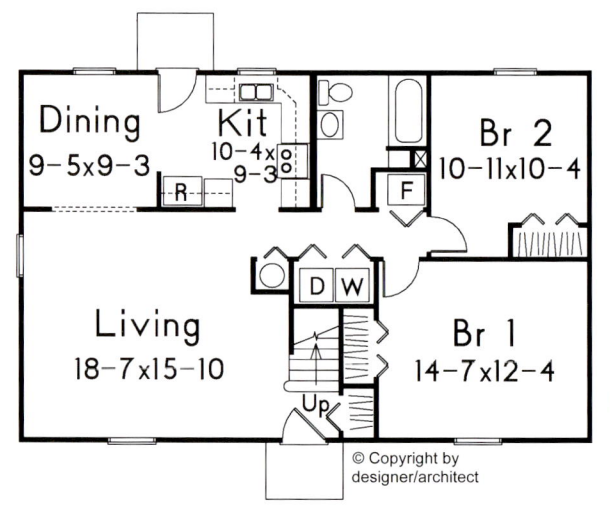

Dining
9-5x9-3

Kit
10-4x9-3

Br 2
10-11x10-4

Living
18-7x15-10

Br 1
14-7x12-4

First Floor
1,040 sq. ft.

© Copyright by designer/architect

To order this plan, visit the Menards Building Materials Desk or visit www.Menards.com

MENARDS

STONINGTON

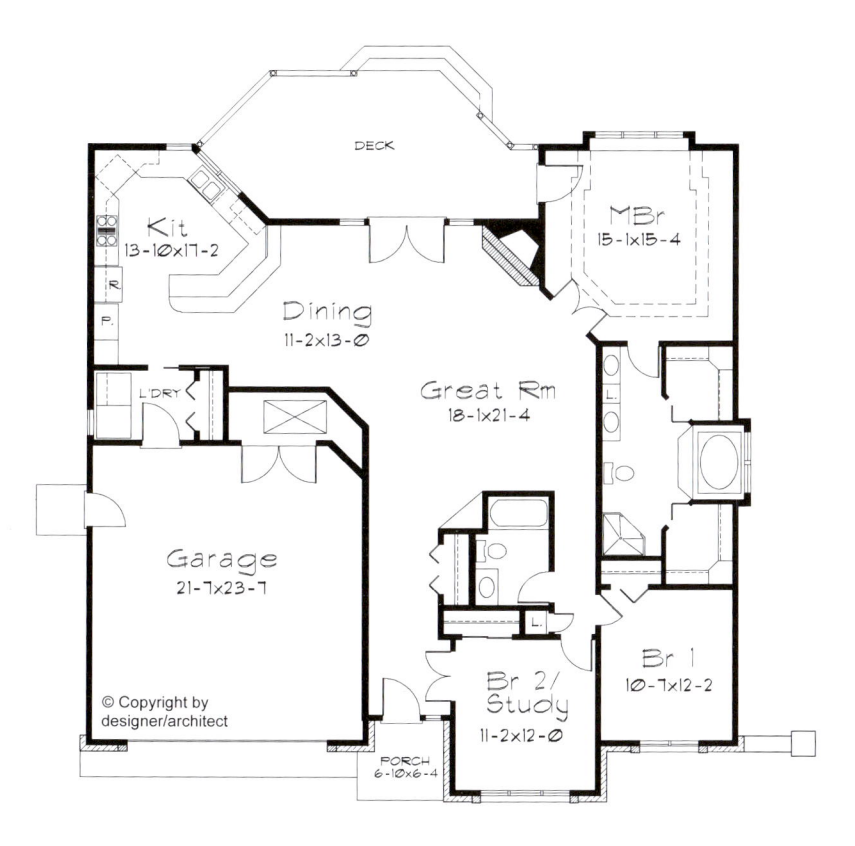

Plan #M09-057D-0019

Stone Decorates Facade

1,838 total square feet of living area

Width: 53'-6"   Depth: 53'-8"

3 bedrooms, 2 baths

2-car garage

Crawl space foundation, drawings also include basement foundation

Special features

Energy efficient home with 2" x 6" exterior walls

The angled great room features a corner fireplace, French doors to the rear deck, and it connects to the dining room for a spacious atmosphere

The wrap-around kitchen counter offers plenty of workspace and room for casual meals

Retreat to the master bedroom where a deluxe bath, walk-in closets, and deck access will pamper the homeowners

Price Code C

To order this plan, visit the Menards Building Materials Desk or visit www.Menards.com.

Holbrook Place

MENARDS

Plan #M09-077L-0081

Open Floor Plan

1,818 total square feet of living area

Width: 63'-4"   Depth: 53'-0"

3 bedrooms, 3 baths

2-car side entry garage

Basement foundation

Special features

Useful and beautiful cabinetry flanks a center fireplace in the vaulted great room

A highly functional screen porch will be enjoyed year round

A corner whirlpool tub highlights the master bath, along with a walk-in closet and a double-bowl vanity

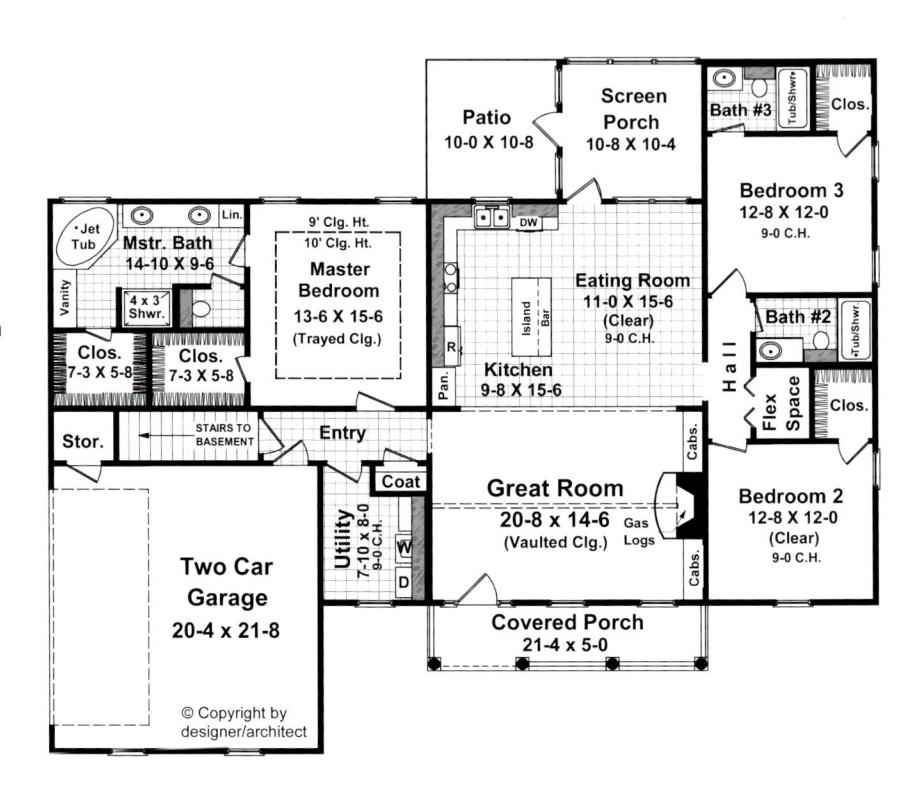

Price Code E

To order this plan, visit the Menards Building Materials Desk or visit www.Menards.com

MENARDS

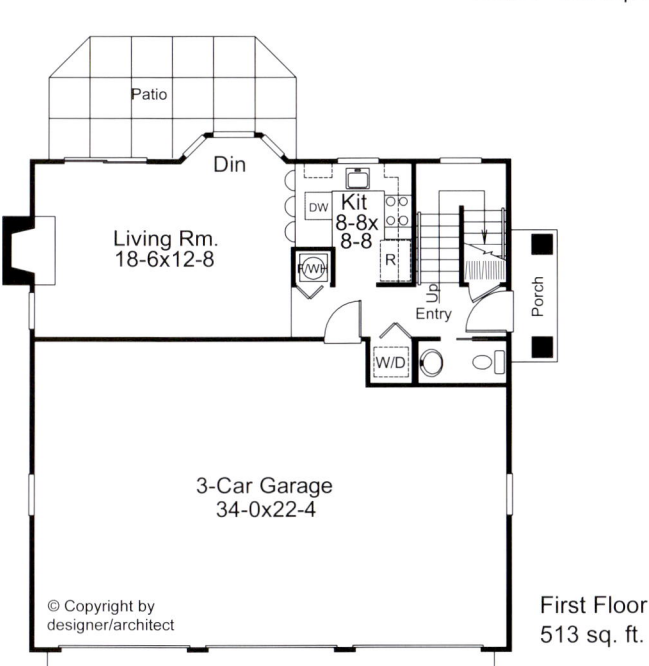

Park House

Plan #M09-007D-0145

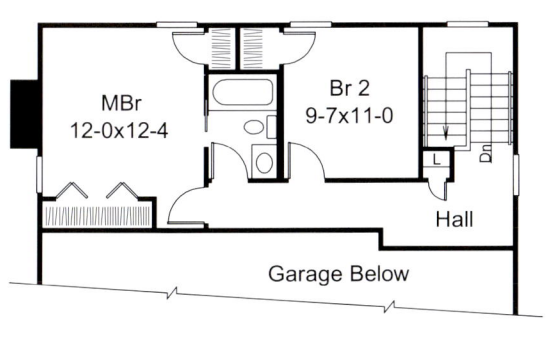

Three-Car Apartment Garage

1,005 total square feet of living area

Width: 40'-0"   Depth: 38'-0"

2 bedrooms, 1 1/2 baths

3-car garage

Slab foundation

Special features

The side porch leads to a hall that accesses the living room, U-shaped kitchen, powder room, and staircase to the second floor

The living room has a fireplace, sliding doors to the patio, a bayed dining area, and opens to the kitchen

The second floor is comprised of two bedrooms and a bath

Price Code AAA

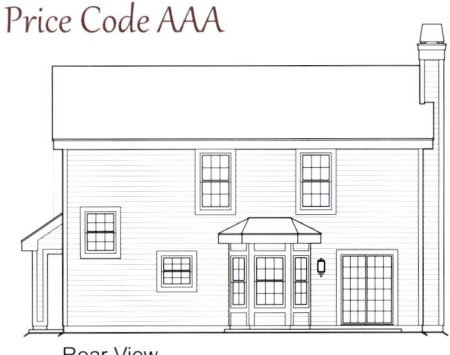

Second Floor 492 sq. ft.
- MBr 12-0x12-4
- Br 2 9-7x11-0
- Hall
- Garage Below

First Floor 513 sq. ft.
- Patio
- Din
- Kit 8-8x8-8
- Living Rm. 18-6x12-8
- Entry
- Porch
- W/D
- 3-Car Garage 34-0x22-4

© Copyright by designer/architect

Rear View

To order this plan, visit the Menards Building Materials Desk or visit www.Menards.com.

195

Cadley

MENARDS

Plan #M09-013L-0136

Lovely Family Area

1,831 total square feet of living area

Width: 50'-0"   Depth: 74'-3"

3 bedrooms, 2 1/2 baths

2-car side entry garage

Slab foundation

Special features

Raised ceilings, arch-top windows, a fireplace, and decorative columns add drama to the combined family and dining rooms

This split-bedroom design offers a master suite complete with a tray ceiling, a plush bath, and sitting area that accesses the screened porch

Two bonus rooms on the second floor offer an additional 798 square feet of living space that can be finished as needed

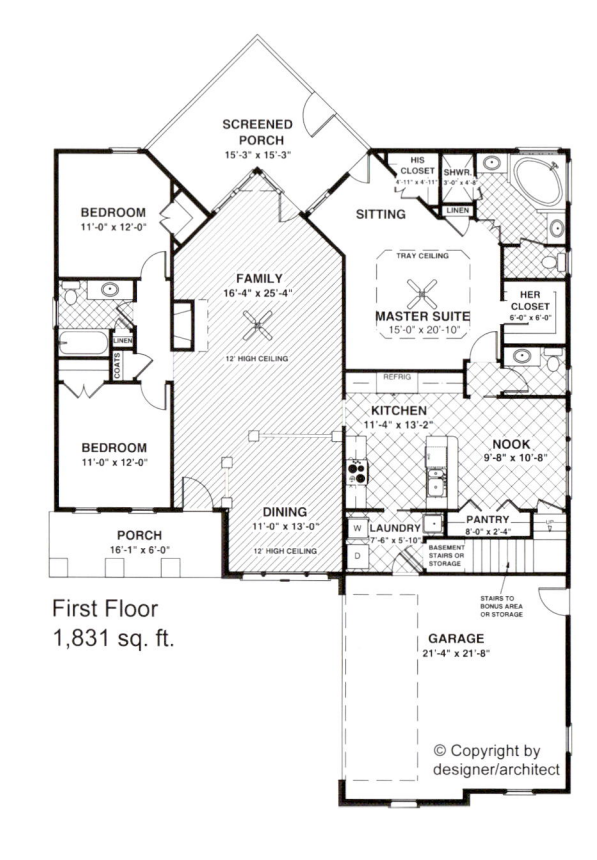

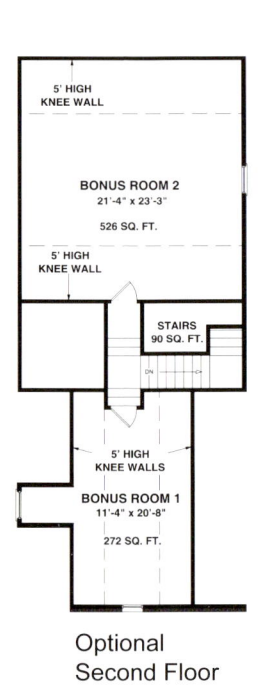

Price Code C

First Floor
1,831 sq. ft.

Optional Second Floor

To order this plan, visit the Menards Building Materials Desk or visit www.Menards.com

MENARDS

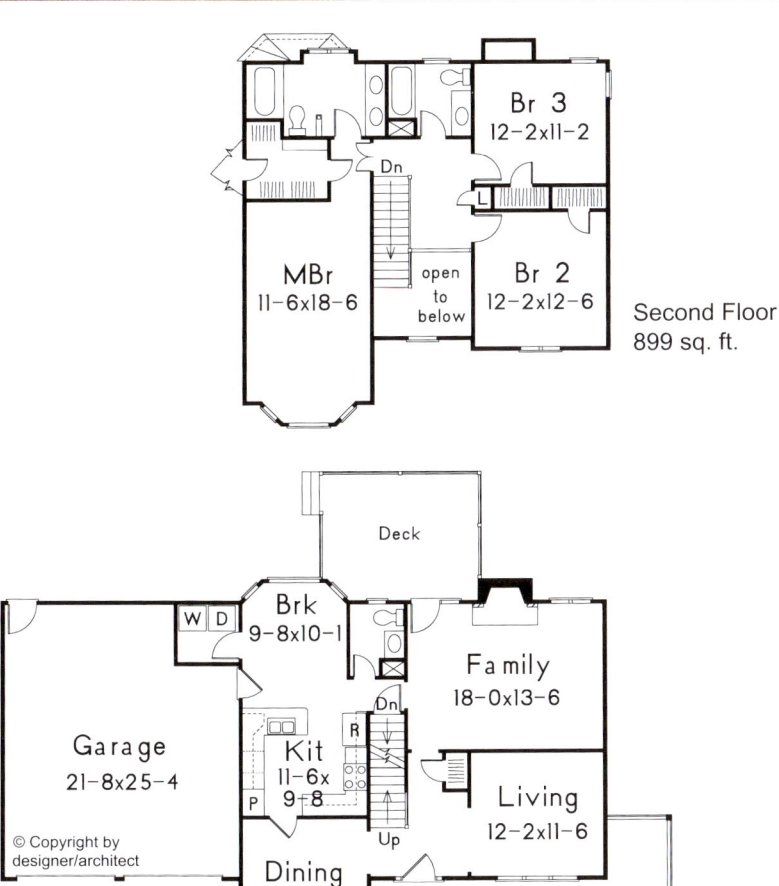

Ridgeview

Plan #M09-053D-0007

Two-Story Foyer Adds To Country Charm

1,922 total square feet of living area

Width: 56'-0"   Depth: 36'-0"

3 bedrooms, 2 1/2 baths

2-car garage

Walk-out basement foundation

Special features

This home's varied front elevation features numerous accents

The master bedroom suite is well-secluded with a double-door entry and private bath

The formal living and dining rooms are located off the entry

Price Code A

Second Floor 899 sq. ft.

First Floor 1,023 sq. ft.

Rear View

To order this plan, visit the Menards Building Materials Desk or visit www.Menards.com.

Foxmyer

MENARDS®

Plan #M09-007D-0134

Affordable Simplicity

1,310 total square feet of living area

Width: 73'-8"   Depth: 32'-0"

3 bedrooms, 2 baths

2-car garage

Basement foundation, drawings also include crawl space and slab foundations

Special features

The combination of brick quoins, roof dormers and an elegant porch creates a classic look

The master bedroom is vaulted and enjoys privacy from the other bedrooms

A spacious laundry room is convenient to the kitchen and master bedroom with access to an oversized garage

2" x 6" exterior wall framing available for an additional fee, please specify when ordering

Price Code A

Rear View

To order this plan, visit the Menards Building Materials Desk or visit www.Menards.com

MENARDS

Plan #M09-008D-0143

Breathtaking Balcony Overlook

1,299 total square feet of living area

Width: 30'-0"   Depth: 32'-0"

3 bedrooms, 2 baths

Crawl space foundation, drawings also include slab foundation

Special features

A convenient storage area for skis and other sporting equipment is located outside the rear entrance

The kitchen and dining room receive light from the box-bay window

The large vaulted living room features a cozy fireplace and overlook from the second floor balcony

Two second floor bedrooms share a Jack and Jill bath

The second floor balcony extends over the entire length of the living room below

Price Code A

First Floor
811 sq. ft.

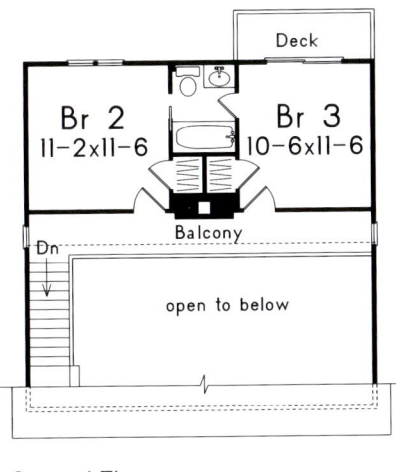

Second Floor
488 sq. ft.

To order this plan, visit the Menards Building Materials Desk or visit www.Menards.com.

Kingsport

MENARDS

Plan #M09-121D-0012

Small Home Packed With Big Style

1,281 total square feet of living area

Width: 37'-6" Depth: 52'-0"

3 bedrooms, 2 baths

2-car garage

Basement foundation

Special features

The well-appointed kitchen enjoys an angled raised counter perfect for casual dining

The great room has an 11' ceiling, a fireplace for warmth, and easy access to the breakfast area

The vaulted master bedroom enjoys a sizable walk-in closet and its own private bath

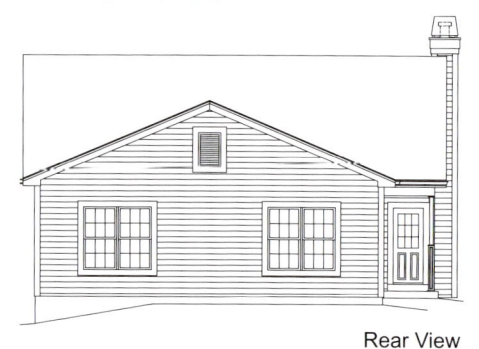

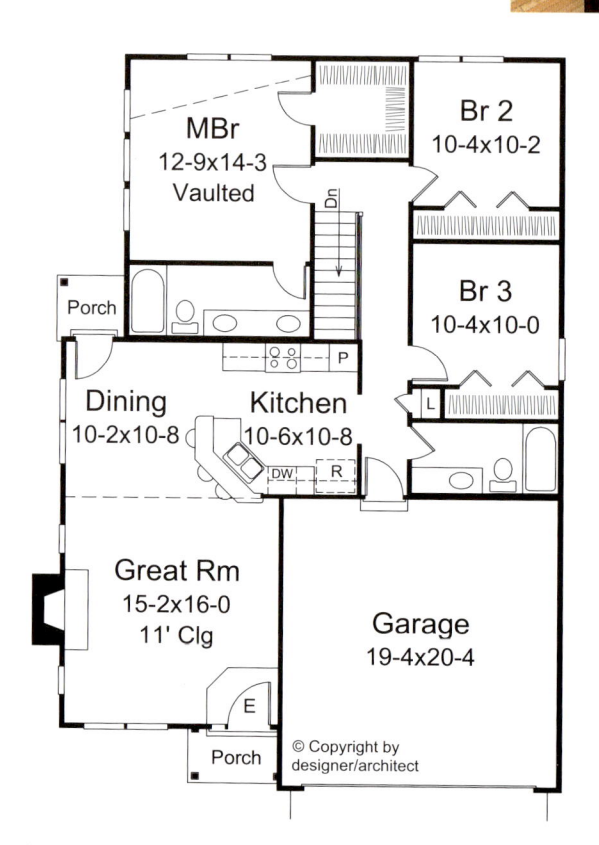

Price Code AA

Rear View

MBr 12-9x14-3 Vaulted

Br 2 10-4x10-2

Br 3 10-4x10-0

Porch

Dining 10-2x10-8

Kitchen 10-6x10-8

Great Rm 15-2x16-0 11' Clg

Garage 19-4x20-4

Porch

© Copyright by designer/architect

200

To order this plan, visit the Menards Building Materials Desk or visit www.Menards.com.

MENARDS

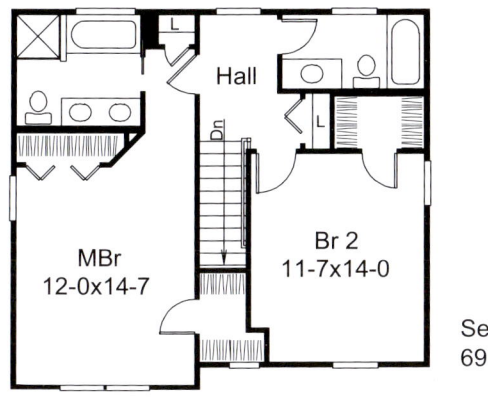

BIRKHILL

Plan #M09-007D-0148

Second Floor
691 sq. ft.

- MBr 12-0x14-7
- Br 2 11-7x14-0
- Hall

First Floor
476 sq. ft.

- Patio
- Brk fst 10-0x10-0
- Kit 7-3x8-0
- Laun.
- Garage 12-0x21-0
- Living 11-7x15-0
- Porch

© Copyright by designer/architect

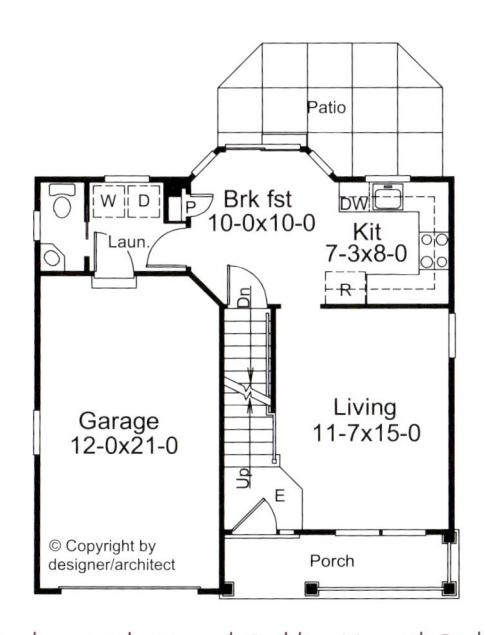

Compact Two-Story Home

1,167 total square feet of living area

Width: 28'-0"   Depth: 30'-0"

2 bedrooms, 2 1/2 baths

1-car garage

Basement foundation

Special features

The sizable living room has a separate entry foyer and view to the front porch

The functional kitchen includes a breakfast room with a bay window, a built-in pantry, and a laundry room with a half bath

The master bedroom offers three closets and a luxury bath

Price Code AA

Rear View

To order this plan, visit the Menards Building Materials Desk or visit www.Menards.com.

Northland

MENARDS

Plan #M09-022D-0022

Perfect Fit For A Narrow Site

1,270 total square feet of living area

Width: 38'-0"   Depth: 54'-4"

3 bedrooms, 2 baths

2-car garage

Basement foundation

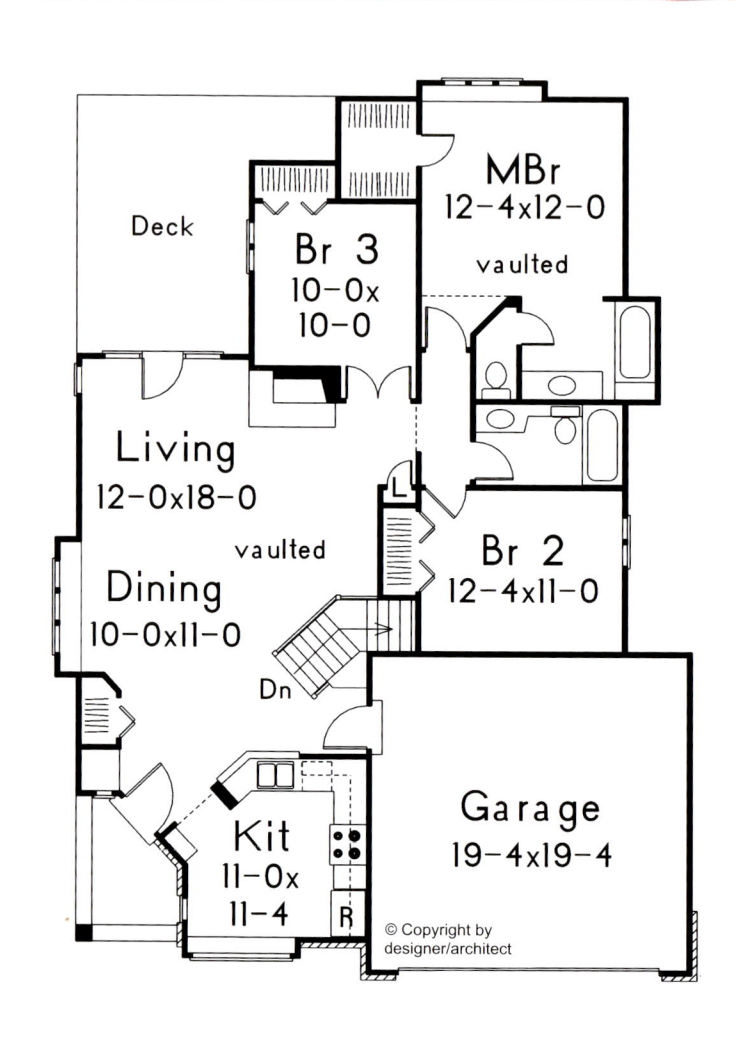

Special features

The spacious living area features an angled staircase, a vaulted ceiling, an exciting fireplace, and deck access

The master bedroom includes a walk-in closet and a private bath

The dining and living rooms join to create an open atmosphere

The eat-in kitchen has a convenient pass-through to the dining room

Price Code A

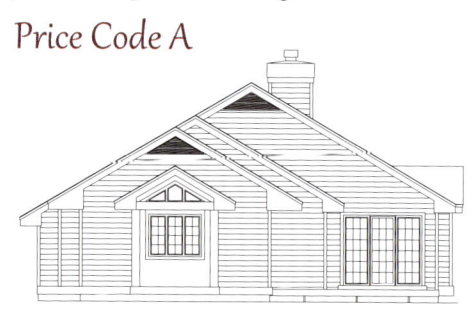

Rear View

To order this plan, visit the Menards Building Materials Desk or visit www.Menards.com

MENARDS

Provider 1

Plan #M09-001D-0039

Perfect Home For A Small Family

864 total square feet of living area

Width: 36'-0"   Depth: 28'-0"

2 bedrooms, 1 bath

Crawl space foundation, drawings also include basement and slab foundations

Special features

The L-shaped kitchen with convenient pantry is adjacent to the dining area

This home has easy access to the laundry, linen and storage closets

Both of the bedrooms include ample closet space

Price Code AAA

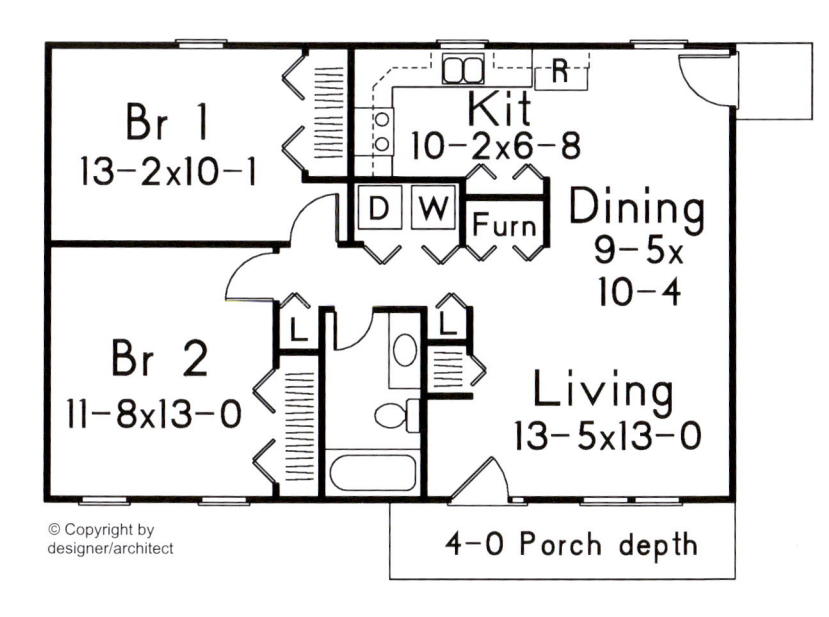

Floor plan:
- Br 1: 13-2 x 10-1
- Br 2: 11-8 x 13-0
- Kit: 10-2 x 6-8
- Dining: 9-5 x 10-4
- Living: 13-5 x 13-0
- 4-0 Porch depth

© Copyright by designer/architect

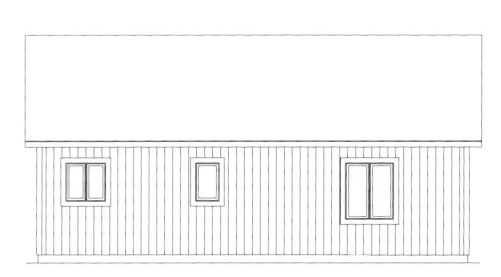

Rear View

To order this plan, visit the Menards Building Materials Desk or visit www.Menards.com.

203

Bonham

MENARDS

Plan #M09-068D-0005

Spacious Living In This Ranch

1,433 total square feet of living area

Width: 54'-0"   Depth: 41'-0"

3 bedrooms, 2 baths

2-car garage

Basement foundation, drawings also include crawl space and slab foundations

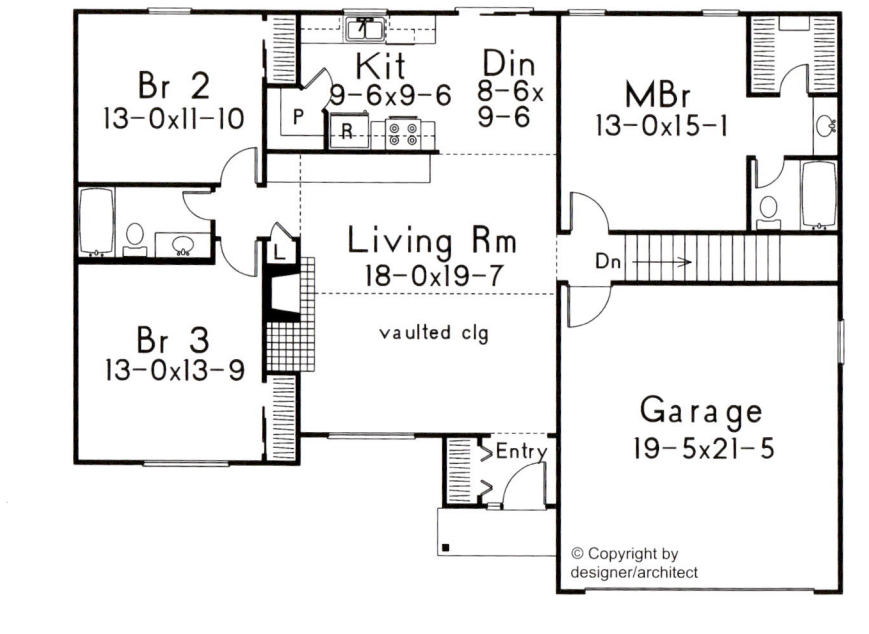

Special features

The vaulted living room includes a cozy fireplace and an oversized entertainment center

Bedrooms #2 and #3 share a full bath

The master bedroom has a full bath and a large walk-in closet

Price Code A

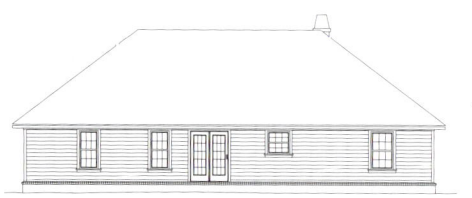

Rear View

To order this plan, visit the Menards Building Materials Desk or visit www.Menards.com

MENARDS

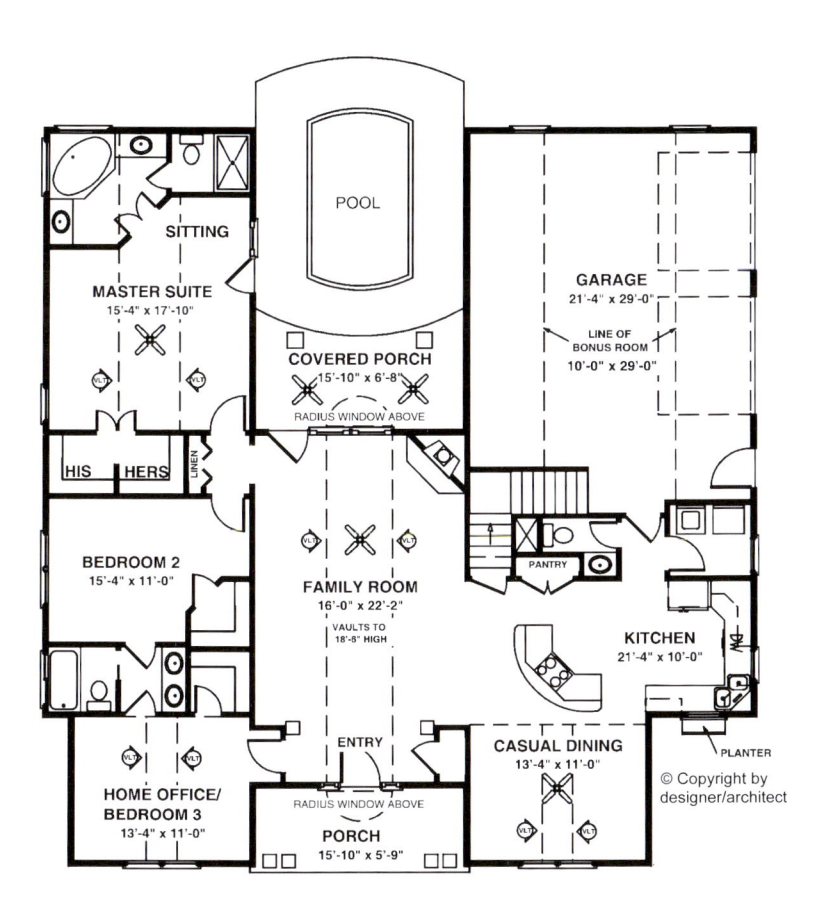

Crandall Cliff

Plan #M09-013L-0130

Exciting One-Level Home

1,798 total square feet of living area

Width: 54'-0"   Depth: 56'-2"

3 bedrooms, 2 1/2 baths

2-car side entry garage

Slab foundation, basement and crawl space foundations available for an additional fee

Special features

A gourmet kitchen, casual dining room, and a rear covered porch overlooking the pool make this home a delight when entertaining

The generous master suite features a sitting area, and a large walk-in closet with separate his and her sections

The front home office can easily become a guest bedroom with its walk-in closet and private bath access

The bonus room above the garage has an additional 328 square feet of living area

Price Code E

To order this plan, visit the Menards Building Materials Desk or visit www.Menards.com.

Wheatland

MENARDS

Plan #M09-058D-0020

Surrounding Country Porch

1,428 total square feet of living area

Width: 46'-0"   Depth: 42'-6"

3 bedrooms, 2 baths

Basement foundation

Special features

The large vaulted family room opens to the dining area and kitchen with a breakfast bar

The first floor master bedroom offers a bath, walk-in closet, and nearby laundry facilities

A spacious loft/bedroom #3 overlooking the family room, and an additional bedroom and bath complement the second floor

2" x 6" exterior wall framing available for an additional fee, please specify when ordering

Price Code A

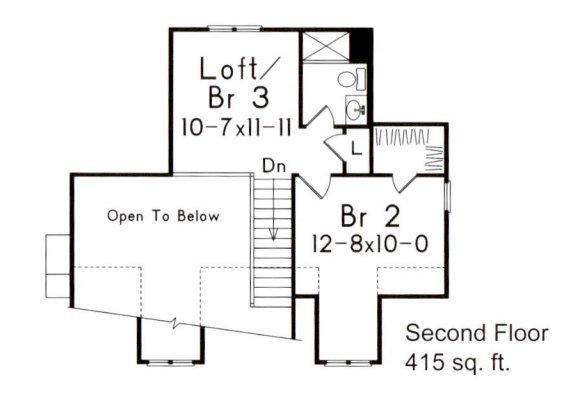

Rear View

Loft/Br 3
10-7x11-11

Br 2
12-8x10-0

Open To Below

Second Floor
415 sq. ft.

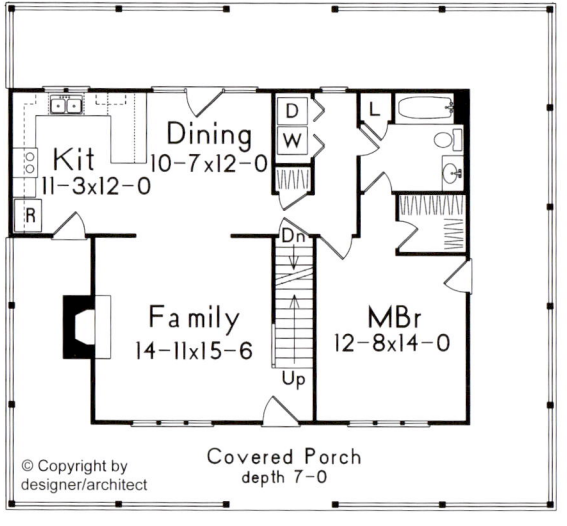

Kit
11-3x12-0

Dining
10-7x12-0

Family
14-11x15-6

MBr
12-8x14-0

Covered Porch
depth 7-0

© Copyright by designer/architect

First Floor
1,013 sq. ft.

To order this plan, visit the Menards Building Materials Desk or visit www.Menards.com

MENARDS

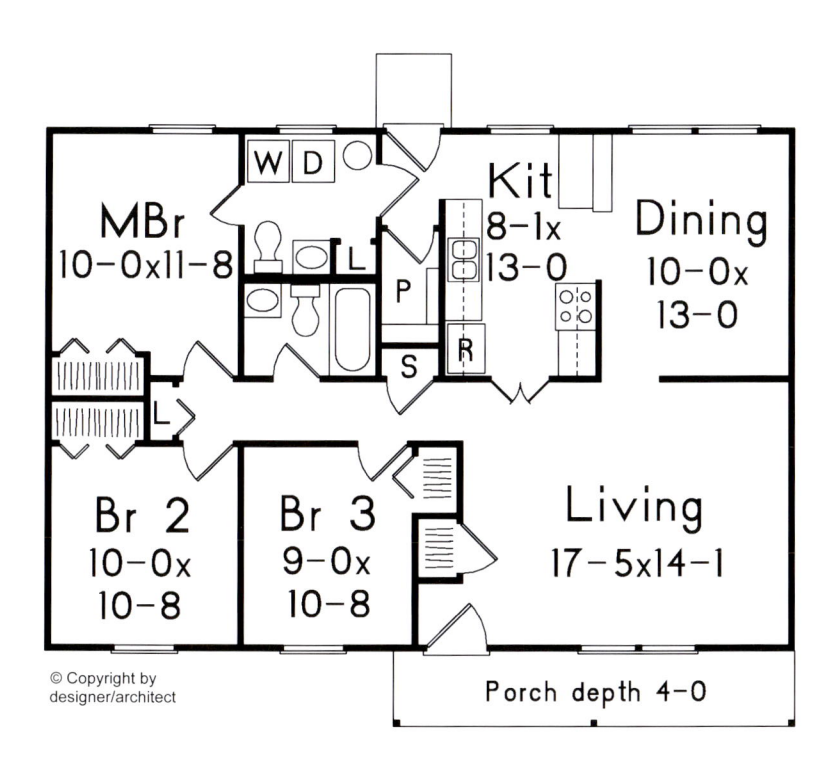

Green Crossing

Plan #M09-001D-0093

Convenient Ranch

1,120 total square feet of living area

Width: 40'-0"   Depth: 32'-0"

3 bedrooms, 1 1/2 baths

Crawl space foundation, drawings also include basement and slab foundations

Special features

The master bedroom includes a half bath with laundry area, a linen closet, and kitchen access

The kitchen has a charming double-door entry, a breakfast bar, and a convenient walk-in pantry

The welcoming front porch opens to a large living room with a coat closet

Price Code AA

Rear View

To order this plan, visit the Menards Building Materials Desk or visit www.Menards.com.

Windingpath

MENARDS

Plan #M09-077L-0105

Compact And Stylish Design

1,100 total square feet of living area

Width: 31'-2"   Depth: 48'-6"

2 bedrooms, 2 baths

Slab foundation

Special features

This home is designed with insulated concrete formed exterior walls providing a tighter construction, conserving heating and cooling energy consumption

The two bedrooms are larger than you would expect for a house of this size, and one includes a private bath with a whirlpool tub

A separate laundry room, pantry, linen and hall closet add convenient storage and workspace to this design

Relax with friends and family on either the front or rear covered porches

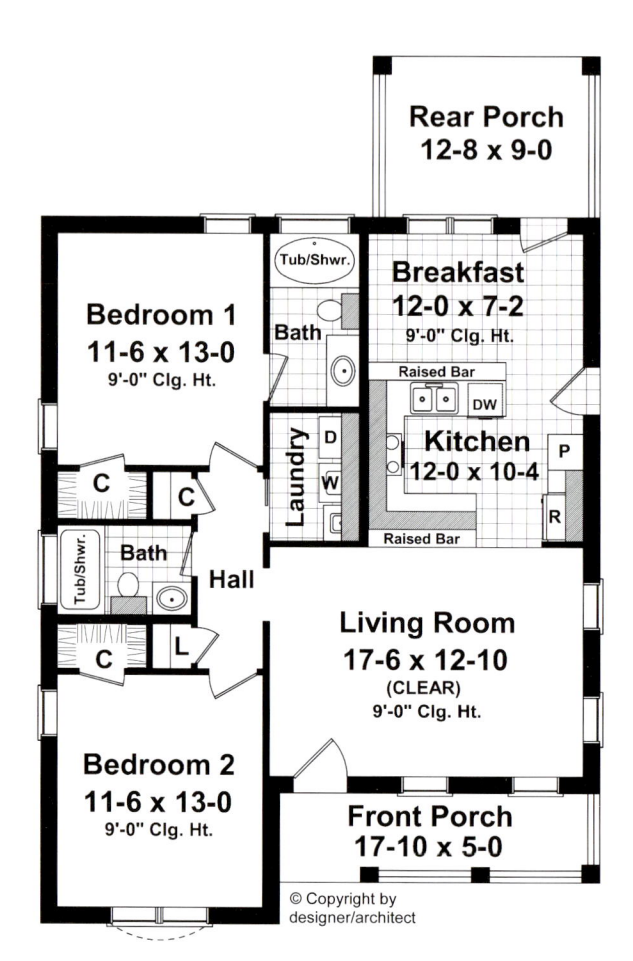

Price Code D

Rear Porch 12-8 x 9-0

Bedroom 1 11-6 x 13-0 9'-0" Clg. Ht.

Tub/Shwr. Bath

Breakfast 12-0 x 7-2 9'-0" Clg. Ht.

Raised Bar

Kitchen 12-0 x 10-4

Laundry

Raised Bar

Tub/Shwr. Bath

Hall

Living Room 17-6 x 12-10 (CLEAR) 9'-0" Clg. Ht.

Bedroom 2 11-6 x 13-0 9'-0" Clg. Ht.

Front Porch 17-10 x 5-0

© Copyright by designer/architect

To order this plan, visit the Menards Building Materials Desk or visit www.Menards.com

MENARDS

Woodridge

Plan #M09-008D-0160

Leisure Living With Interior Surprise

1,354 total square feet of living area

Width: 24'-0"   Depth: 42'-2"

2 bedrooms, 1 bath

Crawl space foundation

Special features

Soaring ceilings highlight the kitchen, as well as the living and dining areas creating dramatic excitement

A spectacular large deck surrounds the front and both sides of the home

An impressive U-shaped kitchen has a wrap-around breakfast bar and shares fantastic views with both the first and second floors through an awesome wall of glass

Two bedrooms with a bath, a sleeping loft and second floor balcony overlooking the living area complete the home

Price Code A

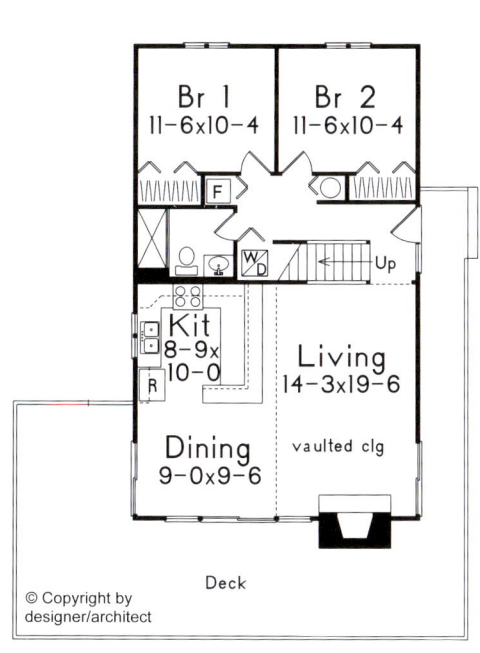

First Floor 960 sq. ft.

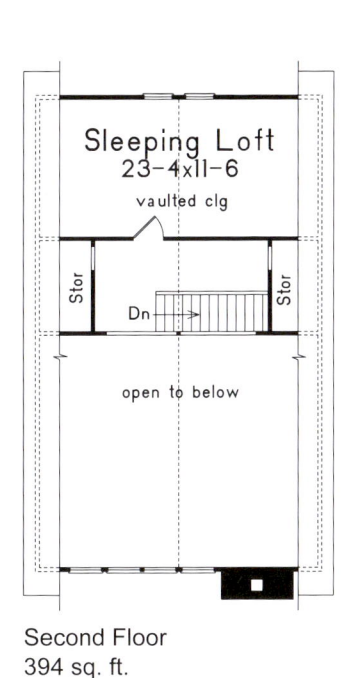

Second Floor 394 sq. ft.

To order this plan, visit the Menards Building Materials Desk or visit www.Menards.com.

Stonehaven

MENARDS

Plan #M09-007D-0161

Earth Berm Home With Style

1,480 total square feet of living area

Width: 70'-0"   Depth: 36'-0"

2 bedrooms, 2 baths

2-car garage

Slab foundation

Special features

Energy efficient home with 2" x 6" exterior walls

This home has great looks and lots of space

Nestled in a hillside with only one exposed exterior wall, this home offers efficiency, protection and affordability

The triple patio doors with an arched transom bathe the living room with sunlight

The kitchen features a snack bar open to the living room, large built-in pantry and adjoins a spacious dining room

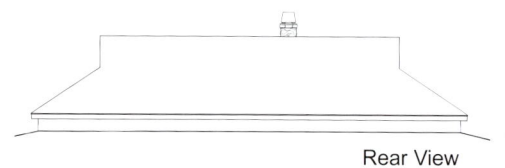

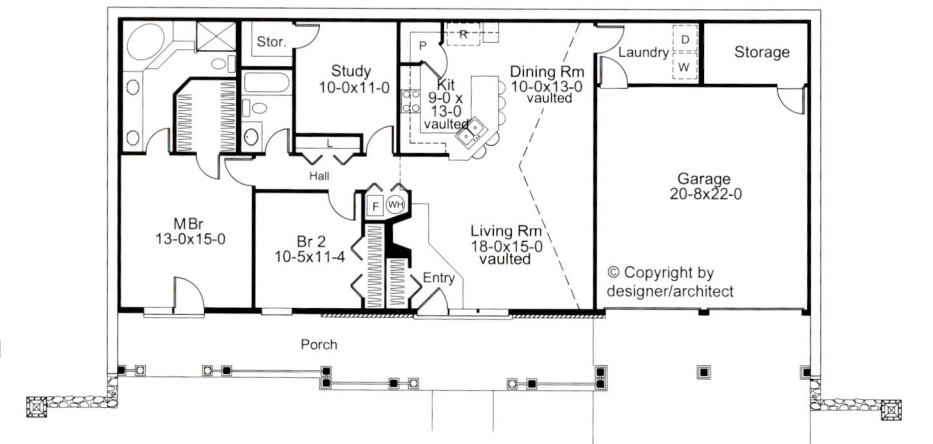

Price Code A

Rear View

To order this plan, visit the Menards Building Materials Desk or visit www.Menards.com

MENARDS

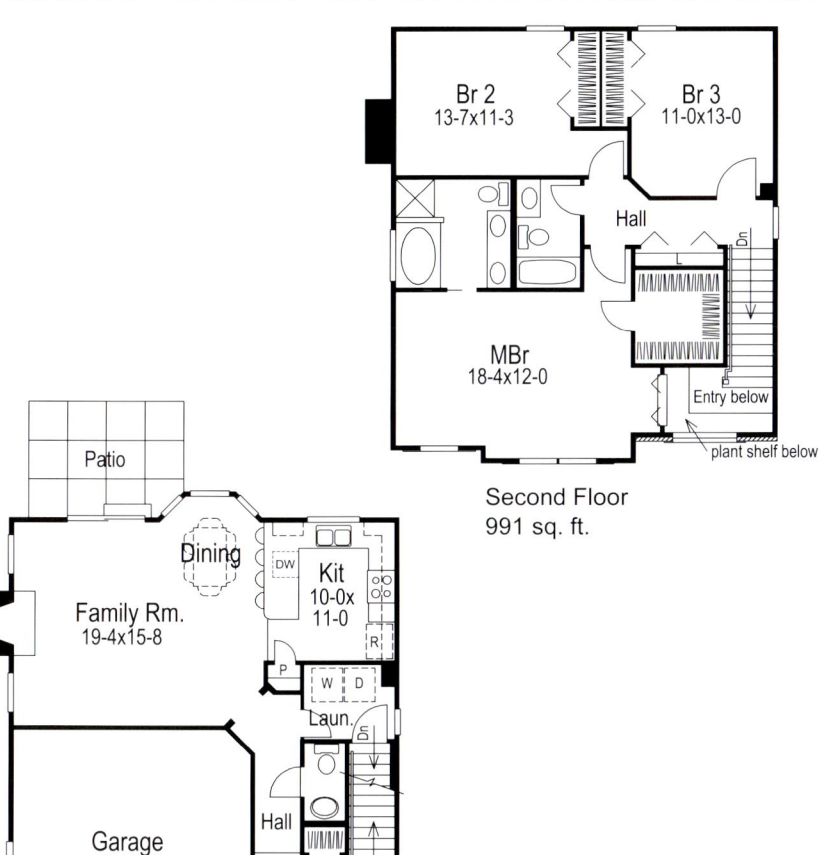

Glencoe

Plan #M09-007D-0114

Gracious Living On A Small Lot

1,671 total square feet of living area

Width: 32-0"   Depth: 39'-4"

3 bedrooms, 2 1/2 baths

2-car garage

Basement foundation

Special features

Triple gables and a stone facade create great curb appeal

The two-story entry leads to a family room, bayed dining area and U-shaped kitchen

The second floor features a large master bedroom with luxury bath, huge walk-in closet, overlook to entry, and two secondary bedrooms with hall bath

Price Code B

Second Floor 991 sq. ft.
- Br 2: 13-7x11-3
- Br 3: 11-0x13-0
- MBr: 18-4x12-0

First Floor 680 sq. ft.
- Family Rm.: 19-4x15-8
- Kit: 10-0x11-0
- Garage: 18-4x20-4

Rear View

To order this plan, visit the Menards Building Materials Desk or visit www.Menards.com

Smithsonian

MENARDS

Plan #M09-058D-0038

Open Floor Plan
With Extra Amenities

1,680 total square feet of living area

Width: 50'-0"   Depth: 35'-0"

3 bedrooms, 2 1/2 baths

2-car garage

Basement foundation

Special features

This home offers a compact and efficient layout in an affordable package

The second floor has three bedrooms all with oversized closets

All of the bedrooms are located on the second floor for privacy

Price Code B

Rear View

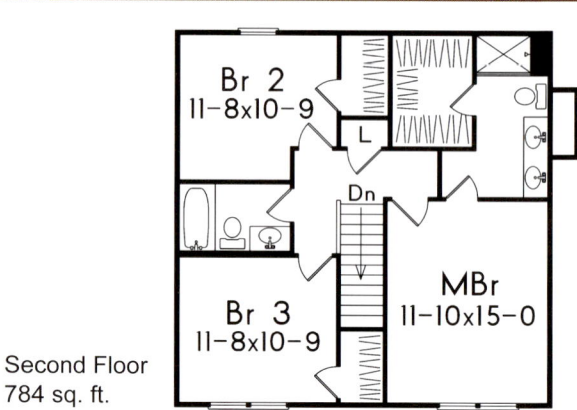

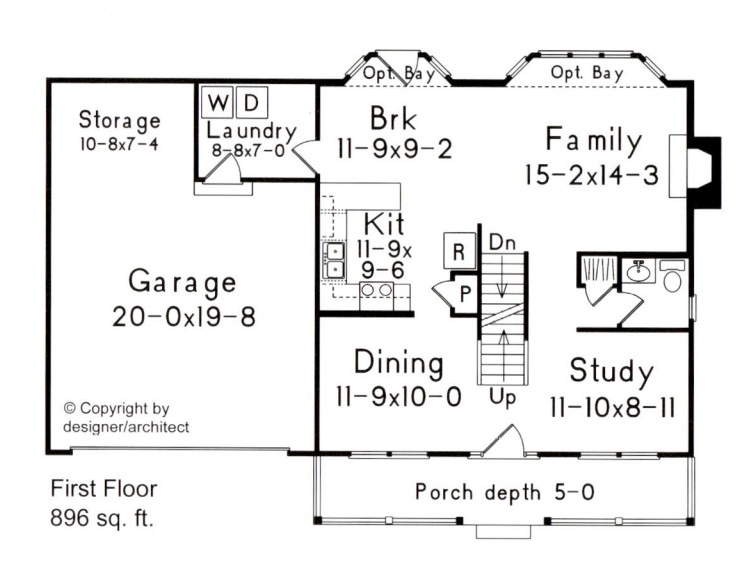

Second Floor
784 sq. ft.

- Br 2: 11-8x10-9
- Br 3: 11-8x10-9
- MBr: 11-10x15-0

First Floor
896 sq. ft.

- Storage: 10-8x7-4
- Laundry: 8-8x7-0
- Brk: 11-9x9-2
- Family: 15-2x14-3
- Kit: 11-9x9-6
- Garage: 20-0x19-8
- Dining: 11-9x10-0
- Study: 11-10x8-11

Porch depth 5-0

© Copyright by designer/architect

To order this plan, visit the Menards Building Materials Desk or visit www.Menards.com.

MENARDS

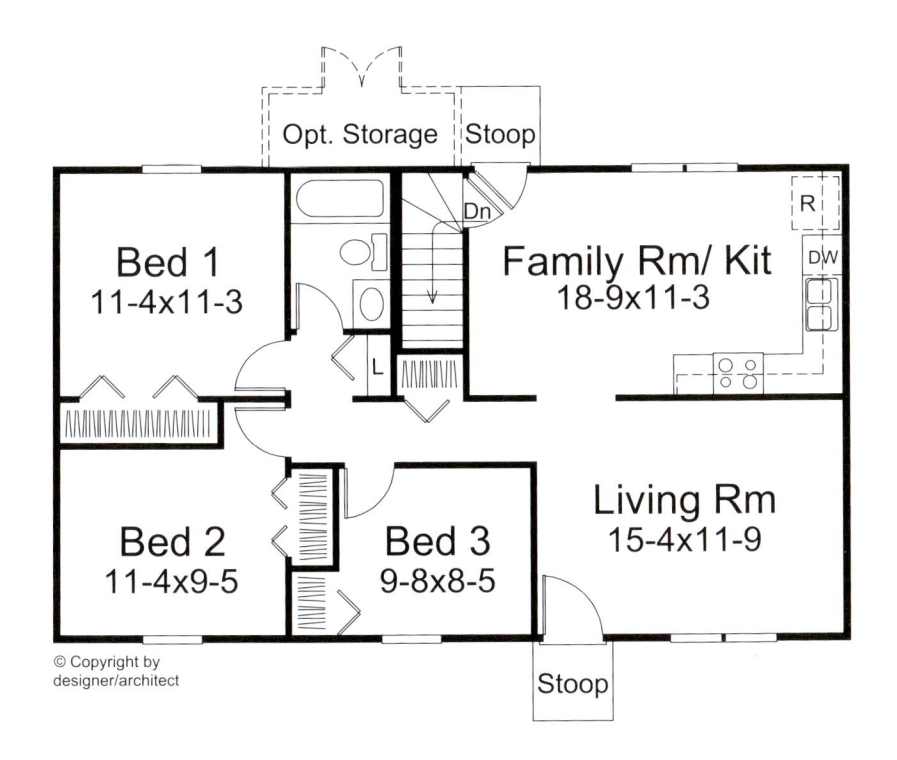

Roseva

Hamlin

Plan #M09-008D-0121

Economize Without Sacrifice

960 total square feet of living area

Width: 40'-0"   Depth: 24'-0"

3 bedrooms, 1 bath

Basement foundation, drawings also include crawl space and slab foundations

Special features

This home's attractive appearance adds to any neighborhood

A nice-sized living room leads to an informal family area with eat-in L-shaped kitchen, access to rear yard and basement space

Three bedrooms with lots of closet space and a convenient hall bath complete the home

Price Code AA

Floor plan:
- Opt. Storage
- Stoop
- Bed 1: 11-4x11-3
- Family Rm/Kit: 18-9x11-3
- Bed 2: 11-4x9-5
- Bed 3: 9-8x8-5
- Living Rm: 15-4x11-9
- Stoop

© Copyright by designer/architect

To order this plan, visit the Menards Building Materials Desk or visit www.Menards.com.

Plan #M09-013L-0011

Appealing Charming Porch

1,643 total square feet of living area

Width: 38'-0"   Depth: 34'-0"

3 bedrooms, 2 1/2 baths

2-car drive under side entry garage

Basement or crawl space foundation, please specify when ordering

Special features

The first floor master bedroom has a private bath, a walk-in closet, and easy access to the laundry closet

The comfortable family room features a vaulted ceiling and a cozy fireplace

The two bedrooms on the second floor share a compartmented bath

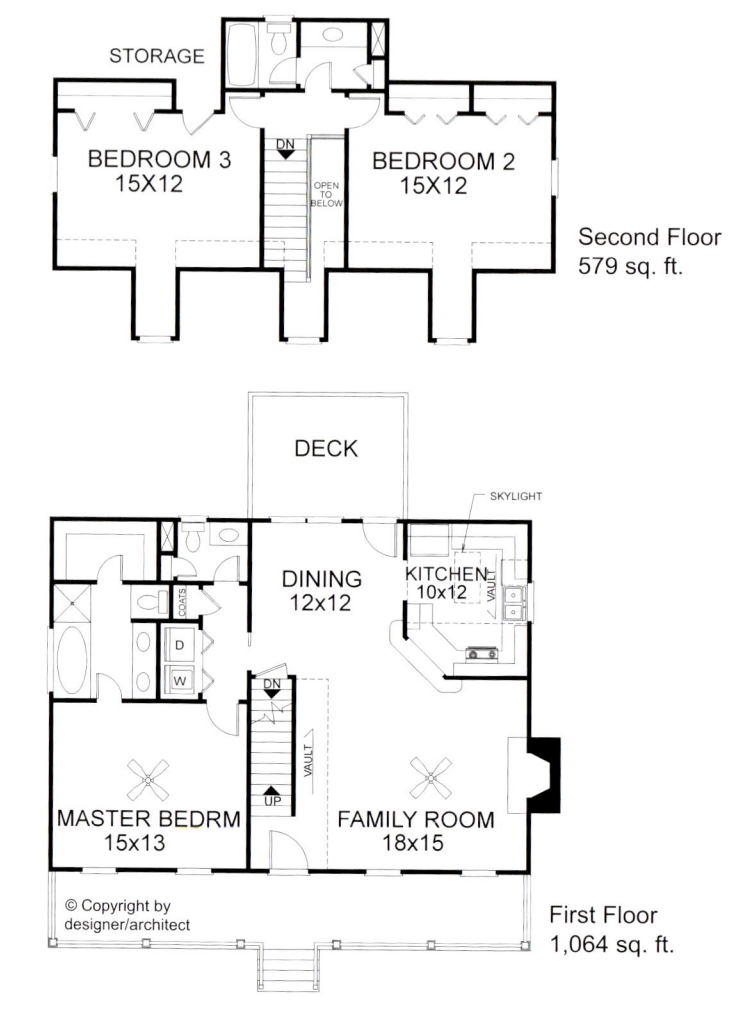

Price Code C

Second Floor
579 sq. ft.

First Floor
1,064 sq. ft.

MENARDS

Lucas Heights

Plan #M09-055L-0053

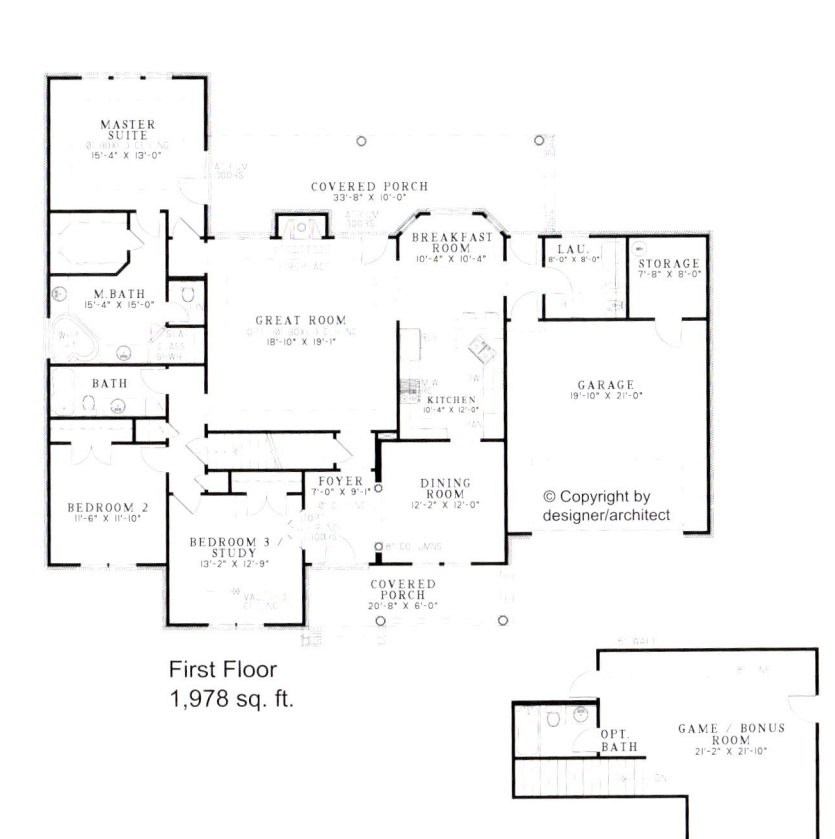

First Floor 1,978 sq. ft.

Optional Second Floor

Second Floor Bonus Game Room

1,978 total square feet of living area

Width: 66'-0"   Depth: 55'-0"

3 bedrooms, 2 baths

2-car garage

Basement, walk-out basement, slab or crawl space foundation, please specify when ordering

Special features

9' ceilings throughout this home create an open atmosphere

The breakfast room with bay window opens to the kitchen with an eating bar

The master suite has a 10' boxed ceiling and atrium doors to the rear porch

The optional second floor has an additional 479 square feet of living area

Price Code C

To order this plan, visit the Menards Building Materials Desk or visit www.Menards.com.

Delmont

Plan #M09-055L-0193

Relaxing Outdoor Areas

2,131 total square feet of living area

Width: 63'-10"   Depth: 72'-2"

3 bedrooms, 2 1/2 baths

2-car side entry garage

Slab or crawl space foundation, please specify when ordering

Special features

The kitchen, great room and dining room create an expansive living area

Bedroom #2 features a charming bay window with seat

The garage includes space for a safe storm shelter

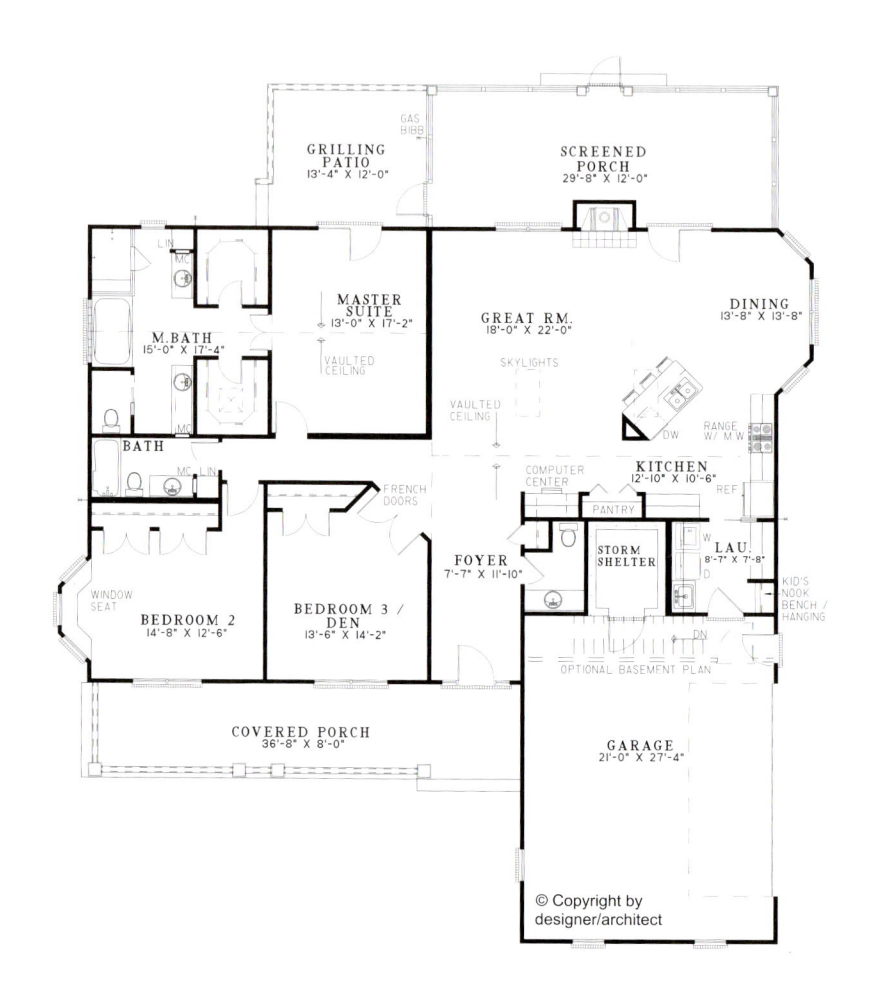

Price Code D

To order this plan, visit the Menards Building Materials Desk or visit www.menards.com.

MENARDS

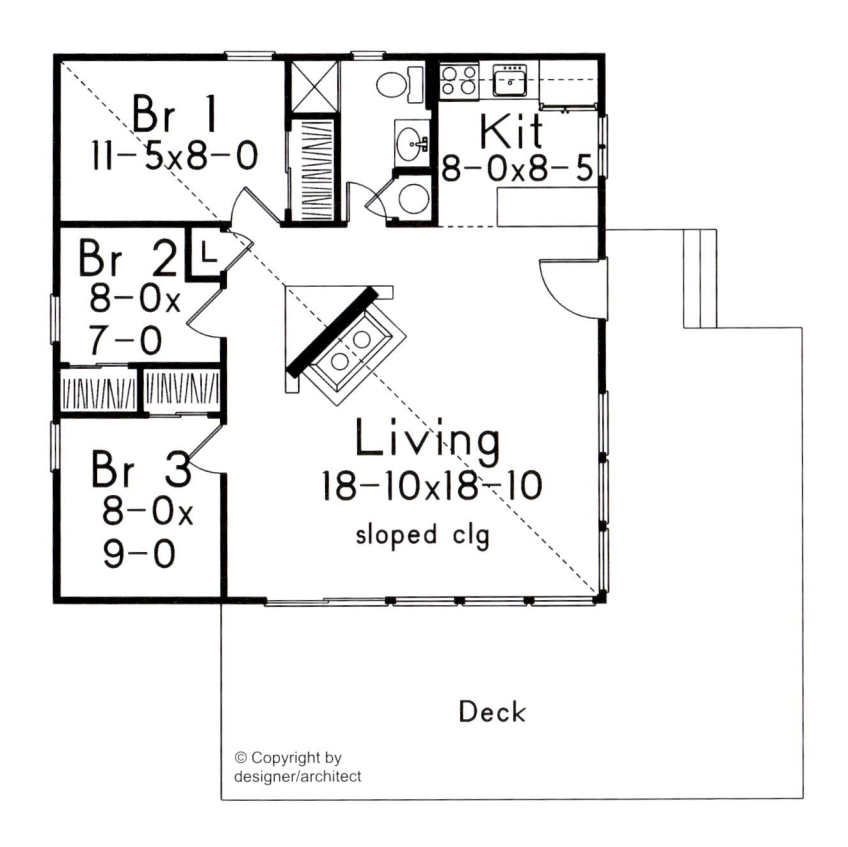

Pinecone

Plan #M09-008D-0148

Corner Window Wall Dominates Design

784 total square feet of living area

Width: 28'-0"   Depth: 28'-0"

3 bedrooms, 1 bath

Pier foundation

Special features

Outdoor relaxation will be enjoyed with this home's huge wrap-around wood deck

Upon entering the spacious living area, a cozy free-standing fireplace, a sloped ceiling, and a corner window wall catch the eye

The charming kitchen features a pass-through peninsula to the dining area

Price Code AAA

Floor plan:
- Br 1: 11-5x8-0
- Br 2: 8-0x7-0
- Br 3: 8-0x9-0
- Kit: 8-0x8-5
- Living: 18-10x18-10 sloped clg
- Deck

© Copyright by designer/architect

To order this plan, visit the Menards Building Materials Desk or visit www.Menards.com.

Summerpark

MENARDS

Plan #M09-007D-0140

Bright And Airy Country Design

1,591 total square feet of living area

Width: 62'-0"   Depth: 45'-0"

3 bedrooms, 2 baths

2-car side entry garage

Basement foundation

Special features

Spacious porches and a patio provide outdoor enjoyment

The large entry leads to a cheerful kitchen and breakfast area that welcomes the sun through a wide array of windows

The vaulted great room has a corner fireplace, wet bar, and patio access

Double walk-in closets, a private porch and a luxury bath are special highlights of the vaulted master bedroom suite

Price Code B

Rear View

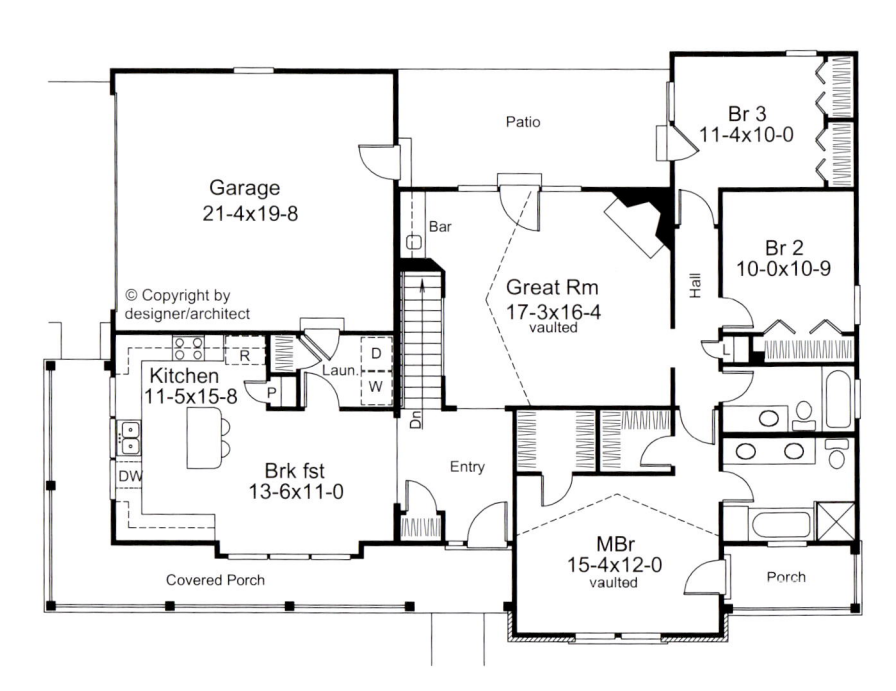

218

To order this plan, visit the Menards Building Materials Desk or visit www.Menards.com

MENARDS

Glen Ellen

Plan #M09-007D-0110

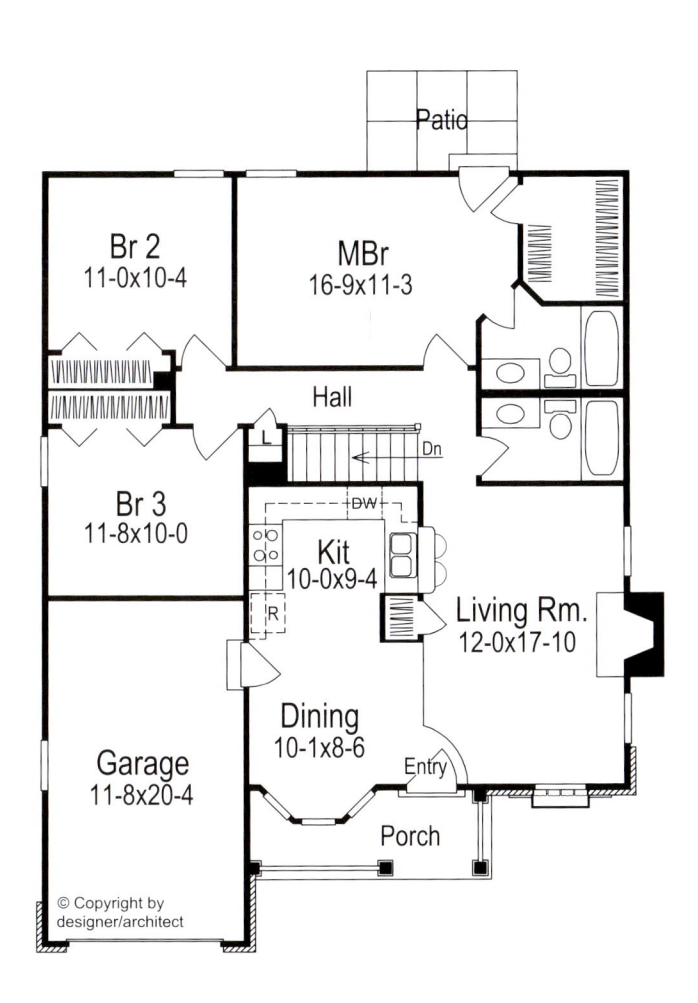

Country Charm For A Small Lot

1,169 total square feet of living area

Width: 37'-4"   Depth: 46'-8"

3 bedrooms, 2 baths

1-car garage

Basement foundation

Special features

This home's front facade features a distinctive country appeal

The living room enjoys a wood-burning fireplace and pass-through to the kitchen

The U-shaped kitchen has lots of cabinet and counterspace and living room views

A large walk-in closet, access to the rear patio, and a private bath are some of the many features of the master bedroom

Price Code AA

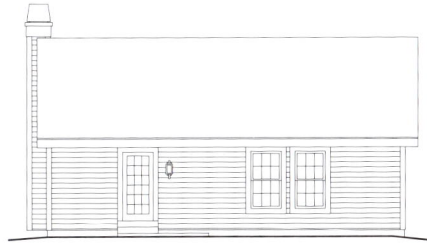

Rear View

Floor plan rooms:
- Patio
- Br 2: 11-0x10-4
- MBr: 16-9x11-3
- Hall
- Br 3: 11-8x10-0
- Kit: 10-0x9-4
- Living Rm.: 12-0x17-10
- Dining: 10-1x8-6
- Entry
- Porch
- Garage: 11-8x20-4

© Copyright by designer/architect

To order this plan, visit the Menards Building Materials Desk or visit www.Menards.com.

Andrew

MENARDS

Plan #M09-013L-0048

Triple Arch Entryway

2,071 total square feet of living area

Width: 63'-0"   Depth: 63'-0"

3 bedrooms, 2 1/2 baths

3-car side entry garage

Basement, slab or crawl space foundation, please specify when ordering

Special features

The entryway dramatically opens to the family room with a high ceiling

The connected screened porch and deck are perfect for outdoor entertaining

The kitchen has easy access to the breakfast area and the dining room

The spacious master suite has a cozy sitting room attached

The optional second floor has an additional 434 square feet of living area

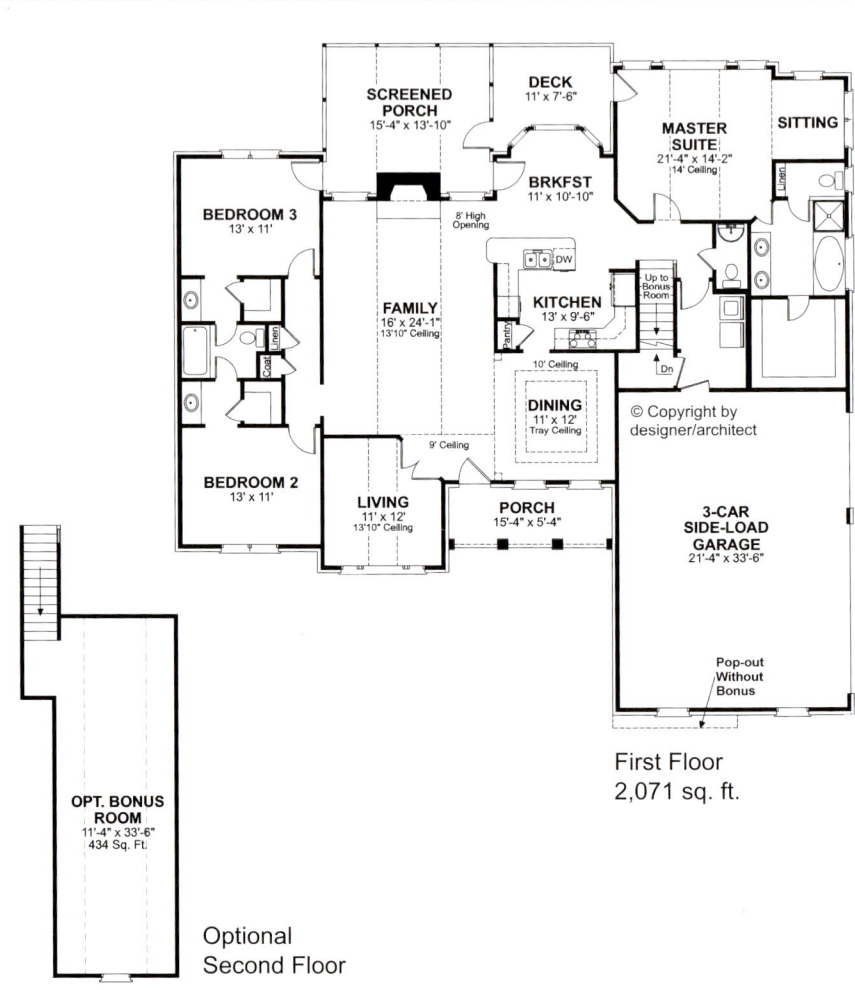

Price Code C

First Floor
2,071 sq. ft.

Optional Second Floor

To order this plan, visit the Menards Building Materials Desk or visit www.Menards.com

MENARDS

Foxland

Plan #M09-045D-0017

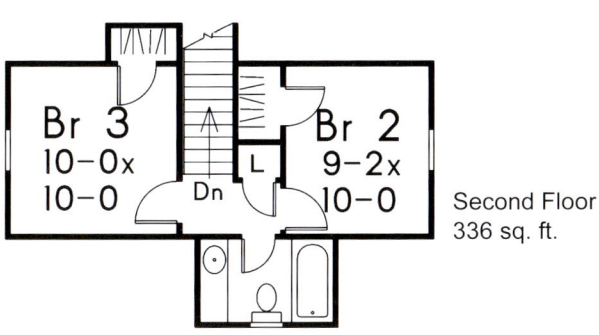

Second Floor 336 sq. ft.

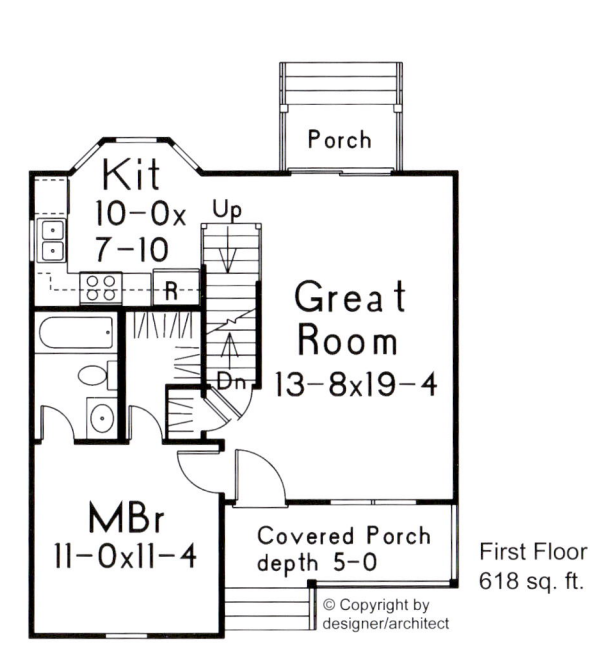

- Br 3 10-0 x 10-0
- Br 2 9-2 x 10-0

First Floor 618 sq. ft.

- Kit 10-0 x 7-10
- Great Room 13-8 x 19-4
- MBr 11-0 x 11-4
- Covered Porch depth 5-0
- Porch

© Copyright by designer/architect

Dormer And Covered Porch Add To Country Charm

954 total square feet of living area

Width: 25'-8"   Depth: 30'-0"

3 bedrooms, 2 baths

Basement foundation

Special features

The kitchen has a cozy bayed eating area

The master bedroom has a walk-in closet and a private bath

The great room has access to the back porch

A coat closet is located near the entry

Price Code AA

Rear View

To order this plan, visit the Menards Building Materials Desk or visit www.Menards.com.

Woodbridge

MENARDS®

Plan #M09-001D-0086

Open Living/Dining Area

1,154 total square feet of living area

Width: 28'-0"   Depth: 30'-0"

3 bedrooms, 1 1/2 baths

Crawl space foundation, drawings also include slab foundation

Special features

The U-shaped kitchen features a large breakfast bar and handy laundry area

The private second floor bedrooms share a half bath

The large living/dining area opens to the deck

Price Code AA

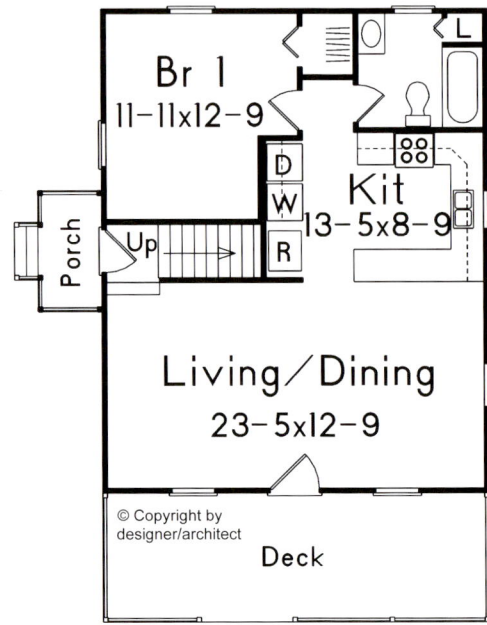

Rear View

First Floor
720 sq. ft.

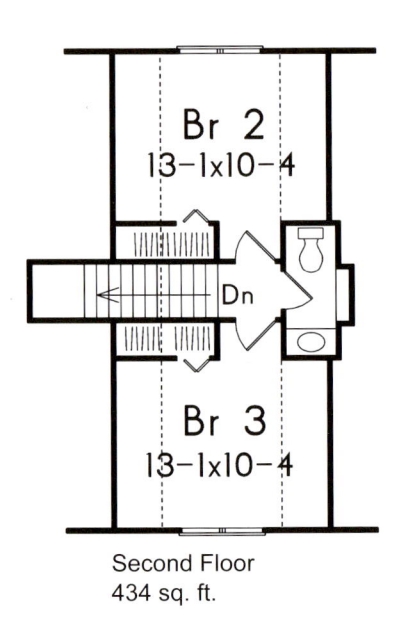

- Br 1: 11-11 x 12-9
- Kit: 13-5 x 8-9
- Living/Dining: 23-5 x 12-9
- Porch
- Deck

Second Floor
434 sq. ft.

- Br 2: 13-1 x 10-4
- Br 3: 13-1 x 10-4

222

To order this plan, visit the Menards Building Materials Desk or visit www.Menards.com

MENARDS

Cambria

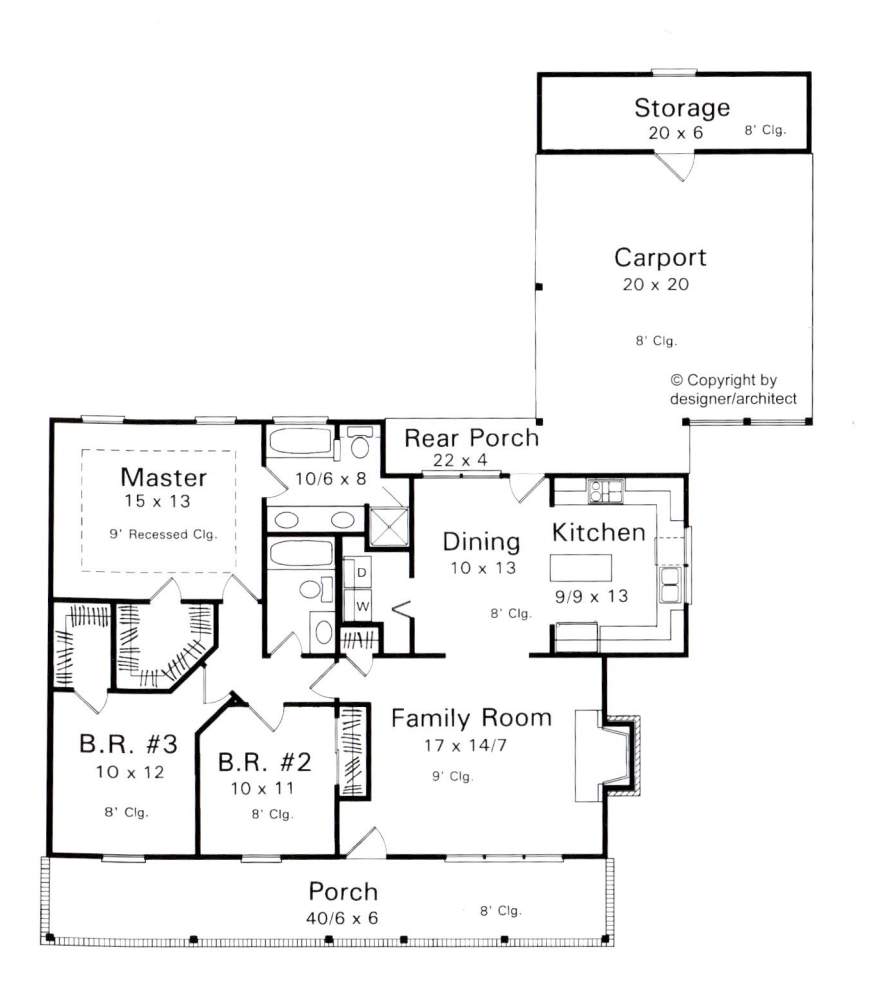

Plan #M09-039L-0002

Carport With Storage

1,333 total square feet of living area

Width: 55'-6"   Depth: 64'-3"

3 bedrooms, 2 baths

2-car carport

Slab or crawl space foundation, please specify when ordering

Special features

Country charm with a covered front porch prevails with this home

The dining area looks into the family room with fireplace

The master suite has a walk-in closet and private bath

Price Code A

To order this plan, visit the Menards Building Materials Desk or visit www.Menards.com.

Home Plan Index

Plan Number	Plan Name	Square Feet	Price Code	Page	Right Reading Reverse
M09-001D-0013	Mooreland	1,882	D	23	
M09-001D-0018	Pineview	988	AA	175	
M09-001D-0024	Brightmoore	1,360	A	156	
M09-001D-0029	Arlington Heights	1,260	A	70	
M09-001D-0031	Mayland	1,501	B	147	
M09-001D-0036	Waverly	1,320	A	95	
M09-001D-0039	Provider I	864	AAA	203	
M09-001D-0040	Provider II	864	AAA	159	
M09-001D-0041	Grass Roots I	1,000	AA	188	
M09-001D-0042	Grass Roots II	1,000	AA	151	
M09-001D-0044	Cumberland	1,375	A	60	
M09-001D-0045	Manchester	1,197	AA	41	
M09-001D-0055	Hatteras I	1,705	B	173	
M09-001D-0056	Hatteras II	1,705	B	192	
M09-001D-0067	Delta Queen I	1,285	B	165	•
M09-001D-0068	Delta Queen II	1,285	B	77	
M09-001D-0072	Burlington I	1,288	A	179	
M09-001D-0081	Pinehurst I	1,160	AA	51	
M09-001D-0085	Highlander	720	AAA	185	•
M09-001D-0086	Woodbridge	1,154	AA	222	
M09-001D-0088	Crosswood	800	AAA	161	
M09-001D-0093	Greenridge	1,120	AA	207	
M09-003D-0001	Wellington	2,058	C	50	
M09-007D-0013	Hampton	1,492	A	97	
M09-007D-0027	Alpine	654	AAA	184	•
M09-007D-0029	Branson Bluff	576	AAA	94	
M09-007D-0031	Hathaway	1,092	AA	79	
M09-007D-0040	Glenwood	632	AAA	164	•
M09-007D-0042	Woodsmill	914	AA	99	
M09-007D-0054	Ashley Park	1,575	B	15	
M09-007D-0060	Ashmont Woods	1,268	B	18	•
M09-007D-0061	Hillbriar	1,340	A	57	
M09-007D-0068	Summerview	1,922	B	166	•
M09-007D-0087	Siminridge	1,332	A	169	•
M09-007D-0088	Brook Hill	1,299	A	66	
M09-007D-0102	Fairmont	1,452	A	104	
M09-007D-0103	Ashridge	1,547	A	67	
M09-007D-0105	Springdale	1,084	AA	98	
M09-007D-0109	Roseport	888	AAA	121	•
M09-007D-0110	Glen Ellen	1,169	AA	219	
M09-007D-0112	Ridgewood	1,062	AA	137	
M09-007D-0114	Glencoe	1,671	B	211	•
M09-007D-0123	Oakbrook	1,308	A	61	
M09-007D-0127	Northhampton	2,158	C	30	
M09-007D-0128	Summerdale	1,072	AA	115	•
M09-007D-0133	Springhill	1,316	A	125	
M09-007D-0134	Foxmyer	1,310	A	198	•
M09-007D-0137	Stonegate Manor	1,568	B	177	
M09-007D-0140	Summerpark	1,591	B	218	
M09-007D-0142	Riverview	480	AAA	109	
M09-007D-0145	Park House	1,005	AA	195	•
M09-007D-0148	Birkhill	1,167	AA	201	
M09-007D-0161	Stonehaven	1,480	A	210	•
M09-007D-0173	Oakford	2,121	C	128	
M09-007D-0175	Shadybend	882	AAA	103	•
M09-007D-0177	Mapleville	1,102	AA	65	•
M09-007D-0181	Greenbay	1,140	A	133	
M09-007D-0189	Stonetrail	713	AAA	172	
M09-007D-0196	Corina	421	AAA	111	•
M09-007D-0198	Lyn Lake	1,142	AA	38	
M09-007D-0199	Briaridge	496	AAA	119	•
M09-007D-0200	Arcadia	1,137	A	72	
M09-007D-0201	Jenny Manor	1,153	A	127	
M09-007D-0210	Forest Ridge	1,942	B	157	
M09-007D-0222	San Saguaro	1,522	A	52	
M09-007D-0233	Yuma Park	1,298	B	63	
M09-007D-0237	Wiseman Park	1,994	B	145	
M09-007D-0238	Cuddington Forest	2,250	E	112	
M09-007D-0244	Marina Bay	1,605	C	140	
M09-008D-0026	Jonesboro	1,120	AA	89	
M09-008D-0069	Cypress Hollow	1,533	B	43	
M09-008D-0078	Woodbine	1,971	C	142	
M09-008D-0085	Kingsmill	2,112	C	81	
M09-008D-0088	Cornwall	1,850	C	154	
M09-008D-0121	Rosevale	960	AA	213	
M09-008D-0134	Breezewood	1,275	A	167	
M09-008D-0139	Grantview	1,272	A	71	
M09-008D-0140	Greeley Cove	1,391	A	131	
M09-008D-0143	Kingsport	1,299	A	199	
M09-008D-0147	Brookwood	1,316	A	160	
M09-008D-0148	Pinecone	784	AAA	217	
M09-008D-0151	Skyliner	1,806	C	170	
M09-008D-0153	Stillbrook	792	AAA	75	
M09-008D-0160	Woodridge	1,354	A	209	
M09-008D-0162	Yukon	865	AAA	37	
M09-008D-0178	Rutherford	1,872	C	87	•
M09-010D-0001	Sherbrooke	1,516	B	56	
M09-010D-0007	Langham	1,427	A	78	
M09-013L-0001	Glen Hills	1,050	B	189	
M09-013L-0002	Briar	1,197	B	68	
M09-013L-0006	Newcastle Falls	1,414	B	90	
M09-013L-0011	Hamlin Park	1,643	C	214	
M09-013L-0012	Driftwood Spring	1,647	C	107	
M09-013L-0014	Evergreen Point	1,728	C	153	
M09-013L-0015	Ellisport	1,787	B	139	
M09-013L-0017	Barnesville	1,992	C	134	
M09-013L-0022	Mannington	1,992	C	20	
M09-013L-0025	Fruitland	2,097	D	33	
M09-013L-0027	Stellaville	2,184	D	26	
M09-013L-0028	Sumner	2,239	D	76	
M09-013L-0043	Newton	1,343	B	171	
M09-013L-0044	Cadwell	1,420	B	116	
M09-013L-0048	Harrison Glen	1,695	C	88	
M09-013L-0049	Carrol	2,071	C	220	
M09-013L-0050	Milner	1,944	C	168	
M09-013L-0129	Sapelo	2,098	D	54	
M09-013L-0130	Crandall Cliff	1,334	D	129	
M09-013L-0132	Baldwin	1,798	E	205	
M09-013L-0133	Fernberry	2,296	F	101	
M09-013L-0134	Martin House	953	A	118	•
M09-013L-0136	Cadley	1,496	E	49	
M09-013L-0154	Canton Crest	1,831	C	196	•
M09-013L-0156	Bogart	953	A	132	
M09-013L-0159	Mount Berry	1,800	B	182	
M09-014D-0005	Oregon Falls	1,992	B	162	
M09-014D-0009	Goodwin	1,314	A	59	
M09-017D-0002	Ivy Place	1,428	A	146	
M09-017D-0007	Sabrina	1,805	D	84	
M09-017D-0010	Iris	1,567	C	176	
M09-022D-0001	Chalet	1,660	C	47	
M09-022D-0007	El Dorado	1,039	AA	39	
M09-022D-0009	Berrybrook	1,246	A	158	
M09-022D-0014	Treebrooke	1,851	D	141	
M09-022D-0022	Northland	1,556	B	16	
M09-024L-0002	Mt. Pleasant	1,270	A	202	
M09-027D-0005	Hermitage	1,405	A	42	
M09-029D-0002	Hickory	2,135	D	19	
M09-033D-0002	Barclay Hill	1,619	B	35	
M09-033D-0013	Mapleview	1,859	D	22	
M09-037D-0009	Springwood	1,813	D	73	
M09-037D-0012	Winford	2,059	C	45	
M09-039L-0002	Cambria	1,661	B	191	
M09-039L-0017	Hyde Place	1,333	A	223	
M09-039L-0027	Carmel Valley	1,966	D	28	
M09-040D-0006	Ferguson	1,612	C	86	
M09-040D-0015	Forestville	1,759	AA	82	
M09-040D-0026	Westrose	1,655	B	150	
M09-040D-0028	Haverhill	1,393	B	62	
M09-041D-0005	Dover	828	AAA	96	
		1,239	A	187	
M09-041D-0006	Concord Grove	1,189	AA	14	
M09-045D-0012	Lexburg	976	AA	152	
M09-045D-0017	Foxland	954	AA	221	
M09-053D-0002	Bay Ranch	1,668	A	69	
M09-053D-0007	Ridgeview	1,922	A	197	
M09-053D-0058	Albert	1,818	A	181	
M09-055L-0017	Eastwood Hill	1,525	D	46	
M09-055L-0026	Brisbane Bay	1,538	C	135	
M09-055L-0043	Eatherton	1,654	C	34	•
M09-055L-0053	Lucas Heights	1,978	C	215	•
M09-055L-0063	Rivers Edge	1,397	B	105	•
M09-055L-0064	Edelton	1,544	C	124	
M09-055L-0067	Wilshire Terrace	1,472	B	114	•
M09-055L-0068	Foxton	1,374	B	123	•
M09-055L-0069	Elderberry	1,400	B	110	•
M09-055L-0070	Verden	1,425	B	113	•
M09-055L-0071	Mesa Mountain	1,542	C	117	•
M09-055L-0105	Moylan	1,023	B	80	
M09-055L-0188	Mona Park	1,525	C	83	•
M09-055L-0193	Delmont	2,131	D	216	•
M09-055L-0196	Casalone Ridge	2,039	D	143	•
M09-055L-0213	Welsberg	1,921	C	138	•
M09-055L-0289	Prestbury	1,504	C	10	•
M09-055L-0350	Kirkland Hollow	1,451	C	92	•
M09-057D-0012	Edison Park	1,112	AA	148	•
M09-057D-0019	Stonington	1,838	C	193	
M09-058D-0004	Summerpath	962	AA	100	•
M09-058D-0010	Dogwood	676	AAA	108	•
M09-058D-0013	Barrett Hill	1,073	AA	174	•
M09-058D-0014	Mayberry Cove	416	AAA	144	•
M09-058D-0020	Wheatland	1,428	A	206	•
M09-058D-0032	Addison Park	1,879	C	53	•
M09-058D-0038	Smithsonian	1,680	B	212	•
M09-058D-0058	Charlemagne	1,865	C	190	•
M09-065L-0002	Oakglen Park	2,101	C	24	•
M09-065L-0006	Wyndhurst	2,082	C	17	•
M09-065L-0062	Bozeman	1,390	A	55	•
M09-065L-0166	Dominique	1,698	B	25	
M09-065L-0173	Coburg Manor	1,969	C	186	•
M09-068D-0005	Bonham	1,433	A	204	•
M09-068D-0006	Caroline	1,399	A	183	•
M09-072L-0013	Kalinda Cove	1,283	D	21	
M09-072L-0024	Boxberg	1,602	D	27	
M09-072L-0036	Hewlett Bay	1,188	D	29	
M09-072L-0058	Galanti	1,800	D	102	
M09-077L-0001	Wakefield Forest	1,638	E	178	•
M09-077L-0026	Morfontaine	1,501	E	40	•
M09-077L-0074	Rosencrest	1,502	E	74	•
M09-077L-0081	Holbrook Place	1,818	E	194	•
M09-077L-0097	Haddonfield	1,800	E	12	•
M09-077L-0105	Windingpath	1,100	D	208	•
M09-077L-0138	Ridgeforest	1,509	E	64	•
M09-077L-0178	Simmons	1,900	E	130	•
M09-121D-0002	Anabel	2,025	B	31	•
M09-121D-0005	Jillian	1,562	A	48	•
M09-121D-0007	Chloe	1,308	AA	149	•
M09-121D-0010	Cassandra	1,281	AA	58	•
M09-121D-0012	Angelina	1,281	AA	200	•
M09-121D-0013	Evelyn	2,100	B	126	•
M09-121D-0015	Rebecca	1,983	B	85	•
M09-121D-0016	Paige	1,582	A	180	•
M09-121D-0017	Melanie	1,379	AA	136	•
M09-121D-0020	Hailey	2,037	B	163	•
M09-121D-0021	Riley	1,562	A	32	•
M09-121D-0023	Zoey	1,762	B	44	•
M09-121D-0025	Sydney	1,368	AA	155	•
M09-121D-0028	Alyssa	1,433	AA	106	•
M09-121D-0040	MacKenzie	1,863	B	120	•
M09-121D-0048	Loraine	1,615	B	91	•
M09-122D-0001	Eureka	1,105	AAA	36	•